The Contemporary Middle East in an Age of Upheaval

THE CONTEMPORARY MIDDLE EAST IN AN AGE OF UPHEAVAL

Edited by James L. Gelvin

Afterword by Moncef Marzouki

STANFORD UNIVERSITY PRESS

Stanford, California

STANFORD UNIVERSITY PRESS

Stanford, California

©2021 by the Board of Trustees of the Leland Stanford Junior University. All rights reserved.

Printed in the United States of America on acid-free, archival-quality paper

Library of Congress Cataloging-in-Publication Data

Names: Gelvin, James L., 1951– editor. | Marzūqī, Munṣif, 1945– writer of afterword.

Title: The contemporary Middle East in an age of upheaval / edited by James L. Gelvin ; afterword by Moncef Marzouki.

Description: Stanford, California : Stanford University Press, 2021. | Includes bibliographical references and index.

Identifiers: LCCN 2020038594 (print) | LCCN 2020038595 (ebook) | ISBN 9781503615069 (cloth) | ISBN 9781503627697 (paperback) | ISBN 9781503627703 (ebook)

Subjects: LCSH: Middle East—History—21st century. | Middle East—Politics and government—21st century.

Classification: LCC DS63.123 .C66 2021 (print) | LCC DS63.123 (ebook) | DDC 956.05/4—dc23

LC record available at https://lccn.loc.gov/2020038594

LC ebook record available at https://lccn.loc.gov/2020038595

Cover design: Kevin Barrett Kane

Cover photo: Ivor Pickett, Panos Pictures

Typeset by Kevin Barrett Kane in 10.5/14.4 Brill

Contents

Contributors

James L. Gelvin is Professor of Modern Middle Eastern History at the University of California, Los Angeles. A specialist in the modern social and cultural history of the Arab East, he is author of five books, including *The New Middle East: What Everyone Needs to Know* (2017) and *The Modern Middle East: A History* (2020); along with numerous articles and chapters in edited volumes. He is also coeditor of *Global Muslims in the Age of Steam and Print, 1850–1930* (2013).

Aslı Ü. Bâli is Professor of Law at the UCLA School of Law and Faculty Director of the Promise Institute for Human Rights. She is the author of numerous law review articles, including, most recently, "Artificial States and the Remapping of the Middle East" (2020) and "Constitutionalism and the American Imperial Imagination" (2019). She is coeditor of *Constitution-Writing, Religion and Democracy* (2017) and the forthcoming volume *From Revolution to Devolution: Identity Conflict, Governance and Decentralization in the Middle East* (2021).

Henri J. Barkey is the Bernard L. and Bertha F. Cohen Professor of International Relations at Lehigh University and Adjunct Senior Fellow at the Council on Foreign Relations. He is the former Director of the Middle East Program at the Woodrow Wilson International Center for Scholars and served on the State Department's Policy Planning Staff.

Joel Beinin is the Donald J. McLachlan Professor of History and Professor of Middle East History, Emeritus, at Stanford University. He has written or edited twelve books, most recently, *A Critical Political Economy of the Modern Middle East* (2021), coedited with Bassam Haddad and Sherene Seikaly, and *Workers and Thieves: Labor Movements and Popular Uprisings in Tunisia and Egypt* (2016). In 2002 he served as president of the Middle East Studies Association of North America.

Aomar Boum is an associate professor in the Department of Anthropology at the University of California, Los Angeles. He is interested in the place of religious and ethnic minorities such as Jews, Baha'is, Shi'is, and Christians in postindependence Middle Eastern and North African nation-states. He is the author of *Memories of Absence: How Muslims Remember Jews in Morocco* (2013). He is also the coeditor of *Historical Dictionary of Morocco* (2016), *The Holocaust and North Africa* (2019), and *Historical Dictionary of the Arab Uprisings* (2020).

Laurie A. Brand is the Robert Grandford Wright Professor of International Relations and Middle East Studies at the University of Southern California, where she has served as Director of the Center for International Studies, School of International Relations, and Middle East Studies Program. Brand is a four-time Fulbright grantee, and the recipient of Carnegie, Rockefeller, and numerous other fellowships. She is author of *Palestinians in the Arab World* (1988), *Jordan's Inter-Arab Relations* (1994), *Women, the State and Political Transitions* (1998), *Citizens Abroad* (2006), and *Official Stories* (2014). A former President of the Middle East Studies Association, she has chaired its Committee on Academic Freedom since 2007.

Nathan J. Brown is professor of political science and international affairs at George Washington University and nonresident senior fellow at the Carnegie Endowment for International Peace. Brown's research focuses on religion, law, and politics in the Arab world. His latest book, *Arguing Islam after the Revival of Arab Politics*, was published in 2016, and his previous book, *When Victory Is Not an Option: Islamist Movements in Arab Politics*, was published in early 2012.

Ishac Diwan is Professor of Economics at Paris Sciences et Lettres (a consortium of Parisian universities) where he holds Chair of the Economy of the Arab World. He currently teaches at the École normale supérieure in Paris. His recent (coauthored) books include *A Political Economy of the Middle East* (2015) and *Crony Capitalism in the Middle East* (2019).

F. Gregory Gause III is Professor of International Affairs and John H. Lindsey '44 Chair at the Bush School of Government and Public Service, Texas A&M University. He also serves as head of the school's Department of International Affairs and as affiliated faculty at the school's Center for Grand Strategy. His most recent book is *The International Relations of the Persian Gulf* (2010).

Lindsay A. Gifford is the Undergraduate Director and Assistant Professor of International Studies at the University of San Francisco and the Coordinator of Middle Eastern Studies. Her research focuses on critical refugee studies in the Levant, Middle Eastern diasporas, and refugee resettlement in the Global North. She has been the recipient of the Fulbright-Hays Doctoral Dissertation Research Abroad Fellowship as well as the National Science Foundation Minority Postdoctoral Research Fellowship. Her fieldwork experience includes research with refugees in Syria, Jordan, Finland, and the Arab communities of California.

Kevan Harris is Assistant Professor of Sociology at the University of California, Los Angeles. He is the author of *A Social Revolution: Politics and the Welfare State in Iran* (2017). Harris is the lead researcher on the Iran Social Survey, a nationally representative polling project for the Islamic Republic of Iran. He is also the coeditor of *The Social Question in the Twenty-First Century: A Global View* (2019).

Harith Hasan is Senior Fellow at Carnegie Middle East Center, where his research focuses on Iraq, sectarianism, religious actors, and state-society relations. He was also a senior research fellow at the Central European University and a fellow at Brandeis University and Radcliffe Institute for Advanced Studies, Harvard University.

Fred H. Lawson is Visiting Professor of International Relations at the Emirates Diplomatic Academy, Professor of Government, Emeritus, of Mills College and editor of the Syracuse University Press series Intellectual and Political History of the Modern Middle East. He is the author of *Global Security Watch Syria* (2013), *Constructing International Relations in the Arab World* (2006), and *Why Syria Goes to War* (1996); editor of *Demystifying Syria* (2009) and *Comparative Regionalism* (2009); and coeditor of *Armies and Insurgencies in the Arab Spring* (2016) and *International Relations of the Middle East*, 4 vols. (2015).

Marc Lynch is Professor of Political Science at the George Washington University. He is Founding Director of the Project on Middle East Political Science, Chair of the MENA Politics Section of the American Political Science Association, and Associate Editor of the *Monkey Cage* for the *Washington Post*. His books include *The New Arab Wars: Anarchy and Uprising in the Middle East* and *The Arab Uprisings Explained.*

Peter Mandaville is Professor of International Affairs in the Schar School of Policy and Government and Codirector of the Ali Vural Ak Center for Global Islamic Studies, both at George Mason University. He is also a Senior Research Fellow at Georgetown University's Berkley Center for Religion, Peace & World Affairs, and a Nonresident Senior Fellow at the Brookings Institution. His books include *Islam and Politics* (3rd ed., 2020) and *Transnational Muslim Politics: Reimagining the Umma* (2001).

Moncef Marzouki is a medical doctor by profession and a human rights pioneer and activist by predilection. Dr. Marzouki founded the Tunisian National Committee for Liberties and went on to become president of the Arab Commission on Human Rights. Elected the first president of post-uprising Tunisia by the newly elected Constituent Assembly, Dr. Marzouki steered that country through its turbulent new beginning, lifting the state of emergency, appointing a prime minister from the moderate Islamist Ennahda movement, and establishing the Truth and Dignity Commission to guide national reconciliation.

The Contemporary Middle East in an Age of Upheaval

Introduction

A NEW MIDDLE EAST?

James L. Gelvin

FORMER SECRETARY OF STATE CONDOLEEZZA RICE COINED THE phrase "the New Middle East" at a press conference held in 2006. She used it to refer to the Middle East that she saw emerging in the wake of the American invasion and occupation of Iraq.[1] The United States had invaded Iraq on March 20, 2003, ostensibly because it suspected Iraq of possessing weapons of mass destruction. By November of that year, however, President George W. Bush supplemented his original casus belli: "As freedom takes root in Iraq," he asserted, "it will inspire millions across the Middle East to claim their liberty as well."[2]

Bush and the neoconservatives he surrounded himself with were, of course, wrong. Besides leaving close to 4,500 Americans and an estimated half million Iraqis dead,[3] the American invasion unleashed sectarian conflict that polarized Iraqi society and culminated in the insurgency of the Islamic State of Iraq and Syria. It also led to the creation of a weak, inefficient, and corrupt government in Iraq that was far from democratic.[4] Adding insult to injury, the invasion left a gaping geopolitical hole in the center of the Middle East: Since 1979, the United States and its allies had found it intermittently useful to use Iraq as a counterbalance to Iran. Since 2003, Iraq has been too weak and divided to counterbalance much of anything, and Iran interferes in the internal affairs of Iraq with impunity. The invasion inspired no one—except, perversely, the founders of ISIS.

1

Rice was, however, correct in one sense: the American invasion of Iraq was one of two events that created what has become known as the New Middle East. The other event took place seven years later.

On December 17, 2010, Muhammad Bouazizi, a produce vendor, set himself on fire in front of a local government building in Sidi Bouzid, a town in central Tunisia.[5] Earlier in the day, a policewoman had confiscated his wares, and he had been humiliated when he went to complain. The self-immolation touched off protests that reached Tunisia's capital ten days later.

At first, President Zine al-Abidine bin Ali, who had ruled for a quarter century, tried to mollify the protesters. In a pattern that kings and other presidents-for-life would repeat time after time in the upcoming months, he promised three hundred thousand new jobs, new parliamentary elections, and a "national dialogue." This did little to appease the protesters. By January 14, 2011—less than a month after Bouazizi's self-immolation—military and political leaders had had enough, and with the army surrounding the presidential palace bin Ali resigned, appointing his prime minister to head a caretaker government before he fled to Saudi Arabia.

About a week and a half after Ben Ali fled Tunisia, young people, many of whom belonged to the April 6 Movement, began their occupation of Tahrir Square in Cairo. (Tahrir Square was one site of many in Egypt where protests took place that day, but it emerged as the symbolic center of the Egyptian uprising.) The security forces and hired goons failed to dislodge the protesters, and the army announced it would not fire on them. Strikes and anti-government protests spread throughout Egypt. On February 11, 2011, the army took matters into its own hands: it deposed President Hosni Mubarak and established a new government under the Supreme Council of the Armed Forces. This phase of the Egyptian uprising—what might be called the uprising's first street phase—was over in a mere eighteen days.

Over the following several months, uprisings and protests spread to almost all states of the twenty-two-member Arab League, demonstrating the loathing many Arabs felt toward the regimes that governed them as well as the commonality of their experiences and problems. Nevertheless, although all states in the Arab world were equally vulnerable to popular anger, they differed in terms of local history, state structure, and state capability. These factors, as well as foreign interference, defined the course of the uprising in each.

Tunisia and Egypt, for example, are the only two countries in the region that have experienced two hundred years of continuous state building. As a result, there were strong institutions—the military in Egypt, the "deep state" (the permanent bureaucracy and power brokers) in Tunisia—that remained intact and stood firm against revolutionary change. While those institutions allowed for the decapitation of the regime in order to be rid of its most provocative symbol—bin Ali in the case of Tunisia, Mubarak in the case of Egypt—they also either slowed the pace of change, as in Tunisia, or reversed it altogether, as in Egypt. In contrast, Yemen and Libya were "weak states" whose government apparatus was relatively feeble and unable to penetrate much below the surface of civil society. As a result, regimes there fragmented: parts of the military and government apparatus remained loyal, and parts saw the uprisings as an opportunity to enhance their standing or settle scores. In the end, both Yemen and Libya descended into protracted civil wars. Then there were Bahrain and Syria, where the ruling cliques, bound together by ties of kinship and religious affinity (both countries are ruled by members of religious minorities), remained unbroken and played the sectarian card to rally as much domestic support as they could until foreign militaries came to their rescue. In other states in the region, the course of uprisings or protests similarly reflected local conditions.

For all the optimism implicit in the commonplace descriptor "Arab Spring," then, the uprisings that broke out in the Arab world between December 2010 and March 2011 hardly had outcomes reminiscent of a sunny, springtime rebirth. In Egypt, the army rebelled after a brief but disastrous experiment in Muslim Brotherhood rule. There, and in all the monarchies as well, the forces of reaction snuffed out the demand for change. Libya, Yemen, and Syria are still suffering from the worst excesses of political violence. It seems unlikely that governments in any of the three will rule over the entirety of their territories or populations within the foreseeable future. In Syria, Libya, Yemen, Iraq, and even Tunisia and Egypt's Sinai Peninsula, the weakening of regimes or the diversion of their attention elsewhere created an environment in which violent Islamist groups, like ISIS and al-Qaeda, have bred. And while protesters in Iraq, Lebanon, and Palestine have mobilized repeatedly to demand accountability from dysfunctional elected governments, those governments continued to prove themselves unable or unwilling to break political gridlock and answer even the most rudimentary needs of their populations.

Across the region, the uprisings led to a rise in sectarianism, fueled in particular by spillover from the Syrian civil war, Saudi-Iranian competition to define the post-uprising regional order and determine the fate of embattled regimes, and the Islamic State's policy of "purifying" its caliphate of those who do not conform to its rigid interpretation of Sunni Islam. In addition, foreign intervention across the Arab world has taken place with impunity, perhaps signaling the beginning of an epochal shift in the meaning of sovereignty and sovereign relations. Such intervention decisively shifted the trajectory of uprisings in Bahrain, Yemen, Syria, Libya, and Egypt. Finally, since 2011 the region has experienced one humanitarian crisis after another. In the most brutal war zones—Syria, Libya, Yemen, Iraq—entire towns and cities have been laid waste, their populations scattered. The number of IDPs—internally displaced persons—in each country tells the story: as of 2019, there were 6.2 million IDPs in Syria, 2.9 million in Iraq, 2 million in Yemen, and 193,600 in Libya.[6] At the same time, the flight of 5.6 million refugees from Syria—more than 1 million to Europe alone in 2015—sparked a xenophobic populist backlash around the world that has yet to dissipate. War and civil disorder not only have taken their toll in terms of civilian casualties but also have destroyed billions of dollars of infrastructure and created a public health nightmare. And particularly in Syria and Yemen, mass starvation—both a consequence and an intentional tool of war—is an ongoing threat, endangering millions.[7]

Tunisia remains the one possible success story of the 2010–2011 uprisings, although the challenges it faces—particularly jihadi violence and poor economic performance—are daunting. This, of course, begs the question: What went wrong? To begin with, it might be too early to write off the wave of uprisings as a failure, particularly since events in Algeria, Lebanon, and elsewhere continue to play out. After all, it might be argued that Europe's revolutions of 1848—also known as the Spring of Nations—did not achieve all they set out to achieve for almost a century and a half, and even now their dénouement must be considered tentative. Nevertheless, in the Arab world, a number of factors have contributed to what the world has witnessed there so far.

From the beginning, protesters and rebels throughout the Arab world faced overwhelming odds, the tenacity of ruling cliques fighting for their lives, the hostility of those dependent on the old order, foreign intervention, lack of foreign intervention, and extremist groups out for their own ends. Furthermore, the very spontaneity, leaderlessness, diversity, and loose organization on which the uprisings thrived proved their Achilles' heel as well. On the one hand, these attributes kept regimes off guard and prevented them from reining in rebellious activity. On the other hand, the same attributes prevented protesters and rebels from agreeing on and implementing coordinated policies with regard to tactics, strategy, and program. Even were this not the case, participants in the uprisings were, more often than not, united by what they were against—the regime—rather than what they were for.

The Italian communist theorist Antonio Gramsci differentiated between a "war of maneuver" and a "war of position."[8] A war of maneuver is a direct confrontation between the old order and those opposing it, as took place during the Russian Revolution. A war of position is the slow, meticulous winning over of a population to one's ideas by infiltrating institutions and structures like the press, trade unions, civic associations, and the like. This enables those who are committed to change to have already created the foundations of a countersociety by the time they assume power. In the case of the Arab uprisings, protesters fought a war of maneuver, not a war of position. As a result, deep states were able to regroup, call on outside support, and stigmatize and isolate their oppositions. In most of the region, this enabled the forces of counterrevolution to overpower the forces advocating change.

A NEW ERA?

Periodization is a contentious endeavor, and the process displays both the subjective predilections of those doing it and the rickety scaffolding against which the historical enterprise rests. Just as it might be argued that the American invasion of Iraq and the Arab uprisings set the stage for and shaped a definably new era in Middle East history, it might just as convincingly be argued that the New Middle East represents the culmination of the postcolonial era in the region and not a break with it.

Take, for example, a hallmark of and impetus for the New Middle East: explosive growth in population. This puts an unprecedented strain on resources, the environment, economic well-being, and the capacity of governments to provide services such as health care and education. According to the World Bank, there were about 133 million people living in the Middle East and North Africa in 1960. In 1980, there were close to 230 million, and in 2018,

531 million—close to a fourfold increase in a little under six decades.[9] Adding to the strain is the peculiar feature of demographic change in the region: the youth bulge. As of 2018, youth between the ages of ten and twenty-four made up 29 percent of the Arab population. Little wonder, then, that about one-third of young people who wish to work are unemployed.[10] Members of the largest cohort in the history of the Arab world face unprecedented competition for education, jobs, and housing, not to mention competition in the marriage market.

Although demographic pressures might be driving the New Middle East, it was the old Middle East that fostered and first bore the strains of the population explosion. The interventionist state that emerged during the period of decolonization brought with it improvements in education, public health, and sanitation. Infant mortality declined, as did the numbers of women who died in childbirth. The children of the baby-boom generation of the 1950s through the 1970s are now paying for these rare successes of the postcolonial state.

Economic stagnation and increasing poverty and income inequality—in large measure the result of the ill-advised and mismanaged application of neoliberal economic policies and rent-seeking behavior—are also defining characteristics of the New Middle East that predate the onset of the twenty-first century. American policy makers began to tout the benefits of neoliberalism, along with its political correlate, human rights, in the mid-1970s, even before Ronald Reagan's presidency. Neoliberal policies got their tentative start in the Arab world in December 1976, when Egypt negotiated a $450 million credit line with the International Monetary Fund, which also gave Egypt the wherewithal to postpone $12 million in foreign debt. In return, Egypt cut $123 million in commodity supports and $64 million from direct subsidies. The result was two days of bloody rioting in which between eighty and one hundred protesters died and twelve hundred were arrested.[11] Similar "IMF riots" broke out in Morocco, Tunisia, Lebanon, Algeria, and Jordan. Although the juggernaut of neoliberal policies was tempered, they continued and, beginning in the twenty-first century, accelerated.[12] After decades of neoliberal "reform," the Arab Middle East was less industrialized at the beginning of the twenty-first century than it had been in 1970, with growth rates lagging the rest of the Global South. It is currently the second least globalized region on Earth, beating out only sub-Saharan Africa.[13]

It might thus be argued that much of what has come to define the region after 2011 is nothing more than a continuation of phenomena that were already present there: Arab states are still rent-seeking and patrimonial, for example, much as they had been before the turn of the twenty-first century. The region is still embedded in a global economic system that gives pride of place to neoliberalism. Arab states are still deficient in human rights, accountability, transparency, and rule of law. Populations still suffer from low human security in much of everything from education and health care to good governance to access to adequate food and water supplies.

All this is true, and it all seems to point to similarities, not differences, between new and old Middle East. But couldn't this be said for every period? Take, for example, the period that followed World War I. Few historians would deny the significance of the region's transformation that took place then. Before the war, the Ottoman Empire ruled, in law if not in deed, Anatolia, the Levant and Mesopotamia, Egypt, and parts of the Arabian Peninsula. In 1918, the Ottoman Empire was gone. By the early 1920s, Turkey was an independent republic, the Fertile Crescent had been divided into separate states under the control of France and Britain, Egypt had evolved from an Ottoman territory and a British protectorate to an independent state, and much of the Arabian Peninsula had been united under the control of the dynasty of ibn Saud. After the war, the Israel-Palestine dispute took its present form. During the war, Jewish nationalism received the support of a great power. This not only ensured its survival; it ensured the persistence of the struggle between Jewish settlers and the indigenous inhabitants of Palestine. Finally, the war brought about a demographic holocaust: upward of one-fifth of the Ottoman population perished during the war years; perhaps as much as one-quarter of the Persian population as well. It would take until after the middle of the century for the region to recover demographically. World War I seems, then, a turning point in the history of the region. Yet in terms of relations of production, social stratification, and meddling by great powers, for example, little had changed since the nineteenth century.

The moral of the story is that when it comes to dividing history into periods based on one or another characteristic, possibilities are limited only by the imaginations of historians. And regardless of whether the phrase "New Middle East" refers to something altogether new and distinctive or the crystallization of earlier dynamics, the fact remains that the American invasion of Iraq, the

Arab uprisings, and even, before them, the end of the Cold War upset the regional order on a number of levels and unleashed destructive forces that are unlikely to be contained anytime soon.

SIX CHARACTERISTICS OF THE NEW MIDDLE EAST

In the chapters that follow, contributors provide their own lists of continuities that link the New Middle East with the old and describe characteristics that distinguish the former from the latter. In the main, their work points to six such characteristics.

First, there is the fallout from the protests and uprisings that broke out in 2010–2011. Although none of the uprisings that broke out in 2010–2011 succeeded (save for possibly Tunisia's), and although it is still too early to know their long-term effects, governments throughout the region that were able to withstand the tumult became more reliant on a combination of raw power, elite cohesion, external support, and bribery to maintain themselves. In Egypt, for example, protesters torched the headquarters of President Mubarak's National Democratic Party, which had dispensed political spoils to the party's constituents (mainly public-sector employees and those living in rural areas). The building is now gone, as is the party. Upon taking power in 2013, General Abdel Fattah al-Sisi decided to cut out the middleman; instead of working through politicians and a civilian party, he relied instead on his own principal constituency, the military and intelligence services. Adding insult to injury, the rubber-stamp parliament he oversees has consistently approved the renewal of a state of emergency, which puts all matters relating to national security—a rather expansive portfolio—in their hands.[14]

Saudi Arabia, in contrast, responded to the first signs of popular unrest with both carrots and sticks. The carrots took the form of pay raises, loan forgiveness, housing assistance, and the like to those whose loyalty the regime considered worth buying; the sticks, violent repression of those the regime deemed less worthy on an order equal to that of Egypt. The Saudi government treated the economically and politically marginalized Eastern Province, where the bulk of Saudi Arabia's Shi'is live, with particular ferocity, firing on protesters and demolishing whole neighborhoods and evicting their inhabitants.[15]

None of the solutions that these or other regimes has found will bring long-term relief to their crisis of legitimacy. The case of Algeria is telling: In 2011, the regime squelched a protest movement when three thousand demonstrators confronted thirty thousand riot police. Eight years later, after the chronically ill eighty-two-year-old president declared for a fifth term, protests broke out throughout the country. In the capital, Algiers, a reported eight hundred thousand protesters took to the streets to express their anger.[16]

In places like Egypt and Bahrain protests and uprisings threatened regimes, but the regimes came through not only relatively unscathed but emboldened. The story is different in Syria, Libya, and Yemen—those states that have been the sites of multiple-sided civil wars fueled by outside powers. The government of Syria, aided by Russia and Iran, took back almost all the territory that had escaped its control, but at tremendous cost. It is likely that Syria's fate will resemble that of Somalia—hence the word coined by Lakhdar Brahimi, former UN and Arab League special envoy to Syria, to describe Syria's future: "Somalization."[17] Syria will have an internationally recognized government that will continue to reign but not rule over a ruined country. Local warlords who fielded militias during the civil war and financed them by grabbing hold of some resource such as oil or smuggling will continue to wield power while the government, impoverished and debilitated by war, can only look on. Libya will probably meet a similar fate, with or without a government (the operative word among analysts being "militiaization"[18]).

Yemen may follow a different path. Outside powers that intervened into the Syrian and Libyan wars did so in order for their proxies to take control of a state apparatus that would rule over the entirety of the state. In contrast, the United Arab Emirates intervened in the Yemeni civil war with the intention of dividing the country and reestablishing an independent South Yemen—a plan with which its ally Saudi Arabia disagreed. Although the UAE subsequently withdrew from the fighting, "Little Sparta" (as American generals call it) maintains big plans for its future in the Red Sea and the Horn of Africa.[19]

As regimes shifted their strategies for holding on to power, oppositional movements paid a heavy price. In Egypt and Bahrain, for example, counterrevolutionary regimes out for revenge crushed mass-based oppositional movements that they had allowed to operate before 2011 or that had emerged publicly during the uprisings. After the 2013 coup d'état in Egypt, President Sisi ordered the massacre of 1,150 supporters of ousted Muslim Brotherhood president Muhammad Morsi who had gathered to protest his ouster in Rabʿa al-Adawiyya and Nahda squares in Cairo. Sisi then had the top leaders of the Brotherhood arrested, disbanded the organization, and confiscated its property.[20]

It wasn't just the Muslim Brotherhood of Egypt that found itself under attack: Muslim brotherhoods throughout the region (the exception being in Yemen) found themselves caught up in the competition between Turkey and Qatar, which generally supported them, and Saudi Arabia and its Gulf allies, which generally did not. In most places (the most notable exception being Tunisia), Saudi Arabia and its friends proved more successful, and brotherhoods were no longer serious contenders for power—a bitter pill for organizations that had sought to avoid such an eventuality by renouncing violence and combining popular appeal with doctrinal flexibility.

As for the activists whose calls for "Days of Rage" started it all in Egypt, Bahrain, Yemen, and elsewhere, the amorphous structure and ad hoc nature of the movements they created only made the repression unleashed by regimes easier. Some activists whom regimes did not kill or imprison went underground. Others reassessed their tactics and goals, and still others withdrew from politics altogether.[21]

In Syria, the uprising weakened, demoralized, and diverted the attention of the military and security services, and the regime lost control of large areas of the country. The collapse of authority created an environment in which the ultraviolent ISIS could emerge. Although born in Iraq, ISIS began its territorial expansion in Syria. From Syria, ISIS's reach spread to Iraq when the army of that unfortunate country refused to defend the corrupt and sectarian regime empowered by the United States there. For a brief moment, ISIS ruled over a caliphate the size of the United Kingdom, comprising upward of eight million people. ISIS applied a draconian interpretation of Islamic law that was rigid even by Saudi standards (in some cases, smokers in the caliphate were flogged; in others, beheaded). It also attempted to purge "apostates" from its territory and kill or enslave "pagans" (those they considered non-monotheists, like Yazidis) within it. Otherwise, the rent-seeking, patrimonial, and autocratic "caliphate" ISIS created was a perfect fit for the neighborhood.

The Syrian civil war and the emergence and expansion of ISIS were two of the factors that contributed to the spread of sectarianism across the region— the second characteristic of the New Middle East. Sectarianism, as this book uses the term, refers to the belief that religious affiliation should be the foundation for collective identity in a multireligious environment. Although there are still commentators who believe that sectarian identities are primordial and that sectarianism has been the automatic default position for the organization of Muslim societies for nearly a millennium and a half, the authors represented here, like most social scientists, take an alternative view. For them, sectarianism as we now understand it first emerged in the Middle East during the nineteenth century, as a result of colonial meddling, new notions of political community that privileged horizontal ties among populations over vertical ones, and efforts of political entrepreneurs who sought to use religious identification for political gain. Those entrepreneurs might be individuals, groups and parties, or governments.

Since its appearance, sectarianism has had a variable footprint across the region. It was woven into the political fabric of Lebanon, for example, but Iraqis had a history of intersectarian cooperation in the political sphere[22]—that is, until 1992, when, in the wake of the Gulf War, Iraqi president Saddam Hussein chose to frame an anti-government insurrection that broke out in predominantly Shi'i parts of the country in sectarian terms.[23] Nevertheless, in their day-to-day interactions, most Iraqis, like most Syrians before 2011, continued to abide by an unwritten code of "public civility," much as many Americans do on the issue of race. As a matter of fact, before the American invasion, 30 percent of Iraqi marriages were between Sunnis and Shi'is.[24] Individuals might have talked trash about members of other sects in the privacy of their own homes, but in their mixed neighborhoods, their mixed schools, and their mixed cafés and markets where they mingled with members of other sects, reference to sectarian difference was boorish.

Since 2011, however, sectarianism has spread throughout the region, mainly as a result of two factors. In Syria and Iraq, domestic political actors deliberately set out to sectarianize society. In the case of Syria, the Alawite-dominated government deliberately stirred up sectarian tensions to rally the support of Alawites and other minorities to its cause. The Syrian regime styled itself for minorities as "the lesser of two evils, or the last line of defence against fundamentalist tyranny."[25] Then it created the conditions whereby that would be true. The regime released jihadis and other Islamists from prison, organized armed "popular committees" to protect Alawite villages, equipped pro-regime militias with weapons to use against unarmed protesters, and deployed the *shabiha*—gangs of Alawite thugs—to provoke tit-for-tat violence against Sunnis. The regime strategy worked, and an intersectarian uprising devolved into a sectarian civil war.[26]

In the case of Iraq, first al-Qaeda in Mesopotamia (whose anti-Shiʻi, or *takfiri*, agenda infuriated the leadership of al-Qaeda central[27]) and then ISIS used sectarianism to their advantage. Al-Qaeda in Mesopotamia's aim was to draw the United States into a sectarian bloodbath as part of the overall al-Qaeda strategy to "vex and exhaust" the "Crusader-Zionist conspiracy." ISIS, in contrast, owed its rapid growth among Iraq's Sunnis in large measure to the anti-Sunni policies of Iraq's Shiʻi prime minister Nuri al-Maliki, who exacerbated tensions between the two communities that the American invasion and occupation had already inflamed. ISIS viewed the elimination of Shiʻis from the territory it conquered as a necessary first step in restoring a Sunni caliphate purified of non-Sunni elements.

Sectarian sentiments spread from Syria and Iraq as the conflicts in Syria and Iraq expanded beyond their borders, as refugees sought safety and fighters sought sanctuary abroad, and as opposition groups sought assistance from coreligionists abroad. Predominantly Sunni militias belonging to the Syrian opposition, for example, crossed into an already-fragile Lebanon seeking revenge against the Hizbullahis who had fought in the Syrian civil war against them. In the coastal city of Tripoli, Lebanon, Sunni and Alawite gangs—the former supporting the Syrian opposition, the latter the government—squared off against each other on a regular basis. In Turkey the influx of Sunni refugees from Syria and the government's support for the Syrian opposition provoked clashes between the police and local Alawites and Alevis, minorities who together make up as much as 40 percent of the Turkish population (the numbers are uncertain).[28]

What makes the current spread of sectarianism in the Middle East all the more tragic is that once sectarianism takes root, it does not simply disappear with the passage of time. People segregate themselves among "their own kind" for safety or comfort (as has happened in Iraq and Syria), or states allocate representation and rights according to religious affiliation (as in Lebanon). And although the mostly young demonstrators in Lebanon and Iraq who demanded an end to sectarian politics during protests in 2019 are a hopeful sign, it is improbable that they will sway the entrenched elites and their constituents who benefit from the system.

Elsewhere in the region, the competition between Saudi Arabia and Iran has driven sectarianism, as each has sought natural allies in its struggle to check the ambitions of its rival. This competition is the third characteristic of the New Middle East.

The roots of Saudi-Iranian competition go back no further than 1979, when, in the aftermath of the Iranian Revolution, Saudi and Iranian interests in the region diverged. Since then, Saudi Arabia has sought to maintain the status quo in the region, which has worked to its advantage. Iran, however, seeks to turn a generally hostile political environment to *its* favor by finding cracks in the system and exploiting them. The American invasion and occupation of Iraq and the Arab uprisings created plenty of cracks. Perhaps the best historical analogue to the current crisis, then, is the Arab Cold War of the 1950s and 1960s, when revolutionary republics like Egypt, Syria, and Iraq struggled to gain regional influence against their "reactionary" opponents like Saudi Arabia.

Saudi Arabia has blamed Iran for stirring rebellion in Bahrain and Yemen, as well as in the Eastern Province of the kingdom and other places. Although it is indisputable that Iran has capitalized on crises in multiple arenas, it has not come close to being the provocateur that Saudi Arabia claims it to be. The Bahrain Independent Commission of Inquiry, appointed by the country's King Hamad in the wake of the uprising, found "no discernable link" between Iran and the uprising against the Sunni king that took place on the predominantly Shi'i island. In other cases, both the Houthi insurgents of Yemen (who have been in revolt, off and on, since 2004) and protesters in the Saudi Eastern Province had accumulated enough local grievances to make Iranian meddling all but superfluous.[29]

If, then, Saudi anxieties are not commensurate with the level of actual Iranian threat, why do they persist? There are three reasons. First, there were the Arab uprisings, which Saudi Arabia viewed as a potential calamity. The uprisings not only threatened to spill over into the kingdom; they jeopardized Saudi Arabia's allies as well as the regional order. Furthermore, by raising the prospect that the realm of democratic and human rights might expand into the region, they rattled the foundations of Saudi Arabia's own legitimacy.

Just as serious for the Saudis, the uprisings threatened to empower Muslim brotherhoods and Muslim Brotherhood–style movements throughout the region. Muslim brotherhoods provide a model for reconciling religion and politics that competes with Saudi Arabia's own vision of the proper relationship between the two. Although the brotherhoods link religion and politics, the Saudi royal family has sought to distance one from the other to prevent the emergence of potentially destabilizing Islamist movements from within and without the kingdom. This has been the royal family's survival strategy since well before 1932, when Saudi religious scholars, acting at the behest of 'Abd al-'Aziz ibn Al Saud, the founder of the current Saudi state, began to promote a doctrine of quietism with increasing urgency. Muslims were to passively obey their leaders so long as those leaders were also Muslim. That is still the Saudi position.[30]

The second source for Saudi anxiety was Barack Obama's Middle East policy. At the time he took office, Obama believed that the United States had expended far too much energy on Middle East issues under George W. Bush and far too little energy on East Asia, which, Obama believed, would be the epicenter of global competition in the twenty-first century. He thus decided to turn away from the priorities of his predecessor and instead "pivot to Asia."[31]

Obama's strategy alarmed the Saudis, particularly his quest to defuse conflicts in the region, a necessary precondition for the pivot to Asia. The Saudis were, of course, used to America's periodic and quixotic forays into the Israel-Palestine issue, but they looked on in horror as the United States signed on to the Iran nuclear deal, which the Saudis viewed as the first step toward inviting Iran's participation in the regional order. They were particularly horrified by the policy behind an interview Obama gave with the *Atlantic*, in which he stated, "The competition between the Saudis and the Iranians, which has helped to feed proxy wars and chaos in Syria and Iraq and Yemen, requires us to say to our friends, as well as to the Iranians, that they need to find an effective way to share the neighborhood and institute some sort of cold peace."

Another aspect of Obama's strategy that alarmed the Saudis was the tactical approach Obama took toward making the pivot. Obama insisted that America's partners in the region take more responsibility for their own defense and that the United States return to its Cold War policy of "offshore balancing."[32] The Saudis took offense to Obama's charge that they had been acting as "free riders" and feared American abandonment.[33] The policy so disturbed the Saudis that they later made sure to capture the ear of Donald Trump, his administration, and his clan early on. Their purpose was to win Trump over to a strategic vision that divided a complex part of the world into binary categories of good (Saudi Arabia, Israel) and bad (Iran). It worked: Trump and his enablers made Saudi and Israeli fears—their Iranophobia, so to speak—the foundation for America's regional policy, vilifying Obama's policy of engagement with Iran as appeasement.[34] And so we have the withdrawal of the United States from the Iran nuclear deal, Trump's veto of a US Senate resolution that would have ended American complicity in the Saudi campaign in Yemen, and his defense of Crown Prince Muhammad bin Salman, whom everyone but Trump believes ordered the murder of journalist Jamal Khashoggi, an American resident.

Finally, the third reason for Saudi anxieties is the collapse of oil prices that threatened the financial underpinning of the Saudi kingdom and fed Saudi concerns about the future. Saudi Arabia depends on oil for 87 percent of its revenue. Between June 2014 and April 2016, the price of oil dropped 70 percent. The price eventually rebounded, but not to the extent that would return Saudi accounts to the black. According to the IMF, oil prices would have to reach $80 to $85 per barrel to fund the 2019 budget. At the beginning of that year, the price was substantially below that level.[35]

The Arab uprisings, the policy of Barack Obama and his administration, and the collapse of oil prices forced the Saudis to rethink policy at home and abroad. At home, Crown Prince Muhammad bin Salman launched Saudi Vision 2030, an improbable scheme to turn Saudi Arabia into a free-market utopia and Saudis into aggressive entrepreneurs in a mere fourteen years. Abroad, Saudi Arabia became uncharacteristically intrusive in the region, intervening into the internal affairs of its neighbors fighting against an often-imaginary Iranian enemy. In the cases of Yemen and Bahrain, this intrusiveness took a military form; in the cases of Syria, Libya, and Egypt, it was financial. For example, Saudi Arabia financed and supplied a number of groups in Syria, including the on-again, off-again al-Qaeda affiliate Jabhat al-Nusra. In Egypt, Saudi Arabia reportedly paid General Sisi $1 billion to launch his coup d'état and, together with funding from other Gulf states, $40 billion over the following two and a half years so that he might consolidate his position by stabilizing the economy.[36]

Saudi Arabia is hardly alone in abandoning the Westphalian principles of respect for state sovereignty and non-intervention. Powers great and small, from inside and outside the region, have also done so consistently in the New Middle East. That this has taken place at all is the result of widespread civil disorder and state breakdown in an environment characterized by intense interstate competition and the absence of a hegemon that might have reserved such transgressions for itself. Indeed, with the American declaration of a global war on terrorism, the US invasion of Iraq, and the UN Security Council's invocation of a "responsibility to protect," coined as R2P, in the lead-up to the NATO bombing campaign in Libya,[37] such practices were practically codified, and even the fig leaf of international approbation for a state's blatant misconduct seems quaint. At one time or another since 2011, Saudi Arabia, the UAE, Qatar, Egypt, Turkey, and Iran, not to mention the United States, its European allies, and Russia, have intervened in one way or another into the internal affairs of Syria, Lebanon, Libya, Bahrain, Iraq, and Yemen against established governments or without their express approval. The widespread abandonment of the principles of respect for state sovereignty and non-intervention marks the fourth characteristic of the New Middle East.

The absence of a hegemon, which might act as a regional stabilizer and mitigate conflicts in the region, also distinguishes the current period from others before it. It is true that America's golden age in the Middle East was more gold plated than solid gold. Significant setbacks tempered American success in the region during the Cold War. The United States was not able to prevent the overthrow of a friendly government in Iran, end the civil war in Lebanon, rein in its Israeli ally, roll back the oil price revolution of 1973, or bring Syria, Iraq, or South Yemen into its orbit. Nevertheless, there is a great deal of truth to Egyptian president Anwar al-Sadat's remark in 1977 that America held "99 percent of the cards" in the Middle East.[38] With the help of its partners in the region, the United States was able to limit and even roll back Soviet influence in the Middle East, its main preoccupation. The United States was successful because it had proxies in the region it could rely on—Israel in the west, Saudi Arabia, and, until 1979, Iran in the east—to act as deterrents against any group or state that sought to upset the status quo, and those proxies had the same overriding goal as the United States: maintaining the status quo.

Then three things happened. First, the Soviet Union imploded, removing the unifying factor that held the alliance together. Then, the United States invaded and occupied Iraq. This, along with the American invasion and occupation of Afghanistan, soured most Americans on further interventions into the region, as poll after poll has indicated. It also demonstrated the limits of American military power—the one power at which the United States excels—to effect determinate solutions to complex problems. Finally, there was the election of Barack Obama and then Donald Trump. Neither president convinced America's partners and adversaries in the region that the United States was willing to play the same role during his administration that it had played during the Cold War—the former through acts of commission (i.e., his pivot to Asia and commitment to offshore balancing), the latter through acts of omission (i.e., his inconsistency and willingness to abdicate responsibility for policy planning and follow-through to America's traditional partners).[39]

It is unlikely that some other power will take up the American mantle in the Middle East. Some have suggested Russia, but a 2017 RAND Corporation report on Russia's ambitions in the Middle East is indicative of why this is not likely to occur: The report uses some variation on the word "transactional" sixteen times and "opportunistic" or "opportunity" eighteen times within the space of eleven pages to describe the bases for Russian policy in the region. It then goes on to conclude that "Russia potentially lacks the economic and military power to sustain a long-term strategy"—an assessment the report shares with Barack Obama, who once dismissed America's Cold War rival as a "regional power" that acts out of weakness, not strength.[40]

Then there is Europe, which others have suggested. The section of the European Union's 2016 strategic program dealing with the Middle East begins with a call to action ("solving conflicts and promoting development and human rights in the south is essential to addressing the threat of terrorism, the challenges of demography, migration and climate change, and to seizing the opportunity of shared prosperity"), but then ignores that call by abdicating primary responsibility to regional actors while relegating Europe to a supporting role. Europe's short-term focus on migration has made it a supplicant rather than a leader when dealing with Middle Eastern regimes.[41]

The final contender for hegemon to replace the United States that media commonly broach is China. They cite China's thirst for Middle East oil and the inroads that China has made in the region with its Belt and Road Initiative, through which China will invest more than $20 billion in the region. Nevertheless, even though Chinese foreign policy has been more assertive of late, China has limited its assertiveness to its own "near abroad"—the South China Sea and its immediate neighbors. There is no reason China should shoulder the responsibilities of a hegemon when it can take advantage of existing security networks and a functioning global economic system sustained by others, as it has in the past. China's role in the contemporary Middle East is, ironically, similar to the role played by the United States in the region during the period between the two world wars. American companies came to dominate the global trade in oil while others—Britain and France—paid the price of hegemons, bearing the cost of providing the stability that enabled the activities of those companies.

In the end, it is worth remembering the particular set of circumstances that at once permitted and compelled the United States to take on the role of hegemon and that obliged states in the region to accept it as such. During the period of American hegemony in the Middle East, the global system was bipolar, the contest to dominate the region played out as a zero-sum game, and the Middle East was a prize worth competing for. The United States was unrivaled as an economic and military power and occupied a preeminent position within the global economic system. There was a core group of states in the Middle East whose interests aligned with American interests and whose very existence the American security umbrella could guarantee. And with the help of some deft diplomacy in the wake of the 1973 Arab-Israeli War, the United States became the only power capable of brokering a land-for-peace deal among the combatants, putting the most populous and militarily capable Arab state, Egypt—previously the region's preeminent spoiler—permanently in America's pocket. Comparable circumstances do not exist for any state or group of states at present. In the absence of a hegemon, local powers—Saudi Arabia, Turkey, Iran—will continue to vie for position within the regional order.

The final, sixth characteristic of the New Middle East is the decreasing relevance of the Israeli-Palestinian conflict. In 2002, Saudi Arabia proposed an Arab-Israeli, Israeli-Palestinian peace plan it called the Arab Peace Initiative. The plan called for the complete Israeli withdrawal from all the territories it had conquered in 1967; the implementation of UN General Assembly

Resolution 194, which endorsed the right of Palestinians to return to the homes they had left in 1948 or to receive compensation; and the establishment of a Palestinian state in the West Bank and Gaza with East Jerusalem as its capital. If the Israelis were to agree to the proposal, the member states of the Arab League would end their states of belligerence with Israel and establish normal relations with it within the framework of a comprehensive peace. As the Saudis probably anticipated, the Israeli government dismissed the initiative (Ariel Sharon, "The Bulldozer," was prime minister at the time), but the fact that the Saudis would launch it in the first place spoke to the regard—even if purely symbolic—in which states of the region held the conflict.

For decades, Arab governments, along with a number of policy analysts and American presidents, have pushed the doctrine of linkage—the idea that instability in the Middle East is "linked" to a failure to resolve the Israel-Palestine conflict. Whatever significance Arab governments might have given to the conflict in the past, however, a number of them, led by the Saudi government, the UAE, and Bahrain have put the conflict on the back burner of their foreign policy concerns, if not having dismissed it altogether. In the true spirit of "the enemy of my enemy is my friend," shared antipathy toward Iran brings Israel, Saudi Arabia, and the members of the Saudi-led "anti-terrorism" (i.e., anti-Iran) alliance together in a common cause.

In April 2018, Crown Prince Muhammad bin Salman told an interviewer that he believed "Israelis have the right to have their own land."[42] In October of that same year, Israeli prime minister Benjamin Netanyahu paid an official visit to Sultan Qaboos of Oman. Four months later, Netanyahu shared a platform with the foreign ministers of Saudi Arabia, the UAE, Bahrain, Yemen, and Oman at the Warsaw Summit, originally convened by the United States to address "Iran's influence and terrorism in the region."[43] And Israel continues to maintain trade offices in Oman and Qatar, along with a renewable energy office in the UAE. Israel provides Saudi Arabia and the Gulf with strategic depth and a technological edge in their confrontation with Iran, not to mention the benefits of Israel's special relationship with the United States. The fact that the Israel-Palestine peace process had stalled, only to be replaced by the Trump administration's so-called Peace to Prosperity giveaway to Israel does not seem to have bothered the states involved in these dealings. Nor did it prevent Bahrain, the UAE, and Sudan from "normalizing" relations with Israel, over Palestinian objections.

While Netanyahu concluded he could count on the support of Trump's America and the support—or at least acquiescence—of Saudi Arabia and the Gulf states in his quest to settle all outstanding Palestinian claims (including the fate of Jerusalem and the right of return) in Israel's favor, crush the Palestinian national movement, and unilaterally fix Israel's borders, Israel has a history of underestimating the resilience of Palestinian resistance—a mistake it may be making once again. Contrary to the beliefs of those ultra-right-wing proponents of Israeli expansionism in the United States who claim that a simple declaration of Israeli victory will end the conflict, the death or suspension of the two-state solution and the attempt to depoliticize the world's longest-running nationalist struggle is a symptom of a disease, not its cure. That disease is dangerous polarization in the region at a time when conventional diplomatic avenues for crisis management are lacking and threat inflation is commonplace among adversaries.

With all of this, the Middle East faces myriad chronic problems that may shift the course of its history forever. Human security in the region is tenuous, made abject by the 2020 COVID-19 pandemic. The region suffers from, or will soon experience, population growth that strains available resources and state capacities; climate change that has already brought about desertification and rising oceans, which themselves threaten to bring flooding to forty-three densely inhabited coastal regions; high rates of poverty along with high levels of income disparity; corruption and a lack of transparency; a democracy and human rights deficit; deindustrialization and poor economic performance; lack of engagement with the global economy; entrenched patriarchy, which economists cite as the number-one block to economic development; high numbers of refugees and the highest number of internally displaced persons of any region in the world—the list goes on.[44] Given the current preoccupations of regional actors and their inability or refusal to engage their citizens in a common project, the prospects that governments in the region will deal adequately with any of the deep-seated ills that face their populations is not encouraging.

Part 1

CONTINUITY AND CHANGE IN THE NEOLIBERAL STATE OF THE MIDDLE EAST

Chapter 1

IS THERE A NEW MIDDLE EAST?

What Has Changed, and What Hasn't?

Joel Beinin

ON JANUARY 14, 2020, THOUSANDS OF TUNISIANS PARADED DOWN the main boulevard of Tunis, festively celebrating the ninth anniversary of the ouster of former president Zine El Abidine Ben Ali. Surrounded by a phalanx of security forces, the crowd did not raise political demands. Rather, it lauded the achievements of the 2010–2011 Jasmine Revolution. A short distance away, several hundred people gathered in front of the headquarters of the Tunisian General Labor Union (Union générale tunisienne du travail), chanting "Work! Freedom! Dignity!"—a revolutionary slogan suggesting that these goals have not yet been achieved. The trade union federation's secretary-general Noureddine Taboubi addressed the crowd, decrying the lack of economic progress since Ben Ali's departure and vowed, "The revolution will go on until the real republic has been established."[1] The Organisation for Economic Co-operation and Development's 2018 Economic Survey of Tunisia confirms that unemployment persists at approximately pre-2011 levels, while real wages in most sectors have declined and annual gross domestic product growth has averaged only 1.7 percent.[2] Tunisia's trajectory exemplifies the continuities in the regional political economy before and since 2011.

Petro-capitalism remains the dominant regime of capital accumulation throughout the Middle East and North Africa. Its power and influence radiate outward from the six Gulf Cooperation Council (GCC) countries, even as they are developing beyond the stage of primitive capital accumulation based on oil and gas rents. The mélange of older and newer forms of governance that regulate this regime of capital accumulation was consolidated during the period between the founding of the Organization of the Petroleum Exporting Countries in 1960 and the oil-price boom of 1973–1981. Gilbert Achcar aptly characterized these forms of governance as "a mix of patrimonialism, nepotism, and crony capitalism, pillaging of public property, swollen bureaucracies, and generalized corruption against a background of great sociopolitical instability, and impotence or even nonexistence of the rule of law."[3] I would add to Achcar's description high military spending, low human development indices, a repressive public culture, and the prevalence of Islamist movements as the main form of political opposition. Hydrocarbon-poor countries are integrated into petro-capitalism via the remittances of their migrant workers, aid, and investments from hydrocarbon-rich GCC countries.

The policies promoted by the international financial institutions (IFIs)—first and foremost the International Monetary Fund (IMF) and the World Bank—and the United States Treasury have sought to integrate this regional regime of capital accumulation into the broader global economy. Despite a post-2011 rebranding, they have remained substantively unchanged. In 1989 a prominent advocate dubbed these policies the "Washington Consensus." Political resistance has often impeded unfettered application of the Washington Consensus program. But in principle, it entails cutting public expenditures, privatizing public-sector enterprises, reducing or eliminating government subsidies on consumer goods, making local currencies fully convertible, and enhancing incentives for foreign investment. Effectively, the policies impose economic austerity and disable public investment in jobs and services, motivated by the dogmatic belief that markets will perform these tasks more efficiently.

Hydrocarbon-poor countries are subject to both the hydrocarbon-rich states and the IFIs. To "encourage" poorer countries to implement Washington Consensus policies, the IMF typically imposes "conditionalities" on loans that it makes to countries in financial distress. During their relatively brief tenure in power following the ouster of the autocratic Ben Ali and Mubarak regimes in Tunisia and Egypt in 2011, Islamists utterly failed to articulate a viable political-economic alternative to the Washington Consensus development model.

THE POST-1967 REGIONAL ORDER

The continuities in the regional political economy across the divide of 2011 are rooted in the historical changes prompted by the Arab-Israeli Wars of 1967 and 1973. Those wars reconfigured the political horizons of the Arab region and initiated the reorientation of Egypt's military-diplomatic posture toward the United States and the formation of the American-Saudi-Egyptian axis, lubricated by the rapid growth of post-1973 oil revenues. The American-Saudi-Egyptian axis ran parallel to, and was sometimes in tension with, the American-Israeli alliance. One post-2011 change is that this tension has been all but removed.

During the lead-up to the 1973 War, Egyptian president Anwar al-Sadat's Corrective Revolution of May 15, 1971 assertively repudiated the Arab nationalism and Arab socialism championed by his predecessor, Gamal Abdel Nasser. Initially, Sadat's diminution of the powers of the secret police won him a degree of popularity. But a student-based New Left soon arose to challenge both his domestic policies and his failure to confront Israel. The Egyptian student movement was part of the regional New Left whose heyday lasted from 1968 to 1975. The movement also included several new communist parties in Egypt and Jordan, the Lebanese Organization of Communist Action, Tunisia's Perspectives/Afaq group and its successors, Ila al-Amam in Morocco, and the Popular Front for the Liberation of Palestine and the Democratic Front for the Liberation of Palestine among Palestinians living under Israeli occupation and in the diaspora, especially in Jordan and Lebanon.[4] Lebanon's descent into civil war from 1975 to 1990 deprived the Arab New Left of its geographical and intellectual center of gravity and discredited its political project.

The active elimination of secular leftist alternatives facilitated the rise of Islamist politics across the region in the 1970s. The Egyptian, Jordanian, Moroccan, and Tunisian regimes all encouraged Islamist political movements as a counterforce to the New Left. Even the ostensible champion of Arab secularism, Tunisia's president Habib Bourguiba, recognized the Society for the Preservation of the Qur'an and allowed it to hold a public congress in 1970.[5] In 1971, Egyptian president Sadat, a former Muslim Brother himself, began to release Brothers who had been jailed by the Nasser regime. He also encouraged the proliferation of "Islamic groups" on university campuses.[6] Sadat ostentatiously proclaimed himself "the believing president" (al-ra'is al-mu'min), falsely insinuating that Nasser had not been a believer. In 1984 Israel recognized al-Mujamma' al-Islami, effectively the Gaza Strip branch of the Muslim Brothers and the precursor of Hamas.

Tunisia's abandonment of its (very limited) "socialist experiment" in 1969 and, much more dramatically, Sadat's announcement of the "open door" economic policy (al-infitah al-iqtisadi) in 1974 heralded the repudiation of state-led development and the gradual reorientation of the political economy of the Arab region. The process did not occur smoothly. Public-sector workers and other beneficiaries of authoritarian populist policies erupted in broad-based, but sporadic and politically disparate, resistance to the new policies. The Egyptian "bread intifada" of January 1977 was among the first of 146 global anti-IMF food riots from 1976 to 1992.[7] It was followed by general strikes in Tunisia (January 26, 1978) and Morocco (June 20, 1981), and by anti-austerity riots in Tunisia (January 1984), Sudan (January 1982 and March 1985), and Jordan (April 1989). Due in part to this resistance, the trend toward diminished government spending as a percentage of gross domestic product began in earnest only in 1982. When oil prices began to fall in 1981 and then crashed in 1985, state revenues declined, and cuts in government spending took on a new urgency.

The fourfold increase in the price of oil from 1973 to 1981 led to massive accumulations of capital in the oil-exporting states. With Arab socialism, Arab nationalism, and alternative forms of leftist secular politics profoundly weakened, Gulf, and particularly Saudi, petro-power, backed by the United States, had a freer hand to remake the economic and social structures and religious culture of the Arab region, a softer version of the Saudi-Emirati post-2011 counterrevolutionary role.

Gulf capital generated by the oil boom ultimately flowed into other Arab countries, especially Egypt, in part because of the strategic added value of deradicalizing Egypt and anchoring it more firmly in the Western camp. In 1975, Egypt, Saudi Arabia, the United Arab Emirates, and Qatar established the Egypt-based Arab Organization for Industrialization with a capitalization of $1 billion to develop Arab military industries. Arab capital investment in Egypt paused temporarily after the 1979 Egyptian peace treaty with Israel until Egypt was "rehabilitated"—with no change in its policies—at the 1987 Arab Summit. In 1993, when Egypt took over the Arab Organization for Industrialization's entire operation, its total capital was valued at $1.8 billion.[8]

Oil-driven profits capitalized a substantial fraction of the new Islamist business class that formed under the aegis of Egypt's open-door policy. By 1980 elders of eight of the eighteen families who dominated Egypt's private sector had Muslim Brothers affiliations. Economic enterprises linked to the Brothers, many concentrated in real estate and currency speculation, may have constituted as much as 40 percent of the private sector.[9]

The oil boom greatly accelerated labor migration to the Gulf. By 1985 the number of expatriates in GCC countries reached 4.1 million; by the 2010s, estimates ranged from 8 to 12 million.[10] Although Asians constitute the largest groups of migrant workers by far—over 7 million—about 3.5 million Egyptians, Yemenis, Jordanians, and other Arabs work in the Gulf as well. During the 1970s, Egyptians earned thirty times more as construction workers in Saudi Arabia than as farmers in Egypt. Engineers earned two to three times more in Kuwait than in Jordan.[11] For workers, peasants, and educated youth who could no longer find stable public-sector employment, working in the Gulf and sending remittances home was an easier option than struggling against the rollback of authoritarian welfarism at home.

So-called Islamic investment companies proliferated in the 1980s. Several originated by serving the needs of Arab migrant laborers who worked in the Gulf oil-producing countries during the oil boom and beyond. The Rayyan investment company, for example, began operating in Saudi Arabia in 1978 by repatriating funds of migrant workers to Egypt. By the mid-1980s, nearly two hundred Islamic investment companies operated in Egypt, with perhaps one million investors. Unsupported estimates of their total assets varied from $20 billion to $60 billion.[12] The capital of Rayyan, the largest of them, was estimated at EGP 5 billion (then officially US$1.00 = EGP .60, with a substantial black market) before the Egyptian government, fearing that they might be funding Islamist movements, shuttered all the Islamic investment companies in November 1986.[13]

In 1977, Saudi prince Mohammed Ibn Faisal established the Faisal Islamic Bank. By 1985, Faisal Islamic Bank and its smaller competitor, the Islamic

International Bank of Investment and Development, held 16.8 percent of the deposits in Egypt's commercial banking system.[14] After a decline in the 1990s due to the disrepute of the Islamic investment companies, they slowly resumed growth. In 2014 Islamic banks held just 8.3 percent of all deposits, but their market share was growing rapidly.[15]

During 2003–2009, the Arab Mashreq countries received over 60 percent of all foreign direct investment (FDI) from GCC countries—a total of €69.2 billion, far more than the €22.9 billion invested by European countries and the €5.2 billion invested by the United States and Canada. In the mid-2000s, these investments comprised over 70 percent of total FDI in Syria and Lebanon, 25 percent in Egypt, and 35 percent in Jordan. Adam Hanieh suggests that Gulf (Khaleeji) capital, much of it closely associated with the Gulf's ruling families, outgrew its rentier origins through such massive investments. In the process, it reformed the class structures of these Mashreq states.[16] This is salient in the banking sector, where Gulf capital is a substantial and often the largest investor in fourteen of Jordan's fifteen largest banks, nine of Lebanon's eleven largest banks, and nine of Egypt's twelve largest banks.

In addition to this influx of capital, the IFIs targeted Egypt, Morocco, Tunisia, and Jordan, along with Turkey, for economic reform and structural adjustment programs. They repeatedly issued overly optimistic reports about the putative successes they believed were the result of implementing, albeit not as rigorously as they advocated, their Washington Consensus policy recommendations.[17] Some of that optimism relied on falsified or unreliable national economic data; some of it came from inability to assess adequately the negative distributional effects of their policies; and some of it came from ideological dogmatism.

CONSOLIDATION OF US HEGEMONY

With the United States unable to contemplate a second Vietnam experience in the Gulf, in 1969 Henry Kissinger devised the "twin-pillars policy" to replace the British forces scheduled to withdraw from "east of Suez" in 1971. Kissinger envisioned Saudi Arabia and Iran as the regional gendarmes maintaining the status quo in the Gulf on behalf of the United States. The 1979 Iranian Revolution dramatically rendered the twin-pillars policy defunct. Unable to rely on Egypt or Saudi Arabia, and unable to use Israeli forces for interventions in the

Arab world, direct US military engagement in the Middle East has gradually escalated since then.

After the Iranian Revolution, bringing Egypt into the Western fold became more urgent. The inconclusive outcome of the 1973 war allowed the United States to establish a diplomatic monopoly over mediating the Arab-Israeli conflict. This was confirmed by Sadat's repeated declarations that the United States held "99 percent of the cards." The 1979 Egyptian-Israeli peace treaty undermined the Palestine Liberation Organization and shelved Palestinian demands for over a decade. Well before the demise of the Soviet Union, the United States became the preeminent power in the Middle East and North Africa. The major exceptions were Iran, Syria, and, until 2003, Libya and Iraq.

The 1979 Egyptian-Israel peace treaty temporarily isolated Egypt from its Arab neighbors and interrupted capital investment from the Gulf. But this was counterbalanced by the regular delivery of American aid. From 1979 to 2016, Egypt received about $30 billion in economic aid and $46 billion in military aid.[18] In 2017 the United States scaled back economic aid to $142 million annually from the 1979–1992 high of about $1 billion or more. Except for a sharp dip—due to short-lived "concerns" about the massive human rights violations of the post-coup regime in 2014—annual military aid has been in the range of $1.3 billion since 1983. Once Egypt no longer threatened Israel, military collaboration with the United States became institutionalized, exemplified by the biennial Operation Bright Star joint exercises initiated in 1980. In 1989 Egypt and Israel were designated "major non-NATO allies," the very year the American government established this designation.

The point of American aid and training was not to enhance the Egyptian military's operational capacity. A 2008 US embassy cable released by Wikileaks reported that "U.S. officers and officials familiar with the military assistance programs to Egypt describe the Egyptian Armed Forces as no longer capable of combat."[19]

THE LIVED EXPERIENCE OF STRUCTURAL ADJUSTMENT
IN EGYPT, TUNISIA, AND BEYOND

I lived and worked in Cairo during the 2000s, including for two years as director of Middle East studies at the American University in Cairo, a privileged position that rendered me an "expert" in the judgment of many journalists.

Corporate media typically uses quotes from "experts" to decorate a story whose frame is predetermined by conventional wisdom or a distant editor. Nonetheless, I took nearly every opportunity I was offered to speak to the media hoping that some useful information and analysis might sneak through.

What did journalists want to know about? First, the status of the Israeli-Palestinian "peace process"; second, the progress of economic liberalization; third, the progress of democratization. My usual response to these questions was:

1. There is no Israeli-Palestinian peace process.
2. While it became much easier for foreign capital to invest and repatriate profits, and the rate of GDP growth in the mid-2000s was impressive, there was no real economic liberalization. Conducting business successfully required loyalty to the regime and political connections to the circle around first son Gamal Mubarak, who controlled the economic ministries in Prime Minister Ahmad Nazif's government (2004–2011).
3. The relatively freer press from 2004 on, the somewhat more permissive 2005 parliamentary elections, and similar measures constituted only a patina of reform and were not signs of a fundamental commitment to democratization.

I repeatedly tried to suggest that, prompted by the Nazif government's acceleration of the sell-off of public assets and implementation of neoliberal economic policies, there was an extraordinary wave of strikes and collective actions by workers. From 1998 to 2003, contentious collective actions by Egyptian workers averaged 118 per year, compared to about thirty-three in the previous cycle of protest from 1986 to 1993. From 2004 until Mubarak's downfall in February 2011, the average annual number of contentious collective actions by workers escalated to 388. While concentrated in the public sector or in the recently privatized textile and clothing industry, by 2007 the movement had spread into every sector of the economy.

"My editor won't let me write about that" was the response of one of the journalists I attempted to persuade that this was a significant phenomenon. Only a handful of stories about the largest and most protracted nonviolent social movement in the Arab world since World War II appeared in the American and European press during the 2000s. Western think tanks also mostly missed the story.[20] Instead, praise for Egypt's annual GDP growth rates, which averaged 7 percent from 2006 to 2008, and the World Bank's *Doing Business* designation of Egypt as one of the top ten "most improved reformers" in 2008, 2009, and 2010 dominated the economic news.[21]

Although I did not personally witness it, there was a parallel story in Tunisia. In 1993 the IMF proclaimed Tunisia "a prime example of the successful transformation of an economy from one heavily regulated by the government to one based on market orientation."[22] French presidents Jacques Chirac and Nicolas Sarkozy hailed Tunisia's economic "miracle." Tunisia's "star pupil" status eased its entry into the General Agreement on Tariffs and Trade in 1990 and the World Trade Organization in 1995. In 1995, the European Union signed an association agreement with Tunisia—the first southern Mediterranean country to achieve this status. However, promising macroeconomic indicators obscured Tunisia's persisting poverty and unemployment, concentrated in the center-west and south of the country and among educated youth, while Tunis and the Sahel region were both richer and politically dominant.

During the 1990s and early 2000s the per capita number of strikes and workers' collective actions in Tunisia was even higher than in Egypt, although they were typically briefer and less intense.[23] The foremost exception was the six-month-long uprising in the Gafsa phosphate-mining basin in the first half of 2008. It received minimal and belated coverage in the French press and no coverage in the major American media. Unemployment in the four phosphate-mining towns ranged from 20.9 percent to 38.5 percent, and poverty rates in the entire Gafsa governorate were 30–40 percent.[24] The Gafsa rebellion originated as a demand for jobs and a protest against unemployment and poverty, both of which neoliberal economic policies exacerbated, as well as a cri de coeur against the local faces of autocracy and corruption—the Gafsa Phosphate Company and the leadership of the phosphate workers' union.

As Tunisia's Gafsa governorate exemplified, the policies promoted by the IFIs failed to set any Arab country on a trajectory of sustainable development. Per capita annual rates of GDP growth in the Middle East and North Africa from 1970 to 2010 were lower than any other region of the Global South except sub-Saharan Africa, although Egypt did significantly better than its neighbors during the oil boom of 1974–1985.[25] The 2003 *Arab Human Development Report* (*AHDR*) concluded that poverty in the Arab region was higher than usually reported by the IFIs.[26] The 2009 *AHDR* estimated that the average poverty rate for Arab countries from 2000 to 2006 was 39.9 percent.[27] Unemployment rates in the region were the highest in the Global South and about double those in Asia during the 1990s and 2000s.[28] Unemployment rates for youth in the Middle East (25.4 percent) and North Africa (23 percent) were more than double those elsewhere in the Global South in 2010, while the proportion of the population under thirty years old was the highest in the world.[29] These macroeconomic indicators suggest a crisis of the mode of capital accumulation, which has not been resolved by the popular uprisings of 2011.

A NEW MIDDLE EAST?

The most notable change prompted by the popular uprisings is the more aggressive role of Saudi Arabia and the UAE in enforcing a regional counterrevolutionary order. Their strategy has been to construct a sectarian "Sunni axis" including Bahrain, Egypt, and, incongruously, Israel, in opposition to Iran and its regional allies—Syria, Iraq, the Yemeni Houthis, Lebanese Hezbollah, and Palestinian Hamas. In 2011 they intervened militarily to quash the pro-democracy February 14th movement in Bahrain.

In Syria, GCC intervention initially supported various Islamist insurgents against the Assad regime. By further militarizing the conflict, GCC states helped marginalize the unarmed popular movement, ultimately creating a politico-military space for al-Qaeda and ISIS.

The Saudis backed the Egyptian military coup of July 3, 2013, against Muhammad Morsi, a Muslim Brother who narrowly won Egypt's first free presidential election just a year earlier. Since then, they have backed coup leader and current Egyptian president Abdel Fattah al-Sisi.

In 2015 Saudi Arabia and the UAE invaded Yemen to fight the Houthi rebels, who had ousted their chosen candidate as president. They simplistically labeled the Houthis Iranian agents, although it was the war launched against them that drew the Houthis closer to Iran. Despite decades of military purchases from the United States, the Saudi and Emirati militaries proved inept, and they committed many potential war crimes in which the United States, which has supplied them with logistical and intelligence support, is complicit. The Emiratis withdrew from Yemen in 2020, although they control powerful militias in the south with secessionist aspirations that the Saudis oppose.

The United States retains about the same number of forces in the Greater Middle East as it did before 2011: sixty thousand to seventy thousand troops, augmented by contractors, in the operational area of the Central Command. But the number of armed actions has increased. Special Forces and drones have been deployed to Pakistan, Syria, Yemen, and Somalia, as well as Afghanistan and Iraq.

Arms sales and military assistance programs have increased. The Obama administration sold Saudi Arabia more than $115 billion in arms, more than any other administration in the history of the Saudi-US alliance.[30] The Trump administration approved at least $1.4 billion more, although it took credit for many of the Obama-era deals.[31] Although Tunisia is not a major arms purchaser, President Obama declared Tunisia a major non-NATO ally following two dramatically lethal terrorist attacks in 2015 and requested that Congress authorize a 200 percent increase in military aid to nearly $100 million.[32] US arms sales to both Tunisia and Egypt proceeded despite their deteriorating post-2011 human rights records.

EGYPT AND TUNISIA: BETWEEN QATAR AND THE SAUDI-EMIRATI AXIS

After the 2010–2011 uprisings, the IMF acknowledged that it had ignored the highly unequal distribution of the benefits of the economic growth model it had promoted since the late 1970s. Its then managing director wrote on the IMF's blog, "Let me be frank: We were not paying enough attention to how the fruits of economic growth were being shared."[33] But in practice, the same basic portfolio of policies that the IMF touted before 2011 has simply been rebranded as "inclusive growth."

The IMF refused to grant post-2011 Egypt a $4.8 billion loan on conditions significantly different from those it imposed over the previous two decades. Morsi's presidency was destabilized when the price increases and other austerity measures the IMF demanded leaked to the press in late 2012. Egypt turned to aid and investment from the GCC countries. As those countries had since the 1970s, they stepped in to maintain Egypt's economic stability, ultimately fortifying the Saudi-Emirati-Egyptian alliance as the backbone of regional reaction against both secular and Islamist democratic political action.

Although Qatar was initially cautious, the GCC countries (except Oman, which is not a significant player) significantly increased their FDI in Egypt after the 2011 uprising.[34] Their shared objective was to prevent secular revolutionary elements from gaining ground. However, tensions among the GCC countries arose because it was widely assumed that Saudi Arabia funded the

Salafi Nur Party during the 2011–2012 parliamentary election campaign, while Qatar funded the rival Muslim Brothers–sponsored Freedom and Justice Party as well as Muhammad Morsi's 2012 presidential campaign.

Two factors roughly determined the timing of FDI from the GCC to Egypt: whether the Muslim Brothers or the military was politically ascendant, and the price of oil and natural gas, which collapsed in the second half of 2014. After assuming office in June 2012, President Morsi abruptly nationalized several Saudi infrastructure and construction projects, resulting in twenty-eight legal disputes with Saudi investors, who controlled over $2 billion in assets.[35] After the military deposed Morsi and launched a far-reaching and deadly campaign to suppress the Muslim Brothers, the parties quickly reached out-of-court settlements. Saudi-Egyptian relations grew closer and the pace of Saudi and Emirati investments quickened in the wake of the coup while Qatari investments declined. After the oil price bust, the Saudis could not maintain their peak investment rate of 2014–2015. Nonetheless, the UAE dramatically escalated its rate of investment, and Qatar did so more modestly.[36]

Foreign direct investment is only a part of the story. During 2011–2012, the Saudi Fund for Development disbursed grants, soft loans, and lines of credit as well: $430 million to finance development projects in several sectors, a $750 million line of credit to ease the state budget deficit, a $1 billion deposit in Egypt's Central Bank, a purchase of $500 million in treasury bonds, $200 million pledged for projects for small and medium-sized businesses, and $250 million in subsidized petroleum products. All told, the Saudi fund disbursed over $3 billion in addition to approximately $500 million in FDI.[37] From 2013 to 2015, Saudi investments and aid totaled some $9.25 billion.

Qatar's single largest contribution to Egypt consisted of deposits of $1 billion–$2 billion as a grant and $4 billion in loans to the Central Bank of Egypt, of which $3.5 billion was to be converted into bonds (in September 2013 Egypt returned $2 billion to Qatar when negotiations on the bond conversion collapsed).[38] From 2011 until the military coup of July 3, 2013, Qatar's total FDI, loans, and grants totaled between $8 billion and $10 billion—more than the Saudis contributed but perhaps not as much as the Emiratis.[39]

Saudi Arabia and the UAE were the leading players at the March 13, 2015, Egypt Economic Development Conference (EEDC) in Sharm el-Sheikh. Saudi Arabia, the UAE and Kuwait promised $4 billion each, of which $3 billion was to be deposited directly into the Central Bank and the remainder earmarked for projects.[40] Since 2014, the UAE has registered the highest ratio of official development assistance to gross national income in the world, with a majority of that assistance going to Egypt.[41] At the EEDC, Dubai's Sheikh Mohammed bin Rashid Al Maktoum announced that the UAE had invested $14 billion in Egypt since 2013, although this appears to include the $4 billion pledged at Sharm el-Sheikh. Qatar pledged nothing at the EEDC.

Capital City Partners, a private UAE-based development company, also proposed to invest $45 billion to design and build Egypt's New Administrative Capital, located halfway between Cairo and Suez.[42] But the Emiratis withdrew in September 2015. Instead, the China State Construction Engineering Corporation will undertake a large part of the project. Egypt's largest private construction firm, Arab Contractors, will build its sewage and water supply lines.

In 2015 total Arab investment in Egypt amounted to nearly $20 billion. Saudis held the largest share—27 percent, worth approximately $5.7 billion. Emiratis came next with $4.5 billion (21.4 percent), followed by Kuwaitis with $2.7 billion (11.2 percent).[43] Before the break in diplomatic relations in mid-2017, Qatar ranked ninth among countries with FDI in Egypt, with over $1 billion.[44] More than half of Qatari investments in Egypt came after 2011, suggesting that support for the Muslim Brothers was a significant motivation.

During Saudi King Salman bin Abdul Aziz's visit to Egypt in April 2016, the two countries signed investment agreements with a total value of $25 billion, although this amount may to some extent be aspirational.[45] In August 2017, Saudi Arabia announced a $500 billion plan to create a business and industrial zone—Neom—extending across its borders into Jordan and Egypt. The Saudis and Egyptians also established a joint development fund capitalized at $10 billion, with the Saudi share earmarked to develop the Egyptian side of the project in the South Sinai.[46] By 2017 total Saudi FDI in Egypt amounted to $7.2 billion, while the UAE's FDI reached $4.9 billion. Support for the Sisi regime was the likely impetus for the accelerated rate of investment.

With oil prices low, a war being waged in Yemen, and the diplomatic row they initiated with Qatar in June 2017, the Saudis and Emiratis alone could not keep Egypt afloat indefinitely. Egypt finally secured a $12 billion IMF loan in November 2016. Following the new script, the IMF's board of directors announced that the loan would "restore macroeconomic stability and promote inclusive growth.["]47 The IMF's conditionalities included floating the Egyptian pound, reducing subsidies on fuel, and adopting a 13 percent value-added tax— measures similar to those it had advocated since the 1970s. After the pound was floated, it lost nearly 50 percent of its value, and annual inflation rates spiked to over 30 percent. After the loan agreement was announced, the government deployed security forces in Cairo to thwart anti-austerity demonstrations.

Tunisia's trajectory differs from Egypt's because before 2011, it received no development assistance from GCC countries, and its exports to them were minimal. Eurozone countries, with France and Italy in the lead, were by far Tunisia's largest trading partners. From 2004 to 2007, the Saudis invested a modest $391 million in four projects: a fertilizer factory, a water-treatment facility, and two oil and gas power projects. Two of the projects were completed late in the Ben Ali era, and two after his ouster. Late in the 2000s, the UAE and Qatar began investing in real estate and telecommunications, but they froze those projects after the 2010–2011 popular uprising.[48]

The Qatar-based Al Jazeera satellite TV channel gave supportive coverage to the uprising that ousted Zine El Abidine Ben Ali. The moderate Islamist Ennahda-led transition regime reciprocated by drawing closer to Qatar. Just as in Egypt, Saudi Arabia and Qatar lined up on opposite sides in Tunisian domestic politics. Qatar supported Ennahda, while the Saudis, after provid-ing asylum to Ben Ali, supported the secularist Nidaa Tounes Party, founded and led by Béji Caïd Essebsi, a ninety-year-old political veteran who had held high offices in the old regime. Nidaa Tounes won a plurality in the October 26, 2014, elections for the Assembly of the Representatives of the People, and Essebsi won the presidential elections the following month. Nidaa Tounes and Ennahda established a coalition government in February 2015.

Their rivalry in Egypt and Tunisia was among the reasons that the Saudis and Emiratis imposed a boycott on Qatar in June 2017. Egypt, Bahrain, and Jordan followed suit. The boycotters alleged that Qatar supports terrorism. But the underlying issue is that Qatar refuses to adopt an antagonistic stance toward Iran because the two countries share the world's largest natural gas field, the South Pars/North Dome field in the Persian Gulf.

Nonetheless, because the stakes were lower, GCC investments in Tunisia were not as highly politicized as in Egypt. Qatari financial support increased substantially when Ennahda emerged as the strongest party in the early post–Ben Ali era. The Qatari National Bank deposited $500 million with the Tunisian Central Bank at 2.5 percent interest to bolster Tunisia's foreign currency reserves. Qatar also invested heavily in Tunisia, including the purchase of a 75 percent stake in the Tunisiana mobile phone company (now Ooredoo Tunisia) for $1.2 billion and the purchase of shares in the Tunisian Qatari Bank, raising its stake from 50 percent to 99.96 percent.[49] In May 2012 Qatar announced plans to invest $2 billion in the construction of an oil refinery at Skhira to refine and reexport Libyan oil.[50] Qatar dragged its feet because of the high cost of the project but renewed its commitment to proceed in 2018. Qatari investments in Tunisia dropped sharply after the removal of Ennahda from power and comprised only 5.43 percent of total nonenergy FDI in 2016, behind France, Germany, the United Kingdom, and Libya, but just ahead of the UAE's 5.07 percent.[51]

Unlike the Saudis, the UAE also significantly increased its investments in Tunisia after 2011. By 2012 they totaled $2.5 billion.[52] The UAE's stake in Tunisia increased further after Essebsi's inauguration as president in late 2014. By May 2015, Emirati FDI comprised 36.3 percent of total Tunisian FDI since 2003. Bahrain was the second-largest source of FDI, at nearly 14.7 percent, followed by France, the United Kingdom, and Italy. These figures are somewhat distorted by inclusion of the energy sector, where Gulf capital is concentrated. But Europeans are also major players in energy. The British Gas Group is by far the largest single foreign investor in Tunisia (until the Qatari refinery is built); its $2 billion stake is twice as large as that of the next-largest investor, the Austrian oil and gas conglomerate OMV. European FDI continues to dominate the nonenergy sectors of the economy.[53]

In June 2013, the IMF approved a $1.75 billion stand-by arrangement for Tunisia, followed by a $2.9 billion loan in June 2016. Echoing the statement that accompanied its loan to Egypt, the IMF announced that the Tunisian loan was "aimed at promoting more inclusive growth and job creation, while protecting the most vulnerable households."[54] But the IMF's conditions for the 2016 loan reiterated policies it had urged since Tunisia adopted its first Economic Reform and Structural Adjustment Program in 1986: reducing the government budget deficit by freezing wages of public employees, devaluing the Tunisian dinar to boost exports, and restructuring—that is, privatizing— public banks because the IMF believes that the market knows best. Six months later the government announced it would sell its shares in three state-owned banks and cut ten thousand public-sector jobs.[55] By March 2018, devaluation had driven up inflation to an annual rate of 7.6 percent.[56]

Qatari and French cosponsorship of the November 2016 investment conference Tunisia 2020 highlighted Qatar's decision to strengthen economic ties with Tunisia, likely to counter Saudi and Emirati influence. At the conference, Qatar promised an additional $1.25 billion in investment and aid, the largest from any source since 2011.[57] Saudi Arabia and Kuwait also made substantial promises: $800 million from the former, and $500 million in soft loans from the latter. In addition, the Kuwait-based Arab Fund for Economic and Social Development promised $1.5 billion in soft loans through 2020. Tunisia's quest for FDI from all the GCC countries, at least in part, explains its proclaimed neutrality in the Saudi- and Emirati-led campaign against Qatar. The European Investment Bank also promised $3.1 billion in loans at Tunisia 2020. These sums are substantial for Tunisia. But because most of the pledges made at Tunisia 2020 consisted of loans rather than investments, they may ultimately deepen Tunisia's economic crisis. Tunisia will need to repay those loans while implementing the austerity economic policies dictated by the IMF.

Egypt and Tunisia represent the polar outcomes of the 2011 Arab popular uprisings that did not culminate in warfare (Libya, Syria, Yemen). Tunisia has been widely hailed as the exceptional Arab success in transitioning to democracy. In Egypt, President Sisi has consolidated a praetorian dictatorship far harsher than the Mubarak-era regime. But the political economies of both countries feature strong elements of continuity with the previous order.

In narrower political terms, Egypt's "officers' republic" established in 1952 persists. The salient change is that the military, which for decades preferred to leave day-to-day governance to civilian political figures and the business class, has assumed a more prominent role in both politics and the economy. Egypt has also become an active partner in the regional counterrevolutionary axis led by Saudi Arabia and the UAE and supported by the United States.

Similarly in Tunisia, significant elements of the crony-capitalist class of the Ben Ali era and much of the pre-2011 administration remain in place. Tunisian democracy is largely limited to matters of electoral procedure. The Administrative Reconciliation Law enacted in September 2017 pardoned civil servants who engaged in corruption during the Ben Ali era, except for those who *personally* benefited from embezzling public funds. It also permitted them to return to positions of power in government. As of mid-2020, the government had not yet established the constitutional court stipulated in the post-2011 constitution. Until his death in July 2019, President Essebsi increasingly presidentialized power, as his predecessors had done, despite the lack of constitutional authority for many of his actions. According to a Gallup Poll taken after the October 2019 elections in which Kais Saied won the presidency and Ennahda won a plurality in the parliament), 64 percent of Tunisians had no confidence in their government, 79 percent said corruption is widespread, and 76 percent said that it is a bad time to find a job.[58]

Outbursts of popular rebellion in Tunisia in 2016 and again in 2018 raised demands and slogans similar to those heard during the movement to oust Ben Ali. These brief Tunisian outbursts of revolt foreshadowed a wave of large-scale, protracted popular protests that swept the Middle East and North Africa from 2016 until it was cut short by the COVID-19 pandemic in early 2020: the Rif movement in Morocco and nationwide uprisings in Sudan, Algeria, Lebanon, Iraq, and more briefly Egypt. These uprisings confirmed that the structural political economy issues highlighted by the 2011 cycle of protest have not been adequately addressed. They raised demands that were simultaneously specific to each country and its history (e.g., Amazigh rights in Morocco; the supply of utilities and dismantling of sectarian political structures in Lebanon and Iraq) and expressions of the crisis of petro-capitalism and its mode of regulation. Until that crisis is resolved, similar rebellions are likely to continue. Their outcomes will be determined by the level of organization of popular power and regional and international conditions.

Chapter 2

WHAT FUTURE FOR THE PRIVATE SECTOR IN THE NEW MIDDLE EAST?

Ishac Diwan

MORE THAN EVER, A DYNAMIC PRIVATE SECTOR IS ESSENTIAL FOR creating the jobs that increasingly educated youth aspire to in the Middle East and North Africa (MENA). This chapter explores the possibility of this happening in the near future. In thinking about the future of the private sector, one cannot escape the need to reflect on how two major recent shocks will reshape the political economy of the region: the uprisings of 2010–2011, their aftermath, and the resurgence of social contestation in 2019; and the oil shock of 2014–2015, which was exacerbated in 2020 with the global COVID-19 pandemic. Both shocks have created imbalances in the macroeconomy and have lowered growth. The prospects of low oil prices in the medium and long terms, and of increased social restlessness, pose fundamental challenges to all countries' development trajectories.

In the MENA region more than elsewhere, political logic infuses the workings of markets. This involves not only concerns about redistribution but also the organization of rent extraction and distribution, as well as control over organizations that might affect regime durability.[1] Arguably, the relentless pursuit of regime durability, which has generated such a high level of distrust among political elites toward an autonomous private sector, makes the MENA region unique. Indeed, the political science literature on the region identifies cronyism as the central mechanism that resolved the contradictions created in the 1990s by the gradual liberalization of the region's economies in environments where political power remained highly autocratic. By the late 2000s, "imperfections" in economic policies became a focus of attention, providing a means to understand how weakening regimes, in alliance with a supportive business elite, managed to redefine the rules of the game, simultaneously creating new sources of patronage and neutralizing possible opposition.[2] Since 2011, however, social movements have started to contest the low economic performance, and rising corruption, of the form of capitalism that emerged.

If political dominance over economics is a characteristic of the region, several important questions arise when thinking about the future of the private sector: What is it in the political environment that gave rise to this drive for control over the private sector? Given the emerging economic and political trends in the "New" Middle East, is this drive for control likely to weaken? Finally, what are the variations observed within the region in this regard, and what explains them?

POLITICAL SETTLEMENTS AND STATE-BUSINESS RELATIONS

To address questions on the private sector in the MENA region, it is necessary both to understand the determinants of the politics of state-business relations and to explore how the social circumstances of each country affect them. A useful frame for this investigation is that of political settlements, a political economy construct that encompasses state-business relations (SBRs), society-state relations, and the relationships between these two domains.[3]

The term "crony capitalism" has come to describe a variety of state-business relations, in the same manner that the term "corruption" has come to describe all sorts of noninstitutionalized relations, ranging from pure theft all the way to informal payoffs that play an important role in stabilizing the political order.[4] Different types of crony relations are prevalent across the world and lead to different types of economic outcomes. This is because relations between state and business can represent different types of exchanges, depending on the type of political system in which they are inscribed. Thus, to understand MENA specifically, we need to start by unpacking its SBRs' terms of exchange.

The state-business relation is best thought of as a patron-client arrangement in which the state is (typically) the patron, business is the client, and the relationship between the two sides is the outcome of bargaining. On the

business side, privileged firms might get, at minimum, a commitment to secure property rights, which might be especially valuable in environments
where state institutions do not function well. These relations tend to be personalized, for example, through matrimonial relations, or institutionalized,
as in an industrial policy that supports those sectors that the state wants to
encourage. Privileges might take a variety of forms, such as a favored treat-
ment by regulatory authorities, trade protection, or privileged access to public
contracts, credit, land, or infrastructure.

What the politically connected firm delivers to the patron in exchange
for economic privileges varies depending on the particulars of the political
settlement. Broadly speaking, privileged firms might provide three types of
payback to politicians.

In the first type, politically connected firms may pay back the favors they
receive by generating economic growth, taxes, and jobs. This is especially
valuable for rulers with long horizons, who are concerned about the long-
term durability of their regimes and are in a position to prioritize long-term
economic growth.

In the second type, politically connected firms might provide a financial
payback to politicians. This might include rents shared by the political elite
to bind them to a governing coalition. It can also include direct support to finance election campaigns and capture the media. More ambitiously, privileged
firms might become the node of a clientelistic network that offers jobs and/or
services to political clients. In all these cases, privileged firms typically operate
in sectors where the state can easily direct favors in discretionary ways, such
as when it procures construction services, or when it licenses extraction rights
for natural resources. To the extent that this type of cronyism is limited to a
small range of rent-thick sectors, it would have a moderately negative impact
on aggregate economic growth.

In the third type of payback, politically connected firms might play an
even more active political role, becoming part of a system of policing markets
with the goal of excluding potential opposition from access to the heights of
the economy. In this case, privileged firms might be pushed to occupy market
spaces precisely in order to deny market opportunities to others. This tends
to happen in particular in sectors with high growth potential, because this
is where the risk to autonomous agents' growth is the greatest. This type of

political management of markets is especially costly in terms of economic performance; it is valuable only for regimes that care more about short-term survival than about long-term performance.

In actual political economies, SBRs will have some elements of each of the three types of relationship. Nevertheless, one type of relationship will likely be dominant. For example, South Korea during its developmental stage had SBRs predominately of the first type, generating growth, taxes, and jobs; countries with high levels of political competition like Brazil or Ghana tend to have SBRs predominately of the second type, financial payback; and hard autocracies such as Russia that rely on repression and populism to survive use the third type of SBRs, political market management, more heavily.

Thus, crony SBRs might have positive or negative effects on growth, depending on the type of payback expected from the client firms, itself determined by the broader political economy perspective. Generally, the question is whether firms—privileged or not—have an incentive to invest in productivity-upgrading methods or in rent-extraction efforts. The first type of SBR favors productivity, the third type pushes toward a rent-seeking economy, and the second type falls in between. Political and economic circumstances affect those incentives. The greater the political risk, and the farther domestic firms are far from the global competitive frontier (in the sense of being much less efficient than their global competitors), the greater are firms' incentives to invest in political relationships and rent extraction.

The MENA region's poor economic performance since the market reforms of the 1990s relates to the prevalence of the exclusionary motive of the third type of payback, market policing or management, and the related narrowness of the region's business elite.[5] To understand better both the genesis and the implications of the narrow form of capitalism that developed in the MENA region, it is necessary to expand the discussion to the broader realm of the type of political settlements in which they have evolved.

Let us define a political settlement as a three-way arrangement between state, business sector, and society that ensures some coherence between power and money in ways that might be sustained without generating self-destructive forces. Political and social conditions might have a positive or negative effect on SBRs. There are at least three mechanisms that matter in this. First, for labor to make a positive contribution to growth, it must be healthy, equipped with marketable skills, and protected from market shocks in ways that foster the type of flexibility that, for example, enables migration to cities and to growing sectors. Second, the provision of social services should be financeable in ways that do not crowd out important investment in competitiveness, such as the provision of adequate infrastructure. Third, social demands should not lead to the type of contestation that unduly increases political risk (as this depresses investment incentives) or creates unsustainable pressures for fiscal expenditures to pacify society.

When social demands rise, reestablishing political stability requires adjustments not only in fiscal and structural policies but also in political strategies (i.e., inclusion or repression), in order to reestablish regime durability. These adjustments test elite cohesion, especially if reforms end up reducing rent extraction. Adjustments might take different forms, depending on social and political circumstances. In particular, political adjustments might include concessions by existing elites, reflected in a broadening of the governing coalition through the social and economic inclusion of particularly vociferous groups. Contrariwise, they might take the form of a narrowing of the ruling coalition and a greater dependence on the stick of political and economic repression. Thus, whether political management of the growth process has positive or negative effects on SBRs depends largely on the scale of social demands and on whether regime survival strategies advantage more accommodation and inclusion or repression and exclusion.

THE CONTRADICTIONS OF CRONY CAPITALISM

In order to appreciate the role played by social discontent in shaping the resulting SBRs, we must explore the political environment of the MENA region in which the reforms of the 1980s took place. During the move from state-run economies to economies in which the market played a bigger role, the massive rollback of the state reduced access to social services and civil service jobs, reversing previous dynamics of social mobility. This represented a clear break from an earlier social contract that was anchored in a growing middle class and connected to state employment.[6] The changing private-public balance sparked social discontent and contestation just when autocratic governments were losing the tools through which they had established their authority. These included not only the mobilization of nationalist, and in many cases, populist, ideology, but also the ownership of state-owned enterprises, large investment budgets, large-scale provision of civil services, and exorbitant military and security spending. This was especially true of the republican revolutionary regimes in Algeria, Egypt, Iraq, and Syria, which comprised elites that hailed from social backgrounds different from those of preceding regimes and that distrusted the old economically and politically dominant classes.

At the same time, regimes were unable to draw the social forces that might benefit from market liberalization into their ruling coalition. Unlike other regions of the world, in the MENA region the regimes in power chose to selectively liberalize their economy but not their polity. They did so because of factors specific to the region: the presence of oil rents, which allowed weakened regimes to expand their repressive apparatus; support from important international actors for autocrats who could protect their interests, be it oil, the fight against extremism, or the Israeli-Palestinian issue; and the institutional legacy of the past, when state intervention facilitated the creation and distribution of regulatory rents. States with populist regimes bore an additional burden: bureaucracies that had inherited an anti-business view from the socialist past.

In the end, economic liberalization took place in the 1990s parallel to a consolidation of state power in most countries. Regimes brought new business elites into the ruling coalition while they pushed out old allies, such as unions and farmers, with the most dramatic examples of this in Egypt, Syria, and Iraq. As the political science literature of the period asserted, the resilience of autocracy in the region depended on the construction of a system of organized co-optation and repression.[7] The combination of carrots and sticks resulted in a deeply polarized society, with a great political divide separating regime supporters and opponents. Although much attention has focused on the repression of political opposition—first against the left, then against groups connected with political Islam—the attempt to control markets was part of the same repressive drive.

The survival strategies adopted by regimes thus resulted in an economic liberalization that rested on a narrow form of capitalism. In addition to a preference for a controlled private sector, other characteristics of the political settlement had implications for the type of SBRs that developed. First, the strategy of social co-optation often took the form of consumption subsidies to the middle class (especially energy), which generated large fiscal deficits, crowding out public investment in infrastructure, with direct implications for the competitiveness of the private sector.[8] Second, as public-sector wages fell in real terms, petty corruption rose, making it easier for rich firms to afford to capture regulatory authority for their own benefit. Third, the rise in social discontent increased political risk, inhibiting private investment but also strengthening the bargaining power of crony firms vis-à-vis their patrons, which demanded increased rents in exchange for keeping up their side of the bargain.

The typical pattern of political settlement/SBR that arose in the MENA region includes a deep differentiation between a small, formal private sector, with protected workers and privileged firms, and a large, totally unregulated and unprotected informal economy. The resulting market segmentation has led to a low-level equilibrium. On the one hand, limited competition reduces the incentive for innovation and accumulation of capital by firms and skills by workers. On the other hand, the dualistic nature of the corporate landscape, and of the labor market, reduced the ability of firms and labor to organize themselves in ways that could legitimately represent their collective interest to demand productivity-enhancing change.[9]

Change introduced by a reformist elite has been rare in the region, and when states have introduced change, the elite has been hesitant and unambitious. The temptation to delay political reforms through repressive means has created tensions among governing elites, pitting reformist moderates against repressive hard-liners and generating additional political risk. With the exception of a few countries, such as Morocco and Jordan, rising political instability empowered hard-liners who were backed by a narrow economic elite, especially when external rents were high enough to finance repression.[10] Internal politics have rarely been supportive of positive change. In particular, losers from reforms have had a lot to lose and have supported the hard-liners, whereas those who stood to gain were fragmented and had little influence, weakening the moderates. It may not have been possible for those who gained from reform to compensate the losers—for example, the political opposition's commitments to allow current elites to benefit from future growth were not credible, a situation that was especially salient in countries where regimes had blood on their hands.[11]

Instead, the push for change came in 2011 from social movements. The up-risings of 2011 were driven by popular discontent over cronyism, low economic performance, and the lack of social justice. An important source of discontent relates directly to the furthering of market segmentation, which increasingly divided new and more educated cohorts of youth into two groups: a minority that attained high-paying jobs in the small, formal private sector and a large group that had to accept low wages in the informal market.[12]

REGIONAL VARIATIONS IN SETTLEMENTS

Although most of the MENA regimes remained autocratic in the aftermath of the economic reforms of the 1980s, there was more variation in political set-tlements than is typically acknowledged. There were several reasons for this. Besides great variation in levels of income and different historical traditions (especially populist revolutionary versus conservative regimes), variations in access to external rents (and in particular to oil revenues) played a determining role in structuring different types of political settlements.

First, consider this question: when do autocratic rulers in oil-producing countries support private-sector development? The incentive of rulers to con-trol the private sector, and thus its resulting narrowness, depends on the size of oil rents per capita. However, the effect is not linear; instead, it resembles a U-shaped curve: countries with middle levels of per capita oil wealth can be expected to repress the private sector more, whereas at both low and high levels of oil wealth, autocrats interested in regime preservation would repress the private sector less.[13]

Thus, when per capita resource rents are high, as is the case for the Gulf oil exporters with small populations, oil transfers to the population tend to be high, rendering the private sector less threatening because its members have less will to rebel. As a result, rulers who transfer higher oil rents in absolute terms to their population foster a political settlement in which more dyna-mism is permitted in the private sector. Similarly, when per capita oil rents are low, as in Tunisia or Morocco, economic growth depends a lot on private sector development, and the political settlement tends to be more open. Conversely, when per capita resource levels are more constrained, as in the Middle Eastern oil exporters with large populations, rulers are more threatened by the rise of the private sector. In these cases, potential political insurgents have less to lose in terms of the destruction of assets and thus greater willingness to rebel, and a rise in private incomes can have a large effect on their ability to mount a successful insurgency. In this context, autocrats tend to restrict private-sector development in order to preempt or suppress threats from outsiders.

The resulting typology resembles that of Henry and Springborg, who distinguish the so-called princes of oil, bunker states, and bully regimes.[14] While the latter two are authoritarian, bunker states use more sticks than carrots, whereas bully states use more carrots than sticks. Bunker states such as Algeria, Iraq, Iran, and Syria rely on relatively modest external rents (e.g., oil, Arab aid) to finance a repressive system that is dependent on a small elite and a narrow patronage network. After the oil bust of the 1990s, the use of repression to control opposition groups has been typically aimed at poorer parts of the population and in marginalized regions, including among constituencies that earlier had been an important component of the ruling coalition, as in Baathist Syria and Iraq. On the other hand, the bully states—Tunisia, Morocco, and Jordan—have had a relatively larger base of productive private-sector firms. The borderline between the two categories is blurred, and also dynamic. For example, Egypt, with access to geopolitical rents (plus Suez and remittances), is in this typology at the margin of each category. Saudi Arabia, where external rents are falling fast, is at risk of moving into the bunker category; in contrast, Sudan may be moving out of the bunker category.

In this discussion, it is clear that economic growth is more likely to take place in countries with low and high rents per capita countries than in the middle oil countries. In these cases, four different models have achieved some measure of economic success. Each has enjoyed episodes of successful economic outcomes post-liberalization, and each faces the challenges of the New Middle East differently.

The first relatively successful model is the one provided by the Gulf Cooperation Council (GCC), in which economies rest on the twin pillars of state capitalism and high levels of oil rents per capita. This model is unique to the MENA region, inasmuch as few other countries are both as autocratic and as rich as those that make up the GCC. In these countries, political stability has rested on supporting a large middle class through public employment, state-delivered services, and consumption subsidies. Among GCC members, the state dominates not only state-owned enterprises but large parts of the private sector as well. Rather than repress the private sector, rulers have tended to nurture it in order to provide incentives for economic elites to support the political order. As a result, the private sector has grown, becoming larger and more sophisticated over time. But it has created few jobs for the national population and relies massively on imported (immigrant) labor. In the New Middle East with low oil prices, the model faces headwinds, as the public sector cannot create new jobs for the educated young people entering the labor market, especially in the countries of Saudi Arabia, Bahrain, and Oman, where space to do this in the national budgets has dramatically shrunk.

But oil did not bring good economic performance everywhere. Indeed, the relative dynamism of the private sector in the GCC countries stands in sharp contrast with the private sector's extreme weakness in a group of countries with large per capita oil rents but also larger populations. These middle oil countries have been hit worse by the "oil curse." They have tended to be dominated by highly autocratic and populist regimes, such as the military-security clan that has ruled Algeria since its independence, Iraq under Saddam Hussein, and Baathist Syria. All three regimes repressed heavily private-sector activity and have instead relied for survival on a powerful security apparatus. In these countries, the only firms that regimes allow to grow are those owned by very close allies of the rulers. Market liberalization, such as occurred in Algeria during the early 1990s, Iraq in the 1980s, and Syria in the early 2000s, was short-lived at best. As a result, private activity takes place in the tightly controlled (and small) formal sector or in the unregulated informal economy. Efficient and competitive firms are unable to take root in such environments.

The second model is that of a controlled but relatively well-managed capitalism. The main cases here are Morocco and Jordan. In Morocco, the narrowness of the middle class has enabled the regime to ignore social demands and to push massive resources—public and private—into investment activities. In Jordan, the ethnic composition of the middle class has allowed the monarchy to expand the private sector without fearing that it will come to dominate politics.[15] As a result, the two monarchies have enjoyed a relatively stable social order—they have generated protest movements, but ones that call for various reforms rather than replacement of the regime. In both countries, however, the growth of the formal private sector has remained relatively modest, with Morocco managing to push some sectors closer to the global frontier than

Jordan (e.g., banking, tourism, value-added phosphates, automobiles). Jordan is grappling with important macroeconomic imbalances as a result of its dependency on remittances and development assistance from the GCC.

The third model is one of a weak state in which the private sector carries out its activities in the interstices of state influence. Lebanon's relatively fast growth until the start of the Syrian war in 2011 illustrates this model best. The Lebanese political system rests on competitive clientelism, but with a small range of politically connected sectors—such as health, education, construction, and mining—where the state retains some influence through regulatory mechanisms.[16] The Lebanese model, initiated by Rafic Hariri in the early 1990s, was ultimately undone by the political polarization brought about in 2019 by the New Middle East. The seeds of the current crisis were planted when the sectarian political elites reacted to the rise in regional insecurity by sharing power in a large inclusive coalition, which made it impossible to achieve decisive economic adjustments, even when it became evident that these were needed to avoid macroeconomic weaknesses exploding into a financial crisis.

The fourth and most successful growth episode in the neighborhood, but not in the Middle East proper, is that of Turkey between 2002 and 2013, when the country experienced extended growth after the Justice and Development Party (or AK Party) came to power. The Turkish model combines democratic populism and economic inclusion. In the case of Turkey, the economic privileges that the AK Party provided to its base of small and medium-sized enterprises, known as "the Anatolian tigers," fostered inclusion and growth. Further stimulating this growth was the proximity of Turkish firms to the global technology frontier, a position spurred by reforms undertaken by the government of Turgut Özal in the 1980s. The success of the tigers, who continued to support the AK Party, provided the regime with durability. On top of it all, populist appeal to the poor through Islamism and, importantly, to the pious middle classes, who enjoyed greater business opportunities, encouraged political stability as well.[17] This period of growth-cum-stability seems to have ended as the New Middle East took shape, but the early era of the political party illustrates the power of including the private sector in order to propel economic growth, as well as the possibility that under particular circumstances, politics might actually foster increased economic inclusion. It is worth considering whether this model could become influential in MENA countries in the future—such a virtuous alignment of politics and economics might be in the cards, for example, in Tunisia, Sudan, Algeria, or Iraq in particular.

The MENA region's political economy has been hit by important macroeconomic shocks, and all three relatively successful models have since been undermined by their own internal contradictions. There are two important dynamics at play: how the collapse in oil revenue plays out and whether a country is democratizing or restoring autocratic rule. The GCC states need to create jobs for their nationals in the private sector. The politically more open and competitive states—which have come to include Tunisia and Iraq— need to muster the strength to reign in their macroeconomic situation. And the countries that have come to rely disproportionally on coercion to stay in power, such as Egypt, need to find ways to entice the private sector to become more active. The main question of interest is whether these new factors will push governments to be more open to private-sector development or, instead, choose repression as a short-term means to survival, at the cost of lower economic growth.

MORE OPENNESS OR AUTOCRATIC RESTORATION?

The governments that emerged from the uprisings of 2011 inherited a system that failed to deliver strong growth but enabled at least a few politically connected firms to flourish. In terms of the latter, the uprisings initially made the situation worse, disturbing, and in some cases eliminating, the existing privileges enjoyed by select private firms. In the countries affected by the uprisings, there was no certainty that the property rights of the elites that had previously been protected from state predation would continue to be protected in the future. In the words of Lant Pritchett, "ordered deals," even when they are restricted to a narrow set of firms, remain, from a business climate perspective, better than "disordered deals," or unpredictable SBRs in which both petty and grand state predation create uncertainty for all firms.[18] Once established privileged relations collapse, there are two ways forward that might again strengthen economic incentives. The first is to move toward fair and well-enforced rules for all firms, a road that is difficult to travel in the shadow of the corrupting influence of an underpaid bureaucracy and a polarized political environment. The other route is for the new regime to rehabilitate the system of privileges around a new circle of loyal cronies.

Both routes are challenging, as illustrated by the cases of Egypt and Tunisia. In Egypt, President Abdel Fattah al-Sisi is, like his predecessor, wary of the political clout of an autonomous private sector. He has therefore patronized friendly cronies whom he trusts. The only difference with the Mubarak regime is that now the army is in charge of managing them. But he remains wary of the proverbial Arab "street" that has repeatedly exploded in Egypt and around the region when economic insecurity becomes unbearable. Because there can be no social dialogue, debate, or compromise with an amorphous "street," the regime delays reforms until they become unavoidable—as happened with the sudden and massive devaluation of the Egyptian pound in 2016, which sent a major economic and social shock through the country. This situation is economically inefficient and politically risky, dependent on populist appeals to nationalism and identity to hide economic failure.

In Tunisia, corruption flourished after the revolution because of a breakdown in bureaucratic discipline and the high financial demands of an overly competitive political system. The power-sharing deal between liberal and Islamist forces may have reduced political instability in the short term, but this came at a high economic cost, as the broad coalition in power was unable to implement the economic reforms needed to stabilize the macroeconomy. This has weakened both state finances and corporate profitability, stymieing a return to growth.

So far, neither Egypt nor Tunisia has improved competitiveness to any substantial degree. In both countries, there is growing public dissatisfaction with economic performance. But over time, this is likely to help Tunisians find new, cooperative solutions while also moving Egypt in the opposite direction by encouraging distributional fights and myopic policies. Although the start-up costs of a new Tunisian political system continue to weigh on the economy, greater inclusion has fostered dialogue, and one might hope that this will end up encouraging win-win bargains between groups with political power. The national debate has become more constructive, focusing on how labor and business might share fairly the burden of a necessary adjustment. Local elections have brought to power new independent groups that are invested more in performance and less in identity politics. The 2019 presidential election brought to power a newcomer bent on accelerating the fight against corruption.

In both countries public debt is on the rise and will soon reach unsustainable levels, but Tunisia's progress toward democratic consolidation appears to be starting to pay dividends. By 2020, just before the COVID-19 crisis, the economy had begun to recover: private investment had increased to nearly 20 percent of gross domestic product, from a low of 17 percent just four years earlier. In contrast, Egypt's economic stabilization efforts were much more successful after the initiation of an International Monetary Fund program in 2016. But private investment in Egypt remained below 10 percent of gross domestic product, among the lowest historical levels, and despite higher growth and a decline in inflation, poverty continued to rise. As a result, Egypt's strategy of autocratic restoration does not offer a sustainable economic path, keeping political risk high and the private sector narrow.

Tunisia remains mired in a state of early democratic development, with excessive competition in the political realm and few institutions with the power to restrain that competition (e.g., the regulation of campaign finance, the enforcement of conflict-of-interest rules). The elections in 2019 resulted in a fragmented parliament and revealed a broad popular dissatisfaction with political elites. Two paths seem possible in the future. The first is a continuation of intense political competition. In its early phases, a competitive system is likely to continue to generate macroeconomic instability. It is possible that the situation will improve over time, but only if institutional arrangements—such as macroeconomic stability and, more ambitiously, the protection of property rights—are reached between the main parties that would commit them to policies that are essential for growth. The second path would come with the dominance of a particular party in the country. In that case, the Tunisian model might end up resembling the Turkish one of growth by inclusion. As in the case of Turkey, a financial crisis that further shakes the confidence of the electorate in the traditional parties might herald such a scenario.

Other countries hit by large shocks could also end up with more political competition or an attempt to restore the old system. The explosion of the economic model in Lebanon exemplifies this choice: it is unclear at the moment whether it can lead to the renewal of the clientelistic political system, as pushed by the street revolt that started in 2019, or whether it will usher a return of sectarian power sharing, albeit in an impoverished form that relies more on security rents than on external flows. In Iran, Algeria, and Iraq, all characterized by internal divisions and deteriorating economic conditions, a broad range of outcomes seems possible in the future, given the weaknesses of regimes in place. In these cases, the currently dominant parties might fracture, but it is unclear whether this would result in increased political participation, a meltdown (as in Syria and Yemen), or autocratic restoration (as in Egypt).

Jordan and Morocco have chosen intermediate strategies, which combine improvements in the rules governing the private sector with selective interventions to promote regime-connected firms. Unlike Lebanon, Jordan has been more resilient to the shock waves created by the Syrian war. But the closing of the fiscal space will require austerity, which will further inflame the street. In both countries, employment growth will remain constrained if short-term political incentives inhibit gains on the economic inclusion front.

LOWER OIL PRICES

The oil-producing countries of the MENA region face the twin challenges of having to stabilize their internal and external balances in the face of a large macroeconomic shock and to reform their economic structure in order to create new sources of growth to complement their still overly dominant oil sector. The specificities of the current shock are its extraordinary size (on average, a 50 percent fall in oil prices after 2014, and a further 50 percent in 2020), the fact that it comes on the heels of a long period of high prices (2000–2014), and the high probability that oil prices will remain depressed in the future. In Saudi Arabia (and also in Bahrain and Oman), the fiscal deficit has been somewhat reduced by slashing public investment, but it remains high at over 10 percent of non-oil gross domestic product, and it is becoming necessary to tax the non-oil economy. In other words, it is no longer possible to shield nationals from the oil shock.

In Saudi Arabia, the Ritz-Carlton episode—during which detained princes and heads of industries had to "pay back" about $100 billion of their wealth—illustrates the policy dilemma ahead. It is possible to view the expropriation of a group that was politically connected and favored in the past as a positive signal of burden sharing fairly. Indeed, the episode reportedly eased opposition to the introduction of a new value-added tax. At the same time, it is possible to read the expropriation as a signal of the weakening of property rights at a time when the business climate needs improvement. In the past, the wealthy ruling elites of the GCC countries have secured themselves and consolidated their power by avoiding high levels of market repression. The question now is whether the current oil shock will strengthen similar incentives or will push Saudi Arabia, in particular, toward the more exclusionary type of political settlement of the middle oil countries.

The current challenge for Saudi Arabia is to find a more productive form of social organization that enlarges the economic pie. It can be argued that the best policy going forward will expand national labor force participation and its productivity. It is feasible to make huge gains on this front because the national labor force is grossly underemployed and increasingly well educated. Currently, only 35 percent of the working-age population works, and when it does, this is largely in low-productivity government jobs. This compares to employment rates of about 60 percent for member countries of the Organization for Economic Cooperation and Development. Low national participation rates are largely the result of women's extremely low participation—although men's participation is not high by international standards either. Projections suggest that with participation rates growing to 60 percent, non-oil national income could double. The addition to national wealth is comparable in magnitude to the kingdom's oil wealth.[19]

How might this be achieved? About 70 percent of nationals work in the public sector, while expatriates fill 80 percent of private-sector jobs. To encourage national labor to work in the private sector, the wages that private firms pay to expatriates need to go up, and national reservation wages need to go down. In this scenario, national labor will, over time, largely replace foreign labor, turning Saudi Arabia into a normal oil economy, with a productive private sector of nationals servicing a large oil-based public sector.

The main challenges to such an ambitious reform program are eliciting social cooperation and avoiding distributional fights. There are two main risks: doing nothing and doing harm. It is entirely feasible that the kingdom might attempt to avoid reform by borrowing. Equally, a mismanaged reform can also end up harmful. In particular, pushing firms to reduce their employment of foreign labor without incentivizing them to invest in the creation of more productive jobs will not allow them to pay higher wages to Saudis and will end up in higher consumption costs. Doing nothing and doing harm will both lead to slow decay and harsher adjustment down the road.

The oil shock will be even harder to digest in Algeria, Iraq, and Iran, which used the last oil boom to stabilize their fragile regimes through a populist consumption drive. In these states, regimes have few options for survival short of increasing the repression of populations and markets. The experience of Syria teaches us that it is impossible to underestimate how far regimes might go in defending themselves against change, especially once they have blood on their hands. Nevertheless, it remains to be seen, on a case-by-case basis, whether lower oil revenues will boost moderates, who stand to gain by placing themselves (or their children) at the heart of a more open form of capitalism, or will induce regimes to seek refuge in a myopic strategy of autocratic hardening, as has happened in Egypt.

For decades, political settlements in the Middle East looked robust, generating a large literature on the resilience of autocracy. The uprisings of 2011 were both unexpected and surprisingly synchronized across countries, revealing a convergence in popular dissatisfaction across the region. However, the modes of governance and the varieties of capitalism that exist in the region have so far prevented the emergence of broad-based reformist regimes. As crony capitalism became entrenched, the formal private sector gave up its role of militating for the upgrade of institutions that govern markets, preferring instead to protect its short-term interests through personalized relations. Elite labor also became protective of its short-term interests and largely gave up its role as a champion for long-term national progress. Moreover, the limited extent of formal employment also weakened and fragmented the structural links between labor and business. This situation exacerbated the distrust between workers and capitalists, and also undermined the potential for class compromise. As the dualism between formality and informality in business and labor relations grew, the countries of the region became stuck in a trap of low equilibrium.

Internal and external pressures post-2011 are increasingly pushing MENA countries to diverge in the form of their political settlement and their economic arrangements. To survive, regimes will increasingly need to deliver economic growth and good-quality jobs. To do so, they will have to stabilize their relations with both the private sector and society at large. In the end, some regimes will manage to renew themselves, and others will likely fail.

In the meantime, the predicament of the private sector everywhere is that it will have to survive in the face of heightened political uncertainty. When other states outside the region have found themselves stuck in this kind of political-economy trap, they have tried to escape in one of two ways. The first approach is to strike an elite deal, as exemplified by the path followed by East Asia. The second approach, championed by the middle class, is to build a broad coalition of workers and firms, as in post–World War II Europe and, more recently, Eastern Europe.

If neither approach is allowed and moderate reformists remain excluded from governing coalitions, change can come only from an alliance between the broader middle class and the poor. In Iraq, Algeria, Lebanon, and Sudan, and perhaps soon in other countries, it is this type of broad social movement that has become the driving force for change. These social movements as coalitions have a long-term interest in upgrading institutions to improve economic and social performance. But whether this can happen in a gradual and peaceful way remains to be seen. The alternative is stark. The experience of the first phase of the Arab uprisings ended in disappointment and extracted large economic and social costs; a failure to bring about change from above will leave rebellious social forces no option but to attempt again, at some point, to force change through revolutionary rather than evolutionary means.

Chapter 3

EDUCATION AND HUMAN SECURITY
Centering the Politics of Human Dignity

Laurie A. Brand

IN THE DECADES FOLLOWING THE SECOND WORLD WAR, THE Middle East and North Africa (MENA) region witnessed a tremendous expansion of national educational institutions at the primary and secondary, as well as technical and university, levels. According to the stylized narrative found in the publications of international development organizations, by the 1980s, what followed were growing budgetary crises that came about in part because of the expansion of the state sector that was financed by external borrowing. Reducing the size of the state, including its role in providing goods and services, became the order of the day. Even those states that maintained their levels of spending on education faced fast-growing populations, which forced budgets to cover more and more students, teachers, and infrastructure, or physical plant. Consequently, educational quality deteriorated significantly, leaving students ill prepared for the labor market, compounding already-serious levels of unemployment and contributing to the scourge of religious extremism in the region.

The poor quality of education and the need for change are certainly well recognized across the region. Indeed, the *Arab Human Development Report, 2016* revealed disturbingly low levels of popular satisfaction with educational quality regardless of the UN Development Programme's Human Development Index rankings (HDI). Among countries with a low HDI, satisfaction was 35 percent in Yemen and 38 percent in Sudan. Among those with a medium HDI, in Egypt satisfaction reached only 40 percent; in Morocco, 41 percent; and in Iraq, 50 percent. Countries with a high HDI ranking still saw troubling levels, with Tunisia at 44 percent; Jordan, 61 percent; and Algeria, 64 percent. Even in several countries with a very high HDI, such as Kuwait and Saudi Arabia, satisfaction reached only 65 percent.[1] Reform proposals aimed at raising educational quality have generally been technocratic in nature, emphasizing improved teacher training, pedagogies that promote critical thinking skills rather than rote memorization, and an upgrading of curricula to better prepare students for the labor market of the so-called knowledge economy. Unfortunately, the stylized account that underpins such reform programs ignores the most important factors that have shaped the region's development, educational or otherwise. One need not delve deeply into Middle East history to see the central role that political repression, regional conflicts, and external interventions have played.

Since independence, the authoritarianism that has characterized the region has meant that the freedom associated with knowledge production, like other freedoms, has been suspect and circumscribed: "Arab regimes' . . . view of knowledge is strictly expedient: knowledge is simply another means to consolidate their power and plans."[2] Although such limitations have not been equal across states of the region, or static, curbs on the independence of the academy have cost MENA societies dearly in terms of lost human development potential.

Even more damaging than repression are the civil wars and insurgencies (Algeria, Iraq, Jordan, Lebanon, Libya, Oman, Sudan, Syria, and Yemen), regional wars (1948, 1967, 1973, 1982, 2014–2016), external military interventions (1956, 1991, 2003, 2014), and episodes of occupation (Egypt, Iraq, Jordan, Kuwait, Lebanon, Palestine, and Syria) the region has suffered. As the discussion that follows makes clear, whichever other sectors may have been transformed by post-2003 developments to constitute a New Middle East, education has continued to bear the brunt of the worst excesses of violence against MENA populations and their basic infrastructure.

EDUCATION AND HUMAN SECURITY

It was the UN Development Programme's 1994 *Human Development Report* that first introduced the term *human security*, defining it as the condition that enables people to exercise safely and freely their choices to be who they want to be, and to be relatively confident that the opportunities they have today will not be lost tomorrow. Shahrbanu Tajbakhash's specification of three components of human security summarizes well the emphases of the now-extensive literature on the concept: *"freedom from fear* (conditions that allow individuals and groups protection from direct threats to their safety and physical integrity, including various forms of direct and indirect violence, intended or not); *freedom from want* (conditions that allow for protection of basic needs, quality of life, livelihoods and enhanced human welfare); and *freedom from indignity* (conditions where individuals and groups are assured of the protection of their fundamental rights, allowed to make choices and take advantage of opportunities in their everyday lives)."[3]

Most of the concerns in the literature relate directly to the component of freedom from want. For example, the lack of education, understood as sound and appropriate forms of instruction, means inferior prospects for employment and thus a higher likelihood of living in poverty. Poor children are also more likely to suffer from hunger and are less likely to enroll in school. Even if they do matriculate, their educational performance is often negatively affected: they may not be able to attend school regularly, whether because of poor health or because their family cannot afford the opportunity costs of the child's being in school rather that working. In addition, such conditions tend to have a disproportionate impact on girls, whose education some still view as less important than that of boys.[4] In addition to poverty alleviation, the solutions proposed to address freedom from want are generally technocratic: a more relevant curriculum, better teacher training, improved physical plant, and so on.

However, when we turn to the other two components of human security—freedom from fear and freedom from indignity—we move away from the primary focus of the traditional literature on education and development and into realms often marginalized in discussions of education in the MENA region. For example, freedom from fear is an obvious concern if the state or an occupier exercises repression directly or indirectly on a campus or in a school, through arrests or other forms of intimidation, or when proximity of conflict makes it dangerous for students and teachers to travel to and from or be in class.

Indignity is seen in the same circumstances. It is visible in the ways that the state shapes elements of identity and belonging, whether national, subnational, or communal. If the repression affects access to education for certain groups or denies cultural (or language or religious) rights in the educational sphere, then human dignity as it relates to the security of culture and community, and by extension, the individual, is threatened.

Thus, the discussion of human security that follows seeks to center freedom from fear and freedom from indignity, and to examine their intersection with the provision of and access to education. By exploring examples of different types of political threats to life and dignity from Turkey (state repression), Algeria (denial of cultural identity), Palestine (settler colonialism, occupation, and war), and Iraq (sanctions, war, occupation, and civil war) the goal is to illustrate how freedom from fear and freedom from indignity have been challenged in the realm of education. Highlighting the relevance of these two components makes clear that to construct the relationship between education and human security as one that can be addressed largely through more resources or better sectoral "governance" is both superficially technocratic and misleadingly apolitical. The secular decline in quality in education and the freedom from want that is so often the focus of reports can be meaningfully addressed only when they are placed within a framework that foregrounds the role of domestic, regional, and international threats to human freedom and dignity.

PURGING THE ACADEMY: TURKEY

According to a 2005 government report, the basic principles of Turkish national education include universality and equality; conformity with the reforms and principles of the Turkish republic's founder, Mustafa Atatürk; and his vision of Turkish identity, nationalism, and secularism, among others.[5] While expressing satisfaction about the gains achieved since the establishment of the Turkish republic, the report nonetheless noted several problems stemming from population increase, rural-to-urban migration, and budgetary constraints: crowded classrooms, suboptimal enrollment levels, the "wasting" of resources on children who fail or repeat a grade, double shifts (i.e., one group of students in class in the morning and another in the afternoon), the need for gender-integrated classrooms, the lack of equipment, inferior teacher training, and the need to change and update curricula.[6] No one reading this litany of problems at the time of the report's issuance in 2005 could have imagined that in 2016 the Turkish state would initiate a purge of precious faculty and staff from the national educational system.

The arrival to power of the Justice and Development Party (AK Party) in 2002 marked a significant turn in Turkish politics away from the staunchly secular orientation of Atatürk's policies. Although Turkey is a multiparty state that holds elections, the country's military had intervened repeatedly (1960, 1971, 1980, 1997) as the so-called guardian of the republic. The coup of 1980 and the period that followed were especially brutal, with hundreds of thousands arrested, dozens executed, and many others tortured or simply disappeared. However, by the late 1990s, with Turkey eager to enter the European Union, the government put in place numerous reforms that served to protect a range of civil, human, and cultural rights.

That said, the state's sensitivity to any critical examination of the historical period of the 1915 Armenian genocide continued, leading to the investigation, prosecution, and dismissal of a number of Turkish academics, writers, and other intellectuals. Indeed, any mention of the genocide, or even a critique of Atatürk, was subject to prosecution under Turkish law on the grounds of "insulting Turkishness." Another issue, that of Kurdish identity in Turkey, was also extremely sensitive: any action that could be construed as support for Kurdish rights opened one up to charges of "making propaganda for a terrorist organization."[7]

However, in a move indicating a shift in one of the redlines of the Atatürk tradition, in the mid- to late 2000s as part of the Ergenekon investigations, the government of Prime Minister Recep Tayyip Erdoğan targeted members of the scholarly community who had been outspoken defenders of secularism.[8] The state then initiated additional steps to undermine faculty governance and interfere in the administration of higher education.[9] By the end of the first decade of the 2000s, indications of what came to be called Turkey's "authoritarian turn" had become increasingly pronounced, including in the educational sector.

A political opening in late 2012 to reach a peace agreement with the Kurdistan Workers' Party (PKK), which the Turkish government considered a terrorist organization, appeared to bode well for resolving that long-standing conflict. However, this initiative was soon caught up in the intricate political linkages between Erdoğan's drive to consolidate his growing power and the Syrian civil war, with its own Kurdish component that threatened renewed instability in southeastern Turkey. The authoritarian turn only intensified.

The summer 2013 Gezi Park protests and the government's reaction to them, including in the educational realm, should have served as a warning—so, too, the increasing moves to silence media opposition voices.[10] Yet it was the initiative of more than 1,100 Turkish academics in January 2016 that triggered a swifter slide into repression and a particular targeting of the academy. The now-famous peace petition entitled "We Will Not Be a Party to This Crime" criticized the government's human rights violations in the largely Kurdish southeast and called for a restoration of the peace process through negotiations.[11]

The government's response was broad and ugly. Erdoğan labeled the petition "terrorist organization propaganda" and the signatories "traitors." As a result, those who had signed the petition suffered a range of threats, disciplinary actions, firings, interrogations, detentions, and prosecutions.[12] As if these measures were not damaging enough, only six months later, the attempted coup of July 2016, allegedly carried out by members of the Gülen movement, a religious order that had formerly cooperated with the AK Party, sent the repressive forces of the state into overdrive.[13] Ties between the two had already soured, and the coup attempt offered Erdoğan the opportunity not only to remove all suspected Gülenists from government but also to charge anyone who had expressed opposition to his policies, including academics, with sympathizing with or supporting terrorism, whether of the Gülenist or Kurdish variety.

A series of emergency decrees followed, and although they targeted Turks across all sectors of society, their impact on education has been particularly destructive. Within the first month following the coup attempt, the government called for the resignation of all public and private university deans (more than 1,500). The government fired more than 15,000 employees in the Ministry of Education and canceled the teaching licenses of 21,000 private school teachers. In addition, state authorities closed fifteen universities and more than 1,500 other educational institutions, including private schools and dormitories, and seized their assets. The state also imposed a travel ban on academics and called upon Turkish faculty working abroad to return. A September 1, 2016, decree announced the removal from their positions of more than 28,000 Ministry of Education employees and 2,346 university academic personnel, including 1,585 professors. The decree also canceled the passports of those dismissed and their spouses, all on charges of being members of a terrorist organization or undermining the national security of the state. No person was afforded any procedural rights, nor was any evidence presented to justify the charges and dismissals.[14] Further emergency decrees issued on October 29, 2016, eliminated the system by which universities elected their own rectors and administrators, replacing it with a system in which the office of the republic's president would select university rectors.[15]

Dismissals of hundreds of faculty continued, as did arrests of students across the country.[16] Not surprisingly, state authorities had to scramble to find replacements for the nearly 60,000 primary and secondary teachers either fired or suspended under the emergency decrees.[17] Yet another emergency decree on July 8, 2018, led to the purging of an additional 206 academic personnel from sixty-three public universities, and 52 academic administrative personnel from twenty-four universities.[18] The impact has been nothing short of a hollowing out of the educational sector. Even with the political constraints of earlier periods, Turkish higher education had distinguished itself with impressive graduates and accomplishments across disciplines. The fear sown by the state authorities in the educational sector and their willingness to sacrifice precious human capital through a range of direct and indirect forms of repression will have devastating consequences for decades to come.

LANGUAGE AND IDENTITY SUPPRESSION: ALGERIA

The issues of language and education have been closely intertwined with the most vexing sociopolitical and economic challenges that Algeria has faced since its independence in 1962. Local and national identity took on political salience during the period of settler colonization, when the French sought to introduce political distinctions between those Algerians whose language at home was a dialect of Arabic and those whose native language was one of a number of Berber dialects.[19] The French narrative regarding the colonized population portrayed the Arabs as the embodiment of backwardness and as opponents of the purported benefits of the French *mission civilisatrice* while also constructing the Berbers as the only superficially Arabized original inhabitants, with affinities to, and perhaps even origins in, Europe.[20] Although at the time of independence the mother tongue of a significant part of the population was not Arabic, and French continued to be an important language among much of the elite, the Algerian Constitution of 1963 named only Arabic as a national language. Furthermore, official accounts of Algerian history ignored or Arabo-Islamized the history of the country and its people prior to the Arabs' arrival.[21] As a result, Berber identity (generally called Amazigh) developed into a sociopolitical fault line and a source of mobilization, particularly among the Kabyle, speakers of Tamazight, the most widely spoken Berber language.

Not until the Printemps berbère, or Berber Spring, of March–April 1980, did the issue of Berber identity impose itself on the country's agenda—threateningly, from the point of view of the regime. This popular mobilization among the Kabyle, which involved demonstrations and general strikes demanding cultural and political rights, left 126 dead and some 5,000 wounded. Although these events shook the regime and led to greater insistence on cultural rights among the Kabyle, the regime did not reexamine critical issues related to language and identity until the country was in the midst of the bloody convulsions of the 1990s, the so-called dark decade. In September 1994 a school boycott by both teachers and students in Kabylia following the fifteenth anniversary of the Berber Spring aimed at securing official recognition of the Tamazight language. The boycott spread to other parts of the country (Aurès and Mzab) during some of the worst violence of the insurgency. Given the regime's interest in securing popular support against its opponents, it reached an agreement in April 1995 with representatives of the Amazigh movement for the creation of the Haut-Commissariat à l'amazighité (HCA). The following year, President Liamine Zéroual's efforts to reach a peace accord through negotiations led to the issuance of the Platform of National Understanding, article 28 of which stipulated: "The state oversees . . . the promotion of the Amazigh language in the different educational cultural and communication sectors."[22]

Nevertheless, it was not until 2002 that the 1996 constitution was amended to make Tamazight a national language, and introducing instruction in it became part of the educational reform program issued that year. It was not until 2016, however, that Tamazight was named an *official* language, with the state thereby committing itself to teaching it in schools. At the time, an otherwise quite critical commentator predicted: "This will help make Algeria's cultural and political national fabric more stable and cohesive. To a certain degree, it will also help the country escape from the cycle of violent conflict over identity, especially among the elites."[23] The relationship of education, culture, and human security could not have been clearer.

However, the obstacles to introducing Tamazight were considerable: a dearth of instructional materials and trained instructors, not to mention hostility from some sectors of Algerian society, most of them associated with Islamist political parties, who continued to oppose the recognition of non-Arab elements of national identity. Nevertheless, new texts introduced in fall 2017, which included elements of Amazigh culture for the first time, were well received by parents, and territorial expansion of Tamazight instruction broadened significantly.[24] By the fall of 2017 Tamazight was being taught in thirty-seven of Algeria's then forty-eight provinces.[25]

Two subsequent developments demonstrated the continuing sensitivity of the official recognition of Tamazight. The first, an announcement that the government intended to reduce the HCA's budget by 0.2 percent for fiscal year 2018 was followed by the rejection by the National Assembly's Finance Committee of a proposed amendment to the draft finance law to restore the HCA's budget.[26] In response, on December 4, university students in the province of Bejaia, in Kabylia, closed the campus in protest. Demonstrations and strikes by university and high school students soon spread from Bejaia to neighboring provinces and ultimately to the capital, Algiers. The protests galvanized civil society beyond the campuses as well, as the popular perception was that the state opposed expanding the teaching of Tamazight. While the strikes and marches were, in many cases, peaceful, police violence against protesters became more common as the demonstrations moved into their second week. Given long-standing sensitivity about the government's marginalization of Amazigh identity in Algeria, the ground was fertile for broad mobilization.

The approach of presidential elections (scheduled for April 2019) in the context of a political elite unable to coalesce around a successor to the ailing 'Abd al-'Aziz Bouteflika, had unleashed rumors of a possible fifth presidential term. In response to the unrest over the Tamazight controversy, Bouteflika made several announcements intended to undermine potential opposition to yet another term among this politicized oppositional community: on December 27, 2017, he announced that the Amazigh new year, Yennayer (January 12), would thenceforth be a national holiday and an official vacation day. Furthermore, he called upon the government to spare no effort in extending the instruction and use of Tamazight "according to the essence of the constitution." He also decreed the establishment of an academy for Tamazight charged with developing instructional materials. Shortly thereafter, the general secretary of the HCA announced that several ministries would soon be issuing documents in the language, and on January 10, 2018, the government issued the first official announcement ever in Tamazight, on the occasion of Yennayer. At the same time, the Ministry of the Interior published on its official site a Tamazight translation of an announcement regarding registration for the annual Muslim pilgrimage, the hajj.[27]

With the recognition of Tamazight as an official language in 2016 and its introduction to schools beginning in 2017, the Kabyles' insistence on the formal recognition of their language had finally borne fruit. The remaining challenge is to ensure that the state move beyond the decades of politico-cultural discrimination to actually deliver quality education to all Algerian children, regardless of native language or cultural affinity. Algerian students' participation in the nationwide Friday political protests (as well as their own demonstrations every Tuesday) that began in February 2019 and continued until COVID-19 began to spread—despite regime oppression and attempts to divide the opposition along ethnolinguistic lines—clearly demonstrated the youth's conviction that the authoritarian regime remains an obstacle to achieving human dignity.

SETTLER-COLONIAL OCCUPATION: THE WEST BANK AND GAZA

External evaluations of the state of education among Palestinian youth in the occupied West Bank and the Gaza Strip (WBG) have often been limited to examinations of textbooks in search of evidence of purported anti-Israeli incitement or anti-Semitic language.[28] Although a case can certainly be made for the need for reforms in Palestinian education, concerns regarding textbook content (of all sorts) need to be placed in a larger framework. The Palestinian reality is that of a diaspora born of dispossession caused by settler colonialism: about half of the total Palestinian population of around thirteen million lives in Israel or, since 1967, under Israel's direct or indirect occupation of the WBG.[29]

During the first twenty years of the occupation, the educational sectors in the WBG experienced severe problems: an insufficient number of schools and qualified teachers, an outdated curriculum and assessment standards overseen by Jordan in the West Bank and Egypt in Gaza, impaired access to educational materials owing to Israeli censorship, and poor overall learning results.[30] The First Intifada, which began in December 1987, with its regular and often extended school closures imposed by the Israelis as a form of collective punishment, also negatively affected Palestinian education.

At a result, when responsibility for Palestinian education was transferred to the Palestinian National Authority (PA) in 1994, the sector, which at the time served around one million students, was in deep crisis. The new Palestinian Ministry of Education and Higher Education had first to unify the two educational systems then in place: Jordanian in the West Bank and Egyptian in Gaza. UNESCO assisted in the ministry's creation, and then with constructing and furnishing new schools, as well as with supporting teacher training, curriculum development, administrative staff salaries, and broader sectoral capacity development. Perhaps most important was the establishment of the Palestinian Curriculum Development Center, which set to work on a comprehensive plan for radical reforms based on the vision of its director, the well-known Palestinian scholar Ibrahim Abu-Lughod. His goal was to develop a modernized curriculum that would serve the purpose of nation building, not through rote memorization, but by nurturing a democratic civic culture.[31] Such an approach would, Abu-Lughod believed, address and eventually overcome the damage and indignity of the long occupation.

However, following the Israeli withdrawal from Gaza in 2004, the Gazan experience began to diverge again from that of the West Bank. Israel removed its forces, but along with Egypt it continued to control land, sea, and air access to and from the coastal enclave and periodically violated its borders. Following Hamas's defeat of the security forces of Fatah for control of the PA in Gaza in 2007, with the support of the United States and other Western states, Israel responded by imposing a siege, turning Gaza into what many have termed the world's largest open-air prison. In the realm of education, the siege has made movement between the West Bank and Gaza nearly impossible, and with exit from Gaza also generally unattainable, students have often been prevented from taking advantage of university admissions, whether in the West Bank or beyond.[32]

The West Bank has faced its own problems. First, the 1993 Oslo Accords opened the way for Israel to cantonize the territory through complex forms of Israeli territorial access and control, complicating or obstructing Palestinians' movement. The West Bank also hosts the headquarters of the PA, which has become increasingly complicit in the occupation. Further complicating this picture is the role of external powers, whose financial contributions and political influence have circumscribed freedom of Palestinian action or decision making.

In addition, military conflicts with the occupier, including large-scale Israeli attacks against the West Bank in 2002 and Gaza in 2006, 2008–2009, and 2014, along with myriad other forms of violence, have taken a terrible toll on Palestinians and their educational institutions. The bombing campaign of 2009 led to the killing of 250 students and 15 teachers, and the wounding of 866 students and 19 teachers. The aerial assaults damaged 16 kindergartens, 217 schools, and all 8 of Gaza's institutions of higher learning. During the assaults in July and August 2014, Israeli forces killed 421 students and 9 administrators, and wounded another 1,128 students and 21 administrators. Israel also destroyed 26 schools, in addition to damaging 122 others, as well as 14 institutions of higher education. The 2014 war also targeted six UN Relief and Works Agency for Palestinian Refugees (UNRWA) schools, killing 47 civilians.[33] Israeli army raids of lesser scale have also regularly damaged or destroyed Palestinian educational institutions, including those run by UNRWA.[34] Moreover, prior to these massive air assaults, Gaza had already been suffering from a shortage of some two hundred schools because the siege had prevented the importation of the building materials needed to construct new facilities to accommodate natural student population growth. The siege, therefore, not only exposed Gaza to repeated, brutal military assaults, but also significantly undermined the population's ability rebuild.

On the West Bank, roadblocks, checkpoints and curfews, and Israeli-imposed school and university closures, have regularly impeded access to schools and classes, sometimes for weeks or months at a time. In addition, there are myriad examples of Israeli army and security forces' conducting arbitrary arrests at and incursions into Palestinian universities; assaulting students, faculty, and staff; and obstructing the education of thousands of students.[35] In addition, severe limitations have been imposed on foreign university faculty teaching in the WBG; and since 2016 the Israeli authorities have increasingly denied visas—both new and reentry—to such academics, to a degree that severely imperils the quality of Palestinian education.[36] The large numbers of children and youth detained and jailed by the occupation have thereby also had their access to education significantly, and in many cases completely, obstructed.[37] The construction of the so-called security wall on Palestinian land in the West Bank has also led to the expropriation of Palestinian university lands and the obstruction of student and faculty access to classes.[38]

There is perhaps no more eloquent summary of the state of Palestinian education, and the continued threat of deadly force that hangs over students and teachers alike, than the first item under "Recommended Advocacy Messages" in UNESCO's report on the damage inflicted upon Gaza during the summer 2014 war. Entitled "Protection and Emergency Response," it includes such proposals as "rigorously monitoring attacks on HEIs (higher educational institutions) and using that information to devise effective, co-ordinated responses"; "establishing preventive measures such as early warning systems and rapid response systems for attacks"; "encouraging HEI's to develop best practices in protecting education from attack"; and "ensuring educators and their families who are displaced are offered protection and encouraged to return." "Prioritise . . . training in emergency and evacuation planning as well as first aid training," the report added. "Prioritise improvements in psychosocial support at all HEIs."[39]

Whether in the West Bank or Gaza, the myriad forms of violence visited on Palestinians renders absurd the notion of implementing a "curriculum reform" to prepare students for participation in the so-called knowledge economy. In Gaza, unrelenting brutality has made mere survival a daily struggle. While in the West Bank large-scale Israeli military assaults have been fewer, the inexorable drive to expropriate Palestinian land and implant more Jewish settlers—combined since 2017 with the Trump administration's unconditional support for Israel's expansionist policies—has made the achievement of the security and dignity once promised by the hopes of a sovereign national state a distant dream there as well.

SANCTIONS, INVASION, INSURGENCY: IRAQ

Despite the devastation caused by the 1980–1989 Iran-Iraq War, Iraqi government health and education programs remained strong. Indeed, before 1990, with education free at all levels, gross enrollment at the primary level stood at

100 percent, and literacy levels were high thanks to successful national campaigns. Thus, in terms of the traditional criteria used to classify educational systems, UNESCO judged Iraq's system to be one of the best in the region.[40] However, the 1991 Gulf War and the expansion of international sanctions in its wake soon devastated the country's earlier achievements.

In the wake of the Gulf War, the northern and largely Kurdish-populated governorates of Dohuk, Erbil, and Sulaymaniyah fell outside the direct control of Baghdad. After April 1995, education there was funded with 7 percent of the revenues generated by the UN-supervised sale of Iraqi oil as part of the Oil-for-Food Programme, which was intended to alleviate the suffering of the Iraqi people under the brutal sanctions. In the remaining fifteen governorates, postwar education was Baghdad's responsibility, and only 3.6 percent of the revenues from Oil-for-Food went to education. As a result, the situation there was far more dire than in the north.[41]

Under the sanctions, salaries diminished and teaching conditions suffered. Some teachers took on additional jobs to supplement their salaries, and "diminished access to professional development resources (periodicals, reference books, and the like) and teaching aids, as well as the minimal opportunities for in-service professional training" further undermined instructor morale.[42] Also contributing to the decline were shortages of educational materials (everything from textbooks and academic journals to paper and chalk) and the deterioration of the physical conditions of the schools. Many teachers simply left the profession and were replaced with less qualified instructors.

Added to these problems was the decline in the socioeconomic status of parents, which compelled them to withdraw their children from school, either because the children were needed to work to assist their families or because the hidden expenses of even a "free" government education—transportation, supplies—were simply too great. In 2000, only 76.3 percent of children between the ages of six and eleven years old were attending primary school. In rural areas, more than 50 percent of girls were out of school (compared with nearly 28 percent of boys), whereas in urban areas the percentages were 20 percent and 12.6 percent, respectively.[43] By 2002, the US Agency for International Development estimated that barely over 50 percent of children were in school.[44] By the mid-2000s, literacy among the population of fifteen- to twenty-four-year-olds was only 82 percent.[45]

Iraq was then further battered by the 2003 invasion, which destroyed hundreds of schools, as well as the Ministry of Education building and all its files.[46] In the wake of the invasion, educational reforms were entrusted to a team of US-appointed Iraqi educators under the auspices of the US occupation–led Iraqi Ministry of Education. Over the summer of 2003 they significantly reworked some 562 texts, including removing every image of Saddam Hussein and the Ba'ath Party.[47] In their haste to have materials ready for the 2003–2004 academic year, rather than carefully addressing controversial subjects, they deleted all references that they judged potentially problematic: any mention of the United States, Shi'a and Sunnis, Kurds, Kuwaitis, Jews, and Iranians was excised. In the case of textbooks on modern history, fully half of the material was deleted.[48] Neither national identity nor human dignity can be secured in the context of an educational system directed by the interests of an occupying power.

The US-decreed dismantling of key Ba'athist state institutions led a variety of actors, many of them educators, to attempt to rework the national curriculum. Some deplored the influence of the occupier, arguing that the US intent was to change Iraqi values and culture. What is clear is that the new space for contention over content enabled the surfacing of a serious rivalry between secular and religious approaches to education, each with its own ideas regarding not only the inclusion of religious instruction in public education but also the content of courses in such disciplines as history, civics, and the sciences.[49]

With the descent of the country into civil war in 2006, sectarianism and ultimately the emergence of the Islamic State of Iraq and Syria not only continued to threaten the physical security of educators, staff, and students but also further entrenched a situation in which the curriculum remained a field of contestation among groups with different sectarian and political orientations.[50] In 2012 the mean number of years of schooling in the country was only 5.6, and only 22 percent of women and 42.7 percent of men had at least some secondary education.[51] The negative implications for postconflict reconciliation and renewed national development promoting human security were clear.

Completing the picture of severe strain on the educational sector is the situation of Iraqi refugees, periodic waves of whom had fled the country since the 1991 war. Many Iraqi refugees have either returned or resettled elsewhere. However, the fight against ISIS, which began in 2014, raised problems of educational access for newly created refugees and the internally displaced. As of 2016, more than one million Iraqi children were internally displaced, only 31 percent of whom had access to education. Of the one hundred thousand who lived in camps, the enrollment rate was 51 percent, much higher than the 29 percent enrollment among children living in host communities.[52]

Three years later, a December 2019 Norwegian Refugee Council paper reported that more than 240,000 Iraqi children had been unable to access any form of education in the previous twelve months. No new teachers had been hired since 2014, leading to a 32 percent shortage. Combined with the damage or destruction of 50 percent of all school buildings in the conflict areas, dropout rates had risen and the need to run two to three shifts of classes to reduce class sizes still left some with as many as 650 students per class. In such circumstances all three components of human security—freedom from want, fear, and indignity—as they relate to the educational realm continue to be compromised.[53]

Each of these cases underlines how a focus on technocratic solutions to serious problems in the MENA educational sector is both misdirected and misleadingly apolitical. The fear and indignity triggered by violence and repression that undermine human security are central elements in them all. In particular, the cases show how some of the most serious threats to the educational sector intersect with narratives of social or national identity that may be understood as foundational to a sense of individual, subnational, or national security and dignity.

In Turkey, education has been a key battleground in the struggle between religious and secular worldviews. The nationalist-secularist narrative that long dominated the state sought to suppress alternative narratives concerning identity, history, and culture, particularly those of the Kurdish and Armenian communities. Indeed, it was the 2016 petition regarding state assaults on the largely Kurdish southeast that led the government to set its sights directly on universities, ultimately criminalizing and purging a whole class of the country's intellectual and cultural capital.

Like Turkey, Algeria has witnessed the ebb and flow of societal and leadership struggles over the elements of identity, history, and culture accepted in defining the country. High schools and universities have been key loci of protests that often have then spread to other sectors of civil society. The Algerian case clearly demonstrates both the degree to which educational issues can be instrumentalized as part of larger political struggles and the dangers to human dignity involved in attempts to suppress societal demands for an expansion of educational—in this case, linguistic and cultural—inclusion.

The West Bank and Gaza illustrate a very different type of challenge. Stateless or second-class citizens in the wake of the dismemberment of Palestine, Palestinian children have had widely varying but generally mediocre educational experiences that further fracture their national identity and history. Not only have their textbooks been scrutinized for any exhortation to resistance to occupation and dispossession, but all manner of administrative, physical, and military obstacles, as well as lethal assaults, have been used to intimidate, obstruct, or destroy access to instruction.

In the case of Iraq, the sanctions regime initiated a process that not only gradually destroyed educational infrastructure and human capital but also obstructed Iraqis' access to knowledge production outside the country. After the 2003 US invasion stoked ethno-sectarian struggles, subsequent attempts to rebuild and rehabilitate national education became even more fraught. Then, out of the destruction wrought by the brutal US occupation, emerged ISIS, with its own vision of education for its new caliphate. The multiple episodes of conflict-driven flight and displacement of Iraqis has only further threatened the possibilities that a meaningful education can contribute to a sense of community, dignity, and freedom.

These are not exceptional cases. This discussion could easily have focused on Libya, Syria, and Yemen for examples of the impact of war, or on other countries of the region for examples of the role of political or cultural repression. The conclusion is clear: political and military threats to education, educators, and students have long compromised the region's prospects for meaningful development, security, and peace. Worse, the fear and indignity that have been so endemic to MENA societies and so injurious to their educational systems in the past show no sign of diminishing in the New Middle East.

Chapter 4

MYTHS OF MIDDLE-CLASS POLITICAL BEHAVIOR IN THE ISLAMIC REPUBLIC

Kevan Harris

ONE OF THE CONCEPTS MOST COMMONLY EVOKED TO characterize and explain the zigzag trajectory of political dynamics in the Islamic Republic of Iran has been the middle class. Recent events including the Tehran-based Green Movement wave of protest against perceived electoral fraud in 2009 and the surprising 2013 electoral victory of Hassan Rouhani as president against a slate of conservative competitors are attributed to the collective social power of Iran's middle class. When this category is utilized, it usually comes packaged with two assumptions. First, the middle class is a coherent social group in both an objective and subjective sense. Second, by collectively participating or refraining from political activity, including through elections or street protests, the middle class is the swing actor in the country's public arena.[1]

Evoking the middle class as a metanarrative to explain political and social dynamics is not unique to the Islamic Republic. Iran's surprising electoral changeovers and dramatic street politics occurred during the same period as large-scale movements across the Middle East and North Africa were also painted with the middle-class brush. Before the 2011 Arab uprisings, and even more so afterward, the concept has done a lot of heavy lifting in social science on Iran with regard to electoral behavior and political dynamics. Yet the term contains numerous assumptions that need to be empirically scrutinized, especially if we believe that the trajectory of a nascent "New" Middle East will depend on actors located in the middle class.

After all, as Göran Therborn has noted, middle classes can be either rebellious or subordinate to the power elite. And this is often true in the very same country, as with post-Thaksin Thailand or post-Mubarak Egypt.[2] Indeed, a recurring finding by social scientists on the role of middle classes in newly independent or democratizing states has been that, rather than being the historical bearer of democracy, they are the most fickle bunch of all.[3] Even more vexing, though also telling, is that there is no scholarly consensus on a fundamental approach to identification and measurement of the middle class. Using arbitrary lines to select households or individuals located above a local consumption floor, drawing from the middle strata of a national income distribution, or categorizing individuals with consumption levels recognized in wealthier countries as "middle class" results in disparate sets of groupings for nearly all developing countries. As a team of economists frustratingly exclaimed, "researchers have employed wildly differing income or consumption thresholds in defining the global middle class."[4]

Sociologists fare no better on a shared definition. As Gay Seidman points out, "Middle-class identities are defined as much by claims to cultural capital and education as by income and consumption—and middle-class anxieties are shaped by an awareness of local inequalities as well as global pressures."[5] Rather than collapsing or conflating a set of different, and often clashing, definitions of middle class, Raka Ray argues that at the minimum researchers should "distinguish between the empirical category 'middle classes' that indicates heterogeneity and the representational category 'middle class' that indicates a singular 'middle class' ideological construct."[6] In other words, the category of "the middle class" is both a category of analysis, one long debated within social theory, and a category of practice, one routinely deployed in political behavior and social distinction. Yet, to paraphrase Rogers Brubaker, most scholarship still unreflexively uses the concept of middle classes as if "they were internally homogenous, externally bounded groups, even unitary collective actors with common purposes."[7]

In the case of Iran, the social categories of "middle class," "youth," and "educated" tend to be conflated and laxly used to analytically describe or theoretically explain large-scale political outcomes.[8] Rarely are these demographic groupings scrutinized or separated. In this chapter, I draw on data from the nationally representative 2016 Iran Social Survey (ISS) to illustrate that these commonly wielded definitions do not explain variation in voter choice for a key political event often ascribed to the participation of Iran's middle class as a collective actor: the victory of Hassan Rouhani in the country's 2013 presidential election.

MIDDLE-CLASS SELF-IDENTIFICATION

As the political scientist Fatemeh Sadeghi has noted, Iranian intellectuals and politicians alike tend to emphasize the historical agency and social power of a modern-looking middle class at the expense of other social categories and actors. As more Iranians engaged in observable consumption patterns and life-styles associated with "middle-classness," it was assumed that this would lead to a process of social change more broadly across the country. In turn, these social transformations would carry into the political sphere, even if those individu-als located in the middle class lacked political organization and resources for collective action. Yet in reality, Sadeghi observed, if there is an actively shared form of middle-class consciousness in Iran, it is more often directed toward the presentation of the self via status distinction and conspicuous consump-tion. The link between middle-classness as a lifestyle and the middle class as a collective agent of political transformation is merely assumed.[9]

Given the distinction between categories of analysis and categories of prac-tice, it is worth considering how the conceptual meanings of middle class vary in everyday usage. In the 2016 ISS, fielded in late 2016 over landline phone to 5,005 adult individuals in randomly sampled households across the country, respondents were asked: "Would you describe your household as upper class, middle class, working class, or poor?"[10] As Figure 1 shows, more than half of surveyed Iranians identified their households as middle class.

This finding places Iran in the same range of middle-class self-identification as a country with more than ten times its income per capita: the United States. In the United States, respondent self-identification as middle class fluctuated between 50 percent and 60 percent on surveys in the 2000s.[11] Yet Iran is not the only middle-income country that exhibits middle-class self-identification sim-ilar to wealthier countries. Cross-national research has revealed wide variation in self-reporting on class identification, with many countries' levels of middle-class self-identification above a 50 percent threshold, which is explained by neither national wealth nor structure of the labor market.[12]

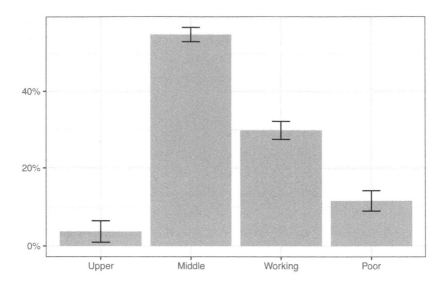

FIGURE 1. Self-identification of household class in the 2016 Iran Social Survey. Note: N = 4,967 respondents based on a nationally representative sample; bars represent 95 percent confidence intervals. The relative distribution of class self-identification is similar when restricting the sample to individuals between the ages of 24 and 55 years old. Source: Harris and Tavana (2017); for survey methodology, see Harris and Tavana (2018).

As a result, although many social scientists unreflexively define middle-class individuals in Iran as either those in the middle strata of a nationally bounded income distribution or those who have attained higher levels of education, these classifications do not capture many individuals who *self-identify* as middle class. As Figures 2 and 3 show, class self-identification in Iran varies by household income and educational attainment, as would be expected. Nevertheless, even among poorer and less-educated Iranians, a sizable portion self-identified as middle class rather than as working class or poor. In Figure 2, respondents in lower-income households self-identify as middle class as commonly as working class. And in Figure 3, among adult Iranians whose educational attainment stood at primary school or less, more than a third self-identified their household as belonging to the middle class.

This lack of congruity between varying definitions of the middle class becomes more problematic when the category is associated with universal theories of political and social change. A common argument among Iranian scholars is that more highly educated and middle-income citizens act as the crucial social base for those segments of the country's political elite that have pushed for political democratization and socioeconomic liberalization. This often comes accompanied with a distinction between the declining "old" middle class, such as artisans and petty traders, who are assumed to be mired in kinship networks or patrimonial relations, and the rising "new" middle classes, which have been produced by the expansion of higher education and technical-professional occupations.[13] As in many middle-income countries, there is a long intellectual tradition of framing popular politics in Iran through an implicit rubric of modernization theory, with the expectation that the middle class is a coherent or incipient political actor.[14]

OFFICIAL ELECTORAL RESULTS IN THE 2013 IRANIAN ELECTION COMPARED WITH SELF-REPORTED VOTING

We know very little about the demographic and class composition of recent political events in Iran, electoral or otherwise.[15] Using data from the 2016 ISS, though, we can test the oft-made claim that the middle class disproportionately

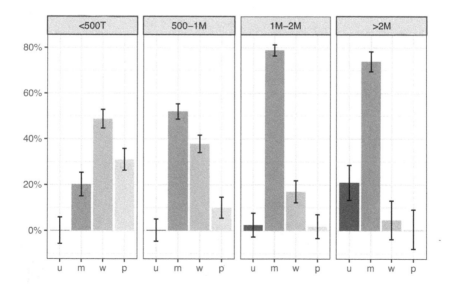

FIGURE 2. Self-identification of household class (upper, middle, working, poor) in Iran by monthly household income (in millions of 2016-year tomans). Note: N = 4,735; bars represent 95 percent confidence intervals. Source: Harris and Tavana (2017); for survey methodology, see Harris and Tavana (2018).

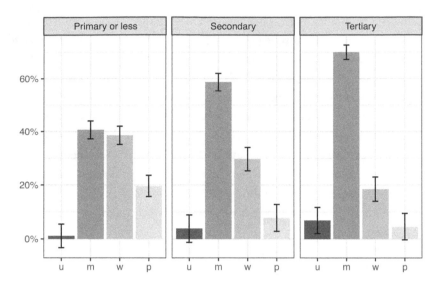

FIGURE 3. Self-identification of household class (upper, middle, working, poor) in Iran by respondent educational attainment. Note: N = 4,967; bars represent 95 percent confidence intervals. Source: Harris and Tavana (2017); for survey methodology, see Harris and Tavana (2018).

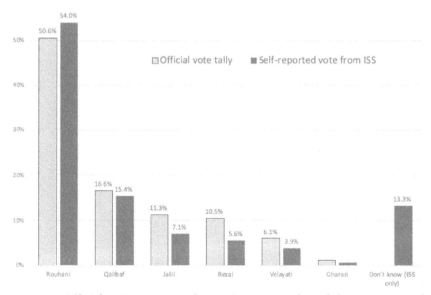

FIGURE 4. Official voting returns in the 2013 Iranian presidential election compared with self-reporting from the 2016 Iran Social survey. Note: N = 3,495. Source: Harris and Tavana (2017); for survey methodology, see Harris and Tavana (2018).

voted in the 2013 presidential race for Hassan Rouhani.[16] Beforehand, though, we should check how closely self-reported voting in the ISS aligns with the officially reported electoral results.[17]

Among most observers at the time, Rouhani's candidacy was associated with domestic political factions pressing for more democratization and socio-economic liberalization. The dynamics of the 2013 presidential race in Iran thus meant that potential voters had a range of choices at the ballot box, albeit choices constricted by the available candidates. Even with a single candidate on the center-left in the guise of Hassan Rouhani and the lack of a consensus candidate on the conservative right, most election watchers predicted that no candidate would win an outright majority in the first round. Yet surprisingly, Rouhani managed to garner a bare majority of votes (50.6 percent) on June 13, 2013, and was certified the winner.[18]

According to Iran's Ministry of Interior, 72.9 percent of the 50.4 million Iranians eligible to participate in the 2013 presidential election voted. In the ISS sample, 76.3 percent of age-eligible respondents reported that they voted in the 2013 presidential election. As Figure 4 shows, the official returns and vote choice reported in the ISS for the 2013 election do not differ by a significant degree.[19] Given the closeness of the electoral campaign and a reliable sample of voters from the ISS, we can test whether individuals in demographic or socioeconomic categories usually associated with the middle class were more likely to vote for Rouhani compared to other candidates.

AGE AND VOTING BEHAVIOR

In reporting after the election, it was often stated that Rouhani's slim elec-toral victory came as a result of his campaign's ability to capture the "youth vote." How accurate was this assessment? In Figure 5, ISS data on voting by age cohort is divided into self-reported votes for Rouhani and for the four conservative candidates other than Rouhani.[20] As Figure 5 shows, there is no youth advantage for self-reporting voting for Rouhani. In fact, evidence slightly suggests that older respondents may have voted for Rouhani at a higher rate than younger respondents did.

Even considering possible types of survey error that might have biased the responses from solely younger respondents, this is a counterintuitive finding. After all, the simple claim made here is that younger voters were no more likely to vote for Rouhani than for his conservative opponents. As with any survey, of course, the data should be scrutinized rather than taken as gospel. Younger respondents were slightly more likely to report that they "did not vote" in 2013 (29.5 percent of age-eligible voters), compared to middle-aged (24 percent) and older (19 percent) cohorts. Some younger respondents who reported "did not vote" may have felt disillusioned with Rouhani and thus did not accurately represent their vote choice to the survey interviewer. Yet a relatively disproportionate number of younger respondents would have had to misrepresent their vote choice to significantly alter the key finding highlighted in Figure 5, which is that the "youth vote" in Iran was not overwhelmingly cast for the center-left candidate. Even if we approach ISS data with a cautionary view of possible biases of postelection recounting of vote choice, younger voters do not seem more likely to vote for Rouhani than for one of his conservative opponents.

EDUCATION AND VOTING BEHAVIOR

Like many middle-income countries that aspired to catch up with wealthier states in Europe and North America, Iran rapidly expanded its educational system over the latter half of the twentieth century. After the 1979 revolution, the government doubled down on the strategy and devoted considerable resources to extending university and college education for larger segments of the population. Consider that Iran's gross school enrollment ratio in tertiary education, which is the number of enrolled students as a percentage of the total school-going population corresponding to the same level of education, stood at only 4.5 percent in 1978. In 2016, the ratio was at 69 percent, according to UNESCO.

Few commentators who remark upon the rise in educational attainment in Iran examine whether educational credentials can reliably be associated with one stream of partisan behavior or another. It is usually assumed that more educational attainment means an increased preference, and even behavior, toward democratization and political liberalization. In Iran, educational attainment rates are repeatedly trotted out in journalists' accounts and think-tank reports without scrutinizing the implied assumptions about what this always-rising level of education is supposed to mean in the political context of Iran.

In Figure 6, surveyed individuals who voted in the 2013 election for either Rouhani or any of his opponents are grouped by educational attainment.

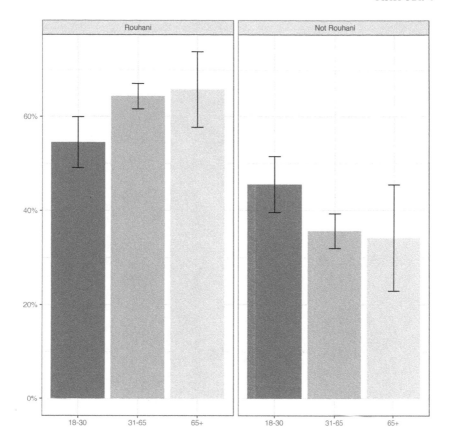

FIGURE 5. Vote choice in the 2013 Iranian presidential election by age cohort (2016 Iran Social Survey). Note: N = 2,621 out of a total of 4,029 (65 percent) age-eligible respondents who recalled their vote choice and reported their age; bars represent 95 percent confidence intervals. Of the remainder, 1,012 (25 percent) reported not voting in the election, and 396 (9.8 percent) answered "don't know." Source: Harris and Tavana (2017); for survey methodology, see Harris and Tavana (2018).

College-educated individuals make up more than 20 percent of respondents in the ISS, yet there is no estimable difference between Rouhani voters with and without a college degree. Individuals from both groups were equally likely to be associated with voting for Rouhani.

As with voting patterns separated by age cohorts, this also may seem like a counterintuitive finding for Iran. But we should question the intuition that produces such a surprise. As access to and attainment of college

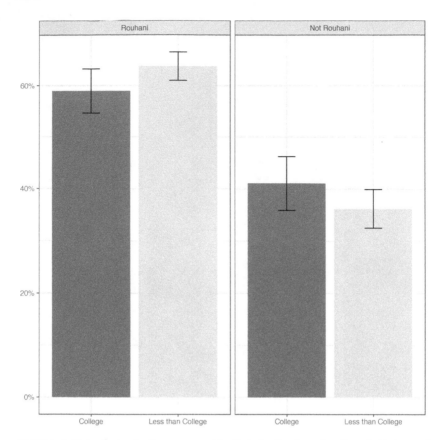

FIGURE 6. Vote choice in the 2013 presidential election by educational attainment (2016 Iran Social Survey). Note: N = 2,621, out of a total of 4,029 (65 percent) age-eligible respondents who recalled their vote choice and reported their education; bars represent 95 percent confidence intervals. Of the remainder, 1,012 (25 percent) reported not voting in the election, and 396 (9.8 percent) answered "don't know." Respondents with more education were more likely to report vote choice, and no significant estimable difference by educational attainment is found between nonvoters and voters. Source: Harris and Tavana (2017); for survey methodology, see Harris and Tavana (2018).

credentials expand in a country, the relative value of the credential itself is likely to decrease. College attainment in Iran is no longer limited to a small segment of the economic and political elite, but rather it is widely attainable. As more and more individuals pursue educational credentials, the collective outcome is what social scientists call "credential inflation." While the social and economic returns to educational credentials do not

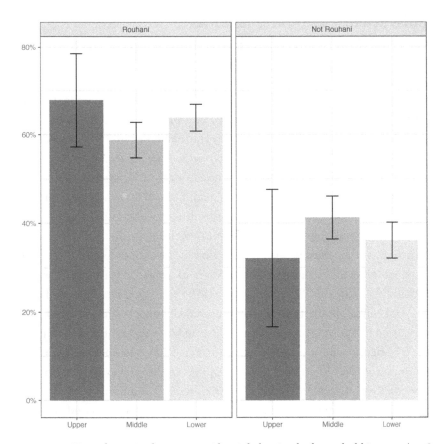

FIGURE 7. Vote choice in the 2013 presidential election by household income (2016 Iran Social Survey). Note: N = 2,551 out of a total of 3,907 (65 percent) age-eligible respondents who recalled their vote choice and reported their household income; bars represent 95 percent confidence intervals. Of the remainder, 979 (25 percent) reported not voting in the election, and 396 (9.8 percent) answered "don't know." Middle- and higher-income respondents were more likely to report vote choice, and no significant estimable difference by income groups is found between nonvoters and voters. Source: Harris and Tavana (2017); for survey methodology, see Harris and Tavana (2018).

disappear amid such a process, the link between educational attainment and partisan social cleavages might not remain constant. In other words, college-educated Iranians seem to be as divided in their political behavior as other demographic groups. In the least, we should take caution, if not wholly reconsider, our expectations for Iranian political behavior as educational attainment continues to rise.

VOTING BEHAVIOR AND CLASS: OBJECTIVE
AND SUBJECTIVE MEASUREMENTS

Figure 7 groups together by monthly household income those surveyed individuals who voted in the 2013 election for either Rouhani or any of his opponents. The low-income group consists of individuals from households under the median reported income, and the high-income group consists of the individuals from the top 5 percent of income earners. The middle-income group consists of those households that are commonly defined as middle class by Iranian social scientists.[21] As Figure 7 shows, there is no estimable difference between Rouhani voters across income groups. Individuals from all three income groupings were equally likely to be associated with voting for Rouhani.

Finally, Figure 8 groups by *self-identified* class position those surveyed individuals who voted in the 2013 election for either Rouhani or any of his opponents. As noted earlier, a larger share of surveyed Iranians classified themselves in the middle class than would be estimated by often-used categories of educational attainment or household income. As far as I know, such a question has never been asked previously in large-scale surveys in Iran. For the 2013 election, however, there is no estimable difference between Rouhani voters across self-identified class groupings in the survey data. Although the point estimate for self-identified middle-class Rouhani voters appears lower than all other class groupings, these points are not estimated precisely enough to claim a large and significant difference. Thus, individuals from all four self-identified classes were equally likely to be associated with voting for Rouhani.

In this chapter, I noted that a common trope in reporting and analysis on Iranian politics is that large-scale political dynamics are collectively driven by young, educated, middle-class individuals mobilizing and voting as a coherent bloc in key elections. However, this chapter has presented evidence that, for the crucial electoral victory of a center-left candidate in the 2013 presidential race, treating these demographic categories as coherent wholes cannot perform the heavy lifting of explanation. Younger, more educated, or middle-class voters did not lean toward voting for Rouhani as compared to voting for his conservative opponents at levels disproportionate to other demographic groups.

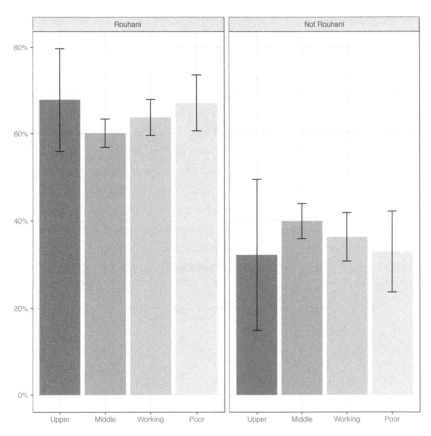

FIGURE 8. Vote choice in the 2013 presidential election by self-identified class position (2016 Iran Social Survey). Note: *N* = 2,607 out of a total of 4,005 (65 percent) age-eligible respondents who recalled their vote choice and reported a self-identified class; bars represent 95 percent confidence intervals. Of the remainder, 1,006 (25 percent) reported not voting in the election, and 396 (9.8 percent) answered "don't know." No significant estimable difference between groups is found between nonvoters and voters. Source: Harris and Tavana (2017); for survey methodology, see Harris and Tavana (2018).

Instead of automatically imputing political trends to demographic ones, we need to more cautiously investigate how political cleavages in Iran are formed and re-formed. In the Iranian case, a portion of voting behavior may be driven by partisan identification with one or another ideological stream of politics in the Islamic Republic, coupled with mobilization cycles that drive turnout on different sides of the political spectrum. Rather than a coherent middle class acting together in a collective effort, electoral outcomes are more likely contingent, spurred on by the rise and fall of networks of electoral activists and mobilizing associations.[22]

In sum, partisan identification and political mobilization are not automatically fashioned from the raw demographic clay of Iranian society. The actors that articulate between demographics and politics are political elites, state organizations, civic associations, social networks, and grassroots movements, often in competition within and between each other for resources, status, rights, and power. It is not impossible that a segment of the lionized young and educated middle classes could act, in a particular place and time, as a coherent political force in Iran's politics. But it is incumbent upon us to document and examine such claims, especially as they tend to be elevated into transhistorical theories that attempt to account for politics not just in Iran but in the entire Middle Eastern region, in lieu of more informative explanations.

Part 2

CULTURE AND COMMUNITY IN THE NEW MIDDLE EAST

Chapter 5

POETS OF THE REVOLUTIONS

Authoritarians, Uprisings, and Rappers in North Africa, 1990s–Present

Aomar Boum

HIP-HOP HAS BEEN USED AS A PUBLIC FORUM BY A GENERATION of North African youth since the 1990s to highlight their social and economic concerns about human rights, repression, legal corruption, educational failures, and unemployment predicaments. Frustrated by the broken promise of their authoritarian leaders and trapped in preadulthood, North African youth deployed hip-hop and rap to challenge local and traditional social and political authorities. North African hip-hop therefore provides a historical archive and documentary resource to understand the social, political, and economic dynamics and transformations within the Maghreb through the eyes of alienated youth before and after the Arab Spring. The turn to hip-hop and rap is in part a rejection of indigenous modes of cultural expression of the 1970s and 1980s. In fact, even though we cannot separate rap and hip-hop as modes of expression from earlier musical forms of political contestation, the appropriation of hip-hop by North African youth highlights the disconnection they felt with their local social milieu.[1] Unlike previous generations of musicians, including Raï (a folk musical style that originated in Algeria) artists who mixed foreign and indigenous popular music, the generation that came of age during the 1990s, benefiting from satellite communication and the internet revolution, settled on hip-hop and rap as global modes of expression. In the absence of local and open political and economic outlets, and given authoritarian restrictions on expression, North African rappers rejected state festivals, television, and public cultural forms, instead mocking state authority while calling for democratic representation.

YOUTH FRUSTRATION IN HISTORICAL CONTEXT

The 1980s was a painful economic period of transition in North Africa. The World Bank and its orthodox economists saw this decade of structural fiscal transitions and social turmoil as part of a natural process of adjustment to correct the budgetary failures of the 1970s. Faced with the global politics of economic recession and structural adjustment, the North African population, in particular in Tunisia and Morocco, initially, though resentfully, was resigned to reduced state subsidies for tea, cooking oil, bread, sugar, and other basic commodities.[2] For example, despite the Moroccan government's efforts to implement its three-year stabilization program to correct the weak national financial system, the decline in revenues from phosphates and in Moroccan workers' remittances, the increase in oil prices and international interest rates, and the costs of the Western Sahara conflict pressured the government between 1978 and 1980 to capitulate to creditors' demands to encourage private investments and limit public expenditures. Subsequently, North African governments' reluctant adjustment to respond to the global crisis of the early 1980s locked the region into a deeper economic dependency to international financial institutions and reinforced their colonial ties to Western governments, especially France. Authoritarian leaders and their governments turned to borrowing, increasing their countries' national debt to avoid the collapse of their fragile economies.

Although these states did avoid protest for a short period, the price of foodstuffs continued to climb, and by early 1984 economic precarity triggered waves of demonstrations led by high school and university students and by workers' unions, whose strikes later turned into violent protest. A series of bread riots broke out first in Tunisia and Morocco, then expanded into Egypt and Sudan as a direct response to high increases in food prices worsened by drought and the decrease in oil and natural gas revenues. The popular unrest was met by an extreme security response as police forces and sometimes soldiers opened fire on the civilian population in major cities. It was clear that North African economies were undergoing a historic makeover and structural shift from a state-driven public economy to new economic model dictated by international lending forces that imposed restrictions on government subsidies and development-oriented public projects.

In the early 1990s, North African governments continued their economic adjustment programs, increasingly slashing social, educational, and health-care services in their annual budgets to meet the mandates and guidelines of Western crediting agencies. A growing generation of young, jobless North African university graduates soon found themselves on the streets of Tunisia, Morocco, and Algeria, forming a generation known as *hittistes* (individuals who spent their time leaning against neighborhood walls).[3] Meriem Verges describes the phenomenon in an ethnographic conversation with the *hittiste* 'Abd al-Haq:

> This is how I came across a young man living in a lusterless universe, lacking both cohesion and a future, who voted for the Islamic Salvation Front (FIS). Without professional credentials or work, 'Abd al-Haq introduced himself as a "professional" *hittiste*. This untranslatable term, a mix of French and Arabic, connotes the young Algerians who hang out, leaning against the wall (in collo-quial Arabic, *hayt*), whose "task" it is to support the walls. Because schools are overcrowded and unemployment runs high; many young Algerians are forced into the streets. A dearth of cultural hangouts like cinemas, theaters and youth clubs helps explain the teeming crowds on the streets of the Algerian capital. 'Abd al-Haq, 26, looks like someone who is out of work. Tall and skinny, he has not eaten much since the previous day: "It's too much trouble." His close-cropped chestnut hair accentuates the angular features of his pale face, em-phasizing the troubled look of a user of cannabis and *kachiete*, the drugs of the poor. To explain his drug use he talks about his anxiety, or *neboula* (anger), and a lack of sleep over the last five years.[4]

Like 'Abd al-Haq, a generation of university graduates in Algeria, Morocco, and Tunisia realized that their educational training failed to deliver economic and job opportunities.[5]

In addition to the pain of structural adjustment, the international eco-nomic slowdown of the early 1980s affected the economies of Algeria and Libya, expanding youth frustration in these rentier states with plummeting oil and natural gas revenues. In October 1988, urban riots against the government's human rights violations and abuse (*hogra*) erupted in the street of Algiers. The song "El harba wayn?" (To escape, but where to?) by Cheb Khalid, Algeria's global face of Raï music, became the anthem of the protests and the expression of the feeling of national crisis, especially after the death of hundreds of civilians. The song notes:

> Where has youth gone?
> Where are the brave ones?
> The rich gorge themselves,
> The poor work themselves to death,
> The Islamic charlatans show their true face.
> So what's the solution? . . .
> You can always cry or complain
> Or escape. But where?
> The good times are gone,
> With their celebrations and prosperity.
> *Baraka* has fled
> And selfishness destroyed solidarity . . .
> Let's stop saying: everything's all right . . .[6]

The state argued that Raï artists encouraged youth social disobedience. In the early 1990s the state introduced censorship on Raï music and encouraged forms of Raï that cohered with its policies.[7] But even though Raï translated the political disillusionment of Algeria's youth, Bezza Mazouzi argues that the genre had a limited revolutionary message.[8] Instead, the vast majority of Raï music continued to encourage leaving (*haraga*) Algeria for Europe and the United States instead of challenging the state abuse (*hogra*).

In his 2005 collaborative album *Partir loin*, Reda Taliani highlights the culture of leaving home in the song "Ya l'babour" (O boat). The song goes:

> O boat, O my love
> Take me away from misery
> In my country I feel humiliated
> I'm tired and I'm fed up with it
> This time I won't miss the chance
> It's been on my mind for a long time

Migration has made me forget who I am
I work on it day and night
Special escape
From Algeria to the West[9]

Throughout the 1990s, a growing trend of rural migration to urban centers added to the size of shantytowns and popular neighborhoods throughout the region. Economic inequality and youth unemployment worsened at the same time that police and security forces increased repression. Some young people turned to political Islam in search of a new social and political model. Initially, security forces succeeded in quelling this threat. Other young people, feeling betrayed by their own governments, opted to leave their families and homes and sought opportunities outside the region through legal and illegal migration. In the meantime, states pursued new models of education and employment to limit the challenge of a youth bulge.

The disenfranchised urban youth of North Africa expressed their frustration with their authoritarian governments, as well as their aspirations, largely as a street movement.[10] Whether they turned to violence, like the ultras (football fanatics), or weaponized hip-hop music, they used stadiums and streets as spaces for challenging the state and its security apparatus.[11] The street thus emerged as a site of youth contestation of neoliberal economic policies, political nepotism, and police corruption. In their songs, hip-hop singers and rappers highlighted the street as a space of refuge and expression away from the family and state institutions. As with Raï, hip-hop expressed frustration, despair, and concern about the economic future. Using a discourse similar to that of hip-hop as "reality" rap, unemployed Algerian and Moroccan rappers challenged official state discourse and turned the medium of internet into a new space to question political parties and state government as early as 1994.[12]

POETS AND POETICS OF REBELLION

"Every social movement," as the popular saying goes, "needs a messenger or soundtrack." In 2011, in their political fight against social injustice and corruption, North African protesters deployed rap and hip-hop as effective weapons for galvanizing broader support, starting with the Tunisian revolution against the regime of Zine el-Abidine Ben Ali. For instance, the rap song "Rais El Bled"

("President of the Country"), composed by Hamada Ben Amor, became the emblematic soundtrack of Tunisia's Jasmine Revolution.

Born in Sfax, Tunisia, and raised by a middle-class family, Ben Amor, known by his stage name El Général, grew up under Ben Ali's authoritarian regime and its neoliberal policies. Ben Amor is a representative of a generation of North African youth that lost faith in political parties and labor unions. He was working class and raised in poor neighborhoods with limited economic and social opportunities. As a rapper, El Général succeeded in escaping the restrictions of the police state through MP3s, YouTube, and other social platforms. His targets are corruption, economic injustice, and police repression.

Released and posted on YouTube in December 2010, "Rais El Bled" gained national and even international popularity. Its lyrics resonated widely and were heard in the streets and squares of Tunisia, Morocco, and Algeria:

> Mr. President, here, today, I speak with you
> in my name and the name of all people who live in misery.
> It's 2011 and there's still a man who's dying of hunger.
> He wants to work to survive, but his voice is not heard!
> Go out into the street and see [how] people have become animals.
> Look at the police with batons. . . . They don't care!
>
> . . .
>
> I see police goons beat women who wear headscarves.
>
> . . .
>
> *Alors!* This is a message from one of your children
> who is speaking with you about suffering. We are living like dogs!
> Half of the people are living in humiliation and have tasted from the cup of
>   suffering.[13]

These words highlight a series of concerns at the center of a new generation of North African youth, including issues such as humiliation, police brutality, political exclusion, economic corruption, wealth disparities, rising unemployment, and an inability to afford starting a family.[14] The impact of structural adjustment policies, the expansion of neoliberal economies, and the privileging of global and private corporations in national economies have resulted in limited opportunities for North African youth who want social and economic mobility. At the same time, "the daddy state" has lost its capacity to dispense patronage. As a result, it can no longer deliver on the economic promises of the early 1960s.[15]

Before the International Monetary Fund and World Bank forced North African leaders to impose neoliberal policies in exchange for bailouts and new loans, North African youth viewed the state as a provider of food, jobs, and security. As this promise disappeared, the state lost their reverence (*hiba*). Over time, young people no longer demonstrated a private or public fear (*khawf*) of the state. Its agents and figures are "mocked and contested" by the new generation of youth who have channeled their disdain through a culture of politicized rap and hip-hop. Today, throughout North Africa, the long-standing authoritarian, bureaucratic, and economic structures of states have limited control over an unemployed generation of youth facing an extended period of "waithood."

Like El Général, many North African hip-hop artists deemed the soundtracks and words of their songs—on and off the internet—as the optimal medium for voicing political demands and sociocultural anguish before, during, and after the recent wave of Middle Eastern and North African uprisings.[16] In Algeria, Morocco, Tunisia, and Libya, rappers and hip-hop artists like Lotfi Double Kanon, El Général, El Haqed, and Ibn Thabit channeled the concerns, fears, and anger of their communities and disseminated their demands for an end to authoritarian rule in the region.[17] The songs of North African rappers yield a trove of archival material that provide those who would listen with detailed information of the quotidian concerns of North African youth as well as their political, social, and economic struggles in the face of social frustration, political disillusionment, and generational despair. These songs are personal accounts of a new generation of North African youth who share a culture of corruption (*chafra*), humiliation (*hogra*), despair (*ihabat*), and disillusionment (*kaybat al-amal*) about the future.[18]

During the 1960s and 1970s, Ahmed Fouad Negm and Sheikh Imam made the "scenes of endemic poverty, deprivation, unemployment and suffering . . . the subject of [their] lyrics."[19] Like others of this generation of rappers and hip-hop artists, Ahmed Fouad Negm was affected by the daily life of the poor, especially the fellahin and workers whose speech and way of life influenced his style of singing. Like their predecessors, rappers and hip-hop artists during the current period demonstrate that, even in the face of renewed political redlines, art remains one of the few means to channel the ire and resentment of North Africa's youth against political regimes and the social malaise that government has produced through failed economic programs.

Largely known for his songs critical of Muammar Qaddafi, Ibn Thabit is the nickname of an anonymous Libyan hip-hop artist whose songs became the soundtracks of the Libyan uprising in 2011. The pseudonym is a direct reference to Hasan Ibn Thabit, an Arabian poet and one of the original companions of the Prophet Muhammad.[20] Arabs of the time deployed the power of poetry to satirize and ridicule rival tribes and their leaders, in the process highlighting the achievements of their communities and caricaturing their tribal enemies. Hasan Ibn Thabit was one of the early poets who defended Islam and its social message. It is no coincidence that that many North African rappers and hip-hop artists looked to Ibn Thabit's poetic defense of Islam and its prophet for inspiration during the early phases of the Arab uprisings.

In his song "Chkoun Yefhamni" (Who can understand me), Lotfi Double Kanon, whose real name is Lotfi Benlamri, highlights his story as a young Algerian rapper and his discovery of rap and hip-hop:

> I rap not for fame . . .
> I lived and saw that in my country
> people are not equal.
> I got enraged.
> That's why I went to rap.
> I transformed my words into "Grad" missiles.
> I told them many times
> I am not a singer.
> I am an educated and struggling individual
> who wrote words brought from Yathrib (Medina).
> I always had the same objective: advice and caution!
> Be patient, oh man!
> On charity stay the course!
> Follow the path of the Prophet's poet
> Hassan Ibn Thabit.

The references to Yathrib and Hasan Ibn Thabit are meant to highlight the similar state of politics and society in the contemporary period with those found during the pre-Islamic *jahiliyya*, or period of corruption and depravation, according to post–AD 622 Islamic accounts. Through rap, North African youth have decided to opt out of media controlled by the state and produce and circulate their own knowledge of the current situation by other means.

Born in Annaba, Algeria, in 1974, Benlamri exemplifies the generation that came of age in the late 1980s. Of modest origins, he founded one of the first groups in North Africa under the name "Double Kanon" in the 1990s. His album *Kamikaz* was released in 1997.[21] It highlights a generation of lost youth who passed their time engaged in drinking and drug use, and underscores the absence of the state and family on the streets of Algeria. Double Kanon sees rap as voice of different social groups irrespective of their ideological background:

> My hip-hop is universal global
> Double Kanon in this country produces popular rap
> My hip-hop, call it social phenomenon
> That's why I have fans from Adrar to Montreal
> My hip-hop is concerned with people from all categories
> . . .
> People with different musical tastes
> Those who drink, those who are religious
> My hip-hop . . .
> Talk about old people who fought the war of Indochina
> Talk about illiterate people who never attended school
> Talk about educated people with high school and PhD degrees
> . . .
> My hip-hop is followed by veiled girls
> Those who wear miniskirts . . .
> Those who love *Star Academy*
> Or those who watch religious program on TV.

Since the 1990s, North African societies have experienced a youth bulge, caused by high birth rates. The result was demographic disequilibrium: more than half of the region's population today is under the age of thirty, and while Algerian, Moroccan, and Tunisian governments have expanded access to modern education, a large segment of youth in these countries remains jobless and underemployed. In 2010, the rate of youth unemployment was over 10 percent in urban centers and more than 40 percent in some rural areas. At the same time, the number of youths who do not seek employment continues to increase. Instead of jobs, they depend upon the support of their families while they earn petty amounts in the informal sector. The tragic story of Muhammad Bouazizi, a street vendor whose death catalyzed the revolution in Tunisia, exemplifies the dire socioeconomic situation of youth throughout North Africa.

The changing family structure demonstrates the emergence of a posttraditional family in which the standing of the family patriarch has declined. In their work on the phenomenon of *tcharmil*—a term derived from the culinary arts (where it refers to meat carved by butchers using large knives), and which is commonly used in Morocco to refer to youth "ultraviolence"—researchers Moulay Driss El Maarouf and Taieb Belghazi note how a new generation of delinquent, marginalized, and unemployed youth in Morocco settle their accounts with state and society by committing acts of violence against the rich.[22] The rising numbers of unemployed North African college graduates during the 1990s; the culture of waithood and youths sitting in coffeehouses and *hittistes* standing on neighborhood corners; the ever-increasing illegal crossings of the Mediterranean by educated youths and university dropouts—all these were early warning signs pointing to Bouazizi's self-immolation.

The recent wave of social and political unrest in North Africa is just the latest chapter in a series of intermittent but frequent occurrences of unrest and social protest that have taken place over the decades since independence. Despite the political and constitutional variations of the countries in the region, young people have encountered common economic difficulties and have participated in common political struggles. The spate of uprisings that took place in the 1980s and 1990s in a number of North African cities pointed to troubles to come. And although states attempted to quell the tide by accommodating protesters and appearing to meet the demands of labor unions and opposition parties, those troubles still came. In his song "Government," Lotfi Double Kanon captures the pre-2011 malaise:

> For the youth,
> the humiliated, and the oppressed.
> Go tell the government:
> Go tell the government why the youth in this country love Rome.

In a plane, a ship, or a felucca, everyone is fleeing from the faces of those
   people.
...
The youth today don't hate their country.
They hate those people who only fill their pockets,
those who got it through connections and clever tricks.
...
The people today know where you get drunk.
The people today know that you're crooks
You guys just relax and we will never remain silent!
The youth today with unemployment are lost.

During and after the 2011 Arab uprisings, Algeria, unlike Morocco and Tunisia, managed to limit its own social protest against the military leadership and corrupt government officials, largely by using oil revenue to subsidize the price of staples such as wheat, sugar, and tea. Despite Algeria's serious social and economic problems, the state succeeded in managing dissent by meeting demands for free housing, electricity, and food. At the same time, the government succeeded in controlling foreign reporting and access to the protests.[23] Yet despite this intervention, the state could not reform its educational system to ensure that university graduates would be equipped to enter the economy. And as the situation became increasingly untenable as the price of oil collapsed, and as Europe developed new sources of energy, conditions continued to worsen, as did the frustration of new entrants to the labor market.

Currently living in exile in Belgium, the rapper Mouad Belghouat, known as "El Haqed" ("The Enraged") became the voice of the February 20 Movement, the organization that sparked Morocco's participation in the 2011 Arab uprisings. His songs spotlighted the concerns of Moroccan youth and did not shy away from criticizing state officials or the monarchy. Born in Casablanca in 1988, El Haqed's songs have targeted not only the police and government corruption but also the king, Mohammed VI. Starting in 2011, El Haqed was arrested and jailed three times for his anti-police song "Klab al-Dawla" (Dogs of the state). In 2014, he released a new album titled *Waloo*. Despite government censorship, El Haqed succeeded in building a large audience of listeners through YouTube.

In his song "Baraka man skat" (No more silence), El Haqed calls for the end of silence and fear:

> If the people want life,
> then they'll stand up to defend their rights. No more silence!
>
> Wake up! Look at the Egyptian people
> and the people of Tunisia. They're lying to you, those who say,
> "Morocco, you're an exception." OK, living is a luxury.
> Their political brainwashing is calculated.
> Debauchery and reality television, among other things, are there to distract
>   us.
> We have no choice but to fight for our rights.
> Silence won't benefit us. I am the child of the people and I'm not scared!
> . . .
> It's for me to choose whom I want to sanctify.
> And if you understand us, come live with us.
> "God, the Homeland, and Freedom"
>
> We want a leader whom we can hold to account
> and not an infallible, sanctified entity.
> . . .
> Give me my rights or give me death.

El Haqed's lyrics call into question the constitutional reform that was introduced in 2011. The "reform" came about in the wake of the Moroccan Constitutional Referendum that followed the urban uprising led by the February 20 Movement, which mobilized crowds as large as sixty thousand across Morocco. El Haqed continued to put the monarchy at the center of his songs, protesting its role and the political corruption it tolerated.[24] Recognizing El Haqed's global popularity and the power of his words, the government focused its attention on fostering fragmentation within the hip-hop industry by co-opting some artists and encouraging divisions within the hip-hop community.[25] This reaction is reminiscent of the intervention of the Egyptian state in the 1960s to co-opt Ahmed Fouad Negm and Sheikh Imam. As Marilyn Booth put it, "Popularity had its price—especially popularity accruing from a skillful satirical challenge to the ruling system."[26]

The Moroccan government succeeded in bringing a group of rappers into the fold, including Tawfiq Hazeb, alias "Don Bigg" or "El Khasser," whom the state allowed to sing out against political corruption, police brutality, and social and economic problems. In 2009, El Khasser performed his famous song "Al Khouf" (Fear), in front of the political leadership of the Socialist Union of Popular Forces, an opposition party during the 1970s and 1980s that had subsequently joined the ruling coalition in parliament. A segment of the song is as follows:

> No more fear.
> Raise your heads, all of you free Moroccans and stop being afraid.
> . . .
> You are afraid of everything but you are not afraid of God.
> There are those who are afraid of the police.
> There are those who are afraid of the district authorities.
> There are those who are afraid of the government's local representative.
> . . .
> There are those who are unjustly sentenced because of their writings.
> There are those who earn billions and pay a dirham in taxes.
> Fear is passed to us from our grandparents, we have to fight it.
> We should work for our country and stop being slaves of corruption.
> My card says Moroccan and Moroccans are proud.
> Those who try to steal my country, I will shout [at] them.

All this is heady, but while El Khasser chose to critique the social and economic conditions in Morocco, he did not cross the redline: the monarchy. El Haqed challenged Moroccan and North African rappers to opt out of the system financially in order to be free to challenge its entrenched political and economic structures of clientelism, patronage, and corruption. The decision to co-opt rappers in Tunisia and Morocco was meant to limit expansion of protests, especially because rappers like El Haqed and Lotfi Double Kanon "became the voice of opt-out movements demanding change."[27]

Rappers and hip-hop artists largely focused on highlighting the realities of youth under corrupt North African governments, but a few of their songs also emphasized the responsibilities of the new generation, its failure to meet the challenges of the time, and its responsibility to change society. In "Nouvelle Generation" (New generation), a song released before the uprisings, Lotfi Double

Kanon mocked North African youth for mimicking the West and for focusing on dress and material objects.[28] At the same time, rappers and hip-hop artists debated Islam and politics in their songs, highlighting the Islamic identity of North African societies but providing a critical portrait of political Islam and its Salafist trend. In Tunisia, Mohammed Guitouni, alias "Guito'N," emerged not only as a representative of moderate Islam but also as a critic of Tunisian Islamic parties, especially after more Tunisians joined ISIS than citizens of any other Arab state outside of Syria and Iraq.[29] His song "Ya mchadad" (You, extremist) captures the political debate about the role of Islam in Tunisian politics:

> For thirteen centuries,
> we Tunisians have lived as Muslims.
> Among us, there are those who drink
> and those who smoke
> and there are those who are pious.
> We've lived with one another.
> We've made revolution with one another
> because we live in poverty and,
> above all, because the people are oppressed.
> In 2011, we went out for revenge.
> As for those who didn't rebel with us
> and said that revolution is *haram*,
> they were in hiding then,
> but they come out now to excommunicate us.
> Muslims and infidels
> this is how they categorize us.
>
> . . .
>
> The Tunisian people are a moderate, Muslim people.
> We remain opposed to extremism. Write what you will!
> Now we understand why Zain (Ben Ali) oppressed you!
> Yo, extremist! Here are two things for you to remember:
> The jihad ain't in Tunisia. The jihad's in Palestine![30]

Guito'N acknowledges the political struggles that Islamism faced during the period of Ben Ali but challenges its leaders to respect the freedom they gained after the revolution. He notes that Islamic activists played only a limited role in the uprisings. At the same time, he criticizes Islamists for taking advantage of the democratic process to make electoral gains after the uprisings and forcing Tunisians to live by their strict Islamic rulings.

Rappers and hip-hop artists touch on other themes as well: Palestine, elections, women, democracy, political participation, citizenship, and immigration.[31] Algerian, Moroccan, and Tunisian rappers such as Lotfi Double Kanon, El Haqed, El Khasser, Muslim, and Guito'N highlighted these issues in the wake of the uprisings, yet they have continued to snub a generation of female Tunisian and Moroccan rappers such as Boutheina Medusa, Nour ben Sultana, and Youssra Oakuf (alias "Soultana") who represent the issues of women and their aspirations.

Since the second half of the twentieth century, riots and protests against state regimes in North Africa have made headlines in every decade. In each uprising, states promised economic change and political inclusion. While youth and workers waited and sacrificed for promises to become reality, education decreased in quality and unemployment increased. Since the early 1990s, rappers and hip-hop artists have directly and indirectly managed to translate the feelings, problems, and aspirations of their generation in their songs. Unfortunately, their call for economic and social justice, political inclusion, and employment continues to be met with resistance from an aging and fragmented political leadership. It is inevitable that, as the political establishment slams the political door in their face, they will continue to find new ways to challenge it and its policies. In addition, as a result of the fragmentation of political parties throughout North Africa—notably encouraged by regimes— states lack political negotiators able to co-opt and integrate those on the other side of the generational divide. As youths continue to lose trust in those states and their bureaucracies, and as those states renege on the social and economic promises they made to quiet rebellion, a maturing movement of those youths gain the advantage.

Chapter 6

ISLAMISM AT A CROSSROADS?

The Diffusion of Political Islam in the Arab World

Peter Mandaville

HOW SHOULD WE THINK ABOUT THE LIKELY FUTURE OF ISLAMISM as an ideology and a political agenda? Only a few years ago, Islamist parties looked certain to be the primary beneficiaries of the Arab uprisings and its associated upheaval. The Muslim Brotherhood and Ennahda seemed set to consolidate their political dominance in Egypt and Tunisia, respectively, with similarly aligned groups emerging as prominent players in other transitional and conflict settings such as Libya, Syria, and Yemen. Today, however, the situation seems to have turned on its head. In Egypt, the Freedom and Justice Party government of Mohamed Morsi was removed from power by force in 2013, the Muslim Brotherhood criminalized as an organization, and the current Egyptian government has been working to systematically eradicate the movement as a social force. In Tunisia, Ennahda relinquished power in 2014 in the face of a dangerously polarizing political environment, only to fail at the ballot box in subsequent elections.

Beyond the question of how Islamists have fared in individual countries, support for political Islam has emerged as one of the defining issues in a new axis of geopolitical division in the Middle East. The United Arab Emirates, Saudi Arabia, and Egypt have branded the Muslim Brotherhood trend as terrorism and pursued a zero-tolerance policy toward the movement. Qatar and Turkey, conversely, have taken a more sympathetic stance toward political

Islam. Furthermore, the trauma and violence associated with the emergence of the Islamic State in 2014 has potentially tainted even mainstream expressions of political Islam in the eyes of populations across the region. In many respects we are presented with an image today of an Islamism that is embattled and, if not defeated, very much on its heels.

But simple narratives of political Islam's decline mask a far more complex reality. If one looks around the Middle East today, the status and fortunes of Islamist groups varies widely. While the Egyptian Muslim Brotherhood is indeed facing a level of political oppression arguably more intense than it has ever seen in its ninety years of existence, its recent experience is not indicative of political Islam's standing in the Arab world more broadly. In Morocco, the Parti de la justice et du développement—a political party with roots in a social movement inspired by the Muslim Brotherhood trend—has led the government since 2011. In Jordan, the Islamic Action Front and other Islamists hold the largest bloc of opposition seats in parliament, while in Kuwait the local Muslim Brotherhood affiliate, Hadas, reentered parliament after years of boycotting elections. And in Tunisia, despite setbacks in 2014, Ennahda performed very strongly in local elections in 2018 and in 2019 became the largest party in parliament. Although it is important to temper our interpretation of these successes—the palace stills holds the real power in Morocco, Jordan's government has co-opted many Islamists, and the electorate's enthusiasm for Ennahda is far from clear—it is evident that Islamism in the Middle East is far from being a spent force. In at least one country, Turkey, Islam-friendly (if not conventionally "Islamist") forces have mostly retained their already-dominant position, with Recep Tayyip Erdoğan and the Justice and Development Party (or AK Party) emerging in that country's 2019 presidential and parliamentary elections—even if the country's failing economy and losses in key municipal elections have revealed some underlying fragility in the ruling party's hegemony.

Factors such as electoral performance and levels of political repression are certainly relevant, but they are also highly situational and, given the enormous volatility that characterizes Middle East politics today, do not necessarily tell the whole story. The purpose of this chapter is to assess these shorter-term, contingent political developments against longer-term trends in the evolution of Islamism as an ideological project and political agenda in order to discern the forces shaping possible futures for political Islam. In short, this analysis suggests that even before the watershed events of 2003 and 2010–2011, the phenomenon of political Islam had been undergoing a longer-term sociological evolution. Although some of the structural features of the "New Middle East" may adversely affect the near-term political fortunes of Islamists, it is clear that Islamism remains a fixture within the societies of the region, and, moreover, one that is perhaps more malleable and adaptable than some observers think.

POLITICAL OPPORTUNITY STRUCTURE

Which broad factors are likely to determine the future of political Islam in the Middle East? Proponents of social movement theory have long recognized the importance of changes in political opportunity structures as one of the most important factors bearing on the success of sociopolitical mobilization.[1] Simply put, a shift in political opportunity structure refers to a change in the political environment that enables social mobilization (including by opposition or other previously excluded groups). Such a change may be created by an all-encompassing and tectonically significant event, such as a political revolution or regime collapse, or by less dramatic developments, such as a tactical decision by an incumbent regime to stop oppressing a particular opposition group, or an intensification of competition among ruling elites. Previous examples of change in political opportunity structure that have had a significant impact on the political fortunes of Islamists include the collapse of the Pahlavi dynasty in Iran in 1979 in the face of popular revolution, decisions by the palace in both Morocco and Jordan in the 1990s to try to co-opt and "domesticate" Islamist parties rather than cracking down on them, the Arab uprisings of 2010–2011 that fundamentally changed the political landscape in numerous countries across the Middle East, and, of course, the 2013 coup in Egypt that removed Morsi and the Muslim Brotherhood from power.

Given the fluid and unsettled nature of politics in the Middle East at present, shifts in political opportunity structure likely represent one of the most important factors determining short-term developments in Islamism. The volatility of Arab politics may present sudden and unanticipated opportunities for Islamists to grow in prominence or increase their political power in some settings, whereas similar dynamics in other countries may lead to a diminution in their political standing. Looking across the Middle East and

North Africa as a whole, it is possible to identify three broad categories of countries in which the ebbs and flows of political opportunity structure are likely to affect Islamist political fortunes in particular ways in the near term.

First is a situation characterized by Islamist stagnation, in which the likelihood of significant shifts in political opportunity structure changing the status of Islamists is very low. The countries in question—Morocco, Algeria, Egypt, Jordan, and most of the Gulf Cooperation Council—tend to be settings characterized by relative political stability, a societal predisposition to avoid political upheaval, and/or entrenched oppression of Islamism. Islamists in these contexts either have very little to no social and political space in which to operate (and little prospect of gaining more anytime soon), or, as in the cases of the monarchies of Morocco and Jordan, have entered increasingly institutionalized bargains with regimes such that they have become effectively denuded of oppositional impulses.

The second category consists of those countries marked by gradual Islamist ascendance. In these countries domestic political developments, coupled with external influences, are likely to produce greater space for Islamist groups to shape political outcomes in the coming months and years. Interestingly, the countries in this category—Tunisia, Lebanon, and Iraq—represent two very different models that can produce positive momentum for Islamists. In Tunisia, Ennahda lost the last parliamentary election in 2014 but stayed within the governing coalition led by Nidaa Tounes and Béji Caïd Essebsi. By remaining in the political mainstream, Ennahda seems well positioned to benefit from the unpopularity of Nidaa Tounes at the next general election—even if, in an effort to affirm their establishment credentials, some of their policy positions seem overly sympathetic to pre-2011 ways of doing business.[2] In Lebanon, conversely, there is a situation in which a perpetually weak government and impasse between the main secularist factions allow a well-resourced and organized Islamist group to wield political influence well beyond its electoral strength. That country's 2018 parliamentary election only further consolidated Hizbullah's position as chief kingmaker in Lebanese politics. In Iraq, Moqtada al-Sadr's surprisingly strong showing in the 2018 elections demonstrates a similar dynamic in which a population disillusioned by a political establishment unable to make progress on the country's pressing needs turns to a relative outsider to shake things up.

Finally, there are those countries in which there is a high potential for Islamist wildcard effects, depending on the direction and outcome of ongoing conflicts or civil unrest. In most of the countries in this category—Libya, Syria, and Yemen—Islamist groups were either prominent in politics before the conflict (Yemen) or have emerged as key power brokers in the context of political upheaval and warfare (Libya and Syria). While the precise role and standing of Islamists post-conflict remains unclear and likely is subject to the terms of any eventual political settlement, local Islamists are likely to be key players if and when the dust settles in Syria and Libya, whereas Yemen's Muslim Brotherhood affiliate, Islah, has lost significant support in the context of that country's civil war but is still likely to have a role in any future government.[3]

At a more mundane level, the politics of most countries that fall into the aforementioned categories are likely to see ongoing instances of cat-and-mouse politics between Islamist groups and ruling regimes. This refers to the day-to-day game of give-and-take as Islamists, secular groups, and regimes react to one another, form temporary tactical alliances around certain issues even as they continue to vociferously disagree about others, and generally jockey for position—in short, the general horse-trading of politics. The net impact of this kind of activity over time on the political standing of Islamists is broadly neutral. On the one hand, it functions to institutionalize and "normalize" the participation of Islamists in everyday politics, but, on the other hand, it also tends to incentivize Islamists to assume increasingly centrist positions that, over time, make their political brand less and less distinctive.

A political opportunity structure-related dynamic more likely to have a broad, systemic impact on Islamist fortunes going forward comes from the aforementioned regional struggle between powerful blocs of pro- and anti-Islamist countries. For nearly twenty years, Qatar and then Turkey have broadly supported ikhwanist-aligned movements, parties, media, and civil society throughout the Middle East.[4] Alarmed by the rapid rise in political strength of these groups after the Arab uprisings, the United Arab Emirates and Saudi Arabia—both of which perceived the Muslim Brotherhood as an existential threat to their respective ruling dynasties—have, since 2012, undertaken a broad-based campaign to discredit, neutralize, criminalize, and generally oppress even mainstream, nonviolent expressions of Islamism. Abu

Dhabi's crown prince Mohammed bin Zayed and, to a lesser extent, Saudi Arabia's crown prince Muhammad bin Salman have emerged as the champions and chief stewards of anti-ikhwanist statecraft. They have provided direct financial support to regional governments that have taken a hard line against Islamists (e.g., Abdel Fattah al-Sisi's Egypt) and have encouraged—mostly to no avail—key global allies such as the United States and the United Kingdom to declare the Muslim Brotherhood a terrorist organization.

Going forward, the intensity of the pro- and anti-Islamist divide in the Middle East and its overall impact on Islamist fortunes is likely to depend on two factors. First, there is the question of the other important geopolitical issue at play within the spat that pits the United Arab Emirates, Kuwait, and Saudi Arabia against Turkey and Qatar, namely Iran. Saudi Arabia and (secondarily) the UAE have viewed Iran as a direct security threat, whereas Turkey and Qatar have taken a more cordial posture toward Tehran (even as both countries oppose its role in Syria). Because the issues that divide the likes of Riyadh and Doha at present are to some extent a package, any progress on one of them—such as the overall trend in Gulf Cooperation Council–Iran relations—is likely to influence other elements within the larger basket, such as the posture that Abu Dhabi and Riyadh strike with respect to Islamism more broadly. Second, the attitude of the UAE and, especially, Saudi Arabia toward ikhwanist groups in the coming years is also likely to be governed by the importance of these groups for achieving Riyadh's desired outcome in a number of regional conflicts, including Yemen, Syria, Libya, and Palestine. If Muslim Brotherhood–linked groups in these countries turn out to be important players for brokering the necessary cease-fires and creating stable political coalitions, then Riyadh is likely to back away from the excesses of its current anti-Islamist campaign and to encourage its allies in the Gulf Cooperation Council to do the same.

POPULAR ATTITUDES TOWARD ISLAMISTS, RELIGION, AND POLITICS

What do popular perceptions of and attitudes toward Islamists tell us about possible futures for political Islam? Here we find a very mixed picture. As the performance of Islamists in elections throughout the region in recent years suggests, the situation varies from country to country. Polling data on this question are difficult to come by, not least of all because many governments in the region are sensitive about survey researchers asking questions about support for Islamism. Using proxy indicators does not get us very far. For example, Pew Research Center data on levels of support for sharia in the Middle East in 2013 found that significant majorities support making Islamic law the official law of the land. However, in several countries the relevant percentages are clearly far higher than are levels of support for Islamists, meaning that sharia supporters have been overpolled or that those who favor Islamic law stay away from the ballot box, or—as is most likely the case—that many who express support for sharia vote for non-Islamist parties.[5]

Several polls, including Pew and the Arab Barometer, ask about levels of support for religious leaders playing a role in government; the Arab Barometer survey shows a clear trend of decreasing support in recent years for religious leaders intervening in politics.[6] Again, however, this does not serve as a meaningful proxy for political Islam, as most respondents likely understand "religious leaders" to refer to religious scholars or clerics and view those actors as separate and distinct from Islamist leaders and politicians. Indeed, many Islamists have criticized the role played by religious scholars in, for example, lending support to authoritarian regimes, so it is likely that the described trend includes many Islamists.

Levels of popular support for Islamist parties and movements, however, is the wrong metric to track in the first place, particularly if the goal is to understand better the more systemic factors and trends shaping prospects for political Islam. Political opinion polls are, after all, notoriously contingent, situational, and volatile. We are perhaps better off asking broader questions about the presence and role of Islam in political discourse in the Middle East and about how peoples' understandings about Islamism and political Islam may be changing.

Part of the challenge in assessing this question arises from a tendency in the study of political Islam to focus primarily on specific organizations, movements, and parties, and the things they say and do. So it becomes relatively easy for observers to explore attitudes of political Islamists toward society (using their statements, behavior, and political strategies) but very difficult for them to know much about popular attitudes toward political Islam beyond electoral performance and occasional opinion polls. Adding to the analytic confusion is the fact that some prominent Islamists have openly questioned the utility of Islamism as an appropriate label or description of what they stand for. A trend started by Turkish leader Recep Tayyip Erdoğan has seen Islamist parties with roots in the Muslim Brotherhood tradition progressively distancing themselves from the label "Islamist." Starting in the mid-1990s, a discourse of *wasatiyya* (centrism) emerged as an alternative to classical Islamist formulations, most prominently in the Hizb al-Wasat faction that broke away from the old-guard leadership of the Egyptian Muslim Brotherhood. Muslim Brotherhood clerics such as Yusuf al-Qaradawi adopted the same language to describe a religio-political trend rooted in Islam but thoroughly pragmatic in its orientation.[7] A different formula proved more successful, however—the "justice and development" trend started by the Moroccan Islamists and later adopted by Erdoğan when he staged his own breakaway from Turkey's old-guard Islamic bloc. Part of the reason for the success of the "justice and development" brand—one since replicated in other countries, including Indonesia—lies in the fact that it eschews the studied vagueness of *wasatiyya* in favor of terminology that gestures toward an actual political platform—"justice," connoting lack of corruption; "development," economic growth. Thus, the phrase captures in a pat formula the two leading concerns of many voters in the Middle East.

Erdoğan was the first prominent Islamist leader to signal a new strategic orientation for Islamist parties when he suggested that the AK Party could not be accurately described as an Islamist party but was rather a socially conservative party comprising public servants whose sense of morality was rooted in their religious convictions.[8] He urged observers of the AK Party to view it as the Muslim equivalent of the Christian democracy movement in Europe; in other words, the religious referent points here to a broad cultural-ethical orientation rather than a specific governing agenda.

Just over a decade later, the leader of Tunisia's Ennahda, Rashid Ghannoushi, announced at the party's 2016 annual congress that members of Ennahda should no longer think of themselves as Islamists but as "Muslim democrats." Ghannoushi's announcement reflected more than a shift in labeling, however; a directive to separate the religious activities of the Ennahda social movement from the work of the political party accompanied it. On one level, Ghannoushi was seeking to reassure skeptical secularists in Tunisia who harbored lingering fears that Ennahda would use its political position at some point to press a religious agenda. On another, this shift is consistent with an emerging pattern in contemporary Islamist thought that, at least implicitly, recognizes religion and politics as separate domains. In both Morocco and Egypt, for example, leaders from the Justice and Development Party and the Muslim Brotherhood have argued in recent years that it is possible for members of specific Islamist movements to create and/or support multiple political parties, including those of non-Islamists.[9] For Ghannoushi, this development reflects a pragmatic approach long present in his writings whereby ideas and solutions from non-Islamic sources or ideologies are perfectly acceptable so long as the effects they yield are compatible with the broad objectives of Islamic law. Translated into politics, this would permit a "Muslim democrat" to collaborate with or, following Ennahda's experience, participate in a coalition with political groups of varying ideological orientations to jointly devise practical solutions to everyday problems unencumbered by a separate proselytizing agenda. With respect to the question of sharia law, for example, this position enables a party such as Ennahda to maintain its commitment to creating sharia-compliant laws instead of sharia-based laws that derive from a specific and separate body of rules that needs to be progressively implemented over time.

LOOKING AHEAD: ISLAMIST TRENDS AND FUTURES

When looking at how changing political opportunity structures, intra-Islamist dynamics, and shifts in popular attitudes toward Islam in politics have played out in various national settings in the Middle East over the past two decades, it becomes possible to discern a number of trends that hold clues to the future evolution of political Islam. They are Islamist self-limiting, internal factionalization and existential crisis, and a shifting sociology of Islamist affiliation.

In terms of the first, it seems likely that in the near to medium term, political opportunity structures in the Middle East will be, by and large, unfavorable to Islamists. At present, there are arguably only two countries in the Middle East in which Islamists are able to compete for power relatively openly and on an equal footing with other political actors under conditions of "normal" politics: Tunisia and Algeria (where an absence of meaningful political competition means that Islamists face no particular disadvantage compared to other groups). All other settings in which Islamist groups and parties are to be found involve one or more of the following: subjugation of all political actors to monarchy (Morocco, Jordan, Gulf Cooperation Council); a ban on Islamist mobilization and political activity (Egypt); active or recent civil war involving the suspension of political institutions (Libya, Syria, Yemen);[10] or the presence of a very weak or failed central government dealing with fundamental issues of social cohesion (Lebanon, Iraq). While it may seem a contradiction to highlight the presence of structural obstacles to Islamist success in two of the countries characterized above as likely to experience gradual Islamist ascendancy (Iraq and Lebanon), the point here is that Islamists can still experience surges in political influence even where they are not able to capture the state. Indeed, the advantages these particular Islamists enjoy are more a function of either their outsider, nonestablishment status (Sadrists in Iraq) or of their ability to adroitly navigate sectarian politics in the face of a severely impaired central state (Hizbullah in Lebanon) rather than their ideological appeal.

This does not mean that it is impossible or unnecessary to track shifts in the political fortunes of Islamists operating in constrained political environments. Indeed, the strategies Islamists employ under such conditions provide evidence of how they think about politics and their capacity to adapt.[11] Rather, the point here is to recognize that in many settings today, as in the recent past, Islamists confront either an enforced political ceiling (especially in the monarchies) or a national political environment defined by conflict, instability, and even fundamental questions of sovereign integrity. It is therefore likely that for the foreseeable future we can expect to see a continuing trend of Islamist self-limiting in various forms.

In monarchies, Islamists will continue to accept the dominance of the palace and its agenda as the price of participation. Across multiple settings in which Islamist political ambition is constrained, we may see these groups pursuing parts of their agenda within the confines of civil society by means of broader Islamic social movements that serve as the bedrock foundation of Islamist political parties. This retrenchment may also lead to increased partnership and collaboration (along ongoing competition) with other Islamic actors working within civil society, including Salafis. Based on the experience of the Egyptian Muslim Brotherhood from 2012 to 2013, many Islamists may conclude that too much political ambition is dangerous and that seeking power or undue exposure is to be avoided.

Even in Tunisia, the country where Islamists appear to have the best short-term prospects, Ennahda is likely to proceed with extreme caution in order to avoid a return to the intense polarization that characterized Tunisian politics in 2012–2013 and ultimately led to its downfall. Islamists there have a strong track record of working in partnership with factions representing other ideologies and dealing with controversial issues in a deliberative, inclusive fashion. Perhaps the greatest risk Ennahda faces is a growing perception on the part of some of its supporters that the party is so concerned with appeasing secularists and remnants of the prerevolutionary regime (both of which remain powerful in Tunisian politics) that it will end up facilitating a return to the very status quo it opposed for so long.

Islamist movements have also faced internal factionalization and existential crisis. In several countries where Islamists have experienced recent waves of oppression or heavy-handed regulation at the hands of the state—notably Egypt and Jordan—Islamist movements have fragmented. In most cases, the basic terms of the internal debate concern differences of opinion over the appropriate response to regime pressure. In Jordan, for example, the chief divide within the Muslim Brotherhood and Islamic Action Front tendency is between one group willing to align itself with the crown in exchange for more political space (à la the Justice and Development Party in Morocco) and another—currently proscribed—that prefers to maintain a more clearly oppositionist orientation. The divide speaks to two very different assessments of Jordan's political future. On the one hand, there are palace accommodationists who see broad stability over time and hope gradually to convince the regime to adopt select planks of their platform in return for placating their constituency. On the other hand, there are oppositionists who are betting on a more fundamental crisis of palace legitimacy in the near to medium term that would permit them to negotiate a higher price for lending support.

Perhaps nowhere in the Middle East today is this internal Islamist factionalization as pronounced and intense as in the case of the Egyptian Muslim Brotherhood. Because the Brotherhood operates almost entirely underground, its internal dynamics are particularly opaque at present. Nevertheless, by tracking the pronouncements of various figures and entities claiming to speak for the group as a whole, it is possible to get a general sense of the major divisions within the movement. One faction, consisting of those who might be called neo-Harakis (a reference to their emphasis on the *haraka*, or "movement"), reject politics, believing that the Brotherhood's foray into the political arena and ascendancy to the presidency was a severe mistake, never to be repeated. They prefer an almost total retrenchment within the Muslim Brotherhood social movement at the level of community and civil society, as well as the renunciation of political involvement. Another group might be called neo-Qutbists (in reference to Sayyid Qutb, the radical Brotherhood ideologue of the 1950s and 1960s). They believe that the experience of the Freedom and Justice Party and Morsi proved that the Egyptian deep state will never accept Islamists in power and that the only way forward involves direct confrontation with the state and, eventually, a new revolution. Some affiliated with this faction have been involved in revenge attacks on the personnel and facilities of the security service protecting the regime. Another revolutionary faction, which consists of those who might be called neo-Thawrists (to indicate their ongoing faith in the possibility of a new *thawra*, or "revolution"), remains open to the possibility of future political participation, perhaps in concert with non-Islamist groups, but only after a new revolution that results in a purge of the deep-state institutions, especially the internal security forces and judiciary. These three groups represent broad, ideal-type orientations. It is difficult to say with certainty how accurately they map on to the sociopolitical reality of Egypt at present. Indeed, as one young former Brotherhood activist put it, the main orientation of most young Egyptians, Islamist or otherwise, is a complete disillusionment with politics and a preoccupation with survival.[12]

The problem of internal factionalization points to a broader crisis of identity and vision that many Islamists deal with today. As the post-Islamism thesis predicts, Islamists seeking to advance their goals through the ballot box and mainstream politics today have had to embrace the political center so thoroughly that they have become ideologically indistinct from most other political groups.[13] In sum, Islamists in the Arab world seem to be at an ideological crossroads. Interest in the ramifications of the classic slogan "Islam is the solution" and advocacy for an Islamic political order based on direct implementation of sharia have worn thin, even among most party faithful. Other than "Muslim democracy" and the nebulous *wasatiyya*, no identifiable or coherent ideological vision has emerged to replace the standard Islamist formulas. Against this backdrop of intellectual stagnation, Islamists have to contend with a significant number of Arabs who believe that Islamists still harbor an extremist or ultraconservative religious agenda, along with others who, having experienced Freedom and Justice Party rule, believe that Islamists just do not know how to govern.

There are those, such as Erdoğan and Ghannoushi, who have sought to parlay this condition into a strategic opportunity by charting what they see as a new course for "Muslim democracy," more or less openly declaring the demise of Islamism. They may yet succeed. But even if Islamist politics can be preserved in one form or another, the range of contexts in which its empowerment would be possible, permissible, or relevant seems very limited, unless and until the broader political landscape of the Middle East becomes more stable, with at least a modicum of political opening.

Finally, the shifting sociology of Islamist affiliation. Issues of factionalization and ideological vision express a top-down orientation to the analysis of political Islam; that is, they presume that organizational dynamics and the agency of movement or party leaders are the key determinants of how Islamism will evolve going forward. But one clear trend, observable since at least the mid-1990s, suggests that bottom-up pressures have played a significant role in shaping the course of Islamism in the Arab world. Thus, we also need to ask questions about who is joining Islamist groups today and why.

Leading scholars of political Islam such as Carrie Wickham and Khalil Al-Anani have emphasized generational differences within Islamist membership as a key force shaping the orientation and internal politics of these movements.[14] As new members joined Islamist groups during different phases in the political history and development of Arab nations, they brought with them different understandings and expectations about what political Islam means and what it could or should deliver. Even the intense ideological indoctrination associated with joining a group such as the Egyptian Muslim Brotherhood has had to contend with the fact that, ultimately, these groups mirror the broader society around them and have to address the issues of the day.

We can discern important clues about possible shifts in the political sociology of Islamist recruitment and affiliation from the work of scholars such as Avi Spiegel. In his book *Young Islam*, Spiegel provides a fascinating portrait of grassroots Islamist mobilization in Morocco.[15] Through conversations with young members and potential recruits to both the Adl w'al-Ihsan movement and the Justice and Development Party, Spiegel discovered that people have a wide range of motivations for joining Islamist groups and varying—even contradictory—understandings of what Islamism means. For many, Islamism does not represent a specific ideology or a clear and distinctive package of political solutions. Rather, they see Islamism in an aspirational sense, as the hope or possibility of an alternative politics—even if its specific agenda and content remain fluid and undefined. For them, Islam functions as a symbol of something more virtuous and authentically "theirs," even if its ideological prescriptions remain undefined. Islam provides a culturally and politically permissible means of registering dissent. This is consistent with views offered by current Egyptian Muslim Brotherhood youth activists. They report a sense on the part of many of their movement colleagues that, in the broad climate of entrenched or renewed authoritarianism in the Arab world, ideological labels such as "secularism," "Islamism," "leftism," and "liberalism" are essentially meaningless. The only relevant political distinction, as they see it, is whether one supports or opposes the regime—and embracing Islamism, even absent any clear ideological conviction or political agenda, becomes one means of registering opposition.[16]

Egypt is, of course, an extreme case at present, and the trend Spiegel describes in Morocco cannot be extrapolated to political Islam across the region as a whole. Similarly, to claim that Islamism is ideologically vacuous today would be inaccurate and unfair. However, it is certainly the case that its proponents have to contend with a shifting marketplace of political expectations, and constituencies look for a "value proposition" that accords with their own social and economic priorities. By and large, this has meant that Islamists have had to back away from a strong focus on religious agendas or the promotion of sharia in favor of a political agenda that broadly endorses liberal economic prescriptions and champions public morality—in short, a relatively conventional agenda of social conservativism. If, however, voting publics start to view the Islamist focus on issues of public morality (e.g., pornography, blasphemy) as a smoke screen masking their inability to address economic woes and bad governance, they will have to struggle to maintain support. Likewise, those gravitating toward Islamism as a generic signifier of an alternative to the status quo will likely lose interest or turn elsewhere if political Islam turns out to be an impotent shell.

ISLAMISM AT A CROSSROADS?

Looking at political Islam in the aggregate, the various trends outlined in this chapter suggest a relatively bleak future for Islamism. In almost all settings where Islamists continue to participate in formal politics, they are subject to political constraints by incumbent regimes or compelled to engage in self-limiting behavior. At the level of ideas, it seems increasingly unclear what Islamists stand for in concrete terms and whether they are able to offer a distinctive vision that can differentiate them from their political rivals. By the same token, it is not even clear that their members, who join for a variety of reasons, understand Islamism to have a coherent political agenda. Finally, Islamists will likely find it increasingly difficult to compete in a diverse and crowded field of actors offering many differing pathways and modalities for pursuing an Islamic way of life.

Given the trend toward post-Islamism and the likelihood of ongoing palace hegemony in Morocco in Jordan, there are essentially three settings in which it is possible that Islam might reemerge as an important political force in the medium to longer term (five or more years). The first of these is the civil war context of Libya, Syria, and Yemen, and the long-standing conflict in Israel/Palestine. In all of these countries, *ikhwanist* groups played a significant role in politics before and in some cases during the conflicts. The Libyan Muslim Brotherhood proved surprisingly resilient in the immediate post-Qaddafi period, and its organizational base will provide it with a comparative advantage following any political settlement in that country's current impasse. In Syria, Islamists of various sorts are prominent within the rebel forces and are likely to emerge as one of the more credible political actors at the popular level if and when stability and a new governing synthesis emerge in Syria.[17] Al-Islah in Yemen has declined in popularity in the context of the conflict there but may yet have a role in helping to hold together any postconflict governing coalition. Any reengagement of the Middle East peace process will require some minimal and sustained reconciliation or power-sharing agreement between Hamas and Fatah. This, in turn, will require that whichever Arab state serves as the process guarantor—most likely Saudi Arabia—find some modus vivendi with Hamas.

Second, despite the draconian crackdown on the Muslim Brotherhood in Egypt, the regime has not succeeded in eliminating it outright as an influential force in society. One opinion poll following the 2013 coup suggested that 38 percent of Egyptians still have a favorable view of the Islamists.[18] This is a precipitous decline from the 75 percent support they enjoyed in 2011, but still remarkable given Morsi's deep unpopularity, the intensity of the regime's crackdown, and the risk of expressing support for a banned organization. Despite the intense factionalization, it appears that the Brotherhood continues to operate in Egypt, albeit quietly, as a social movement at the community and neighborhood levels. While its Egyptian-based leadership, which managed to avoid detention, has maintained an underground presence, it is questionable how much control it has over the day-to-day operations of the movement. Likewise, exiled Brotherhood leaders have not refrained from bold declarations and rhetoric, but it is not clear whether the rank and file in Egypt are paying attention. The most likely scenario for Islamists' reemergence in Egypt involves an accommodationist faction of the movement striking a bargain with the regime, similar to the deal they made with Sadat in the 1970s. It is not impossible to imagine an increasingly beleaguered Sisi (or even his successor), unable to make progress in addressing the nation's economic challenges, reaching out to rehabilitate the Brotherhood in order to shore up support. Such an arrangement would likely look similar to Egypt in the 1980s and 1990s—a Muslim Brotherhood banned from politics but increasingly prominent in civil society—and could provide the Islamists with a new foundation on which to build.

Finally, it will be important to keep an eye on Tunisia as the one context that might provide a sustainable model for the normalization and integration of Islamists into electoral politics and successful power sharing. Ennahda has won one election, overseen a vexed but ultimately successful and widely supported constitutional process, experienced deep political polarization and negotiated to voluntarily relinquish power, lost the subsequent election but joined and supported the resulting coalition government, and enjoyed success in local and municipal elections—positioning its members well for the next general election. This is an impressive record of accomplishment and one that suggests a rapidly growing political maturity that may allow Ennahda to provide a road map for Islamists elsewhere looking for a new strategic and operational paradigm.

The combination of regional upheaval and the associated volatility in the political fortunes of Islamist parties make it a particularly difficult time to predict the future of political Islam with any certainty—even when some of the broad trend lines are clear. This effect is compounded by the fact that the political vision and identity of Islamism had been subject to considerable debate and diffusion for some time before the Arab uprisings. While Islamism may well be at a crossroads today with little prospect of near-term dominance in the region, it is also clear that political Islam will continue to exert significant social and political influence in the New Middle East—even if (or perhaps because) the nature and meaning of political Islam continue to be subjects of vociferous debate among its supporters and detractors alike.

Chapter 7

ISLAMISTS BEFORE AND AFTER 2011

Assuming, Overlooking, or Overthrowing the Administrative State?

Nathan J. Brown

ONE OF THE ODDEST THINGS THAT THE ISLAMIC STATE (PREVIOUSLY called ISIS), a political entity that claimed to be like no other in the world and to be based solely on Islamic teachings, did was to call itself a "state" (*dawla*). And while there is some ambiguity in the term,[1] the Islamic State's leaders, officials, and bureaucrats behaved as if this meant an administrative state in the fullest modern sense.

What did it mean to regulate traffic, building codes, social media, e-commerce, and traffic in SIM cards in an Islamic manner? Confronting a host of regulations, instructions, official structures, and chains of command, one electrical engineer who worked in the Mosul municipality discovered: "The Islamic State was a terrorist state, but it was also a modern state. They dressed and talked like they lived in early Islam, but administratively they were excellent and ran the state efficiently."[2]

The administrative state—with its laws, bureaucracies, ministries, courts, officials, procedures, and regulations—is assumed in debates about the relationship between religion and state, but until recently it has often been simultaneously all but invisible. In this chapter, I seek to bring this invisibility fully to light, aided in part by developments since 2011. In his introduction to this volume, James L. Gelvin discussed ways in which the upheavals of 2011, the rise of groups like ISIS, and the decline of respect for state sovereignty were all possible characteristics of the "New Middle East"—but he also invited readers to consider how much continuity might also be in evidence, especially when taking a longer-term historical view.

THE REALITY OF THE ADMINISTRATIVE STATE

A modern administrative and regulatory state seems an almost inevitable part of governance in the twenty-first century. What does it mean to construct it along Islamic lines? If a ruler, regime, or state claims to base itself on Islamic principles, there is a well-established (if sometimes contentious) debate about what this means for legislation and adjudication. But what does it mean for administration—for issuing driver's licenses, promulgating building codes, calculating pensions, designing curricula, and fostering safety in the workplace?

Can an Islamic state do these things within the bounds of the Islamic sharia? Does it do so in any distinctive manner because it is Islamic, or does it simply follow the same patterns as other regulatory states? Are there any boundaries on what it can and cannot do? Are there any regulations—or manner of issuing regulations—that it must follow or avoid? What does it mean to be an Islamic polity and a modern administrative state at the same time?

It is not merely the Islamic State that has faced the question in a manner that fascinated many. Some more mainstream Islamists have gone beyond holding an occasional cabinet seat (as occurred in a few countries in the past) and actually taken on significant executive authority—in Palestine they formed the cabinet in 2006 and have governed Gaza since 2007; in Egypt they held the presidency in 2012; in Tunisia and Morocco they have taken on a far greater executive role in the years since 2011.

But it is not merely governing that has raised the problem of what Islamic administration looks like. Islamists accustomed to assessing the legitimacy of the political system in terms of an individual ruler or in terms of the compatibility of the legal system with the Islamic sharia suddenly face the realization that more complicated questions are involved. In Saudi Arabia, a series of political and legal changes, some quite subtle, such as qualifications for judicial office or the geographical distribution of sharia faculties, are reconfiguring the ways that religious scholars inform, guide, and instruct officials. In Syria and Yemen, the prospect of eventual political reconstruction of the state apparatus will raise far more questions than simply who will occupy top offices or which law codes will be restored. And in Egypt, Islamists have come to understand that it is the "deep state," and not merely the chief executive and the law code, that is at issue.

But if there is a growing realization of the breadth of the modern state and the tremendous scope of its administrative apparatus, these developments are not producing clearly Islamic approaches or even clear lines of debate.

In the summer of 2017, I sat far from away from Islamic State rule in Mosul but instead in the Riyadh home of 'Isa al-Ghaith, a member of the Saudi Consultative Council. Al-Ghaith, a judge and the son of a former leader of the country's religious police, had made a name for himself over the previous few years by staking out progressive positions on Islamic legal questions and opposing more conservative forces and positions.

I probed him in particular about his view that in an Islamic state the only sharia-based strictures that should be enforced are those on which all religious scholars agree or—in the absence of clear consensus—those that the ruler has clearly endorsed.

At first, his position seems uncontroversial. The idea that the political authority of the community enjoins virtue and forbids vice—and that "changing with the hand" is a religiously required task that should be assigned with great care and generally to the ruler—is a well-established one in Muslim communities. And of course, the implicit targets of al-Ghaith's criticisms— Saudi judges who resist codification, or members of the religious police who claim that they have been deputized by the ruler to prevent vice—would not disagree with his position.

The punch of al-Ghaith's argument was packed in something far subtler: the claim that it is the ruler himself who must declare personally which contentious interpretations are binding. In other words, judges and religious police officers should not act on their own understanding of the Islamic sharia but instead only on those understandings explicitly endorsed by the ruler himself. Muslims might come to their own opinion on what God requires, but it is only the ruler's will that can be enforced; this is an authority that cannot be delegated.

In short, what does it mean to be an Islamic and an administrative or regulatory state? Can they be combined, and if so, how? What is most interesting about this question is how infrequently it has been posed.

THE *WALI AL-AMR* AS FATHER AND STATE: RELIGIOUS
SCHOLARS AND JURISTS BEFORE 2011

What struck me in my discussion with al-Ghaith was that what appeared to be the crux of the disagreement—who has authority to speak for the state—was almost never at the center of the argument. When al-Ghaith made headlines (and he seemed to enjoy being provocative) by tangling with more conservative religious scholars, it was over his positions on gender relations or other sensitive matters. The seemingly more technical issue—though politically actually quite far reaching—of when the ruler's authority operates personally and when it operates through state institutions draws no attention in public debates and al-Ghaith elaborated on it only when pressed. This should not have surprised me—the inattention to such questions was hardly a new discovery.

Indeed, the discussion brought to mind a striking element I had come to notice in a 1995 decision issued by Egypt's Supreme Constitutional Court (SCC) in a case involving women's head covering. The minister of education had barred the niqab (full-face veil) from Egyptian schools; the father of two sisters expelled under the ban, acting as the *wali al-amr* (legal guardian) for them, filed suit against the principal, the school, and the minister. He claimed the ban violated article 2 of the Egyptian constitution, which states that "the principles of the Islamic sharia are the main source of legislation." The SCC turned back the challenge, arguing that in matters of the Islamic sharia, except for those few rules certain with regard to their authenticity and meaning, the *wali al-amr* (here meaning the ruler) is authorized to enforce the interpretation consistent with the general goals of the Islamic sharia that is most appropriate for the society at that time.

There are many issues that attract attention here—the constitutional clause; women's dress and the way it serves at the touchstone for so many controversies about religion; the court's views on Islam, sexuality, and other matters. But what stands out about the nature of authority is the use of the phrase *wali al-amr*. It is used both for the father (because he acts legally on behalf of the students who are expelled) and for the ruling political authority—an elision in terminology that makes that political authority appear paternalistic in the most literal sense. Furthermore, the term in the second sense is undefined but seems to refer at various times to the ruler, the minister of education, the court, the parliament, the constitutional authority, the entire state, or any state authority. In seeking to ground reasoning in Islamic political and legal terminology, the SCC has neither the language nor the interest to distinguish among these things.

The Islamic sharia, understood as a pious discourse among religious scholars and specialists, historically has operated alongside of—and with some distinctiveness from—the political authority of rulers and states. But academic specialists in Islam and law have long noted that modern states, by codifying law, establishing hierarchical court systems, inserting constitutional provisions for observing Islamic law in some areas (e.g., personal status), or making the Islamic sharia a source of law, raised a challenge for how the Islamic sharia had been understood and informed political practice.[3]

By focusing on issues such as sovereignty and source of law, academics explore a strong tension that can emerge between the Islamic sharia (with its legal nature and the implicit, or sometimes explicit, assertion that sovereignty lies with God) and the modern state (with its penchant for positive law and insistence on state or popular sovereignty). Academics have probed the awkwardness, tensions, and even contradictions that occur by overstepping the way in which the Islamic sharia is a scholarly discourse partly autonomous from governing and inserting it into the legal framework of the state. Indeed, the transformation is so profound that Wael Hallaq has staked out the increasingly strong claim that the Islamic sharia as it was understood for much of Islamic history is essentially extinct and that the modern state is fundamentally and essentially incompatible with it.[4]

Hallaq's position is sufficiently extreme that it is rejected by most academics. More subtly, Clark Lombardi titled his book on Islamic law in the Egyptian legal and constitutional order *State Law as Islamic Law in Modern Egypt*—and by using that title, he clearly suggests that the forms of Islamic law that come out of the attempt to fold it into the modern state have to be taken seriously as Islamic law and that Islamic law as expressed in the positive law of states (derived, to some extent, from Islamic *fiqh*, or jurisprudence, but following very different processes, accepting different sources of authorities, and taking very different forms) is how many Muslims encounter Islamic law in the world today.[5] Most academics hew more closely to Lombardi's views than to Hallaq's in that they avoid viewing the Islamic sharia simply as it existed in historical (or perhaps fossilized) or essentialized forms. Indeed, they show far greater reluctance to render categorical and moral judgments on what the Islamic sharia is than Hallaq insists on doing. Instead, they examine how the Islamic sharia has been remade, expressed institutionally, and understood in different ways—exploring those forms as part of a living tradition rather than dismissing them as corruptions.[6]

But the sharpness of the debate often distracts attention from the nature of the terrain. This scholarly discussion turns our attention to very specific structures: constitutions and courts take center stage; codes of law attract extended attention. Rulers, judges, legislators, and sometimes senior religious scholars in state institutions are the main characters. Hallaq's modern state is much more about sovereignty and law than public administration and bureaucracy; his more nuanced opponents evince similar interests.

But of course modern administrative states are often far-flung affairs, and the Islamic sharia appears in numerous guises. It can be, of course, the subject of legislation and adjudication. But it is also taught to schoolchildren in curricula developed by ministries of education; it is studied by law students as a discrete subject in the lecture halls of state universities; it is preached by imams who are trained in state institutions and monitored by ministries of religious affairs (and sometimes by ministries of interior); it is propounded by fatwa-giving bodies that are supported by the state; it is the subject of broadcasts and other state-operated media outlets.

How are these officials and bureaucracies supposed to operate? On these matters, *fiqh* gives only the most rudimentary guidance. It does have some teaching on the duties of the ruler—what the *wali al-amr* must and must not do, how to deal with a *wali al-amr* who deviates from Islamic teaching, and so on.

But this conflates ruler and state in a way that simply looks past much of what actual administrative states do. How are identification cards supposed to register religion? How are endowments to be audited? How should grades in religion classes be factored into students' academic records? How many minutes should sermons last?

These are all matters on which administrative states are active and sometimes quite precise. When studying, praying, lecturing, assembling, celebrating in a religious manner, often a state bureaucracy (and sometimes more than one) has something to say and some regulatory framework to enforce.

Islamic legal and political thought does offer the doctrine of *siyasa shar'iyya* (governance according to sharia) as guidance, allowing rulers to do what is necessary to help a society operate in accordance with a sharia-based social order. That provides a sense of the ethics of rule but leaves the administrative details in the hands of a would-be virtuous ruler.

The SCC moves between the *wali al-amr* as legal guardian for minors and the *wali al-amr* as the state in a manner that is clear; it is less obvious but of tremendous significance that it uses a term that originally referred to an individual (the ruler or father) to describe various parts of the entire state apparatus, some of them only dimly aware of what other parts are doing. How are the parts of the state to relate to one another? How is the ruler selected, and how are parts of the state to relate to the head of state? What is the authority of various state bodies and where does it come from?

These are questions that folding the Islamic sharia into the state—making Islamic law a form of state law, to use Lombardi's title—would seem to force onto the agenda. But they are also ones that the restricted focus of the academic debate focusing almost exclusively on law (and sidestepping administration and regulation) do not lead us to probe or consider.

And academics are not alone. Islamists have betrayed a similar blind spot.

ISLAMISTS TAKING THE ADMINISTRATIVE STATE AS A GIVEN BEFORE 2011

It is remarkable that the question—what happens to the Islamic sharia when it is folded into the legal apparatus of the modern state?—that occupied academics seemed for so long to be of so little concern to many of the most prominent movements that seek to bring Islam in general, and the Islamic sharia specifically, to play a greater role in public and political life. Is codification an abomination? Can God's sovereignty be exercised in a state that also proclaims popular sovereignty? To be sure, some of these questions did sometimes elicit some debate. Codification has been an issue in Saudi Arabia but virtually nowhere else.[7] The "contradiction" between divine and popular sovereignty has been raised on occasion by some Salafi leaders and some jihadist groups. (Intellectuals also write on the subject, often seeking ways to explore the way that God's commands can be seen as empowering popularly-based institutions.)

But the larger and more mainstream Islamist movements stayed away from the subject, not so much out of fear as of lack of interest. Even when constitutional clauses have attracted very great attention (especially those specifying the Islamic sharia as *a* or *the* source of law), Islamists paid little attention to the fine print or implementing bodies. They demanded, in short, a very strong verbal and symbolic commitment to Islamic law, but they have not looked so much to that commitment to be the basis for structuring the state. Hierarchical court systems, parliaments, ministries of religious affairs, secondary school examinations—all these aspects of state structure, all the tools of public administration—did not attract much attention at all; they were simply taken for granted with the assumption that if they were to put into pious hands, good things would result.

There are some exceptions. One Arab state, to be sure, did create a structure that is based on a premodern state institution quite directly. Saudi Arabia's "religious police"—formally known as the Committee to Promote Virtue and Prevent Vice—is a direct attempt to take the post of *muhtasib* (a market inspector and enforcer of morality in public places) and render it into a bureaucratic structure, complete with regulations that spell out its precise authority and relationship to other state structures.[8] But the bureaucratization of the religious police occasioned little controversy in Saudi Arabia. (The precise nature of its authority and where it fits in to the state bureaucracy is a matter of constant tinkering, but not its conversion from an individual deputized by the *wali al-amr* into a bureaucratized structure whose regulations more closely resemble those of a safety inspectorate or than anything found in *fiqh*. Only when the tinkering seemed designed to diminish its stature—when it was deprived of the power of arrest in 2016— did much debate arise).

When Islamists throughout the region—chiefly those I call "mainstream" movements, which refers to those that attempt to appeal to broad constituencies while participating in existing systems—sought to move their agendas through electoral participation, as many did in the decades prior to 2011, they peppered the political scene with all kinds of policy proposals but remained maddeningly vague in their positions on the nature of the state. They certainly demanded an Islamic political system, but asking what that meant in practice provoked almost platitudinous responses about serving the needs of the society, ending corruption, and rejecting oppression. When it came to fundamental constitutional questions—how they view the legitimacy of parliaments, bureaucracies, ministries, state regulation of mosques, and the other structures modern states have established that play a religious role— there was a clear but unspoken answer: they were good with all that. They did worry about what such structures would do and who would be in charge, but not about their existence.

There was, to be sure, a strong interest in governance on the part of such mainstream movements (and some less mainstream movements as well) and an attempt to draw on Islamic themes in addressing issues related to governance. But that interest did not often extend to issues of procedure and structure. The more common approach was to assume a state, demand a virtuous ruler, and then ask what a state (or ruler) guided by virtue should do.

In conversations with Egyptian Islamists and Egyptian SCC judges in the years prior to 2011, I was struck by how similarly they referred to article 2 of the Egyptian constitution. The interpretation laid out in the niqab case insists that the *wali al-amr* should not promulgate a law that contravenes a clear sharia-based rule or the general goals of the Islamic sharia; on all other questions where there is no definitive sharia-based rule, the *wali al-amr* should select the interpretation most appropriate for the needs of the society. When I was given a similar argument by ʿAbd al-Munʿim Abu al-Futuh (then on the Guidance Council of the Brotherhood) in 2006, I responded that his views sounded very much like that of the SCC; he responded that he had been unaware of that agreement. When I reported the conversation to a justice of the SCC, he raised his eyebrow and said with apparent irony, "Praise God."

The reason, of course, for SCC justices' lack of interest in (and perhaps even hostility to) their apparent agreement with the Brotherhood on the role of the Islamic sharia in the Egyptian legal order was that it masked a profound disagreement on the identity of the ruler. The difference was less doctrinal than it is political. It was not *what* the state should be or *what* the Islamic sharia is that divided them but *who* should exercise state authority. The SCC was comfortable with the regime; the Brotherhood wary of it. Conflating the *wali al-amr* and the state personalizes the state and moves the center of debate from that which academics focus on (can the Islamic sharia operate in a modern state?) to the personal (who should guide the ruler and how should the ruler wield authority in a manner that supports the development of a sharia-based society?).

This is why Islamists can seem so hard to pin down. Their proposals can indeed be vague on the details that constitutional academics have trained themselves to ask—how to select a leader, how to pass a law, who should build a road, who should determine what is consistent with the Islamic sharia—and they generally simply deflect such procedural and substantive questions by placing an enormous emphasis on how virtuous and learned individuals should behave when in authority and whom such rulers should listen to.

THE PROBLEM AFTER 2011: ENGAGING THE STATE OR AVOIDING IT?

This is not to say that Islamists have had no reaction to the state. But it is to say that it is not the administrative state that generally attracted their attention. When they argued about how to approach the state, they did so in some ways that were easy for many observers to miss. Their debates tended to focus on two political questions (ones with doctrinal overtones to be sure, but generally ones that varied far more according to political judgments than religious interpretations): How much should politics be emphasized in their efforts to Islamize society? And how legitimate is the current regime?

The lack of a full Islamist theory (or set of theories) of the state often led us to overlook these debates. They were, however, quite lively in the pre-2011 period. They have continued after 2011 but are colored by the aftermath of the upheavals of that year: the entrance of Islamists into government in Tunisia and Morocco (with attendant concerns about co-optation), the rapid rise and dramatic fall of the Brotherhood in Egypt (and the repression and violence beginning in August 2013), and the rise of the Islamic State.

The first question—how much should politics be emphasized?—is often missed by political scientists because those Islamists who de-emphasize politics are, unsurprisingly, less visible politically. And the debate, such as it is, often takes place through actions, not words. Put differently, there is less explicit doctrinal argument about the primacy of politics among various orientations (although that takes place, to be sure) and more of a different pattern of behavior in which politically oriented Islamists canvass, organize, and strategize about how to use political opportunities to Islamize society and less politically oriented ones ignore, avoid, or roll their eyes at such efforts.

But if the difference is sometimes expressed more in body language than in words, it still has stood at the core of differences among Islamists. The effort to build a society on an Islamic foundation can take many forms—small-group work; social and charitable organization; pious works; studying; serving as a model; proselytizing; advertising; political mobilization; writing, tweeting, and discussing; and campaigning are all among frequently used channels. They are not, of course, mutually exclusive except in the sense of limitations imposed by time and resources; they can even be mutually reinforcing (as different forms of publicity in particular might all help to raise the profile of an Islamist project in the media and in an election campaign).

Are those politically oriented Islamists (like the Muslim Brotherhood in recent years) realists, doers, and efficacious, or are they politicians first and Islamists second, running the risk of co-optation, and superficial in their understanding of religion? Are those less inclined toward politics (like some but not all Salafis) focusing on what can actually be done, motivated by piety rather than power, thoughtful, and making a real difference? Or are they armchair intellectuals, sidetracked into harmless platitudes, well-intentioned charitable works, or textual exegesis, not grappling with the realities of corruption and oppression? At the core of such debates are very different judgments about which opportunities exist in the political world and the effects of pursuing them.

The question on which Islamists differ greatly is their understanding of existing regimes. Are existing rulers who might deviate from the path that Islamists recommend mistaken but legitimate, or have they lost their claim to serve as the *wali al-amr* of the political community? In debating such issues, there is a rich tradition of Islamic legal and political thought on which to draw, but the roots of that thought reach deeper in historical time than does the modern state. In other words, Islamists tend to focus on the ruler and his actions rather than on the vast array of institutions, rule-making bodies, security forces, economic enterprises, educational apparatuses, broadcast arms, and bureaucratic structures that exist today. This can make for some curious elisions. Sayyid Qutb's *Ma'alim fi al-Tariq* (*Milestones on the Road*) dismisses all existing regimes for their embrace of nationalism and socialism, their failure to follow the sharia, and their replacement of divine with human sovereignty (all arguably aspects of the modern state) but also suggests that Muslims have been misled almost since the end of the era of rightly guided caliphs. Is it Gamal Abdel Nasser, his regime, the administrative Egyptian state that emerged in the nineteenth century, or everything since the Abbasids that troubles him? He gives the careful reader little guidance to make such distinctions.

To be sure, these contemporary debates about politics do have premodern debates to draw from—on "changing with the hand," the qualifications of the *wali al-amr, takfir* (the act of declaring a Muslim a nonbeliever), and so on. But again, the inclination to look past distinctions among ruler, regime, and state often blunts the sharpest disputes or leads interlocutors to talk past one another. Turning again to Sayyid Qutb, his charge that *jahiliyya* prevails everywhere and that there is no Islamic political system today is taken to be the starting point for much of the contemporary resurgence of *takfir.*[9] But his apologists often claim that Qutb actually avoided accusing individuals of apostasy—indeed, he does not mention anybody by name. Perhaps that is an indication of a distinction between the ruler on the one hand and either the regime or the state on the other, but if so, it is a distinction that has been lost on almost all of his readers.

Such political judgments lead to different strategies and outlooks, but not to many attempts to probe what it means in procedural or institutional terms to ensure that the administrative state behaves in a way that is consistent with an Islamic society. Most Islamists take the administrative state as a given and ask what is to be done about it. Those who are more politically inclined often seek to guide it (perhaps volunteering themselves for that task); those less interested in politics seek ways to bypass it or cope with it. Those who decry political systems rarely distinguish (as we have seen) among ruler, regime, and state.

The experiences of 2011 shifted the terms of the debate. In Tunisia and Morocco, Islamists who emphasized politics—the Party of Justice and Development in Morocco and Ennahda in Tunisia—actually entered government. In the former case, the step was taken by an existing regime and exposed the party to the criticism that it was being co-opted in return for a share of political power by a regime that was only willing to share limited authority. In the latter case, the step came after the overthrow of an existing regime, but it also occasioned concerns that the political focus was leading the movement to invest in politics to the exclusion of its religious and cultural mission. Ultimately it led to a decision to form a separate political party and movement, but it is not yet clear if that step will lead to any easing of the tension between political and nonpolitical goals.

Ultimately the experience of Egypt and the Islamic State may have more far-reaching effects on Islamist political thought. And those effects may be leading many Islamists away from mainstream politics and in sharper opposition to current regimes. Those Islamists who reject the Islamic State—and most of them do—can still feel pressured by its ability to present itself as an uncompromising movement. For those who offer a different path, they must persuade potential followers that their path is more efficacious or authentic. And the experience of Egypt—and the bitterness brought about by the violence used against the Brotherhood and its supporters since 2013—also point in a radical direction.

ISLAMISTS IN THE NEW MIDDLE EAST: THEORY OF THE STATE, THEORY AGAINST THE STATE

The political project of the Islamists did sometimes hold out some pressure to develop more clarity in thinking about an administrative state. In the period before 2011, for instance, Islamists in Egypt debated whether women could hold the position of judge or head of state. Those who held close to traditional *fiqh* insisted that only men could hold such positions. But others—some within the Islamist camp—argued that such positions were based on an outmoded premodern conception of those positions (in which the ruler, for instance, served as prayer leader) and did not anticipate the modern state in which such offices were better seen not in personal terms but as institutions that might be staffed with different individuals. In that way, Islamists who approach positions of political authority sometimes develop some flexibility, generally accommodating themselves to the procedures and institutional framework in place and developing doctrines to support that accommodation. That path might still be viable in places like Morocco and Tunisia.

But since 2013 there have been murmurs of a more radical orientation—gestating not so much among those traditionally seen as radicals (the jihadists) but among those who emphasized politics but came to turn against existing regimes. Again, Qutb leads the way but in a manner that was submerged until quite recently. *Ma'alim fi al-Tariq* has several themes, but one of the most powerful ones is the evil of humans dominating other humans. Qutb shows a great suspicion of any kind of authority that is guided by human whim rather than divine will. And he is maddeningly vague on how an Islamic society would actually be administered. What comes across is a strong suspicion of all political forms in existence and a simple but hopelessly vague offer that pious and learned individuals could lead a community of Muslims on a path that frees humans of domination by other humans.

To be sure, this aspect of deep distrust of the state has been noted by others. Ellis Goldberg has written of "the arbitrary power of the state symbolized by the Pharaoh" in Qutb's writings, explaining that "Qutb's understanding of community and agency was profoundly conditioned by the experience of watching a powerful but nationalist state intrude into society as the colonial regime had never been capable of doing."[10]

This is less a theory of the state than an aesthetic against the state. But it is one that may be springing to life in a post-Rab'a world. In 2015, I traveled to Istanbul and met with young Islamist activists clustered in circles dominated by Egyptian Brotherhood members. What struck me in our discussions was the way in which Qutb-like denunciations of state domination figured in their rhetoric. Their mistake in 2011–2013, many averred, was in thinking that they could use the democratic process to take control of the state and use it to better society. But they had come to realize that they had misunderstood the way that basic state structures—and the judges, officers, police, and bureaucrats who staffed them—used their authority in corrupt and oppressive ways. They no longer seemed to want to guide the state so much as dismantle it. They used Islamic and sharia-based language on occasion, but what really stood out was a harsh and radical political judgment that the modern Egyptian state must be dismantled and rebuilt from the ground up in a manner that eschews domination and exploitation, and that those (not necessarily all in the Islamist camp) who would join in that process were their allies.

Even more than the Islamic State (which seemed quite content to mimic some aspects of a modern administrative state in its internal operations), the new trend, rooted in strains of Brotherhood thinking and less in Salafism, jihadism, or other approaches, seems to be finally addressing the nature of the administrative state, animated more by a spirit of anarchism than a careful study of doctrines of *siyasa shar'iyya*. It is too soon to tell whether this vengeful post-Rab'a impulse will produce its own theoreticians and strategists, but if it does, it could fill the lacunae of Islamist political thought in an explosive way.

Chapter 8

HOMELAND (DIS-)ENGAGEMENT PROCESSES AMONG THE NEW SYRIAN DIASPORA

Lindsay A. Gifford

SINCE THE INCEPTION OF THE SYRIAN WAR IN 2011, OVER THIRTEEN million Syrians have been forced to flee their homes. Historical Syrian diasporas have been transformed with the arrival of newcomers, and new diasporas have formed in different places. In seeking to understand any New Middle East, it is imperative to inquire about those whose lives have most directly been affected and jarringly changed by the 2010–2011 uprisings and their aftermath. Among those are Syrian exiles in the new diaspora. How do diasporic Syrians understand what is taking place in their home country? How are they involved in the struggle (or not)? What do they expect the future of Syria will hold, and will it include those who fled?

This chapter presents qualitative interview data from Syrian exiles whose plight is one of the most representative and disheartening aspects of the New Middle East. One of the characteristics of large-scale displacement in and from the New Middle East is that old diasporas are reshaping and growing with the arrival of ethnic compatriots, and new diaspora communities are rapidly forming in places that had not seen high levels of Middle Eastern resettlement prior. Syria's neighboring states have taken in millions of Syrian refugees, indelibly altering their demographic composition and incurring broad social and political pressures in areas such as environment, economy, housing, nutrition, education, and security.

The data analyzed in this chapter largely come from a series of interviews with first-generation members of the new Syrian diaspora conducted in early 2018. I define the new Syrian diaspora as those who migrated or were displaced due to the Assad regime and Syrian uprising, in contrast to the Syrian diasporas established in the nineteenth and early twentieth centuries. I also draw from field research over the past decade with Syrians in Syria, the Middle East, Europe, and the United States. All respondents were born in Syria and migrated within the past twenty years, most within five to ten years. Some were activists, others not. Their professional backgrounds include auto mechanics, elder care, geospatial analysis, hairdressing, human rights assistance, human resources, information technology, medicine, and sales. All names are pseudonyms to protect respondents and their families from retribution, and interviews have been truncated for brevity.

I explore the ways members of the Syrian diaspora act and think as "agents of diasporic imagination."[1] Early engagement with the war effort is followed by complex processes of distanciation. "Stretched" transnational social relations, especially in conflict, can reach their limits and spring back to more immediate surroundings.[2] This chapter seeks to illuminate the ways that the broad historical arcs of the New Middle East reverberate in the lives of Syrian exiles.

EXIT, VOICE, LOYALTY, AND TRAUMA IN THE SYRIAN DIASPORA

The trauma literature identifies a pattern that has been dubbed "purposeful distanciation" for individuals who are experiencing post-traumatic stress disorder. Among populations with collective experiences of conflict, "the survival of war demanded emotional numbing to maintain a psychologically safe distance."[3] Diasporic engagement with home countries has often been understood through Albert O. Hirschman's paradigm of loyalty, voice, exit.[4] Some, such as Stephen Lubkemann, have explored the ways that trauma affects these various modes of engagement for refugees and how loyalty and voice strategies are not mutually exclusive but rather manifest on a continuum.[5]

Hirschman's typology poses strategic options for behavioral decision making. He argues that when individuals confront an undesirable situation, they can leave (exit), speak out to change the rules (voice), or try to achieve goals by working within the status quo (loyalty). Each strategy poses risks: political-economic structures (often states, but also nonstate actors such as businesses, organizations, or families) can "exact a high price for exit" ranging "from loss of life-long associations to loss of life."[6] For Syrians, exit can entail high levels of risk both within and outside the country, as internal security forces (*mukhabarat*) operate among the Syrian diaspora.[7]

In the original framework, exit, voice, and loyalty were conceived as mutually exclusive, yet globalization has facilitated the possibility of exercising these strategies in concert.[8] Diasporic Syrians have exited the state, but they do not necessarily become disengaged from political concerns or movements in the homeland, as they can still express loyalty or voice as supporters of the regime, the opposition, or *al-sha'b al-suri* (the Syrian people).[9] For diasporic Syrians it is the exit itself that allows for the expression of loyalty or voice in ways that were not possible in the authoritarian state (while recognizing that loyalty to the regime, or at least "acting 'as if'"[10] is generally necessary for survival in Assad's Syria). Exit provides a safe distance from which to engage in protests or to demonstrate loyalty without direct exposure to the authoritarian state or war.

For diasporic Syrians, exit allows for activation of the loyalty-voice continuum, and strategies can shift so that loyal actors come to express greater voice, and vociferous actors come to express greater loyalty. This process of change can muddle one's core identity and lead to a new understanding of self and society. Diasporic Syrians may not readily become agents of development in the homeland but rather focus on integration and emplacement in the country of resettlement. Members of the new Syrian diaspora may differ from older ones by disengaging from the homeland, while established diasporas have the psychological and physical distance necessary to reengage. Although it may seem that those temporally closer to the homeland would be more inclined to maintain stronger levels of engagement, conditions of conflict greatly affect that possibility. The classic exit-voice-loyalty paradigm is thus expressed in a processual and flexible manner by Syrians in the new diaspora, rather than either-or choices, and is deeply imbricated with traumatic distanciation.

DIASPORIC ENGAGEMENT WITH THE SYRIAN CONFLICT

When the uprising broke out, both recent and long-established diasporic Syrians began to think about what the future would hold for themselves and their homeland. For some, this meant supporting the regime and the status quo.[11]

Members of historical Syrian diasporas, such as in Latin America, could safely express loyalty to the regime without having lived under its authoritarian rule.[12] For others who migrated more recently to avoid military service, who were members of opposition parties or supporters of democratic reforms, or who left as a result of violence, the uprisings offered an opportunity to effect change in the homeland that often directly spoke to their reasons for migrating. Concepts of modern diaspora, incipient ethno-national, and new diasporas have been used to distinguish between established diasporas and those that are still forming, as in the Syrian case.[13]

Since 2011, the Syrian diaspora has established several hundred grassroots organizations worldwide.[14] Because the regime harshly suppresses civil society, diasporic organizations often stimulate public discourse back home.[15] I provide several ethnographic examples here. Ashraf, who had moved to Britain to pursue higher education and avoid military service, was working in the nonprofit sector. When the war started, he quit his job and began a humanitarian position with a major transnational nongovernmental organization in Syria:

> I was running the mission; but I found everything was corrupt. A drug that costs five *lira* would be charged at one thousand. They said they had to import these drugs, the local quality was not high. Of fifteen or twenty staff, only one or two would show. And they all had the same last name. So I shut it down. My driver, an intelligence officer, I told him to take me to the airport. Then they arrested me.

Rafeeq met an Italian student while he was studying at Damascus University. They moved to Italy and married, but when the uprisings broke out, Rafeeq felt the need to work directly on the struggle in Syria. He had been a critic of the regime and its internal security apparatus, and his father had spent much of his childhood on the run for opposition political activities. Rafeeq joined the staff of a major international aid organization and moved to Turkey, where he helped run a humanitarian unit focused on northern Syria. He and his wife divorced.

Tariq, a freelance journalist and filmmaker, had moved to Germany to escape Syrian government oppression and violence. As a member of an opposition party in Syria, he had been detained and tortured. When the war broke out, he was active in protests and opposition mobilization.[16] He returned to Syria to document the Battle of Aleppo in 2012, but as he was filming, he was shot by a sniper, and recorded himself the moment he was fatally struck.[17]

Stories like his serve as a warning to members of the diaspora who would dare to return to engage in the struggle for the new Syria.

DISTANCIATION FROM THE CONFLICT

Although some diasporic Syrians remain directly involved in the struggle in the homeland, respondents express distanciation over time after initial engagement. Professional and volunteer work might be reoriented to issues or methods less salient to the conflict. Intellectual distanciation occurs through vernacular conflict analyses. Understandings of Syrian society as an ethno-religious mosaic are presented as distant from current realities. Narratives of self and identity become distanced from prior representations. In this section, I discuss varied modes of diasporic Syrian distanciation.

First, there are lessons learned in conflict and aid efforts. Although small and large-scale efforts to supply aid from the diaspora have been blocked, these efforts still shed light on the war economy, which has made the conflict seemingly intractable. As exiles lose trusted connections in Syria, greater degrees of social distance make it difficult to establish new networks in the country and reduce the likelihood of successful advocacy.[18] Imad relays his experience from Turkey:

> I had a friend who I would send [money] to, but he was killed. We tried to send stuff to Homs, like blankets and . . . milk [for babies]. But there was a corrupt regime officer who said I can let you go in with weapons, but you cannot take in any medications or milk. They want people to fight and to die.

After Ashraf was detained, as recounted earlier, he was held by the regime and tortured. Because of his connections in Britain, his case was publicized in English by friends and colleagues on social and mainstream media.[19] Eventually the regime allowed him to leave Syria on bail. He then began to engage with the crisis by monitoring human rights violations. He says:

> The role of the diaspora, number one, is to raise awareness. And they give money to the needy. Another friend, he is somewhat wealthy, he started an NGO for people who lost their limbs.

Diasporic professionals have found a way to use their skills to support the Syrian struggle. Health-care initiatives by medical professionals of Syrian or Arab descent are well-known examples.[20] Awwad provides another from Germany, where he moved in the late 2000s. Working in information technology, he used his skills to create an open-source archive that collects amateur video clips of possible human rights violations in Syria; his hope is that this resource will serve as documentary evidence of war crimes. His activities cohere with Moss's articulation that "cyberspace can provide a 'free space' that permits diasporas—particularly those who have emigrated out of authoritarian states—to embrace 'voice,' communicate shared grievances in a safe arena, and mobilize on behalf of home-country causes."[21]

Amal, in Finland, offers a counterexample.[22] She reoriented her nonprofit work from diasporic concerns of Syrians in Nordic states to direct engagement. After migrating for marriage twenty years ago, she founded a local nongovernmental organization that provided a social-educational outlet for Syrian-Finnish children, but when the war started, they began to provide direct aid.[23] Amal's work shows a process of reorienting the Syrian diaspora community away from domestic concerns to those back in the homeland, in contrast to the experiences of more recent migrants. Similarly, Moss argues, "the stronger the transnational ties to the home country, the greater the probability that diaspora members will self-censor; once these ties loosen or fade over immigrant generations, concerns about getting on the sending-state's radar from abroad are likely to decline."[24]

Diasporic Syrians also undergo a process of intellectual distanciation from the conflict as they make sense of the powerful interests behind it through vernacular conflict analyses. The economic dynamics generated by the war—both domestic and international—contribute to its intractable nature, creating a complex web of ties that must be disentangled for de-escalation to occur. Hamed and Omar, a barber and a mechanic, respectively, living in Saudi Arabia relate the following explanation:

> HAMED: I'll tell you who benefits from this. Those who are armed. This is really important. From the checkpoints, stealing from this house or that. They are happy!
>
> OMAR: People make their own checkpoints. You have to pay money. It's forbidden to bring in anything, except with money.

Rafeeq argues that the state will use mass displacement to pursue a land grab in order to reconsolidate regime power. He has since relocated from

Turkey to Germany, and his natal family has resettled in the Netherlands: "My family still has land, but I can't register any of it to my name. Soon the government will start confiscating all the land of the families who have fled." Indeed, Law No. 10—Syria's Absentee Property Law—was passed on April 2, 2018, requiring that all landowners provide proof of ownership to the Syrian government within a limited time frame; otherwise, the properties would be forfeited to the state.[25]

Syrian refugees have become embedded in political economies of capital accumulation and consumption. Hamed notes that "Syrians have become the labor for the Middle East and Europe," whereas Ashraf describes a complex dynamic in which regional state actors and transnational corporations benefit by exploiting displaced persons:

> In Turkey there are sweatshops filled with minors; they produce clothes for international brands. The Turkish economy is booming. There is a lot of money being made. But they are blaming Syrians for being a burden. It is the same in Lebanon and Jordan. Even in Saudi, they say Syrians gain "so much benefits," free schooling and so on, but in fact they have to pay large sums of money for their residency. I know someone who moved his factories to Lebanon for the same reason.

Syrians constitute a multireligious, multiethnic, and socioeconomically diverse population. Those in the diaspora identify a divide between what exiles recall as authentic Syrian demographics and intercommunal relations versus wartime shifts.[26] Rafeeq argues that a process of ethnic cleansing is transpiring:

> What is really going on is a huge demographic change. They tried to divide us in the twentieth century, and they did, there was an 'Alawi state for a while. But the reality is that we are mixed. Sunnis are being pushed out, and 'Alawis and Shi'is are left. The Kurds have also participated. It will be twenty years before an 'Alawi can go to Idlib or Deir al-Zur. The minorities are with Assad mostly, it's really sad.

Not all observers agree with Rafeeq's generalizations regarding minority allegiances,[27] but there is evidence that ethnic cleansing has transpired, particularly against Sunni Muslims, Christians, Turkomans, and Yazidis.[28] Preexisting boundaries between ethnic and sectarian communities have hardened.

Hamed views the conflict largely in Sunni-'Alawi terms, arguing that it will take significant work to rebuild trust and dismantle hatreds that have built up from witnessing war atrocities: "The Sunni have a hundred reasons. And the 'Alawi same thing. There is hatred that will not go away." He notes that the current war is taking place in a historical context that includes the Hama uprising of the early 1980s, which the military violently quashed:

> There was a previous crisis. In the 1980s right? There was Hafez al-Assad and his regime. But after the crisis things were resolved. They hated us [Muslims] in general. But the Muslims have power. But afterward things became natural between 'Alawis and Sunnis.

Similarly, Ashraf notes the 1980s uprising as a benchmark to measure Bashar's political leadership skills:

> Syria is not safe for anyone. Not pro-Assad forces, not anti-Assad. It's not one government anymore. There is fragmentation, even in the intelligence apparatus. Assad is weak. His father had leadership skills. He suppressed the 1980s revolution in a few months. But Bashar is dependent on others. He's not a leader, he inherited power. And he had to kill the old guard.

Ashraf goes on to argue that collective Syrian national identity has been lost, with communitarian identities rising to fill the void among an inverted class structure. He also notes that communalism and xenophobia may intensify for those monitoring the conflict online from the diaspora:[29]

> There has been a loss of identity. People don't believe in Syria. They retreat to racial relationships, tribe, religion. The Kurds became fanatic for the Kurdish cause. It's not the Arabs or the Kurds who have been victimized more. Everyone has suffered. So we have the Sunni radical cause, with ISIS or Nusra Front. And outside Syria the news is amplified. Online you can utter racist comments, hate speech, but not when you meet someone. People who were poor have gotten rich from the war trade, but they are not educated. The educated have become poor.

For Imad, the various strategic positions of different sectarian communities further solidified divisions in Syrian society. He said: "Sunnis have been used as a ground weapon, and Shi'is and Christians too. Druze were very smart. They are good fighters. But they mostly stayed out of it. Mostly we lost good 'Alawi, Shi'i male fighters." The repair of communal relations is a key issue in reestablishing Syrian identity and national stability for diaspora members. As

Imad stated: "Justice is to be together again, Christian, Sunni, Shiʻa, ʻAlawi, whatever. But even if Bashar goes, we are going to keep fighting."

In addition to forcing Syrians in the diaspora to think about the nature of the Syrian "mosaic," the civil war has shifted their attitudes toward self and society. The moral gray zone of the Syrian war has muddled respondents' personal values and conceptions of self.[30] Whatever it would take to end the violence, even if that runs contrary to one's fundamental values, becomes desirable. Personal or intellectual conflicts and cognitive dissonance are irrelevant in the gray zone.

While Syrians in conflict experience a gray zone of survival, those in the diaspora experience a different kind of moral ambiguity regarding what they would be willing to compromise to achieve a resolution. Democracy activists begin imagining the possible advantages of dictatorship, atheists call for supernatural intervention, former critics become loyalists. According to Rafeeq, "Honestly, there is no power in this world that can fix anything in Syria anymore"; although he is an ardent atheist raised in a communist family from an Ismaʻili background, Rafeeq now looks to the supernatural for intervention for the first time in his life. Imad, a nonpracticing Muslim merchant, also looks to supernatural intervention: "At this point I think it has to be something in religion, like a miracle. Man cannot fix it anymore."

Although he is a human rights and democracy activist, Ashraf has come to see value in dictatorship, an oppressive system that he struggled against for years:

> [I] left to avoid military service, education was a pretext. At the time I was frustrated with the people; I thought they were cowards. Now I realize they were right. It is total destruction for millions of people. And democracy wouldn't do any good. We need a dictatorship with a slow transition to democracy. We can't build democracy in a failed state.

Josef worked in the shop of his Syrian-Armenian family as a luxury car mechanic in Damascus. As small-business owners who occasionally worked on regime cars, the family was solidly upper-middle class and enjoyed a flat in the capital as well as a villa in the Christian countryside. In Syria, Josef did not hesitate to critique the regime, Bashar al-Assad, or the system of *wasta* (connections) and corruption that organized Syrian society. But with the onset of the war, he fled to Kuwait and became an ardent Assad supporter, frequently posting pro-regime propaganda on social media and referring to Assad and his inner circle as "Titans" of Syria.

These examples demonstrate the complex negotiations of identity and moral personhood that take place in the gray zone of war and diaspora. Meaningful identities and beliefs are called into question in the ambiguities of violence and rapid social change, and individuals become willing to suspend long-held values in search of conflict resolution.

QUESTIONING THE DIASPORA'S ROLE IN RECONSTRUCTION

Despite the growing international discourse that the war in Syria is losing steam, members of the diaspora vehemently disagree. Respondents do not perceive that the time for Syrian reconstruction is anywhere near, nor do they think that reconstruction is incumbent upon them, despite academic and policy arguments framing diasporas as "agents for development."[31] The following examples demonstrate how diasporic Syrians think about the possibilities for postwar drawdown and reconstruction:

> RAFEEQ: It makes me so angry when journalists go to nightclubs and say life is coming back. The Syrian diaspora doesn't want to come back. They are rebuilding their life abroad. Trying to integrate where they are. There is no country after Assad.[32]
>
> ASHRAF: Rebuilding Syria is not for me. I feel like the corporations who took part in the war will, like there is a major construction project in Damascus, led by China and Iran. Those who participated in the war will reap the rewards with contracts.

Although academics and policy makers may argue that the Syrian diaspora will be instrumental to any reconstruction effort, exiles do not necessarily feel the responsibility or desire to take on that project. The war has been led by internal and external forces that they do not control. For Syrian exiles, it is untenable to lay the burden of reconstruction on the new diaspora.

PONDERING RETURN

The possibility of return for Syrians in the new diaspora is highly uncertain. For those who have made their way into the Global North and regularized their migration status, repatriation is unlikely. However, many would welcome the opportunity to visit their homeland without fear. Respondents in Saudi Arabia were clearer about a desire to return should conditions permit. Because Syrians in most Arab states are only afforded temporary status, structural conditions for exiles in the Middle East may create a greater impetus to return. Yet there is still much ambivalence expressed regarding the possibility of repatriation, as demonstrated in the following examples:

> ASHRAF: I don't know. I love Syria. I want to visit. Then I could assess the situation in person. It's a matter of when will I be allowed.
>
> HAMED: If my family [in Syria] said it's OK to go back then we will go. If you are a young man, it will be the end of you. You have children, they have grown up outside. They are living a tragedy. And to go back to the same rule? They don't want to go back.

In the same conversation, Hamed vacillated between remaining in exile and repatriation: "If Bashar falls then I will go back. After the war for sure. We will go back, we will not stay here. We'll make a home, a shop, work. We'll help!" His friend Omar agreed: "If there is a solution I will go back. If Bashar falls or he goes." Choices between exit and return are fraught with uncertainty and directly shaped by diasporic conditions.

THE NEW SYRIA: THE VIEW FROM THE DIASPORA

Much of the anger, despair, fear and uncertainty generated during the conflict coalesces in the idea of the New Syria. This concept points to the radical changes that have taken place in Syrian society since the start of the war, making the country unrecognizable to exiles who left only a few years ago. Widely dispersed respondents agree that it will take a generation for life in Syria to stabilize. As Imad stated: "The new Syria is not Syria. You cannot say Syria without Syrians. More than half the country [is gone]! And foreigners are in charge of the country." The following examples aggregate thoughts on the new Syria:

> RAFEEQ: There is no new Syria. It's not one country anymore. The media is saying that the "war is finishing" but this is not true. Syria is divided, it's occupied, there is mass depression. You allow a criminal to kill half a mil-

lion people, the UN even stopped counting. You have a generation without education. You have hundreds of thousands in jail without daring to ask where they are. Because this was allowed, Assad will be more horrible. What will he do with the militias afterward? How will he control them? The Kurds will separate. And why not? Why should they live under a fascist state? In Germany the world had an interest to reconstruct the country, not in Syria. And Hitler was dead. In Syria, Hitler won. He's still alive.

ASHRAF: A hellish place. New doesn't mean good. Assad will expand his territory, and he will kill Syrians as he does. There is the challenge of radicalism. A lot of men have had a tough experience in the war, and they will carry that. There will be huge numbers of disabled Syrians. And there will be long-term sanctions. The international community has allowed Assad to win, but the sanctions will punish the average Syrian.

HAMED: Because of the war everything changed. They took our homes and gave them away to the military. The first thing I think of is the past. Our streets. Our memories come back, my childhood. The guys. Sweet things. To remember is to get upset. It's not going to come back. It's just a dream.

INTERNATIONAL RESPONSIBILITY

Some members of the diaspora focus on making the case for international engagement in de-escalating the conflict and resolving the crisis. This includes the question of what will happen to Bashar al-Assad. Exiles argue that the world often downplays the international nature of the war. Syrian interlocutors do not generally use the term "civil war" (*harb ahaliyya*) as English-language media do; they simply use "the war" (*al-harb*). At the same time there is a deep mistrust of the international community. International actors have increased the violence and longevity of the Syrian war, making it difficult to trust the international community even as it is needed to negotiate. The prospect of returning to the status quo without sustained diplomatic engagement looms large. The following examples demonstrate how Syrian exiles view the relationship between the international community and the conflict:

RAFEEQ: The US, Russia, Europe, and Iran have the responsibility to rebuild Syria. I got into an argument with someone at the US Department of State. He said, "It's you guys killing each other" so it's *our* responsibility to stop it. But it's not. It's you guys *preparing the ground* for us to kill each other. The European Union says there will be no reconstruction money without a transition plan. The people who are against Assad are not there anymore. They destroyed the opposition. [But] he has Iranian protection, so no one can get close to him. He is a puppet.

ASHRAF: It is clear that Assad is winning. They are taking territory. But they can't take Kurdish areas, not without a lot of help. The Russians can provide some help, but they can't provide boots on the ground. [But] there is no international acknowledgment of the regime. I have lost all trust in the international justice system. All I want is for Syria to be united, and to stop killing, to be able to return, rebuild. And to have a leader who suits Syria. Justice means Assad in prison. And to have a proper leader. I believe in negotiation to rebuild the infrastructure, and especially the military, so that they will fight *for* Syrians, not fight Syrians.

BURNOUT AND DIASPORIC INTEGRATION

For many, the final stage of diasporic distanciation is to turn focus toward local integration. As Kodmani has found, "from coping with the hardships of violence and insecurity, Syrians are now looking at how to rebuild themselves, their immediate family circle and their local environment."[33] After engaging with the Syrian struggle, recognizing the economic and political forces behind it, and losing local contacts in the country, Syrian exiles attempt to avoid the war, heal themselves, and focus on the present. Unfortunately for many Syrians in the Global North, the country of asylum is no panacea, as Rafeeq knows too well: his younger brother recently committed suicide. For others, economic struggles preoccupy the mind with immediate needs, making war imagery no longer pervasive. If "what defines a diaspora is participation in activities designed to sustain linkages to the homeland,"[34] this burnout is significant for future Syrian diasporic engagement. The following examples demonstrate the diasporic turn to the immediate present and local environment:

RAFEEQ: Now it is just how can you eat, feed the children. In Europe they are worried about integrating, to not be labeled "Syrian refugee." The rest are focused on studying, or they turn to drugs, alcohol. People are worried about finding a job. I will just work on healing myself, my brother issues. I just want to not care for a day or a week about everything.

IMAD: I've been in Turkey for five years. I'm the kind of person who likes to work, I cannot just take charity from a government. We tried to [establish] something for Syrians here [in Istanbul], so that we could hold our ceremonies together, like weddings or funerals. I spent years thinking about it so now I don't. I had to burn some memories. But I'm really pleased with myself at where I am. I'm alive, I can make a living.

ASHRAF: They have to feed their family in Syria, so they want to avoid the news. You start to shut off. You are excited at the beginning, you think that things can change. But then you don't want to be a part of it anymore.

HAMED: We don't help, we don't do anything. The most important thing is to live. You have children; you can't think about anything worse. You can't watch the news; it hurts your head. You get upset for your country; your country is gone.

Near the end of his interview, Hamed spent several minutes worrying about the price of gas in Saudi Arabia, car maintenance, residency paperwork, and trying to find work. Focusing on the present is a coping mechanism to deal with the traumas of war and displacement. Diasporic Syrians are looking for life alternatives to block out the fog of war.

Syrian exiles in the new diaspora demonstrate the critical intersection of loyalty-voice-exit strategies with traumatic distanciation. Diasporic exit from the authoritarian state allows for voice and loyalty strategies to be activated from relative safety. The new diaspora differs from the established diaspora because of its members' temporal proximity to the conflict and sociopolitical connections with the homeland, which colors their actions and thoughts regarding the war and any forms of activism or engagement they pursue or avoid. The New Syria has experienced massive population loss and demographic change, as the surviving displaced have formed new, expanding, and changing diaspora communities directly affected by the war while struggling to establish lives elsewhere. Part of those new lives can involve new conceptions of self and identity contrasting with formerly held values in the diasporic gray zone.

Members of the new diaspora state that their homeland is substantively different from antebellum Syria, which was a diverse ethnic, religious, and sectarian community ruled by a strong authoritarian regime. The previous social mosaic has been reshaped through ethnic cleansing, community segregation, and the arrival of nonindigenous combatants. The regime is also weaker and less centralized, led by an uncharismatic president by inheritance, in a classic cycle of power as identified by the medieval Arab historian Ibn Khaldun in which strong charismatic leaders generate solidary allegiances but pass on authority to feebler uninspiring heirs. Syrian exiles in the new diaspora resist calls from the international community to be mobilized as an instrumental tool in their home country's postconflict rebuilding. Agents of diasporic imagination choose to engage or disengage in the struggle for the new Syria in varied and contingent ways over time. Perhaps more important for exiles is the struggle to establish the new *Syrians* as individuals and communities rather than the new Syria as a postconflict nation-state.

Part 3

OLD STATES, NEW DILEMMAS

Chapter 9

SAUDI ARABIA

How Much Change?

F. Gregory Gause III

THE SAUDI ARABIA OF KING SALMAN BIN ʿABD AL-ʿAZIZ AL SAUD, who came to power in January 2015, is much different from the cautious, conservative, and reactive country of previous decades. The leaders of Saudi Arabia, the quintessential oil state, began not only talking about lessening the economy's dependence on oil but also doing things about it. The home of Wahhabism, a puritanical and reactionary interpretation of Islam, saw unprecedented moves to increase the role of women in public life and loosen social restrictions. From a foreign policy characterized by an extreme reluctance to expose itself to risk, Saudi Arabia engaged in a war of choice in Yemen, initiated a crisis with Qatar, and, very briefly in 2017, kidnapped the Lebanese prime minister. While much of the "New Middle East" analyzed in this volume was experiencing revolutions from below, Saudi Arabia's new leadership was promising its own brand of revolution from above.

Most explanations for these changes center on the crown prince Muhammad bin Salman. His father, the king, elevated him to this position in June 2017, leaping him over older relatives, and gave him enormous power in all elements of policy. Still in his thirties, MBS (as he is known in the West) cut a very different figure from the septuagenarians and octogenarians who had been governing the country since the 1970s. He portrayed himself as the face of a new Saudi Arabia—more progressive socially, more aggressive in foreign policy, more of a risk taker in terms of the economy, although not more democratic politically.[1]

Personalities are important in absolute monarchies. But understanding the changes that have occurred in Saudi Arabia during the reign of King Salman also requires an understanding of the context in which the king and his crown prince came to power. They faced an acute fiscal crisis stemming from the plunge in world oil prices in late 2014. With 2015 oil prices averaging 50 percent below their 2014 levels, the imperative for economic change was self-evident. In the region, the collapse of the state in so many places presented opportunities for Iran, Saudi Arabia's main regional rival, and threats to a number of Saudi allies. Although Saudi foreign policy had succeeded in sustaining its fellow monarchies during the Arab uprisings, it had failed to contain and roll back Iranian influence in the Arab world. The United States, Saudi Arabia's main security ally for decades, was, under President Barack Obama, negotiating with Iran and avoiding serious involvement in the Syrian civil war. In 2015, it looked like Saudi Arabia would have to pursue very different policies both at home and abroad to sustain the regime.

But just how far away from past Saudi practice the king and the crown prince are willing to go remains an open question.[2] Oil prices recovered in the late 2010s, reducing the immediate need for major economic changes. But the subsequent collapse of the world oil market during the COVID-19 pandemic of 2020 brought the economic challenges of oil dependence back to the forefront. The failures of MBS's aggressive foreign policy have not resulted in a return to the caution of previous years, but might temper his willingness to pursue new adventures. Change is happening in the kingdom, but not as much change as some observers think. And certainly not political change, as King Salman's rule has seen a reassertion of royal autocracy.

CONTEXT

King Salman came to power in 2015 amid two crises: a political crisis represented by the weakening or collapse of state authority in the Arab world and an economic crisis represented by the collapse of oil prices. The first crisis did not begin with the Arab uprisings of 2010–2011. Lebanon and Yemen were always weak states. The US invasion of Iraq in 2003 destroyed the Baathist regime without building an alternative that could effectively govern the country. But the uprisings created a whole new set of political vacuums in the region—civil wars in Libya, Syria, and Yemen that drew in regional and international actors. The weakness of these states provided political and geographic space for the Islamic State, al-Qaeda, and other Salafi jihadist groups to thrive.[3]

This crisis of state authority was not limited to civil wars. Regimes friendly to the Saudis in Egypt and Tunisia fell. In Morocco and Jordan kings promised political reform and successfully defused protests. In Bahrain there were massive public demonstrations calling for political reform, put down by Bahraini security forces supported by Saudi troops.[4]

Saudi Arabia's rulers were not challenged to the same extent during the Arab uprisings. Demonstrations were limited to the Shi'i areas of the Eastern Province and were relatively small. But King Abdallah left nothing to chance. He authorized the spending of over $100 billion domestically to keep Saudis off the streets and supported fellow Arab monarchs financially and politically. With Iraq still reeling from the American occupation and Egypt consumed with its own internal problems, Saudi Arabia was the only Arab state in a position to confront the spread of Iranian power in the region.

The political crisis thus thrust Saudi Arabia into a leadership position in the Arab world for which it was ill prepared. Riyadh historically preferred to act within at least an alliance of Arab powers, if not an Arab consensus. Now the Saudis were largely on their own. Their efforts to take the lead during and after the Arab uprisings had decidedly mixed results. Where money was enough to get the job done, the results were positive from the Saudis' perspective. They supported cash-strapped Jordan during the uprisings and helped preserve the Hashemite monarchy there. Billions of dollars of aid from Saudi Arabia and other Gulf states helped secure the military coup in Egypt that brought down the elected Muslim Brotherhood president, Muhammad Morsi, and put Abdel Fattah al-Sisi in power. Their modest troop deployment into Bahrain in the spring of 2011 supported the faction within the ruling Al Khalifa that implemented the tough security response there.

However, where power beyond the financial was needed, the Saudis failed. Despite spending billions on modern arms, Saudi Arabia's military was not strong. Unlike the Iranians, who had extensive organizational and ideological ties with a number of Shi'i militias, the Saudis had no loyal nonstate-actor allies in the regional civil wars. The groups ostensibly closest to the Saudis ideologically were the Salafi jihadists: al-Qaeda and the Islamic State. But they hate the Al Saud and want their overthrow. The Saudis thus largely stayed out of the scramble for influence in Iraqi politics, ceding the field to the Iranians. They tried to roll back Iranian influence in Syria, supporting various factions in the Syria civil war. However, without their own forces to deploy (as the Iranians used the Quds Force) and without committed allies and proxies, the Saudis could not dislodge Iran's ally, the Assad regime.[5] In Yemen, the Saudis led the international effort that eased 'Ali 'Abdallah Salih from power and installed a compromise government led by 'Abd Rabu Mansour Hadi.[6] But as the country descended into civil war, Riyadh seemed powerless to halt the rise of the Houthi movement, which was increasingly allied with Tehran.[7]

The second crisis King Salman faced upon coming to power was economic. At the end of 2014 oil prices fell precipitously, from around $100 per barrel to below $60 per barrel.[8] Prices continued to fall through 2015 and into 2016, with the average price per barrel over that later year at less than $45 per barrel.[9] Saudi Arabia could mitigate the immediate effects of the collapse in oil prices. It had over $750 billion in financial reserves and an extremely low ratio of debt to gross domestic product (below 5 percent). It could draw down reserves and borrow to sustain state spending. However, the effects of the price collapse on the country's fiscal situation were striking. Between 2012 and 2016, government revenue fell by almost 60 percent.[10] Even with Saudi Arabia's considerable economic and fiscal resources, it could not sustain its levels of spending for very long.

King Salman came to power upon the death of his half brother, King Abdallah, in January 2015. He is the last of the series of half brothers who have ruled the country since the death of the founding king, 'Abd al-'Aziz "Ibn Saud" in 1953. His career spans the modern history of the country. He became governor of Riyadh, the country's capital and now most populous province, in 1963. He was part of the conservative and cautious group of senior princes who guided the kingdom for decades. He might have been expected to follow the muddle-through strategy of incremental change and spending large sums of money that had successfully brought the regime through crises of the past. However, he chose a more ambitious and risky course, empowering his son MBS to undertake a number of initiatives that changed the structure of power within the ruling family, set a course for economic change, altered the country's conservative social policies, and thrust the kingdom into a number of foreign policy confrontations.

THE RULING FAMILY

The most radical political change King Salman has undertaken is within the Al Saud itself. The intrafamily struggle that culminated in the replacement of King Saud by Crown Prince Faisal in 1964 established a system of rule by consensus. King Saud was suspected of wanting his son to succeed him. Faisal rallied the majority of his half brothers to oppose this intergenerational transfer of power.[11] An unofficial committee of senior princes, all sons of King 'Abd al-'Aziz and all holding important government positions bestowed by Faisal, passed the kingship horizontally down the line by seniority from Faisal through Abdallah. Salman, one of the youngest members of that group, is the last in that line. Many observers thought that these senior princes would eventually re-create the committee system among their own sons. Under King Abdallah it appeared such a system was forming. Abdallah's own son Mit'ab took command of the National Guard, a position Abdallah had held since 1963. Muhammad bin Nayif inherited his father's position as minister of interior upon the latter's death. Khalid bin Sultan appeared poised to inherit his father's position as minister of defense, acting as deputy minister.

King Salman upended these expectations. When he became crown prince in 2013 he also took the defense ministry, blocking Khalid bin Sultan's ascension. Within a matter of months of becoming king he removed his half brother Prince Muqrin as crown prince and replaced him with Prince Muhammad bin Nayif, signaling that the kingship would pass to the next generation. In June 2017 he removed Muhammad bin Nayif and made his own son crown prince. King Salman concentrated power in the hands of MBS in a way unprecedented in modern Saudi history. Not only did the king appoint MBS as defense minister; he also placed the young prince at the head of a cabinet committee charged with the development of the country's economic and oil policies.

Gone are the days of consensus rule by a committee of senior Al Saud princes. The sons of prominent princes of the older generation have been shunted aside. There are now fewer senior princes in the cabinet than at any time since the rule of King 'Abd al-'Aziz. The foreign ministry, headed by King

Faisal and then by his son Prince Saud Al Faisal for a total of nine decades, was led under Salman by two commoners and is now led by a member of a cadet branch of the Al Saud, not a direct descendant of ʿAbd al-ʿAziz. The interior ministry is led by a fourth-generation royal, a nephew of the deposed Prince Muhammad bin Nayef.[12] MBS is cultivating a new power base within the ruling family, placing princes closer to his own age, frequently from a generation below him (great-grandsons of the founding King ʿAbd al-ʿAziz), in government positions. Many of them now hold governorships and deputy governorships in the provinces.[13] But in the central government, decision-making power is tightly held by the king and the young crown prince.

The stability of this new arrangement is the most important question facing the political future of the kingdom. The previous effort by King Saud to consolidate succession for his son sparked an intrafamily struggle that led to his deposition. There have been public hints of dissatisfaction in ruling family circles about the rise of MBS.[14] Nevertheless, there has yet to be any sign of serious moves within the family to oppose the crown prince or prevent his ascension to the kingship. This is one area where King Salman seems to have succeeded in significantly altering the course of politics in Saudi Arabia.

SOCIAL ISSUES

In June 2018 Saudi Arabia lifted its ban on women driving automobiles. For decades the inability of women to drive was the marker of the strict policies of gender segregation and public piety enforced by the Saudi state and its infamous "religious police," officially known as the Committee for the Promotion of Virtue and Prevention of Vice. The legal change on women's driving is part of a broader set of initiatives by the crown prince aimed at, in his own words, "returning to what we were before—a country of moderate Islam that is open to all religions and to the world."[15] At his direction, the powers of the religious police have been curtailed; strict gender segregation has been loosened (though not eliminated); new public entertainments, such as movie theaters and musical concerts, have been permitted; and women have been encouraged to take a more prominent role in the workforce and the public sphere.[16]

The origin of these social changes predates the Salman era. In the wake of the September 11 attacks in the United States, the government sought to distance itself from the jihadist ideology of al-Qaeda and its Saudi founder, Osama bin Laden. King Abdallah and other Saudi officials and clerics claimed that their official brand of Islam, known to outsiders as Wahhabism, was actually a religion of moderation—*wasatiyya* in Arabic, a "middle way."[17] The king named women to the appointed Saudi Consultative Council in 2013, a quasi-legislative body without much real power, and gave women the right to vote in municipal elections, the only elections to political office held in the country, in 2011.[18] However, he did not substantially change the central role of the religious establishment in Saudi social life.

MBS has gone much further in opening up Saudi society. He wants to bring more Saudis into the workforce, particularly the private sector, reducing reliance on foreign labor and increasing local productivity. That requires a larger role for women in the economy and, thus, in society. The ban on women driving was a major obstacle to female labor force participation. MBS wants Saudis to spend more of their money at home instead of traveling abroad for entertainment. He wants to attract both domestic and foreign capital into the Saudi economy. Projecting a more "normal" sense of Saudi social life and promoting the investment opportunities in the entertainment sector are part of that effort. These social changes are part of his own self-image as a representative of Saudi youth, a generation that he contends is yearning for greater social freedoms.[19]

The crown prince's contention that these social changes are simply a "return" to the Islam of the Saudi past, before the "extremism" of recent decades, is self-serving historical reinterpretation. Wahhabism was extremely conservative and puritanical before 1979, the year MBS sees as the beginning of the "extremist" phase. But by couching his social changes as simply reestablishing the old traditions, he is trying to minimize the backlash from clerical and social conservatives. The social changes are real and substantial, but the new openness has not turned Riyadh into Dubai. Saudi Arabia remains very conservative. Elements of the male guardianship system, under which women are required to have the permission of a male relative to study, travel, or open a business, are still in place. There have been a number of missteps and false starts in the effort to provide more public entertainments.[20] But in the social realm the changes introduced by King Salman and the crown prince are historic.

ECONOMIC ISSUES

MBS's initial approach to the fiscal and economic problems facing Saudi Arabia was as ambitious as his initiatives on social policy. In early 2016 he introduced Vision 2030, a plan to reduce the centrality of oil in the Saudi economy and the government's budget, increase the role of the private sector, and create more jobs for Saudis in it. The headline-grabbing element of Vision 2030 was the proposal to sell 5 percent of the state oil company, Saudi Aramco, to international investors, with the goal of creating a huge sovereign-wealth fund for Saudi investment at home and abroad. But other goals in the document were just as radical in the Saudi context: reduced subsidies on electricity, water and gasoline; a value-added tax on consumer purchases; a reduced public sector, where the vast majority of Saudi citizens work; complete privatization of a number of state-owned entities. Fully realizing the goals of Vision 2030 would create a new Saudi political economy, vastly different from the oil-based welfare state constructed by Saudi rulers during the oil boom of the 1970s.[21]

The "fully realizing" part is, however, the catch. Aside from the privatization of a small percentage of Saudi Aramco, almost all of the goals set out in Vision 2030 have been present, in one form or another, in every Saudi planning document since the 1970s. The problem has been the political will to implement the policies, because each of them involves pain for Saudis. Cutting subsidies hits every Saudi citizen through higher prices. Taxes do the same. Reducing the size of the public sector means fewer jobs for Saudis. Pushing the private sector to hire more Saudis disrupts a very successful business model that relies on foreign labor, which is cheaper than Saudi labor. Past Saudi leaders have not had the political will to impose these costs.

MBS, at least at the outset of the Salman era, demonstrated that political will. By the end of 2016, Saudis were paying more for their basic utilities. The government implemented a direct-payment system for lower-income Saudis, called the "citizen's account," to lessen the burden of the price increases, but there were still plenty of complaints in Saudi public opinion about the new expenses.[22] A number of steps were taken to raise the cost of foreign labor, including more expensive visas and stricter enforcement of quotas for Saudi employment in certain sectors of the economy. Salaries and perks for government employees were cut. Real pain was being enforced.[23]

As time went on, however, some of that political will dissipated. The privatization of that small piece of Saudi Aramco was delayed and then whittled down to an even smaller percentage of the company, sold not to Western investors but to Saudi and Gulf investors.[24] As oil prices increased in 2017 and 2018, the fiscal pressures created by the price collapse of 2014 lessened and the public's willingness to accept austerity lessened with it. In 2018, the government backed away from plans to cut the "bonuses" that Saudi government workers normally receive and increased monthly salaries for a range of government workers.[25] King Salman went back to the previous practice of bestowing cash gifts to government employees on holidays. Rather than cut spending further, government borrowing on both domestic and international markets increased, with total government debt as a percentage of gross domestic product reaching 20 percent by the end of 2018 (from below 2 percent in 2014).[26]

In late 2016 Saudi Arabia reversed course in its oil policy as well, working with Russia to cut production to push prices up. The price collapse of late 2014, largely the result of increased American oil production, led the Saudis to propose to Russia and Iran a coordinated production cut. When they demurred, the Saudis sustained their output, which exacerbated the price fall. Riyadh chose at that time to ride the price down, hoping that lower prices would decrease investment in American fracked oil.[27] Then, in late 2016, after experiencing two years of low prices, the Saudis went back to the Russians with a new proposal for what became known as "OPEC plus"; the proposal involved production cuts, shared by members of the cartel and Russia. The venture succeeded, and prices rose from below $30 per barrel in January 2016 to more than $70 per barrel in mid-2018. The Saudi backtracking—restoring some benefits, increasing government borrowing, and using oil diplomacy to drive up prices—is more characteristic of the old Saudi model of an oil-financed welfare state than the Vision 2030 goal of economic transformation.

The difficulties in changing the Saudi political economy were brought into sharp relief by the dramatic arrest in November 2017 of over three hundred princes, billionaires, and high-ranking government officials—a large slice of the Saudi business and political elite. They were detained in the most luxurious jail in the world, the Ritz-Carlton Hotel in Riyadh, but their plush circumstances belied the seriousness of the crackdown, orchestrated by the crown prince. Those detained were accused of corruption, although no specific charges were ever made public, and forced to pay large sums and/or turn over shares in their businesses to the government.[28] Saudi officials portrayed this unprecedented assault on the country's elite as a necessary step to clean up corruption and return funds to ordinary citizens.[29]

While the "Ritz-Carlton roundup" certainly added to the coffers of the government, its effects were negative for the Vision 2030 goal of a larger and more vibrant Saudi private sector. The episode called into question whether investors, domestic or foreign, could imagine their assets in the country to be safe.[30] While Saudi Arabia had substantial corruption in its business-state relations in the past, the informal rules of the game were well known. Private-sector actors were free to take their capital out of the country as they wished. That assurance, paradoxically, encouraged them to keep a substantial proportion of those assets at home. The arrests shattered the old rules but without a clear signal as to the nature of the new rules. Capital flight from the country has increased, although reliable figures on exact amounts are hard to come by.[31]

The collapse of the world oil market caused by the COVID-19 pandemic of 2020 returns Saudi Arabia to the bleak fiscal picture of 2015. With Vision 2030's ambitions scaled back over previous years, Riyadh is even less prepared to face the wrenching challenges created by oil prices below $40 per barrel. The choices are not pleasant: a vastly scaled-back welfare state and a shrunken private sector that will bring economic hardship to every Saudi or a run-up of debt and a spending down of reserves that can only be sustained for a few years. In either case, Vision 2030 will likely take its place next to past plans of Saudi economic reform, gathering dust on the bookshelves of government bureaucrats.

FOREIGN POLICY

When King Salman came to power in January 2015, Saudi Arabia was entering its fifth year of dealing with the Arab uprisings that had unseated regimes in Tunisia, Libya, and Egypt and led to civil wars in Syria, Yemen, Libya, and, less directly, Iraq. Moreover, Saudi Arabia's major international ally, the United States, was in negotiations with Iran and other world powers that would lead to the Joint Comprehensive Plan of Action, the "Iran nuclear deal" that lifted international sanctions on Tehran. Riyadh worried that the Obama administration would use the nuclear agreement to open a new political relationship with Tehran, in effect acknowledging Iran's leading regional role. The Saudis were also upset that the Obama administration had supported the removal of Egypt's President Hosni Mubarak, a longtime American and Saudi ally, and had welcomed Egypt's democratic turn that led to successes for the Muslim

Brotherhood. The fact that the administration was publicly lukewarm toward the Saudis—President Obama described the relationship as "complicated"—did nothing to reassure Riyadh.[32]

The new king and MBS immediately took a more aggressive stance against Iran on a number of fronts. Most notably, in March 2015 the Saudis and the United Arab Emirates launched a military campaign in Yemen, where the combined forces of the Houthis and troops loyal to former president Ali Abdallah Saleh had taken the capital, San'a, and were marching on Aden. Emirati ground forces, supported by the Saudi air force, landed at Aden and pushed the Houthi-Saleh forces away from the city.[33] Saudi Arabia executed a well-known Saudi Shi'i dissident clergyman, Nimr al-Nimr, in January 2016, an act condemned by Iran and other Shi'i governments and movements. In retaliation, mobs in Tehran burned down the Saudi embassy as Saudi-Iranian tensions reached a high point.[34] Saudi cooperation with Turkey, the other major Sunni state backing Syrian rebels, on Syrian issues increased in 2015.[35] Earlier, in 2013, when King Salman was crown prince and minister of defense, Riyadh had committed $3 billion in aid to develop the Lebanese Army as a counterweight to Iran's ally Hezbollah.[36]

These early initiatives did not work out as planned for the Saudis. The Yemen campaign was an initial success, but the coalition was unable to defeat the Houthis and their allies decisively. The Houthis continued to hold San'a throughout the fighting. The civilian casualties of the conflict and the humanitarian crisis that ensued came to be seen by many in the United States and internationally as primarily the responsibility of Saudi Arabia. António Guterres, UN secretary-general, called Yemen the world's worst humanitarian crisis, with eight million people threatened with famine.[37] Saudi Arabia remained bogged down in Yemen, unable to defeat the Houthis, unable to find a diplomatic solution, and increasingly subject to Houthi missile attacks into Saudi territory. The expense of the campaign weighed on the Saudi budget, particularly with the 2020 collapse in oil prices. The Iranians were able to cause the Saudis enormous problems with a very small investment of support for their Yemeni allies.

The Saudi initiatives in Syria and Lebanon also failed to achieve their objectives. While the Turkish-Saudi cooperation did help the rebels unite their forces in early 2015 and go on the offensive against the Assad regime, Russia reacted by increasing military support to its Syrian ally. By 2020 the regime held the battlefield advantage in almost all of the country. The Saudi effort to dislodge Assad and roll back Iranian influence in Syria had failed. Likewise, the effort to use Saudi aid to build the Lebanese army as a counterweight to Hezbollah also failed. In February 2016 Riyadh suspended the aid package, upset that the Lebanese government had not aligned itself with Saudi Arabia against Iran more enthusiastically.[38]

One area in which the new Saudi approach to its regional conflict with Iran held more hope for success was Iraq. Here the approach was not more force, but more diplomacy. King Abdallah had refused to deal with the government in Baghdad, viewing it as hopelessly in thrall to the Iranians. In effect, the Saudis ceded the field in Baghdad to Iran. King Salman changed that course. The Islamic State offensive of 2014 that captured Mosul and threatened to spread south toward Baghdad brought home to the Saudis the dangers of a weak Iraqi government. Both the Obama and the Trump administrations pressed Riyadh to reengage with Iraq, to balance Iranian influence, and to support the campaign against the Islamic State. Saudi Arabia moved cautiously at first, sending its ambassador back to Baghdad in 2017 and receiving Iraqi leaders in Riyadh. The most dramatic evidence of the new Saudi approach was the visit of Shi'i cleric and political maverick Muqtada al-Sadr to Jeddah in July 2017, where he met the crown prince.[39] The visit demonstrated that the Saudi effort to compete with Iran for influence in the region was not limited to military actions and proxy wars. It also provided a clear sign that MBS was moving away from the sectarian framing of the Saudi rivalry with Iran.[40] The continued political chaos in Iraq has limited Saudi influence building there, but prospects for improvement remain.

While MBS displayed a talent for deft diplomacy toward Iraq, his style is more usually characterized by threats and confrontation. In June 2017 Saudi Arabia and the United Arab Emirates, joined by Bahrain and Egypt, cut off diplomatic relations with Qatar and declared a land, sea, and air blockade of the country. While Qatar is a fellow member of the Gulf Cooperation Council, tensions with Riyadh went back some years. The Saudis (and the Emiratis) objected to Qatar's maverick foreign policy—its support for the Muslim Brotherhood regionally, its close ties with Iran, its support for the Al Jazeera network that broadcast the events of the Arab uprisings throughout the Arab world.

There were past diplomatic ultimatums from Riyadh to Doha, but problems were always resolved. The crisis of 2017 was different. The Saudi-Emirati front rejected efforts by other Gulf monarchs to mediate and ignored American entreaties to end the dispute.[41]

In November 2017, as the detention of so many Saudi elites in the Ritz-Carlton continued, Prime Minister Saad al-Hariri of Lebanon visited Riyadh. Hariri is a longtime Saudi ally whose father, Rafiq, made a fortune in the kingdom and then went on to become Lebanese prime minister. In a bizarre televised speech from the Saudi capital, al-Hariri resigned as prime minister. This was clearly a Saudi power play meant to put pressure on the Lebanese political system and deal a blow to Hezbollah. It backfired, with Washington and Paris pressing the Saudis to de-escalate the crisis. A few weeks later, al-Hariri returned to Beirut and rescinded his resignation.[42] The Qatar boycott and the Hariri resignation—strong-arm tactics that failed—gave the crown prince a reputation for recklessness in foreign policy.

Saudi relations with the United States improved considerably with the election of Donald Trump as president. President Trump's harder line on Iran resonated with the Saudi leadership. The Saudis reached out to the new administration immediately after the election, if not before.[43] Saudi Arabia was the first foreign country visited by President Trump, and he pledged tens of billions of dollars in arms sales to the Saudis. Although Riyadh has not supported every Trump administration initiative in the region, particularly moving the American embassy in Israel to Jerusalem, the Saudis were pleased by the president's withdrawal from the Joint Comprehensive Plan of Action, the new sanctions and increased pressure on Iran, and the continued American support for the Saudi-Emirati military campaign in Yemen. The Trump White House was solicitous of MBS from the outset, scheduling a personal meeting for him with the president in March 2017 and publicly supporting his elevation to crown prince, which occurred shortly after Trump's visit to the country.[44] The mutual embrace of Trump and MBS has soured many Democrats on Saudi Arabia, which has never had many friends in American political life (outside of the White House). The October 2018 killing of Saudi dissident journalist Jamal Khashoggi—a resident of Washington, DC, who was well known to American political and media elites—at the Saudi consulate in Istanbul further alienated many of those elites and turned the generally positive American perception of

MBS substantially negative.[45] With the election of Joe Biden, the relationship with Saudi Arabia is in for a reassessment.

WHAT HAS REALLY CHANGED?

In one area, there has been absolutely no change in the Saudi Arabia of King Salman—political reform. Political life is as authoritarian, if not more authoritarian, than it had been under King Abdallah. The limited but real increase in freedom of political speech under Abdallah that followed the September 11 attacks began to be rolled back during the Arab uprisings. But the rollback accelerated after 2015.[46] The Ritz-Carlton roundup was preceded in September 2017 by the arrests of a number of prominent Saudi activists, including Islamists, liberals and civil society leaders. As women prepared to get behind the wheel legally in June 2018, the government arrested a number of the activists who had pushed for the change.[47] Even Saudis who supported many of the crown prince's initiatives began to believe that less political freedom was too high a price to pay for social and economic change.[48]

The rule of King Salman and his son the crown prince has ushered in real changes in other areas of Saudi life. Centralizing power in the hands of the crown prince and marginalizing numerous other senior princes is a significant change in how Saudi Arabia is governed. It is hard to imagine the more cautious decision-making process of the past producing policies like granting women the right to drive, the imposition of the value-added tax, and the military campaign in Yemen. There are few opportunities left for potential blocking alliances within the family to prevent MBS from eventually becoming king. He could be calling the shots in Saudi Arabia for decades to come.

The changes implemented by the king and the crown prince in social life are also real. It is hard to exaggerate the long-term consequences of lifting the ban on women driving for Saudi economic and social life. Greater workforce participation by women is essential for the private-sector growth the crown prince's Vision 2030 foresees. The introduction of new public entertainments can also increase the private sector's role in the economy. Other social changes, such as true legal and social equality for women, are less likely. Conservative forces remain important players in the country's politics, and a backlash could be expected. But the trajectory of social change under King Salman and the crown prince is clear and will be hard to reverse.

Changes in foreign policy are significant, but they do not add up to a fundamental shift in the goals and methods of Saudi national security. The military campaign in Yemen is the most notable departure, but its deviation from past Saudi practice is easy to exaggerate. The Saudis have not committed significant ground forces to the campaign. Yemen is the regional hot spot where the Saudis are least likely to confront the Iranians directly. The Saudis have not flexed their military muscles in Syria. The methods the Saudis have used to wield regional influence in the past—money, diplomacy, propaganda—will remain their primary tools for regional influence. Despite the confrontation with Qatar, the Saudis are still committed to other monarchical regimes, as the quick moves to bolster Jordan financially in the wake of public protests there in June 2018 suggest.[49] Iran remains the focus of Saudi regional concerns, as it was under King Abdallah. The Saudi-American relationship remains central to King Salman's foreign policy, a core element of continuity in Saudi foreign policy.

The most uncertain area of change in the King Salman era is in the economic realm. MBS's Vision 2030 proposes a radical change in the political economy of Saudi Arabia. The steps taken so far to implement the Vision—reduction of subsidies, imposition of the value-added tax, efforts to increase the cost of foreign labor—are significant. However, as oil prices rose in 2017–2018, the momentum for economic transformation slowed. The arrest of many of the leading lights of the Saudi private sector in the Ritz-Carlton roundup chilled the investment atmosphere. The collapse of oil prices in 2020 might refocus Saudi leadership on the need for economic transformation, but it also reduces the resources they have at their disposal to accomplish it. Steffen Hertog observed that no state with an economy as dependent upon oil as Saudi Arabia's has ever successfully transformed itself into a non-oil economy.[50] It is unlikely that Saudi Arabia will achieve the most significant economic changes the crown prince set out in Vision 2030.

The scorecard for the Salman era so far is mixed. There have been significant changes in some areas, no change toward greater political reform (just the opposite), and a mixed record elsewhere. The more dramatic accounts in some Western media sources about the extent of the changes that Crown Prince Muhammad bin Salman has been able to bring about are, at best, premature.

Chapter 10

ERDOĞAN, TURKISH FOREIGN POLICY, AND THE MIDDLE EAST

Henri J. Barkey

DURING THE FIRST DECADE OF THE TWENTY-FIRST CENTURY, thanks to some deft thinking, luck, and timing, Turkey successfully strove to assume an important and very visible role in international and especially regional affairs. In Europe and elsewhere, the accomplishments of the ruling Justice and Development Party (AKP), especially in seeking to democratize and improve links with the European Union, were widely feted. Turkey's widespread appeal among Middle Eastern publics had become a source of soft power and an important tool in Turkish diplomacy. The heyday of Turkish diplomacy may now appear to be in the distant past as Turkey finds itself at odds with myriad former and current allies, ranging from the Persian Gulf monarchies to the United States. This new reality, however, does not accord with the ambitions and stated goals of its reminted president Recep Tayyip Erdoğan.

From the moment the AKP came to power under Erdoğan's leadership, it focused primarily on building domestic coalitions and strengthening its base—it had only won some 34 percent of the national vote in 2002—and it faced opposition from formidable entrenched interests. The focus on domestic policy notwithstanding, Erdoğan undertook foreign policy overtures not just to seek legitimacy and protection abroad as an insurance policy against potential domestic opponents, but also because, coming off the 2001 economic crisis, he sought to improve Turkey's economic fortunes, open new markets for Turkish goods, and gain access to foreign capital markets.

Under Erdoğan, foreign policy "accomplishments" became an important part of the domestic narrative designed to enhance the government's and ruling party's domestic stature. The new opening to the West in particular would help to blunt potential foreign criticisms of traditional Turkish stances on various issues, ranging from Cyprus to the Kurdish problem.

Erdoğan did, indeed, face challenges at home; in 2007 the military tried to interfere in the presidential elections, in 2008 a Constitutional Court case unsuccessfully sought to close down the AKP, in 2013 the massive Gezi protests shook the AKP's confidence to the core, and again in 2013 damning revelations concerning crimes and misdemeanors among Erdoğan's tight entourage were made public. Erdoğan fought off all of these challenges successfully, but the 2013 events, especially the corruption allegations, demonstrated to him that even his own close allies could turn on him. The unsuccessful coup attempt of July 15, 2016, gave him the wherewithal not only to institute an ongoing ruthless and unprecedented purge of state and society of "undesirable elements," but also to configure the institutional edifice to ensure his regime's long-term survivability.

The period of formal domestic consolidation has since ended. A constitutional referendum in 2017 and presidential elections in 2018 transformed the Turkish republic from a parliamentary into a presidential system that effectively subordinates every single state institution to the president and does away with any semblance of separation of powers. Erdoğan, who expects to remain in power for a significant interval, is busily expanding his control to what remains of civil society. In the new authoritarian Turkey, the old adage can be modified to "L'état c'est Erdoğan."

The transformation did not, of course, happen overnight. Erdoğan worked assiduously to acquire more power, putting his imprint on all matters big and small, including foreign policy. Over time foreign policy has increasingly come to reflect his personal views and preferences. This chapter argues that Turkey's new foreign policy will assume a far more important role in Turkish politics for two reasons. First, choices made in economic and foreign policy since 2013 have resulted in unprecedented challenges and dilemmas. The policy of maximizing growth, often at the expense of greater indebtedness, has resulted in a severe economic crisis that has been aggravated by the COVID-19 pandemic. The resolution will necessarily require greater international cooperation, often with powers that Erdoğan claims are hostile to Turkey's interests.

Second, there are structural reasons: Erdoğan's firm control over state institutions notwithstanding, there remains strong opposition to him, as evidenced by the 2019 defeats in the Istanbul and Ankara municipal elections. The loss in Istanbul, the city that launched him, was traumatic. When Erdoğan forced a repeat of the elections on spurious grounds, the AKP lost it twice, the second time by even greater majority. Foreign policy offers him a new arena of contestation to construct a narrative of accomplishment, whether real or imaginary, that serves to keep the focus on him and bolster legitimacy at home. Erdoğan uses foreign policy—formulated as an appeal to nationalism and Islamism—to buttress domestic support and insulate himself from domestic critics.

To achieve this objective, Erdoğan has had to push the boundaries of Turkish activism, first in the Middle East, then beyond. This has the added benefit of amplifying his own (and in his mind, Turkey's) global stature and importance. This, despite the fact that his new foreign policy initiatives, ranging from his massive and multifaceted interventions in Syria and Libya to new activism in the eastern Mediterranean and the Red Sea, have antagonized foes and allies alike.

Turkey's activism is not new. Erdoğan and his immediate entourage have always had an inflated opinion of their and Turkey's international standing and role in history. Erdoğan saw Turkey first and foremost as the natural leader of the Middle East, if not also of the Muslim world. Almost from the moment he assumed power, he has argued that Turkey deserved greater global recognition and commensurate responsibilities. The road to a global role, however, would have to go through the establishment of an implicit hegemony over the Middle East.

Foreign policy activism was intended to underscore Turkey's importance. In one notable example, in May 2010, Erdoğan and Brazil's President Lula da Silva blindsided President Obama with an unsolicited intervention into the Iran nuclear diplomacy that threatened to undo months of painstaking US-led negotiations. This initiative, like many others, failed to earn Erdoğan the global recognition he yearned for but was emblematic of the new role he envisioned for himself.

The outside world also serves as a foil for domestic failings; blaming the multitude of "enemies abroad" is a vital part of Erdoğan's discourse and legitimation process. He has often intimated that the July 2016 coup was instigated by Washington. His foreign policy parallels the domestic one; they are both laced with acrimony and indignation.

Activism, often for the sake of visibility, led to unnecessary risk taking. Erdoğan did not shy away from testing the limits of his relationship with Washington. For example, in August 2018 he provoked an unnecessary crisis by detaining an American pastor, Andrew Brunson, and three Turkish employees of the American embassy and consulate system on bogus charges of trying to overthrow the government. Turkey paid a heavy price for this miscalculation when a frustrated President Trump, who generally was sympathetic to Erdoğan, levied sanctions on Turkish exports because Ankara failed to follow through on a deal to release Brunson. The sanctions exacerbated Turkey's then economic woes, adding additional pressure to a weakened Turkish lira and an economy suffering from capital flight and high inflation.

A far more strategic misstep occurred when NATO member Turkey, though forewarned, opted to purchase the sophisticated Russian S-400 air-defense system that could compromise the security of the new US frontline fighter, the F-35. Turkey, which had been a key customer of and participant in the F-35 manufacturing, was forced out of the program and potentially lost billions of dollars in export revenue, not to mention opportunities for technology transfer. Erdoğan has used these fights with Turkey's primary ally to galvanize his base, heighten Turkish nationalistic passions, and off-load blame for a deteriorating economic landscape on Washington's "foreign currency assassination" policy.[1]

DOMESTIC POLITICS AND FOREIGN POLICY

Erdoğan and his supporters are singularly focused on demonstrating that his ascendancy is legitimate and a reflection of the people's desires. His consolidation of power has come about through legal means; that is, elections, referenda and constitutional changes in what Kim Lane Scheppele has called "constitutional legalism."[2] The emergence of charismatic leaders willing to up end existing rules and undermine institutions as they secure their rule is not unique to Turkey; as Marianne Kneuer argues, it fits "those states that have undergone democratic erosion, where existing democratic institutions are undermined (e.g. through vote rigging), horizontal accountability is damaged in favour of expanding executive power, and the rights of citizens and the opposition are restricted."[3]

Both the 2017 referendum that fashioned the executive presidential system and the 2018 presidential elections that culminated with Erdoğan's victory were fraught with irregularities, if not outright fraud.[4] Nothing about the circumstances of the 2018 elections could be characterized as fair; Erdoğan monopolized print and electronic media outlets while the opposition received scant coverage. One presidential candidate campaigned from jail while the country was under a state of emergency, which enabled authorities to ban opposition rallies and control access to the ballot box.

Immediately following his electoral "win," Erdoğan promulgated a series of directives designed to further centralize all power at the presidential palace. Scores of organizations and institutions big and small found their charters rescinded or upended to have them reporting directly to him, and he appropriated the right to make all appointments to state institutions, including universities, without any parliamentary oversight. Perhaps the most egregious of these faits accomplis was his assumption of complete control of the Turkish Sovereign Wealth Fund with his son-in-law Berat Albayrak, who is the minister of economy and treasury, and a coterie of cronies populating the fund's board. The fund has in its possession some of the most important Turkish companies and vast tracts of public land, which it can sell and administer at will.[5] In effect, Erdoğan has initiated the most significant and rapid process of deinstitutionalization in modern Turkish history. This development parallels the construction of a state clientelist system in which businesses favored by the AKP have received the bulk of state contracts, especially infrastructure-related ones.[6]

The twin processes—the quest for personal legitimacy and the deinstitutionalization of the state—have come to define and drive Turkish foreign policy. Purges, politicization, and the intrusion of other agencies into policy resulted in the foreign ministry losing its preeminence in terms of both expertise and role in decision making.[7] Not since Kemal Atatürk, the founder of the modern Turkish state, has one individual had such overwhelming influence over the formulation and course of the country's foreign policy.

A snapshot of Turkey's current foreign policy reveals a great deal of uncertainty, instability, and absence of direction. The current picture is dramatically different from what Erdoğan and the AKP projected at the beginning of their rule. From what was, unquestionably, a position of regional influence, Ankara finds itself isolated, in search of transactional alliances and, more important, at odds with its traditional allies. In 2018 alone, Ankara has gone from calling European nations "Nazi remnants" to courting them again as potential allies against the United States as relations with Washington deteriorated.[8]

A process of change that began with the end of the Cold War, shaking alliance patterns and threat perceptions, and continued with the Iraq War compelled Turkey to adapt and react. The adaptation has been difficult, although at times successful. Turkey adjusted to the emergence of the Kurdish Regional Government in northern Iraq and managed to turn it to its advantage, bringing temporary domestic respite to its Kurdish question and economic benefits. However, at the root of the most profound changes rest the Arab uprisings. Turkey's expectations from these uprisings failed to materialize. As Gencer Özcan has argued, Erdoğan and the AKP presumed that the uprisings would allow Turkey to showcase itself as a model for the region and simultaneously increase Turkey's influence there.[9] Bashar al-Assad, whom Erdoğan had initially backed and then turned on, has persevered.

Turkish euphoria that greeted the fall of Egypt's Hosni Mubarak and the emergence of the Muslim Brotherhood–backed president Mohammed Morsi was short-lived; the latter was overthrown in a military coup a year after assuming power. Abdel Fattah al-Sisi, the former defense minister and new president, in many ways represented what Erdoğan feared the most: a coup, not just in Egypt but also at home. Morsi's imprisonment was accompanied by the massacre of some eight hundred demonstrators in Rabaa Square by security forces. For Erdoğan, Morsi's fate became a paramount issue; he stressed that relations with Egypt would only improve upon Morsi's release from incarceration. He made it a domestic issue by repeatedly flashing the four-finger symbol of the Rabaa massacre in public and inviting his audience to join in. Frustration with the outcome of the Arab uprisings led to old friends becoming rivals, if not perceived enemies, which happened with conservative Arab monarchies. Correspondingly, Turkey found itself isolated and often ignored by local partners who saw it as being far too demanding and even too ideological.

Domestically, the government and the media have projected a very different image. The supplicant Turkish press is replete with wildly exaggerated stories of successful Turkish leadership in the Middle East and beyond. It is not just the victories that dominate everyday headlines but also anger at the West in general and the United States in particular. The West is at the heart of a voluminous conspiracy literature propagated by the government that has it conjuring all kinds nefarious plots. Yet in what can be classified only as a case of extreme cognitive dissonance, the same Turkey under "pernicious Western attack" continues to maintain its alliance with the West and its NATO membership.[10]

President Erdoğan is driving both the narratives of success and victimization. As Turkey has transitioned toward a personalized, one-man political system, Turkish foreign and domestic policy preferences have become synonymous with his predilections and needs. To be sure, there are long-standing interests, some archaic and some vital, that all Turkish governments have pursued. And Turkish domestic politics has long cast a shadow on the country's role in the region and beyond, as well as on the competition with other states, be they in the Gulf, North Africa, or the Levant. Yet the degree of personalization of foreign policy in Turkey is new. While Erdoğan has always been confident in his own knowledge of foreign affairs and his own abilities to tackle these issues, what is different is that the institutions that mediated his preferences and the priorities of the state and society, albeit sometimes with limited success—such as those of the foreign ministry, the military, and economic actors—have all been sidelined, tamed, or subdued. Erdoğan inhabits an echo chamber of sorts. In the near term, this will translate into policy making that is simultaneously fast moving yet prone to potentially serious errors in judgment as well as ordinary mistakes. Its long-term consequences are difficult to discern at this stage.

TURKISH FOREIGN POLICY THEN AND NOW

Erdoğan and the AKP have their roots in Turkey's Islamic movement, specifically in Necmettin Erbakan's National Salvation Party. Erdoğan and many of his political companions entered politics with Erbakan, an unabashed Islamist. Erdoğan broke with his mentor to set up his own party when it became evident that the military would never give Erbakan a path to power.

Conveying a more moderate image, Erdoğan and his colleagues nonetheless aspired to discard the straitjacket that the military establishment had imposed on Turkish foreign policy. The military had always preferred to have as little to do as possible with the Middle East, focusing instead on transatlantic ties, competition with Greece, and the strategic and domestic threat that of the Soviet Union and later Russia posed. In what would be dubbed a policy of "zero problems with the neighbors," Erdoğan and Ahmet Davutoğlu, his initial foreign policy aide, foreign minister, and prime minister before his unceremonious dismissal, charted a proactive regional policy that sought to improve relations with all. This policy embraced democratic values, increased economic integration and trade, and, as a beneficiary of the advantages of belonging to NATO, "complementing" American foreign policy.[11] Although not openly articulated, an underlying theme was a new emphasis on Islam. This message, though subtle, was in contrast to the AKP's more traditional and secular predecessors, who eschewed any expression of an attachment to Islam, lest they be tainted in the eyes of the military. In fact, the AKP understood that it was the intersection of its Islamic roots with its democratic credentials that would appeal to many across the Middle East.

The transformation of Turkish foreign policy under Erdoğan would not have been possible without the economic reforms introduced by Turgut Özal, first as an adviser to the 1980 military regime, then as prime minister and president. The military, in what was a Latin American–style bureaucratic, authoritarian coup, had sought to abandon import substitution industrialization and open up the economy. The transition to a more globally competitive economy would take the better part of a decade and a half. By the time Erdoğan became prime minister in 2003, the economy had become more diversified and the private sector more dynamic as new firms emerged that took advantage of the export-friendly policies. Özal's legacy included the empowerment of new business enterprises, nicknamed "Anatolian tigers," that surfaced in towns and regions long considered the hinterland, such as Konya, Kayseri, and Gaziantep, away from the industrial centers of Istanbul and Izmir. These areas also tended to be both politically and culturally more conservative in outlook and, as such, would ultimately provide critical political and electoral support to the AKP.

The AKP's economic policy emphasized both economic growth and integration with the global system. As a sign of its success, Turkey joined the G-20, the group of the twenty largest global economies. Erdoğan and the AKP aggressively promoted Turkish business interests abroad, and companies that benefited from the party's largesse, especially new ones, became AKP's supporters. The once close Erdoğan ally but now much vilified Gülen group, through its business confederation, TUSKON, worked in tandem with state institutions to support Turkish businesses abroad. TUSKON, along with MÜSIAD, another business confederation put together by self-described Muslim businesspersons, were empowered by the AKP as alternatives to the entrenched and powerful Istanbul and Izmir-based business organization TÜSIAD. These efforts paid off handsomely: Turkish exports to the Middle East jumped from $4.4 billion in 2002 to $43 billion in 2018, and overall exports grew from $37 billion in 2002 to $168 billion in 2018.[12]

The ups and downs of Turkey's relationship with Syria best exemplify the challenges Erdoğan has faced since 2003 in engineering a new foreign policy. Erdoğan and the AKP started by upending the traditional Turkish approach to Syria and its ruling Ba'ath Party. Erdoğan injected a level of dynamism and openness unseen since the days of former president Turgut Özal. Turkey, with its "zero problems with the neighbors" approach, managed to pave the way for a new and potentially productive relationship with the states of the Middle East—one that better suited post–Cold War realities. Erdoğan went out of his way to court and form a close relationship with Syrian leader Bashar al-Assad, initiating a policy euphemistically termed "one nation, two governments." His charm offensive in the Middle East notwithstanding, Erdoğan pragmatically eyed Turkey's economic interests, which meant that he chose to cooperate with all kinds of authoritarians in addition to Assad.[13]

When Damascus failed to heed his advice following the outbreak of the Syrian uprising, Erdoğan quickly jettisoned Assad to align himself with the opposition. In due course, he created and armed his own militias in Syria whose membership include large numbers of Islamist extremists. The Syrian civil war was a profound disappointment for Erdoğan. Assad, whom he expected would quickly be replaced by the Sunni opposition, slowly gained the upper hand with the help of his allies, the Iranians, Russians, and Hezbollah. The Syrian civil war saddled Turkey with two new problems. The first was the emergence of the Syrian Kurds as a factor, thanks, in part, to the United States. The second was the inflow of refugees. Turkey has provided shelter for as many as 3.5 million Syrian refugees and remains vulnerable to the influx of more should Idlib, the opposition's last remaining bastion, fall. By the end

2017, Erdoğan sought to mastermind another about-face: frustrated by the failure of the Syrian opposition and angered by US support for the Syrian Kurds, Erdoğan pivoted in search of allies against America's new protégés. The best he managed to accomplish was tacit understandings from Vladimir Putin, who in turn used him to score points with Washington.

The Syria crisis encouraged Erdoğan to take risks, especially in Kurdish-inhabited northeastern Syria. In 2014, the Islamic State (ISIS) swept through northern Iraq and Syria, capturing vast expanses of territory, including Iraq's second largest city, Mosul. When ISIS forces threatened Kobani, a Kurdish town on the border between Turkey and Syria, the Obama administration sought Turkish help to contain the threat. Erdoğan refused, preferring, as he made clear then, ISIS to the Kurds. Erdoğan had seriously underestimated the alarm in Western capitals caused by the advance of the Islamic State. Obama decided to arm and train the People's Protection Units (YPG), the militia affiliated with the Democratic Union Party (PYD), which itself was affiliated with Turkey's domestic Kurdish insurgent group, the Kurdistan Workers' Party (PKK). With the assistance of a small number of US combat personal, the PYD ultimately defeated ISIS in Syria.

Such collaboration was anathema to Erdoğan, who ratcheted up his rhetoric against Washington to the point of threatening to intervene into areas where US troops were based, hoping that this would induce the United States to change its approach. Taking matters into his own hands, he ordered the Turkish military and its local allies into Kurdish-inhabited areas of Syria twice. The first of these interventions, in Afrin in January 2018, not only pushed the YPG and its Syrian allies out, but the subsequent occupation led to the eviction of Syrian Kurds from their homes and the forced "Arabization" of the area.[14] After President Trump pulled US forces out of the area around Tal Abyad further to the east in October 2019, Turkish forces again invaded Syria.[15]

Because of Turkey's deep-rooted Kurdish problem, along with its unwillingness to resolve it, Erdoğan perceives Syrian Kurdish gains as a strategic threat. Syrian Kurds are strongly aligned with their Turkish kin, and Turkey fears the possibility of a Syrian Kurdish autonomous zone backed by Washington, perhaps under the guise of a Syrian federal arrangement similar to that in Iraq. While Erdoğan was willing to accommodate Iraqi Kurds and make them dependent on Turkey, two contiguous Kurdish autonomous zones on Turkey's southern border could feed demands for autonomy among Turkey's Kurds as well. The fear of such an eventuality led Erdoğan to abandon the peace process he had initiated with Turkey's Kurds. Erdoğan's Syrian gamble has paid off so far only because Trump acquiesced to it, despite strong opposition from Europe and from within the US government and Congress. As Ankara seeks to undo Syrian Kurdish advances made under an American umbrella supported also by the United Kingdom and France, it has confronted the Syrian military in Idlib to prevent the latter from capturing the province. Turkey is now party to the Syrian conflict; it risks getting further entangled and unable to control its outcome.

The eastern Mediterranean is another area in which Ankara has aggressively asserted its regional interests. Turkey has sought to prevent Cyprus, Egypt, Greece, and Israel from searching for and exploiting gas reserves by extending its own economic exclusion zone (EEZ) to such an extent that it overlaps with internationally recognized territorial waters, and by deploying warships to chase away drilling and exploratory vessels. Ankara has also negotiated an agreement with the Libyan government that conjoins the two countries' EEZs to prevent the construction of pipelines from the eastern Mediterranean to Europe. This has made Turkey party to a second civil war in Libya: Erdoğan gambled and won big by deploying thousands of Syrian jihadist mercenaries and Turkish military wherewithal, including drones, to support the Libyan government, which subsequently blocked the advance of the opposition general Haftar on Tripoli. This puts him at odds not only with most Europeans, who have to worry about the introduction of jihadist elements so close to their shores, but also with Egypt, Russia, and the Gulf powers, which support Haftar. Civil wars are messy; there is no guarantee that Erdoğan's allies will, in the end, carry the day.

As these examples demonstrate, Erdoğan has shaken up Turkish foreign policy by combining risk taking with belligerency. With the notable exception of Russia, Ankara has made a habit of bullying those who might stand in its way, threatening to send Syrian refugees to Europe and intervening militarily in Syria and the Eastern Mediterranean. Still, Erdoğan's gains in Syria and Libya remain tentative and may prove costly down the road. His bet on the Muslim Brotherhood and hope to harness the Arab uprisings has alienated many regional conservative regimes. With the exception of the beleaguered state of Qatar, which Turkey has supported by deploying soldiers there, and

Hamas and Sudan, Ankara does not have many friends left in the region. Nevertheless, recent Turkish behavior in its immediate environment is likely to raise the question of whether or not Ankara has transformed itself into a revisionist power.

AUTOCRACY AND FUTURE FOREIGN POLICY

Erdoğan's foreign policy to date has been characterized by both strong ideological pronouncements and positions as well as by pragmatism. He has changed course when needed. Still, pragmatism notwithstanding, there is a consistency to his vision. Neo-authoritarian leaders, argues Kneuer, create "missions" as constructs to legitimize their rule. Missions constitute "the political programme of an authoritarian government, namely its performance-focused objectives—national security, international security, economic growth/prosperity, solutions to social problems," as well as the "ideational-identitarian narratives designed to achieve effective appeal and generate an allegiance to the regime."[16] In contrast to hard ideological approaches, missions are inherently flexible, as they make no sweeping claims of validity and are easily adaptable. In other words, missions do not offer comprehensive analytical explanations or uniform policy options.

Erdoğan approaches almost everything as a mission. Foreign policy, therefore, should be seen as a mission unto itself. It is not any different from Erdoğan's decision to build a powerful navy complete with a Turkish-made light-aircraft carrier, and the numerous mega-infrastructure projects ranging from a gargantuan airport in Istanbul to bridges across the Bosporus and the Dardanelles to the controversial Canal Istanbul, a man-made parallel waterway to the Bosporus.

Erdoğan's missions consist of performance-focused objectives whose ultimate goal is to reconstitute the glory of an imaginary past. The incessant allusions to and commemoration of the past—not just the Ottoman past but also the past of the Seljuks and others—contributes to the ideational aspect of his rule. He also seeks to fashion a Turkish identity that Lisel Hintz terms "Ottoman Islamism": "The social purpose of the Ottoman Islamist identity involves increasing the space allowed for Islam in the domestic public sphere, and acting in solidarity with Turkey's Muslim brothers internationally."[17] The underlying theme that is dominant is the defense of the homeland against its enemies, new and old, real or imaginary. At the 947th anniversary celebration of the Battle of Manzikert in 2018, Erdoğan argued: "Thus, we have to be powerful in politics, diplomacy, economy, trade and technology. Otherwise, put this homeland and geography aside, they won't give us a single day to live in this world."[18]

This sense of insecurity may mean that the next "mission" threshold might be nuclear. Erdoğan has been contesting the UN system, arguing that "the world is greater than five,"[19] in reference to the UN Security Council's five permanent nuclear members. In fact, in 2017 he outlined concrete proposals to revamp the Security Council, arguing before the UN General Assembly that the world has moved on since the days of the post–World War II order.[20] Equally unacceptable to him is Israel's undeclared status as a nuclear state.[21] Nuclear weapons would not only bestow the great power status he craves; they would confirm Turkey's dominant position in the Middle East. Because they would jeopardize Turkey's relationships with its allies, such a decision has a downside as well.

In many respects, Erdoğan most resembles the late Hugo Chávez of Venezuela, who conjured a new construct, the Bolivarian state, and appended his oil-based clientelist state to the glories of Simón Bolívar. Turkey, of course, does not have oil, but Erdoğan has managed to structure a similar form of clientelism by dispersing state resources among people and enterprises that are bound to be loyal to him even if their world and social views do not always correspond to those of the leader's. A mission-style system, focused on performance and obtaining results, is both more engaged than a traditional charismatic regime and also inherently more suitable to a charismatic leader who seeks to consolidate and institutionalize power over a longer time frame.

Especially since the June 2018 election that finalized his ascent to power as the sole uncontested leader, Erdoğan has gone out of his way to conjure an image of himself as defender of the nation and faith, appearing in a variety of military uniforms, even at events that are primarily civilian. Similarly, he has also tried to eliminate the separation between the state as an institution and himself; he is not just a temporary occupant of a position in the state hierarchy but the personification of the state. The press, which he almost completely controls, amplifies this message, and the flow of information makes it clear that all decisions are taken at the presidential palace and nowhere else. What has changed is that before June 2018 some institutions had limited autonomy by virtue of their place in the constitutional framework. These included the offices of the prime minister and other ministers, and the parliament, or at least the parliamentary leadership. Some previous occupants of these positions, such as Ahmet Davutoğlu, used the power of their office to make decisions in an attempt to shape the national discourse. No one other than Erdoğan is empowered to do this today, and cabinet members have been reduced to simple office managers executing the leader's wishes.

The contour of Erdoğan's mission has been in the works for some time, although over time some of its characteristics have gained greater definition. Among these is what Kneuer calls, "antagonizing 'Western' liberal democracies" as "an increasingly successful legitimation strategy."[22] Erdoğan antagonized the Europeans by likening them to Nazis not only because they refused to go along with his wishes to extend presidential campaigning to Europe but also because they were critical of his human rights violations, including purges and incarcerations of tens of thousands of his opponents. Similarly, he has been trying to devise a way to bypass the American dollar as the medium of exchange. As his son-in-law Treasury and Finance Minister Albayrak wrote, Turkey is spearheading an effort to create a common strategy against the United States to "build a sustainable future."[23] Carving out a new "independent" foreign policy course that is increasingly antagonistic to his traditional allies, without breaking with them and exiting the NATO alliance, while improving relations with others, is the next goal.[24] Ironically, the Turkey Erdoğan has built is very dependent on external (Western) capital and sources of financing. He cannot, therefore, afford a geopolitical pivot from these sources.

Erdoğan's greatest challenge lies in the autocratic system he has built. The system is bound to be challenged at home, especially if economic and social conditions deteriorate, polarization increases, and, most important, the elimination of avenues for dissent results in increased civil disobedience and oppositional activities that are difficult to contain. A critical actor will be Turkey's middle class, which, by virtue of the country's recent history, geographical location, and economic linkages with the West, has the greatest stake in continued stability and economic prosperity.[25] A regime feeling threatened will seek to protect itself by externalizing its challenges. The regime has not forgotten the 2013 Gezi protests that erupted over the threatened destruction of a popular park in downtown Istanbul and became the single most important popular public challenge it faced in its eighteen-year rule. It continues to litigate that event by prosecuting some of the participants, accusing them of having foreign connections, including "the Hungarian Jew George Soros."[26] Kneuer suggests that external legitimation strategies may also include military aggression. This, too, has already occurred in Syria and Libya.

Turkish foreign policy in the years to come is sure to vacillate between autocratic pragmatism and bouts of autocratic belligerence. The conflation of Erdoğan's own interests with those of Turkey's—a process unmediated by institutions but supported by individuals who owe him their power, their well-being, their positions, and the totality of their careers—not only increases the chances for errors but also compounds them. In the meantime, Erdoğan's articulation of performance-based missions will help deflect attention at home from the slow but real transformation in foreign policy. Given current constitutional provisions, Erdoğan could remain president for a while to come. What is clear, however, is while there may not be another Erdoğan waiting in the wings, there are plenty of Nicolás Maduros, leaders with none of their predecessors' influence.

Chapter 11

THE SYRIAN CIVIL WAR AND THE NEW MIDDLE EAST

James L. Gelvin

THE SYRIAN UPRISING AND SUBSEQUENT CIVIL WAR WAS BOTH A symptom of, and catalyst for, the emergence of the New Middle East. It was a symptom, inasmuch as the uprising and civil war erupted in response to the same economic, political, and social malaise that ravages most of the Arab world; fostered a new, overt sectarianism; compelled or provided opportunities for outside meddling in the internal affairs of a sovereign state; and demonstrated the post–Cold War, post–Iraq invasion impotence and indecision of American policy makers. It was a catalyst, inasmuch as it triggered the strengthening, shifting, and straining of prevailing alliances—Syria with Russia and Iran in the first instance, Saudi Arabia and Israel in the second, the United States and Turkey in the third; spilled out over Syria's boundaries to challenge the stability, economic capacity, and demographic and sectarian balance of Syria's neighbors; and spawned a political vacuum in the heart of the eastern Arab world in which armed groups of jihadis might breed before striking out elsewhere.

SECTARIANIZATION, MILITARIZATION, PROXY WAR

Overall, three characteristics have defined the Syrian uprising: its militarization, its sectarianization, and its nature as a proxy war.

In the very beginning, the regime depended most heavily on the security services to put down the uprising. The services broke up demonstrations and arrested protesters. Although security personnel were effective where deployed, such tactics could not and did not prevent protests from leapfrogging from town to town, village to village.

This forced the government to reconsider its tactics. Realizing that its campaign to isolate and punish pockets of resistance using lightly armed security personnel had done little to stamp out the resistance, the regime literally brought in the heavy artillery. The regime handed counterinsurgency over to the armed forces, which, in the manner of militaries throughout the world, are more adept at wielding a meat cleaver than a scalpel.

The army used scorched-earth tactics to pound the insurgents into submission. The test case proved the district of Baba Amr in the city of Homs, which called itself the capital of the revolution. Using all the firepower under its command—tanks, helicopter gunships, artillery, mortars, heavy machine guns, and snipers—the army first cut off the city from the outside world, then softened up the rebel stronghold, reducing much of it to rubble. Finally, it stormed the district, killing about 250 rebels and driving the remainder out.[1]

Its mission a success, the military began applying the same tactics elsewhere, escalating the level of violence with the occasional use of poison gas and barrel bombs (barrels filled with TNT and dropped from the air indiscriminately). Partly as a result of these tactics, the government was able to regain the initiative. By 2014 it was in control of the line of cities that stretched from Damascus in the south to Aleppo in the north. The government also dominated the coastal areas to the west, particularly those heavily populated by Alawites—the minority sect to which most of the ruling elite belonged. Unable to seize control of much of the countryside and border areas, however, the government proved incapable of uprooting the resistance once and for all.

The military was not the only force that learned a lesson from the change in tactics. As it became increasingly clear that the brutality of the regime against its own citizens knew no bounds, the resistance also changed in form. At the outset, protests had been localized and largely peaceful affairs. Each rebel village or district had its own "local coordination committee."[2] To protect demonstrations from snipers and informants, protesters staged rallies at night. Organized militias, made up of local fighters who had deserted from the Syrian army, provided further protection. This proved futile once the army replaced the security services as the regime's main tool to combat the uprising.

With their communities under siege or bombardment, local militias were often forced to retreat from their own neighborhoods and regroup and fight wherever they sensed regime vulnerability. This was the origin of the "Free Syrian Army"—the rebel group backed by the United States and its allies—which former president Barack Obama once derided as comprising "former farmers or teachers or pharmacists who now are taking up opposition against a battle-hardened regime."[3] The close connection between local militias and their civilian counterparts became increasingly tenuous. Civilians lost control of the uprising, and the balance of power within the opposition tipped in favor of the fighters.

In addition to militarizing the uprising, the regime effectively sectarianized it. It did this by exploiting both the heterogeneous character of Syrian society and the homogeneous character of the ruling group, which was bound together through ties of family, sect, and place of origin (in or around the village of Qardaha in the Latakia Governorate). This limited the probability that one member of the regime would turn on the others, effectively "coup-proofing" it.[4] Rule by members of a minority sect also affected the way the ruling elite approached members of the broader Alawite community and members of other minority groups (Christians, for example, make up about 10 percent of the Syrian population). Because the regime was identified with a minority sect, it could count on the support of members of that and other minority sects who feared massacre at the hands of the majority Sunni population should the government fall. The United Nations' Regional Bureau for Arab States calls this dynamic "legitimacy of blackmail" (more properly rendered "legitimacy by blackmail"): "Stick by us or they'll kill you."[5]

The uprising had begun without reference to sectarianism.[6] Protesters focused on the removal of a regime they considered repressive and corrupt. This is hardly surprising. Before the uprising Syrian society as a whole was not divided along sectarian lines. Members of sects of course recognized their religious differences and, in the privacy of their homes, might have made derogatory comments about one another. But they mingled with members of other sects in markets, public schools (where they all wore the same uniforms), coffee shops, and on public transportation. The regime therefore deliberately set out to polarize Syrian society—and the uprising—into opposing sectarian camps.

The regime adopted a number of tactics to accomplish this. As soon as the uprising broke out, the regime labeled its opponents, among other things, Salafis, Islamists, terrorists, jihadis, and agents of Saudi Arabia. To ensure this would be a self-fulfilling prophecy, as early as spring 2011 the regime released Salafis, Islamists, and jihadis, including those associated with al-Qaeda, from prison. Many ended up in the on-and-off al-Qaeda affiliate in Syria, Jabhat al-Nusra, or in ISIS.[7]

The regime also deployed violence to sectarianize society. It organized armed "popular committees" to protect Alawite villages, and it equipped pro-regime vigilantes with knives and clubs for use in street battles with mostly unarmed protesters. And it used the *shabiha* (a name probably derived from the Arabic word for "ghosts")—Alawite thugs who hailed from Assad's home town and its immediate vicinity—to provoke tit-for-tat violence against Sunnis.[8] In July 2011, nine died in Homs after an Alawite mob surrounded a Sunni mosque in one of the first recorded instances of sectarian conflict during the uprising. That was just a harbinger of worse to come: in Baida and Banias, for example, *shabiha* massacred 248 Sunnis, and in the village of Aqrab opposition fighters slaughtered at least 125 Alawites.[9]

The intervention of Iran, Hizbullah, and Russia on the side of the Syrian government and the West, Saudi Arabia and the Gulf states, and Turkey on the side of the opposition also served to define the contours of the uprising and civil war, prolonging it and making it bloodier and more lethal. In the case of the former group, intervention was both direct and indirect. Iran's close relationship with Syria stretches back to 1982, when Syria became the only Arab state to side with Iran in the Iran-Iraq War. Russia's goes back even further, to the early days of the Cold War, with the polarization of the Arab world between the so-called moderate and revolutionary camps. Along with Hizbullah, both had a stake in the survival of the regime: among other benefits, partnership with Syria enabled both Russia and Iran to project power abroad and disrupt a Middle Eastern status quo that held little benefit for either. A friendly government in Syria was vital to Hizbullah because it provided a land bridge across which Iran could ship a continuous stream of arms to its ally keeping Israel off balance.

Thus, all three intervened on the side of the regime directly. The Iranians provided the Syrian regime with intelligence and advisers deployed to instruct the Syrian military on tactics and on controlling cyberspace (techniques which the Iranians perfected putting down their own antigovernment protests— the Green Revolution of 2009). Iran established an air bridge that resupplied the Syrian army with ammunition, weapons, and even refurbished attack helicopters. And Iran, along with Hizbullah, sent troops to assist the Syrian regime (at one point there were eight thousand to ten thousand soldiers from the Islamic Revolutionary Guard Corps and its elite Quds Force fighting in Syria, along with five thousand to six thousand from the regular army[10]).

Russia also provided Syria with weapons (within the first three years of the civil war, Russia had contracted for close to $5 billion worth of arms to sell to the Syrian government) and advisers. And like Iran and Hizbullah, Russia participated directly in combat operations. Russian warplanes not only flew missions in support of the Syrian army, but Russia deployed Special Forces, artillery units, and tanks to back it up. And Russia's presence on the UN Security Council prevented the sort of diplomatically sanctioned foreign intervention that brought down Muammar Qaddafi in Libya.

Iran and Hizbullah organized, imported, and underwrote pro-regime militias as well. Among the most notorious of the Iran-supported groups were the Fatemiyoun Division (comprising fighters from the Afghan Shi'i community in Iran), the Heydariyoun (Iraqi Shi'i fighters), and Zeynabioun Brigade (made up of Pakistani-Shi'is), and the locally recruited Baqir Brigade. Iranian-backed militias provided the critical firepower on the ground to re-take Aleppo, Syria's largest city, from rebel militias at a time when the Syrian army was so overstretched it lost Palmyra to ISIS.[11] Hizbullah was particularly useful to the regime organizing local militias. Because it is itself a popular militia, Hizbullah possesses a level of expertise vital to the training of the pro-regime popular committees that protect Alawite and Shi'i villages in Syria. And unlike Iranians, members of Hizbullah have the added advantage of speaking Arabic.

Outside powers supportive of the opposition likewise financed and advised militias whose ideological stance—when they had any—reflected what their paymasters were willing to support or, at least, wanted to hear. The non-Islamist Free Syrian Army, the darling of the West, never acted as a cohesive fighting force and underperformed throughout the civil war as a result of an ineffective command structure, corrupt leadership, the superior capabilities and experience of hardcore Islamist fighters, shifting ideological winds, and, most important, spotty American support and commitment. In contrast, the Harakat Ahrar al-Sham al-Islamiyya (the Islamic Movement of the Free Men of Syria, commonly called, simply, Ahrar al-Sham), the largest militia fielded by the opposition (at its height it comprised about twenty thousand men), proposed turning Syria into an Islamic republic. It received the backing of Qatar and Saudi Arabia (in a rare instance of collaboration) and Turkey. Needless to say, Islamization within the opposition camp, coming so soon after the Libyan debacle, undercut support in the West—particularly vital material support—for the rebels and contributed to their defeat.[12]

TURNING THE TIDE

Overall, the transformation of the Syrian civil war into a proxy war ultimately affected the course of the war and narrowed the field of possible outcomes. At the beginning of 2015, for example, the Syrian civil war was, according to the *New York Times*, a "chaotic stalemate."[13] Neither the government nor the opposition forces arrayed against it was able to gain the upper hand. Battlefield gains were reversed, regained, then reversed again. Battles fought between the two sides more closely resembled a war of attrition than a war of movement.

By the summer of that same year, however, the situation on the battlefield had completely shifted in the rebels' favor. In 2014, the United States, Jordan, and Saudi Arabia set up a joint Military Operations Command (MOC) in Amman, Jordan. Commonly known as the "operations room," MOC collected intelligence, financial and logistical assistance, and military know-how from the United States and Saudi Arabia. It then coordinated the flow of information and assistance to opposition groups fighting on the southern front in Syria. MOC, in effect, unified the operations of those groups not only on a tactical level but on a strategic one as well. The coordinated effort that MOC supervised ensured victory in the Southern Storm campaign, which led to the rebel seizure of a vital Jordanian-Syrian border crossing.[14]

Opposition groups throughout Syria began copying MOC by setting up their own operations rooms. This enabled them not only to achieve a brief tactical coordination, but it made it possible for them to wage major campaigns that spun out over time. By autumn of 2015, the Syrian army was reeling. The opposition had pushed it back to a defensive line that was steadily shrinking. Then the reversal was itself reversed.

In July 2015, Bashar al-Assad made a formal request to Vladimir Putin, asking for direct Russian intervention to fight "jihadi terror" in Syria.[15] The Russians responded by sending in warplanes, tanks, and artillery a month later. Russian operations continued for months thereafter, even after Putin announced that he had achieved his goals. Russian jets, artillery, and even cruise missiles pounded opposition positions—Islamist, jihadi, and non-Islamist alike (in spite of Russian protestations to the contrary, initially 85 percent to 90 percent of Russian targets were non-ISIS related).[16] As a result, the Syrian army and supporting militias regained both the initiative and territory, particularly in the north and along the vital Damascus-Aleppo highway. Once again, foreign intervention had changed the course of the Syrian civil war.

Negotiations among parties involved in a civil war—the most common sort of war since the end of the period of decolonization—can succeed in ending hostilities only when each side views a battlefield victory as impossible and continued warfare as injurious to itself as to its opponents—what is called a "mutually hurting stalemate."[17] If one side or the other thinks its goals can be achieved on the battlefield, however, there is little possibility of reaching a settlement. After all, why compromise if there is still the possibility of taking it all? Only after all sides in a civil war realize there is no possibility of achieving their goals through violence is the time ripe for negotiations. Analysts point to a number of examples of civil strife—in Northern Ireland, Bosnia, and elsewhere—which, they assert, prove this.[18]

Foreign intervention into a civil war makes it difficult to achieve a mutually hurting stalemate and thus makes it difficult to achieve "ripeness." Losing belligerents will naturally look to their foreign patrons to help them turn the tide, and those patrons are usually only too willing to help. Foreign backers of each side view the stakes not only in terms of a winning or losing proxy but also in the wider, more critical context that made them get involved in someone else's war in the first place. Both Saudi Arabia and Iran, for example, viewed the Syrian civil war as one front in their battle for regional dominance. They were unlikely, therefore, simply to throw up their hands at the first signs of setback. Rather, under such circumstances they were more likely to ramp up assistance to their proxies. When they did, their opponent was more likely to do the same, thus increasing the level of violence and further delaying the ripe time. The proxy nature of the civil war in Syria foreclosed the possibility of a negotiated settlement.

DOMESTIC RAMIFICATIONS

What, then, might the future bring for Syria? When the uprising morphed into a civil war and the magnitude of the Syrian crisis became apparent, policy makers and analysts began spinning out scenarios concerning an endgame. They came up with five possibilities: The Syrian regime or the opposition wins an out-and-out victory on the battlefield, leading to a total collapse of one side or the other; Syria is either de facto or de jure divided; all interested parties reach a negotiated settlement; the conflict continues, with periods of greater or lesser violence among the various parties; the Syrian government puts down the revolt in all but name but is unable to reassert its political control over society at prewar levels. Setting aside the intervention of some deus ex machina (pandemic, anyone?), the proxy nature of the conflict and the battlefield successes of the Syrian regime and its allies made the possibility of all but the final two options unlikely.

Interestingly, Lakhdar Brahimi, the United Nations and Arab League envoy to Syria, warned of this very eventuality as early as December 2012. "I am unable to see another solution out of two possibilities: either a political solution that is accepted by the Syrian people which meets its aspirations and legitimate rights, or Syria to be transformed into hell," he began. He continued: "People are speaking about a divided Syria into many small states like Yugoslavia. Absolutely no! This is not what is going to happen. What is going to happen is 'Somalization'—warlords and the Syrian people persecuted by people seizing its fate."[19]

Coming as it did before the regime's battlefield gains of 2015, Brahimi did not foresee the resilience of the Syrian government, enabled by foreign assistance. Yet that makes his Somalia analogy even more apt. It is probable that Syria, like Somalia, will have a single government that will reign, but not rule, over the entirety of its territory. It is probable that it will have a permanent representative to the United Nations, issue passports and print postage stamps, and even, if it so desired, send a team to the Olympics. However, as in the case of Somalia, it is also probable that armed militias will control large swaths of territory outside the control of the government. There would be no established boundaries between the territories. Militia leaders will engage in chest thumping and perpetual warfare against each other or sign on to informal truces. The world will inherit another failed state, this time in the heart of the Arab east.

The character of the insurgent forces gives credence to Brahimi's vision. Of the close to 150 groups listed in an October 2015 report published by the Institute for the Study of War, fewer than one-third had a presence in more than one governorate, and about half of those were located in only two.[20] What this indicates is that over the course of the civil war, much of the indigenous opposition (along with indigenous militias supporting the government) came to consist of locally recruited fighters loyal to their neighborhood power broker whose authority enabled him to wrest control of resources—oil, wheat, refineries, tolls from border crossings, protection money—from rival power brokers and the government. Together, the fighters and the power brokers inhabit a self-perpetuating war economy upon which they depend.[21] As one observer has noted, "Opposition-held Syria is Mad Max meets the Sopranos."[22] Unable to dismantle this system or overwhelm autonomous power brokers, the weakened government will likely have to learn to cope with them.

What will further frustrate the Syrian regime's attempt to reimpose itself on society is the parlous state of the Syrian economy and the damage brought about by civil war. Since the 1960s, Syrian governments subjected Syrians to a variety of economic models, but all of them depended on a combination of patrimonialism and rent-based capital accumulation. In 2005, the Syrian government, bowing to the neoliberalization of the global order, introduced what it called a "social market economy." The government consulted with the International Monetary Fund in drawing up the new economic blueprint, whose purpose it was to shift Syria away from a command economy closer to a free market one. The result was an economy that combined the worst aspects of both systems, replete with crony capitalists (such as Rami Makhlouf, the president's first cousin, who became the principal owner of the mobile communications giant Syriatel) and burgeoning income inequality.[23] The social market economy yielded lackluster results. The World Bank reported that in 2010 Syria's gross domestic product grew by less than 3 percent. It also estimated that the GDP would have to grow at an annual rate of 7 percent merely to absorb new job seekers.[24]

Then came the uprising and civil war. According to the International Monetary Fund, from 2010 to 2015 alone, Syria's GDP plummeted from $60 billion to $14 billion; government fiscal revenue likewise fell from $21 billion to $6 billion, and gross public debt skyrocketed from $30 billion to $150 billion. Oil production and exports fell by 98 percent and 92 percent, respectively. The only product whose export increased was copper and copper alloys, presumably looted from factories and private houses, then sold abroad, mostly in Egypt.[25] Overall, 2016 estimates put the total economic loss as a result of the conflict at $275 billion, along with an additional $180 billion in infrastructural damage.[26]

From where the Syrian regime will be able to come up with these huge sums in a region that has witnessed more than its share of devastation is a question that currently has no answer. The West, Saudi Arabia, and the Gulf states, which have the financial resources, are not anxious to reward Assad and his allies for out-brutalizing the regime's opponents. The United States, which had pledged $230 million to help "stabilize" territories no longer under the control of the regime, withdrew that pledge in August 2018, deferring to the generosity of its Arab allies. For its part, Saudi Arabia refused to pick up the slack, holding to its initial pledge of $100 million.[27] The Assad family has had a long history of affirming its loyalty or good behavior to Saudi Arabia in exchange for financial assistance, only to renege later on. Such pledges were a drop in the ocean anyway.

That would leave Assad's allies, Russia and Iran, holding the proverbial bag—although neither is capable of providing the sort of financial largesse Syria requires for reconstruction. Over the course of the war, the regime increasingly abandoned investment in wealth-producing sectors of the economy and spent lavishly on public-sector salaries and military expenditures to buy the loyalty of those sectors. Russia and Iran have helped defray the cost of current accounts, but even if, for example, Iran's $6 billion to $10 billion credit line from 2011 to 2017 goes down in the ledger as a strategic investment, it is not sustainable in the long term.[28] To help defray the cost of its outlays, therefore, the Syrian government has begun selling off assets: a Russian company bought a 25 percent stake in Syria's oil sector, and both Russia and Iran have invested in gas and phosphate operations.[29] These sales are not inexhaustible and can hardly be expected to generate the sort of revenue that would have a long-term impact on an economy that still focuses on the short term.

Although Assad himself has raised the possibility that China might act as a white knight, there is little indication that China will be willing to do so. So far, China has pledged $23 billion in loans for the Arab world as a whole and pledged an additional $90 million in aid for reconstruction and care for internally displaced persons to Syria, Yemen, Jordan, and Lebanon.[30] Furthermore, the tendency for China to leverage loans to poorer nations into ownership of strategic industries should give Syrian officials pause before they mortgage off Syria's future.

Even if the Syrian regime found donors or creditors willing to subvent the country's physical reconstruction, Syria's problems would not end there. In the words of the World Bank, "Capital destruction, by itself, accounts only for a small share of the conflict's economic impact." The larger share belongs to the destruction of economic networks and human capital and connectivity.[31]

In February 2016—one month before the fifth anniversary of the Syrian uprising—the Syrian Center for Policy Research released the last in a series of reports about the impact of the Syrian civil war on the lives of Syrians and on the Syrian social fabric.[32] According to the report, by the end of 2015, there were 470,000 war-related deaths (2015 was the last year in which a count was attempted). Syrians with war-related injuries numbered 1.9 million. This means that 11.5 percent of the prewar population ended up as casualties. The war had uprooted about 45 percent of the population, including 6.36 million internally displaced persons (as of spring 2018, that number had risen to 7.2 million).[33] Displaced persons frequently lack access to health care, family networks, employment opportunities, and schooling (around 45.2 percent of children no longer attended school). They also strain the economies and social fabric of their sites of relocation and suffer disproportionately from depression and post-traumatic stress disorder. Syria's mental health crisis is one of the great unwritten stories of the civil war.[34]

The war spread poverty and unemployment. According to the report, the overall poverty rate was 85.2 percent. About 69.3 percent of the poor lived in "absolute poverty" (defined by the United Nations as "severe deprivation of basic human needs"). About 35 percent were even worse off, living in "abject poverty" (unable to meet their basic food needs). In 2011, unemployment had been 14.9 percent; by the end of 2015, it was 52.9 percent. Of those working, more than one-third participated in the "conflict economy" as fighters, suppliers, smugglers, and the like. As a result of unemployment, poverty, and the breakdown of vital infrastructure and social networks, life expectancy at birth dropped by about fifteen years. And diseases that had been under control—including typhoid, tuberculosis, rabies, hepatitis A, and cholera—are no longer. Diseases that had been eradicated, such as polio, have returned.

Compiled, as they were, before 2016—the year Syria's largest city, Aleppo, fell after a massive air assault that destroyed more than thirty-three thousand buildings[35]—these figures should be taken as a touchstone, not an accurate reflection of the current state of devastation.

GLOBAL RAMIFICATIONS

The aftershocks of the Syrian uprising and civil war spilled out over Syria's borders, roiling not only Syria's neighbors but Europe and North America as well. By the beginning of 2018, more than six million refugees had decamped from Syria, straining economies in the Middle East and provoking xenophobic backlash elsewhere. The civil war had left large areas of Syria ungoverned and lawless, enabling ultraviolent jihadi groups such as Jabhat al-Nusra and the Islamic State, which sought to upend the regional state system, to spawn and incubate. Both the presence of large numbers of refugees, which upset often-fragile sectarian balances in their host countries, and the presence of jihadis committed to purifying conquered territories of Shi'is and select minorities, exacerbated sectarian tensions throughout the region. Finally, as the war within Syria wound down, outside powers scrambled either to cash in on the victory of their side or to reposition themselves in the wake of the loss.

Perhaps the most visible reminder of the Syrian crisis are the refugees, scattered throughout the world but disproportionately located in surrounding states. By the beginning of 2019, more than 85 percent of Syrian refugees worldwide lived in Turkey (3.64 million), Lebanon (about 1 million), Jordan (680,000), Iraq (250,000), and Egypt and North Africa—and those were just the ones registered with the UN High Commissioner for Refugees. Most of them had left Syria between 2013 and 2016, when urban warfare was at its height.[36]

From the beginning of the Syrian uprising to the end of 2018, Turkey spent $35 billion on refugee assistance.[37] Other sites of refuge paid comparable amounts. While the international community picks up some of the tab, the burden for providing municipal services such as lighting and road building, health care, educational services, and the construction of infrastructure necessary for delivering clean water falls heavily on host countries. According to a report of the World Bank, published in 2016, the influx of refugees sparked a doubling of Lebanon's unemployment rate (to 20 percent), increased the number of Lebanese living below the poverty line by 170,000, and caused an additional $7.5 billion in economic losses.[38] In Jordan, where upwards of 500,000 refugees live outside camps and are thus not wards of the international community, unemployment increased by 34 percent among native-born Jordanians between 2011 and 2014; between 2012 and 2014, the price of housing increased by 25 percent.[39] Jordan has been home to ongoing anti-austerity protests and seven different governments between 2011 and 2018.

Although international law prohibits the involuntary repatriation of refugees, governments in the Middle East and Europe have used both carrots and sticks to encourage what American presidential aspirant Mitt Romney once called "self-deportation." Germany uses the carrot of providing financial incentives; Lebanon, the stick of denying work permits to refugees and demolishing the "semipermanent" housing they construct. Turkey has chosen to ignore international law altogether. In 2018, the Turkish government began deporting mostly young, undocumented Syrian men to the northern Syrian territory occupied by the Turkish military, despite UN warnings that Syria was still too dangerous for them.[40]

Nevertheless, the refugee crisis is unlikely to go away soon. The joint Russian-American plan for repatriation negotiated by Vladimir Putin and Donald Trump in Helsinki in July 2018 was stillborn,[41] and although 89 percent of Syrian refugees in Lebanon expressed interest in eventually returning home, few were prepared to do so in the near future. Overall, in spite of pressure from the Lebanese government, from 2016 through June 2019 only 40,230 Syrian refugees in Lebanon returned home—even with a Lebanese government plan to facilitate their departure—about 4 percent. The proportion for refugees in Jordan is slightly better—close to 6 percent.[42] And who can fault them for their wariness? There are few opportunities and little safety for returnees in Syria, and it has been reported that the Syrian government has a list of 1.5 million expats who are to be arrested upon arrival (not to mention the fact that all men between the ages of eighteen and forty-two are liable for military conscription). Besides, the Syrian regime is in no hurry to repatriate refugees it regards as mostly hostile to the regime and has thrown up roadblocks to prevent their return.[43]

The refugee crisis is one reason for the rise in sectarian tensions in the region. In Turkey, for example, the arrival of Syrian Alawites fleeing anti-Assad forces and ISIS has sparked sectarian resentment among Turkey's own Alevi and Alawite populations, many of whom fault their government for supporting the rebels and favoring the Sunni refugee community at the expense of endangered Syrian Alawites. But it is not just refugees who are responsible for renewed sectarianism. In Lebanon, anti-Assad forces and ISIS have crossed the border from Syria, targeting Hizbullah and the Shi'i community it represents, the former as payback for Hizbullah's support for the Syrian regime, particularly its role in the 2013 Qusayr campaign, the latter as part of its general war against Shi'is. And in both Syria and Iraq, local residents, Kurds, and imported Shi'i militias have targeted entire communities whom they claim harbored ISIS members or cooperated with ISIS, sparking counterreprisals.[44]

ISIS emerged in Syria in 2013 after Syrian-born members of the Islamic State of Iraq returned home to fight against the regime (they later split from ISIS to found the autonomous Jabhat al-Nusra). Its original core comprised remnants of al-Qaeda in Iraq, Syrian Salafis whom the Assad regime had released from prison, and, perhaps most important in terms of ISIS's military capabilities, former Ba'athist military officers who had served under Saddam Hussein. ISIS's first major victory was the conquest of the provincial capital Raqqa, in north-central Syria, which it took from other insurgent forces that had taken the city from government forces. It was from there that ISIS began its rapid conquest of territory in Syria and Iraq, abetted by the Syrian government's preoccupation with combat elsewhere and the collapse of the Iraqi army. In 2014, Abu Bakr al-Baghdadi, the group's leader, proclaimed the reestablishment of the caliphate (which, except for its Salafi-jihadist ideology, differed little from any other autocratic state in the region) with himself as caliph. Having briefly consolidated a territorial state, ISIS established outposts elsewhere in the Middle East (the most active being in Libya, Tunisia, the Sinai, Algeria, and Yemen), Africa and North Africa, and Central and South Asia.

It was the threat ISIS posed to the state system in the Middle East that provoked the American-led campaign there,[45] and over time that campaign came to include a multitude of actors, including militias supported by the American coalition (including the predominantly Kurdish Syrian Democratic Forces) and by Iran, along with armed forces from Turkey and Russia, which have used the campaign to justify their pursuit of unrelated geopolitical interests. By mid-2017, the caliphate was all but defeated, leaving in its wake an ongoing insurgency, counterinsurgency, and revenge killings in Syria and Iraq; the weakening of states and state institutions there and wherever else ISIS had set up shop; a global counterterrorism campaign and xenophobic response that far outweighs the threat posed by those who might continue to identify with ISIS; the fraying of the American-Turkish and perhaps American-Kurdish alliances; and the destruction of ancient minority communities and much of the ancient cultural heritage in the heartland of the Arab world. The state system, however, remains intact.

FROM CENTER STAGE TO BACKDROP

With the caliphate gone and Donald Trump's announcement of the withdrawal of American troops from Syria (along with his ill-considered remark that Iran "can frankly do whatever they [*sic*] want there"[46]), Israel and Turkey directly entered the lists in Syria, transforming the proxy war there into something else entirely. In January 2019, Israel began two days of attacks—around seventy in all—against Iranian and Syrian targets in Syria following the launching of a missile from Syria against Israel. Israeli strikes in Syria were nothing new, but claiming responsibility was. Before these attacks, Israel had adopted a policy of "ambiguity"—that is, not claiming credit for its actions in Syria. The January 2019 announcement was an indication that Israel had moved away from the policy of ambiguity and instead adopted one of deterrence. The Israelis were unambiguously informing Tehran that the establishment of permanent Iranian bases in Syria would be crossing an Israeli redline.[47]

Then, it was Turkey's turn. In October 2019, Turkish forces established a second, vastly larger bridgehead in Syrian territory, 120 miles to the east of the territory Turkey had occupied in 2016. The stated aim was twofold: to create a longer buffer zone between Syrian territory and Turkish territory that would be free of the Syrian Democratic Forces, which the Turks claim is dominated by partners of the Kurdistan Workers' Party, and to dump one million Syrian refugees in Turkey into the corridor.[48] Accompanying the Turkish forces was the Syrian National Army, a remnant of the Free Syrian Army that harbored more than its share of criminals, sociopaths, and Islamists. The Turkish invasion and occupation threatened Rojava, the Kurdish protostate in northern and eastern Syria, which, according to its blueprint, the Charter of the Social Contract in Rojava (Syria), was to be the locus for a radical experiment in democratic decentralism and women's rights.[49] Soon after the Turkish invasion, the Kurds threw themselves into the arms of the Syrian government for protection. Whether at the hands of the Turks or at the hands of the Syrian government, Rojava is doomed.

Over the course of the civil war, Syria had morphed from the site of an uprising to the site of a civil war to the site of a proxy war. Finally, it became the site where regional powers could fight out their own battles.

Chapter 12

STATE BUILDING, SECTARIANIZATION, AND NEO-PATRIMONIALISM IN IRAQ

Harith Hasan

WHEN THE GROUP THAT CALLS ITSELF THE ISLAMIC STATE OF IRAQ and Syria (ISIS) took over Mosul in June 2014 and began its march southward—threatening to invade Baghdad and topple the government—the Iraqi state seemed to face an existential challenge. This was not merely an insurgent group fighting the central government; it was a movement defying the very legitimacy of the state while offering an alternative concept of statehood—one in which "Iraq is not for Iraqis and Syria is not for Syrians," in the words of Abu Bakr al-Baghdadi, ISIS's self-declared caliph.[1] ISIS found fertile ground in Iraq and Syria to form its state based on the utopian myth of the Sunni caliphate. The weakness or disintegration of the state in both Iraq and Syria created vacuums of authority that allowed ISIS and other paramilitary groups to operate more freely, invoking all kinds of ideologies that evolved on the margins. The collapse of a dominant center in both countries allowed internal and external frontiers to reconstitute themselves around their own centers. At the same time, both countries experienced a sectarianization of political struggles along with popular mobilizations, which gave increased salience to the Shi'i-Sunni divide.

These dynamics aggravated a process of disintegration and reconfiguration that intensified after the American invasion of Iraq in 2003, although some of that process had begun years, if not decades, before. American officials portrayed the occupation as the beginning of a new Middle East, one in which a democratic, pluralistic, and pro-Western Iraq would transform a region long depicted as stagnant, authoritarian, and resistant to change. This proved a promise unkept. Iraq slipped swiftly into a long period of violence, and the United States found itself trapped in a war against multiple foes. This is the setting in which ISIS originated and eventually evolved to its ultimate incarnation. Likewise, this very context produced a shift in the American narrative about Iraq and the Middle East. Administrations after that of George W. Bush abandoned the 2003 missionizing discourse of democratization. Criticism of "nation building abroad" became recurrent themes in the Obama and Trump administrations. They both adopted an approach prioritizing security, stability, and national interest. The Trump administration customized this approach with a combination of cynicism and dogmatism revealed in its pragmatic deals with Arab autocrats and a more confrontational stance toward political and ideological foes of the United States and Israel.

But while the United States had the luxury of abandoning "nation building abroad," Iraqis continued struggling with the realities created by the American invasion. Since the fall of Saddam Hussein in 2003, various groups competed to influence the process of state reconstruction and emerging configurations of power. Soon after the restoration of territories from ISIS, militias and paramilitaries acting both within and outside the state became a new challenge. As some of these groups were allied with Iran, the escalating US-Iranian competition placed a huge pressure on the country, which became one of their major battlefields. Meanwhile, the Iraqi state has been trying to claim its uncontested authority over its territory and legitimize its monopoly of violence, a challenge that is yet to be fully realized.

Events that unfolded in Iraq after April 2003 and culminated in the rise of ISIS in 2014 must be put in the context of attempts to reshape the Iraqi state, restructure power relations within and beyond, and redefine its legitimizing principle. Facile explanations for Iraq's situation—for example, blaming Iraq's internal conflicts on the primordial irreconcilability of its various ethnic and sectarian groups, or on the artificiality of its borders—fail to grasp the complexity and plasticity of the country's sociopolitical landscape. Similarly, approaches that view transformations in Iraq solely from the perspectives of democratic transition or ethnic conflict or neoliberal state building often provided reductive and insufficient explanations.

This chapter addresses post-2003 dynamics in Iraq from a sociopolitical perspective, underscoring the relationship between sectarianization and the reconfiguration of state authority. I argue that sectarianization came about as a result of two processes. First, there was a historical shift in state-society relations, which produced a system of governance that institutionalized ethno-sectarian categories. Second, the collapse of the state in 2003, the ensuing struggles to fill vacuums of authority, the rise of nonstate actors, and inter-communal violence triggered new forms of boundary demarcation. I go on to discuss the contradiction between state reconstruction and ethno-sectarian representation, focusing on the crisis of the current regime. Finally, I explore the potential for the emergence of postsectarian politics as the country moves to face a different set of challenges, including intracommunal rivalries and complex socioeconomic conditions.

FROM THE MODERNIZING STATE TO PATRIMONIALISM

The invasion of Iraq resulted not only in regime change; it transformed the foundation upon which the Iraqi state had theretofore stood. Since the found-ing of the Iraqi state in 1921, its ruling elites faced the challenges of sociocul-tural heterogeneity and weakly developed national identity, yet they employed divergent approaches and discourses of nation building. Although most of these elites embraced modernization and homogenization, there was disagree-ment over the manner and the scale with which these objectives were to be pursued. As in other postcolonial states, the project of nation building in Iraq rested on the assumption that the state would be the main agent of change. The fundamental task was to transform local "traditional" communities into a modern, secular, and homogeneous society. This is how Iraq's first monarch, King Faisal I, envisaged his government's role in a widely cited memorandum sent to members of the Iraqi political class. He lamented that in Iraq there was "no Iraqi people" but "masses of human beings, devoid of any patriotic idea, imbued with religious traditions and absurdities, connected by no common tie.... [Of] these masses we want to fashion a people."[2]

Although not without setbacks, centralization, formalization of structures and institutions, and secularization reshaped Iraqi society and altered the rel-ative weight of societal forces.[3] These processes produced a new middle class that embraced the modernizing agenda of the nation-state, although it was divided by competing ideological preferences. After the fall of the monarchy in 1958, republican regimes advanced this agenda more vehemently, adding to it an explicit populist and anti-colonial tone. Socialist and nationalist republican elites believed that their mission was to fight imperialism and dismantle the alliance between the "colonialists" and internal "reactionary forces,"[4] which they saw as the main obstacle to ensuring the "sovereignty of the people." The land reforms and the progressive family law adopted by 'Abd al-Karim Qassim's government (1958–1963), as well as the abolition of the use of tribal names during the early Ba'athist period and the stigmatizing of the sectarian diversity in the public discourse were only few examples of how populist regimes of the republican period carried out state-led, top-down modernization. Setting aside political liberalization, the revolutionary discourse of the ruling elites focused on facing real or imaginary enemies both inside and outside the country.[5]

Over the course of the past four decades, the power of populist developmentalism waned for three reasons. First, between the 1950s and 1970s, Iraq completed its transformation into an oil-dependent rentier state. In 1977, oil revenue mounted to 86 percent of governmental budget. This easily-gained rent provided ruling elites with effective tools for social control and patronage.[6] As Isam al-Khafaji argues, it altered the balance between state and society to the detriment of the latter.[7] Eventually, the ideological underpinnings of the Ba'athist regime lost their significance as the patrimonialist practices came to prevail. Second, the military adventures of the regime of Saddam Hussein wreaked enormous destruction and socioeconomic devastation, especially since they provoked the 1991 American-led bombing campaign and harsh international sanctions that lasted for thirteen years (1990–2003). The middle class began its rapid decent in the 1990s, and as a result of an international embargo on the sale of Iraqi oil, the state abandoned most development projects.[8] Third, the end of the Cold War and the global shift toward neoliberalism discredited the socialist mode of development. The modernization paradigm came under attack both politically and intellectually, accompanied by the rise of alternative approaches that decentered the state-building project and its homogenizing logic. These approaches held the state to be a tool of domination and suppression used by ruling elites based in the capital to marginalize or exclude large segments of the population.

The regime of Saddam Hussein became the quintessence of the now-maligned model of authoritarian developmentalism, especially as the news of its brutal suppression of Kurdish and Shiʻi oppositions began to attract international attention after the deterioration of its relations with the West. This created an opening for revisionist readings of Iraq's past. Some argued that the failure of nation building in Iraq was an inevitable product of the artificial nature of the state. Others searched for the original sin in the colonial imposition of Sunni minority rule over other groups.[9] The sectarian narrative about Iraq's history became more appealing as an analytical tool, often obviating the process- and context-bound effects of sectarianization.

These readings were reductive and simplistic. Sectarianism was not the dominant political frame in the 1950s and 1960s. As Eric Davis and others have shown,[10] conservative and revolutionary alliances privileged other social categories such as class and national identity (pan-Arabism versus Iraqi nationalism). Undeniably, sect-based solidarities always existed, influencing behind-the-scenes alliances and sociopolitical preferences. But other forms of solidarity mitigated and even superseded them. This began to change because of the increasing patrimonialist characteristics of state authority, especially in the times of Saddam Hussein, who leaned, for pragmatic rather than ideological reasons, toward regional-tribal clientelist networks mostly consisting of Sunni Arabs. This dynamic, in turn, enabled sectarian subjectivities to politicize and operate as alternative mobilizing strategies, especially among the Shiʻi Islamist movements. Further encouraging this trend was the Iranian Revolution, which put on display theological-doctrinal disparities between Shiʻism and Sunnism. The anti-Iranian alliance uniting Saddam Hussein with Gulf countries during Iraq-Iran War in the 1980s further inspired segments of the Iraqi/Shiʻi Islamist opposition and solidified their ties to Iran.

TOP-DOWN SECTARIANIZATION

By 2003, a new language and understanding of the state had already emerged. American policy makers and the mostly exiled leaders of Iraqi opposition groups made the pluralist model the natural alternative to the past dictatorship in their discourse.[11] Importantly, however, the way they visualized this model was through the lens of identity politics, a politics based on an ethno-cultural and ethno-religious interpretation of plurality. This became manifest in the upsurge of a political language centered on ethnicities and sects—called euphemistically *mukkawinat* (cultural components)—to define the building blocks of Iraqi society. Ending the homogenizing tendency of authoritarianism, of which Ba'ath rule was, perhaps, the epitome, required giving recognition to subnational identities. These identities became the authentic, representative forms of social reality. Thus, to prevent the reemergence of a dominant, oppressive state, ethnic and sectarian "groups" would maintain their internal autonomy, while sharing power with the center. The underlying assumption was that Iraq comprised separate ethno-sectarian groups—Shi'i, Sunni, Kurdish, Turkoman, Christian, and other minorities—and the best way to democratize it was to base political representation on these cultural categories. Political scientists call this arrangement "consociationalism," a term first used by Arendt Lijphart as a formula of representation in divided societies.[12] Accordingly, the selection of members of the first Iraqi institution formed after the invasion, the Iraqi Governing Council, corresponded to their ethno-sectarian identities. Similarly, the three most important government positions—president of the republic, prime minister, and speaker—went to a Kurd, a Shi'i, and a Sunni, respectively.

Tacitly, the category of "Iraqi" unlinked to a specific ethnic or sectarian qualification was alien to the new regime. The consequences of this arrangement became apparent in 2010, when a coalition called al-Iraqiyya, led by a secular Shi'i, Ayad Allawi, and composed of mostly Sunni parties, won largest number of seats in the parliamentary election. The coalition, however, did not secure the majority necessary to form the government. Instead, a grand Shi'i coalition formed after the election, the National Alliance, gained the majority. Former prime minister Nuri al-Maliki secured his second term in office as the head of a "national unity" government, a euphemism for a government distributing its ministerial positions mainly on the basis of ethnic and sectarian affiliation. When negotiations began over the positions al-Iraqiyya's politicians would hold in the government, a controversy ensued regarding whether it should be considered a Sunni coalition and given the "Sunni share" of positions, or should continue to be identified, as its leader wanted, as a cross-sectarian coalition—an identification that was difficult to quantify in the ethno-sectarian formula of power sharing. In the end, the Sunni parties in the coalition removed their cross-sectarian hat and resigned themselves to recognizing their "Sunnism" in order to receive their due. And when protesters stormed the squares at the end of 2019 demanding the end of *muhasesa* (apportionment of positions among ethno-sectarian parties), most Kurdish and Sunni parties opposed the formation of a nonpartisan government, arguing that the protesters were predominantly Shi'i and their demands should be addressed only by Shi'i parties. The elite found it difficult to absorb and decode the nonsectarian character of the protest movement and the fact that it was driven by a different conception of representation derived from socioeconomic status rather than ethno-sectarian background.

Notwithstanding the inherent contradiction between the individualism of neoliberalism—the conceptual frame dictating the thinking of US policy makers—and the collectivism of ethno-sectarian politics, the two intersected so long as the objective was to deprive the central state of its dominance.[13] Advocates of both positions viewed the state with suspicion or, at best, as a venue for negotiation and power sharing among representatives of ethno-sectarian communities. That is why it was expected that central state elites would not act independently of their communities.

Although the central state was redesigned to abandon top-down homogenization and secularization, an alternative process of internal homogenization began to take root within each subnational group. As the state abandoned its earlier attempts to fashion its own Iraqi "people," it adopted an alternative engineering designed to turn cultural subgroups into valid political categories, thereby preventing the development of cross-communal solidarities. Thus, the formula invoked in Iraq as a solution for "divided societies" ended up deepening the presumed divisions. In his theoretical model, Lijphart argued that consociationalism is better suited for countries in which boundaries between subcultural groups were well defined. [14] This was not the case in Iraq, where the mere idea of sectarian representation was widely rejected in public discourse. Fearing the political harm it would do, none of the mainstream parties used explicitly sectarian language or publicly emphasized their sectarian affiliation. Nevertheless, ethno-sectarianism was eventually institutionalized through ethno-sectarian power sharing, an electoral system based on proportional representation, and the eventual predominance of parties composed exclusively of members of one subnational community.

SECTARIANIZATION FROM BELOW

Sectarianization was not simply a top-down process. In the conditions of systemic collapse that followed the invasion, religious actors emerged as social leaders, both in their localities and at the communal level. On the one hand, this was a by-product of Islamization and the upsurge in religiosity that had accelerated in the 1990s throughout the Middle East as a result of the decline of the state's role as a secularizing agent.[15] On the other hand, the level of social control and political oppression exercised by the regime of Saddam Hussein prevented the evolution of autonomous civil society organizations, let alone political parties. After the fall of the regime, religious actors, especially those that were Shi'i, activated their preexisting networks of representatives and offices to reach out to a wider public in need of guidance and a sense of order.

The collapse of the central state prompted a movement from the margins to form new centers, that is, creating alternative configurations of relationships of power and realizing them in public sphere. For example, soon after the invasion, Saddam City in Baghdad was renamed Sadr City after Muhammed Muhammed Sadiq al-Sadr, an ayatollah with broad support in the poorest and most peripheralized Shi'i areas.[16] Pictures, murals, and the names of other Shi'i religious personalities appeared on the public landscape. Among those so celebrated were the grand *marja'* Ali al-Sistani; the Qum-based ayatollah Kadhum al-Hairi; the leader of the Supreme Council for Islamic Revolution in Iraq, Muhammed Baqir al-Hakeem; and Sadr's student and disciple Muhammed al-Yaqubi. The increasing Islamization of public space with emphasis on Shi'i particularities and mythology led to further sectarianization, even though that may not have been the intention. Furthermore, the visibility accorded various leaders and clerical networks, identified with different socioeconomic and sociocultural configurations, resulted in the further fragmentation of public space and the absence of a dominant narrative even at the Shi'i communal level. This dynamic evolved in a fluid context characterized by the absence of a dominant center of power. Therefore, since 2003, the process of creating a Shi'i center went hand in glove with state building, enabling Shi'i Islamists eventually to emerge as the dominant group.

On the Sunni side, the process of sectarianization was much more disruptive and destructive. Under Saddam, the regime had built effective clientelist networks among the Sunni Arab population, which, along with the heavy security grip, left very limited opportunity for the emergence of autonomous actors, religious or otherwise. Although Sunni Arabs had a dominant position in the Ba'athist government, they did not secure their position by an ideological commitment to Sunnism. Rather, recruitment to the regime was the outcome of pragmatic and opportunistic alliances based on a combination of tribal-geographic loyalties and identification with the state. This latter form of recruitment had antecedents in Ottoman times. Thus, at the time the regime fell, Sunnism was not yet an effective mobilizing political ideology.

After 2003, sectors of the population that came to be identified as Sunni felt a growing sense of alienation, triggered in large measure by a combination of a power vacuum, a disruptive foreign invasion, the spread of Shi'i and Kurdish triumphalism, and the increasing salience of Shi'i cultural symbolism after years of repression. This alienation found expression in two channels. First, there was a rejection to the new political realities. Sunnis, for example, boycotted the January 2005 election of the Transitional General Assembly and overwhelmingly voted no in the constitutional referendum of October 2005. Second, there was the toleration of, or at best indifference toward, the emergence and activities of insurgent groups, including jihadi factions, and their deployment of a radical and increasingly sectarian discourse.[17]

Violent rejectionism identified with "Sunnis" provoked counterviolence identified with "Shi'is," leading to the solidification of sectarian boundaries. One manifestation of this was increasing spatial segregation in Baghdad, where a process of intense sectarian "cleansing" took place between 2005 and 2008. Neighborhoods that had identified with class or socioeconomic commonalities became neighborhoods that identified with one or another religious-sectarian identity.

In this context of systemic collapse and widespread violence, the most radical groups found an opportunity to flex their muscles and operate freely, spurred on by the absence of a strong state capable of monopolizing the legitimate use of violence or a communal center that could rationalize the exercise of violence. But when the state and communal centers (especially on the Shi'i side) grew stronger, the most radical and anomalous elements were pushed to the margins in the newly constituted sphere of normality. By 2008, the Iraqi government, backed by the American army, allied with tribal and former insurgent fighters in Sunni communities to fight al-Qaeda in Iraq. Shortly thereafter, then prime minister Nuri al-Maliki led a military campaign against the Mahdi army and other Shi'i paramilitary groups in Basra in an attempt to impose government's control there. Levels of violence began to decrease significantly, raising the hope that Sunni rejectionism would crumble at the same time Shi'i groups, which occupied dominant positions in the government, would marginalize their more radical counterparts.

STATE-BUILDING AND ETHNO-SECTARIAN GOVERNANCE

The increasing sectarianization of regional politics was another factor that drove Iraq's own sectarianization. The implosion of Iraq after the American invasion altered the previous geopolitical balance, thereby intensifying the Iranian-Saudi rivalry. This further politicized the Sunni-Shi'i divide, a process that was aggravated by the transformation of the Syrian uprising into a civil war and a regional proxy war. Indeed, the Syrian conflict, framed as it was in sectarian terms, energized the mood of rejection among Iraqi Sunnis, especially as some regional players, such as Qatar and Turkey, sought to increase their influence in the shadow of Iranian-Saudi competition. A year of sit-ins and protests in Sunni areas, occasionally led or addressed by radical voices, generated a mobilization which Maliki's government failed to address constructively.[18] Regional tensions facilitated the rise of ISIS, which managed to take over Mosul and most Sunni cities in a few days, thereby exposing the state's crisis of legitimacy as well as its internal corruption. Suddenly, the government found itself dependent on nonstate actors, such as Shi'i clerics and Iranian-backed militias, to mobilize a strong fighting force that could face ISIS—ample proof of the effects of weak institutions and the fragile formula of ethno-sectarian power sharing.

The results of the general elections of 2014 and 2018 showed that electoral constituencies have become further and further split along sectarian lines, with competition taking place principally within each constituency. However, the top-down sectarianization continued to face some resistance on both political and societal fronts. The protest movement that forced Adil Abdul Mahdi's government to resign in 2019 represented the biggest challenge to the ethno-sectarian paradigm because it appealed to alternative notions of state-society relations centered on good governance and social justice.

After 2003, the idea of "Iraqism" did not vanish, although its meaning became more fluid. As McGarry and O'Leary argue, despite the strong consociational element of Iraq's 2005 constitution, there was resistance to the formal institutionalization of sectarian and ethnic categories.[19] This resistance was visible in the adoption of constitutional articles suitable for majoritarian systems. Majoritarianism assumes a degree of cultural homogeneity, and unlike consociationalism, majoritarianism does not prioritize the principle of managing a "divided society." This created a tension between groups prioritizing consociational arrangements and groups adhering to majority rule. Understandably, defending their earned autonomy, the Kurdish parties were the main advocates of the former, whereas most Shi'i parties embraced the latter, for they viewed majoritarianism as the best way to "represent" the Shi'i demographic preponderance.[20]

The Kurdistan Regional Government (KRG), led by the Kurdistan Democratic Party, considers Kurdish nationalism its main political ideology and source of legitimacy. Thus, its political agenda concentrated on defending and maximizing Kurdistan's autonomy rather than reconstructing Iraqi nationalism. Kurdish parties in Baghdad worked to advance consociationalism and prevent the reemergence of a dominant center in the capital.

Over time, some Sunni parties came to the conclusion that challenging Shi'i domination in the center was unlikely to succeed. They joined the KRG by embracing an anti-centralist approach. In contrast, Shi'i groups, some of which were supportive of consociationalist arrangements for the fear of the return of a "Sunni dictatorship," came to embrace majoritarianism and a more central approach. This is what lay behind Nuri al-Maliki's push to end the *muhassesa* (quota) system and form a majoritarian government.[21] Indeed, in preparation for the 2018 election, almost all major Shi'i groups adopted an anti-*muhassesa* position, although they differed on whether the alternative should be a majoritarian or a technocratic government.

Two parallel processes explain these political shifts. First, the Sunni Arab community gradually overcame its initial resistance to being reductively categorized as Sunni, which would, of course, reduce its members to a minority within Iraq. Sunni political leaders defended their communal share of political power and sought more independence from Baghdad, as exemplified in Sunni politicians' occasional circulation of the idea of forming a Sunni region, or increasing the autonomy of predominantly Sunni governorates, such as Nineveh and Anbar, from Baghdad. Second, the Shi'i factions began to back away from their defensive posture as they managed to consolidate their dominant political position in Baghdad. They grew more supportive of a centralizing and homogenizing approach, which could only redound in their favor. Their confidence got a boost after the liberation of ISIS-controlled areas and the failure of the KRG to declare independence, a development that reinforced the authority of the central government in territories previously defined as "disputed."

Access to resources influenced political discourse and attitudes as well. Indeed, the fact that Iraq remained a rentier state that depended on oil resources was an important element in the changing relationships of power. The Iraqi government secures about 95 percent of its revenue from oil rent, which reinforces the state's position as the strongest economic actor and the largest employer and spender. Consequently, groups that had better access to state resources managed to improve their positions vis-à-vis those with less access. Whereas the *muhassesa* system helped reproduce the dominance of ethno-sectarian parties within their constituencies, the accumulation of oil rents in the central government's budget gradually strengthened centripetal forces. The Da'wa Party, which provided three prime ministers, expanded its influence in the state bureaucracy and military. Particularly under Maliki's premiership, clientelist networks connected to the prime minister infiltrated most central institutions and enhanced Maliki's centralizing tendencies.

Nevertheless, intra-Shi'i rivalries among the Da'wa Party, the Sadrist Movement, the Badr Organization and its allies, and al-Hakeem's group prevented the emergence of a Shi'i consensus on key issues. The war against ISIS and its aftermath generated new dynamics that will be critical not only to intra-Shi'i dynamics, but also to the future trajectory of the Iraqi state and the choice between ethno-sectarianism and Iraqi nationalism, on the one hand, and consociationalism and majoritarianism , on the other. By defeating ISIS, extending the central government's authority to disputed areas, and preventing the disintegration of Iraq, a power center dominated by Shi'i groups consolidated, although not to the extent of preventing its potential disintegration should a serious internal crisis emerge. This power center should not be mistaken for an institutionalized central government; rather, it is a configuration of relationships of power that includes state and nonstate actors. This broad reconfiguration, shaped by sectarianization and the attempt to articulate an Iraqi nationalism salient to the Shi'i community, lies at the root of what Fanar Haddad calls Shi'i-centric state building in Iraq.[22]

However, this came with a price of deepening the intra-Shiʻi divide as a new generation of Iranian-allied paramilitaries gained more power throughout the war against ISIS and dominated the Popular Mobilization Forces. They became more embedded within the Iraqi state, their networks entrenched in the security organs and their pan-Shiʻi worldviews embraced or propagated by some of those organs. They are opposed by groups that are more Iraq-centric and less inclined to completely align their political futures with Iran. This division became more pronounced after the 2019 protests whose discourse was critical of Iranian intervention in Iraq and of nonstate actors hijacking the Iraqi state to serve the interests of a foreign power. The competition between Iraq-centric groups, including segments of the new protest movement, and pan-Shiʻi groups working to obscure boundaries between Iraq and Iran in the name of revolutionary Shiʻism, has become the main polarity in Shiʻi politics and will influence the future of the Iraqi state.

In this reconfiguration, Shiʻi clerical authority gains extraconstitutional status. It acts as both a moral guide and, occasionally, the ultimate political broker among Shiʻi forces.[23] Paramilitary groups have entered into a complex web of relations with the state. They backed the formal military and security forces in the war against ISIS while simultaneously contesting the state's monopoly of violence when it threatens them. Through the Popular Mobilization Forces Law and other formal and informal arrangements, Shiʻi paramilitaries evolved into hybrid entities that operate on the borderline between formality and informality.[24] This contingent arrangement is reminiscent of Kurdish Peshmerga in Kurdistan, which act formally as the region's guard but, in fact, answer to their partisan leaders.

These arrangements clearly challenge the common view of state building that focuses on formal institutions yet neglects the role played by other societal actors in shaping and constraining the state through conflict and negotiation. Surely, states do not derive their legitimacy just from constitutions and formal legal rules; rather, states must navigate complex context-bound effects. The reconstitution of authority in the broader sociopolitical order also depends on redefining and discursively framing the role of the state, not only on the basis of constitutional and legal principles but also on the basis of that which is normatively accepted. Cultural forces shape the normative, whereas forces that are hegemonic in society propagate it.

NEO-PATRIMONIALISM AND STATE-SOCIETY RELATIONS

In contrast to the deep divisions that sectarianization brought on, another form of non-identity-based mobilization is germinating that might enable a postsectarian Iraq. This mobilization and the discourse that appeared with it were manifested in protests in Baghdad and southern Iraqi cities. These protests demanded the government fight corruption and improve governance. Secular protesters even invoked the idea of a "civil state"—a state that is not dominated by Islamist groups or militias.[25] Observers saw the demonstrations that took place in mostly Shi'i areas as an indictment of the Shi'i political elite. But similar events unfolded in Kurdistan, where a series of protests, brought on by the region's economic crisis (exacerbated by the decline of oil prices) and the rampant corruption of the two dominant parties in Erbil and Sulaymaniyah, erupted in 2015.[26] The protests echoed some of the dynamics of the Arab Spring: They were mostly led by the youth, used social media for mobilization, were decentralized and leaderless, and contained a clear socio-economic component. They reflected an increasing disillusionment with the system and existing modes of conducting politics.

However, these events also showed the difficulty of injecting meaningful reforms in a system of power sharing that exempted ethno-sectarian elites from accountability. In theory, ethno-sectarian elites represent—and therefore respond exclusively to—only their subcommunities. This was a moment in which the ethno-sectarian formula clashed directly with demands for socio-economic reforms. On the other hand, ceasing the *muhassesa* system, which was the protesters' main demand, might very well end up deepening the ethno-sectarian rift if used by ethno-sectarian entrepreneurs either to exclude their rivals or to claim that the power allotted their community was appropriated by others. This would be the outcome if Kurdish and Sunni groups considered the change in the power-sharing system an attempt to deprive them of the right of choosing their representatives in the central government. Dismantling the patronage networks of ethno-sectarian parties could threaten the fragile balance of the system.

The low turnout in the 2018 general election indicated an increasing disillusionment with a system in which ethno-sectarian parties always managed to maintain their power within their communities and at the national level. These parties rely on patronage and traditional loyalties derived from kinship and regionalism, and they are often backed by paramilitary groups whose survival depends on their patrons' access to oil rent. These groups do not just depend on electoral laws that are favorable to maintaining the system; rather, they use extralegal means to win elections and make it difficult for newcomers to challenge their authority at the ballot box.

All this is typical of neo-patrimonial systems, in which formal and constitutional bodies and practices run in tandem with informal and extralegal practices.[27] As a result, the legal/political process is not up to the task of shifting the fundamental configuration of power. As a senior member of the Patriotic Union of Kurdistan, Mullah Bakhtiar, put it, "Regardless of the number of seats we win, whether one or 100, we will continue to be the PUK . . . we have weapons and nobody can take them from us."[28] Nevertheless, while the neo-patrimonial system has reinforced the ethno-sectarian formula, it has also mitigated sectarianism on some occasions. This was evident in Sistani and Sadr's opposition to Maliki's policies, and in the role played by Sistani to prevent Maliki from securing a third term in office.[29] Ideology does not drive actors in neo-patrimonial systems—what drives them is the need to sustain their domains of authority. This might be seen by their sometime resistance to ideologically sectarian state actors.

Increasing fragmentation within ethno-sectarian blocks can, however, reduce the effects of sectarianism and might even serve a desectarianizing function. Take, for example, Sadr's attempt to strike a deal with senior Kurdish and Sunni politicians to vote Maliki out of office in 2012. Although these rivalries reflect, to a large extent, patronage and personalized relations, they also might function as an alternative foundation for alliances that might challenge the ethno-sectarian arrangement in the future. There was a preview of this in the 2018 election, during which both the Abadi-led coalition and the Sadr-backed coalition included Sunni factions. To the extent campaign rhetoric is relevant, both coalitions advocated new arrangements that challenged the ethno-sectarian system.

In post-2003 Iraq, the dismantling of the highly centralized system of authority created multiple centers of power, formal and informal. Federal and local rules formally granted the KRG and the provincial administrations powers previously monopolized by Baghdad. Ethnic, religious, and tribal actors, as well as political parties and civil society organizations, gained a considerable degree of autonomy from the state. The absence of a dominant authoritarian center has increased political mobility and allowed, to a certain extent, the distribution of resources among multiple centers of authority. These arrangements unfortunately failed to produce effective institutions of public governance. As one economic adviser to Iraq's prime minister pointed out, the state became a primitive machine of rent distribution rather than of governing.[30] Among the multiple examples of this is the large number of Iraqis who receive salaries and pensions from the state. The Iraqi economist Ali Mirza noted that, between 2007 and 2014, the public sector employed 62 percent of new employees. He also estimated that salaries and pensions of about five million current and former public-sector employees consumed 48 percent of the 2016 governmental budget.[31] According to Iraq's Ministry of Planning, the public sector alone employs 40 percent of Iraq's workforce.[32] In 2020, following a drastic decline in oil prices, the government announced that oil revenue no longer provided liquidity to pay salaries of public employees, and the minister of finance considered the reduction of those salaries essential for the economic survival of the country.[33]

Despite the large public sector, observers often describe state institutions as weak and ineffective. Corruption and a sclerotic bureaucracy stand as key impediments to economic reform and the growth of the private sector. Since 2003, the system of patronage has created entrenched interests, often in the form of clientelist and crony capitalist networks consisting of politicians, bureaucrats, and private entrepreneurs. Two factors facilitated the evolution of these networks: First, state contracts, state-sanctioned import licenses, and the central bank's currency auction have provided the foundation for the largest and most economically rewarding activities. Second, the system of power sharing that led to the distribution of ministries and public institutions among political parties facilitated the evolution of fiefdoms within the state structure. Political parties, including those with armed wings, have used the positions they acquired as tools for patronage that served to sustain them financially. Each major political party formed what is often called an "economic committee," responsible for ensuring that state contracts issued by the ministries they control go to allied companies. According to an Iraqi economist, 38 percent of registered companies are either dependent on state contracts or operate as economic extensions of political parties.[34]

The gap between population growth, which fuels the demand for jobs and services, and the resources available to meet that demand is Iraq's most pressing challenge. Although Iraq has not conducted a census since 1987, most calculations estimate a population today of thirty-seven million. Demographers estimate that that number will increase to fifty-three million by 2030, with an average annual growth of 2.75 percent. The fertility rates in Iraq continue to be among the highest in the world—4.27 percent between 2015 and 2020.[35] Almost 40 percent of the population is under fourteen years old, 20 percent is under twenty-four, and 34 percent is between the ages of twenty-four and fifty-four. The estimated rate of unemployment among youth is 30 percent, and this number is likely to increase in the coming years.[36] The national poverty line, which the World Bank established at 22.5 percent in 2014,[37] has steadily risen as a result of conflict, the decline in oil prices, displacement, drought in southern Iraq, and rapid demographic growth.

Statistics also reflect growing disparities among provinces, which increases migration between regions and cities and intensifies instability by expanding peripheral zones and adding more pressure on depleted infrastructure. Economically attractive cities such as Baghdad and Basra have already experienced an increase in migration and the expansion of shantytowns at their margins. The lack of resources to deal with migration often leads to the expansion of ungovernable margins, as well as the spread of criminal groups and paramilitaries that sometimes become radicalized but always pose a threat to economic development and stability.

The ethno-sectarian system will remain under pressure to respond to these challenges. This pressure might lead Iraqis to adopt strategies of mobilization that would eschew identity-based politics, as demonstrated in the 2019–2020 protests. This, in turn, might encourage the eventual desectarianization of politics. The failure on the part of ruling elites to respond to this pressure or accommodate new forms of mobilization will further delegitimize the system, which might result in more radicalized action from newly mobilized groups.

The process of sectarianization in Iraq was not simply the result of the existence of various ethnic and sectarian communities. It was largely shaped by the movement from the paradigm of the modernizing state to authoritarian patrimonialism under the rule of Saddam Hussein, and then the adoption of an ethno-sectarian model of governance after the American occupation. Rather than the state acting as the main engine of development, as postcolonial elites assumed it would, it became the main venue for representing and negotiating the demands and interests of increasingly essentialized ethno-sectarian groups. This led to the institutionalization of sectarianism and the emergence of identity-centered politics, diminishing the state as an actor independent from its subcultural components.

A weakening of civil society and the decline of the middle class since the 1990s accompanied the transformation of the state. As a result, religious, tribal, and other "traditional" networks took on functions once jealously guarded by the state, thus filling the authority vacuum. Along with post-2003 process of state building and the violent conflicts that accompanied it, a neo-patrimonial model, incorporating state and nonstate actors, has evolved. Neo-patrimonialism in Iraq was sectarianizing, but it also mitigated the effects of sectarianization by preventing the consolidation of power by sectarian state actors. The combination of ethno-sectarian politics and neo-patrimonialism produced a largely dysfunctional state that is facing increasing pressure to reform itself and become more effective in dealing with deepening socio-economic challenges. This has already created demands to move toward a politics that is not centered on identity. The failure to do so would likely lead to increasing authoritarianism or a new round of radicalization and conflict.

Part 4

GLOBAL AND REGIONAL DYNAMICS OF THE NEW MIDDLE EAST

Chapter 13

THE POST-UPRISING TRANSFORMATION OF INTERNATIONAL RELATIONS IN THE MIDDLE EAST AND NORTH AFRICA

Fred H. Lawson

INTERNATIONAL RELATIONS IN THE MIDDLE EAST AND NORTH Africa (MENA) changed in three notable ways following the wave of popular uprisings that swept across the region beginning in the winter of 2010–2011. First, states throughout MENA became more truculent in their dealings with one another. Second, the dominant mode of regulating interstate disputes shifted from an admixture of diplomatic initiatives and economic statecraft to the exercise of military force. Third, the MENA regional security complex—or more precisely, the four overlapping regional security complexes that make up the MENA supercomplex—expanded to incorporate four adjacent interstate conflict zones. Taken together, these developments entail a transformation of the basic structure of the pre-uprising regional order.

HEIGHTENED TRUCULENCE

In the aftermath of the 2003 Gulf War, Iran, Turkey, Saudi Arabia, Egypt, and Algeria adopted comparatively accommodative postures toward one another and neighboring countries alike. The authorities in Tehran made sustained overtures to both Turkey and Iraq, and engaged in a marked rapprochement with the Kurdistan Regional Government (KRG) of northern Iraq. Relations with Saudi Arabia remained frosty, yet Tehran's long-standing rivalry with Riyadh exhibited a substantial degree of restraint, most notably with regard to contests for influence over internal affairs in Iraq and Lebanon. When war broke out between the Lebanon-based Party of God (Hizbullah) and Israel in July 2006, the Islamic Republic pointedly refrained from intervening in the conflict and dispatched its foreign minister to Istanbul and Cairo to explore ways to end the fighting. Meanwhile, the strategic doctrine and force structure of both the regular armed forces and the Islamic Revolutionary Guard Corps (IRGC) highlighted territorial defense, along with retaliatory deterrence, in a deliberate attempt "to avoid antagonizing [the country's] neighbors."[1]

As Henri Barkey shows in his contribution to this volume, Turkey in 2003–2004 launched a broad campaign to mitigate or resolve outstanding problems with neighboring countries, largely as a way to brighten the prospects for Turkish trade and investment in the MENA region. Particularly striking was the rapid improvement in relations with Syria, which had previously bordered on open warfare. Only marginally less remarkable was the sustained rapprochement between Ankara and the KRG. Turkey's relations with Iran improved as well. Under these circumstances, Turkey's steady alienation from Israel reflected—and reinforced—its broadly conciliatory approach to the other states of the region.

Egypt joined Saudi Arabia in castigating Hizbullah for engaging in inordinately provocative behavior in the run-up to the 2006 war, and both Cairo and Riyadh voiced intense animosity toward Hizbullah's primary patron, Iran. On the whole, however, Egyptian officials restrained themselves in regional affairs and tended to "stress the importance of inter-Arab economic cooperation through trade, joint ventures, and direct investment. [They also] encouraged the establishment of economic high commissions between Egypt and many Arab states."[2] At the same time, Gregory Gause observes that "the Saudi approach toward the rise of Iranian power, to the end of 2008, [consisted of] a subtle effort to both engage and contain Iran. The Saudis have avoided direct confrontation with Tehran."[3] King 'Abdullah bin 'Abd al-'Aziz Al Sa'ud took the extraordinary step of traveling to Ankara in November 2006 to discuss how Saudi Arabia and Turkey might reconcile their policies toward the Islamic Republic. Algeria similarly set out to resuscitate the moribund Arab Maghreb Union: it dampened its historical enmity toward Morocco; forged closer connections with nearby Mauritania, Mali, and Niger; and engaged in a halting reconciliation with Iran.

These five states implemented much more combative foreign policies in the wake of the 2010–2011 uprisings. Iran reacted to charges on the part of Arab Gulf governments that it was stoking popular discontent in Bahrain, Saudi Arabia, Kuwait, and the United Arab Emirates by redoubling efforts to solidify control over three islands that command the northern entry to the Strait of Hormuz, Abu Musa and the Greater and Lesser Tunbs, which the Iranian armed forces had occupied at the moment of the UAE's independence in December 1971. Officials in Tehran stepped up material and moral support for the beleaguered authorities in Damascus and adopted an overtly antagonistic posture toward their counterparts in Ankara as Turkey gravitated toward backing the Syrian opposition. The Islamic Republic pursued an equally truculent course of action toward Azerbaijan, then antagonized both Azerbaijan and Turkey by cultivating closer ties to Armenia.

More important, Tehran took steps to gain a strategic advantage vis-à-vis the Arab Gulf states by accelerating its medium-range ballistic missile (MRBM) program. An upgraded version of the Shehab-3 MRBM, code-named the Emad, was tested in early October 2015. The new model boasted a range of 1,700 kilometers and incorporated a guidance system that enabled it to strike distant targets with a degree of precision unprecedented for weapons manufactured in the Islamic Republic. The appearance of the Emad came shortly after a senior commander told reporters, "Iranians must not be afraid of enemy threats. We won the [1980–88] war with Iraq with the least [sophisticated kinds of] military equipment, but if ['Ali] Khamenei gave the orders today to attack Saudi Arabia, we have 2000 rockets ready to set off from Isfahan."[4] Iran's state television in January 2016 broadcast images of Speaker of the National Assembly 'Ali Larijani touring an underground storage facility that looked to be fully stocked with Emad missiles.

Furthermore, Tehran adopted increasingly belligerent tactics in its jockeying with Riyadh for influence inside Iraq. Iran-sponsored components of the Popular Mobilization (al-Hashd al-Sha'bi) advanced into Iraq's southern marches and took up positions well within striking distance of Saudi territory. IRGC units concurrently set up a forward base in the province of al-Anbar to train the Abu al-Fadl al-'Abbas Brigade Iraq Formation (Liwa Abu al-Fadl al-'Abbas Tashkil al-'Iraq); they then invited Hizbullah cadres to take charge of protecting east-west traffic along the desert highways between the Iraqi pilgrimage city of Najaf and the border with Syria. These provocative initiatives accompanied the deployment of short-range missile batteries outside the western city of al-Ramadi, which were reportedly operated by the Iraq-based Battalions of the Party of God (Kata'ib Hizbullah). Additional Iranian-built and Iranian-supplied missiles were deployed to Iraq's southern and western provinces during the summer of 2018.

Turkey's relations with surrounding states became more truculent as well after 2010–2011. Rapprochement toward Iran and Syria was replaced by renewed combativeness, and rivalry intensified vis-à-vis Saudi Arabia and Egypt. In his chapter, Barkey provides a detailed analysis of how Ankara, arguably frustrated by its inability to capitalize on the Arab uprisings, assumed an increasingly belligerent tone with friends and foes alike.

As Gause demonstrates in his contribution to this volume, Saudi Arabia adopted an equally pugnacious posture in the aftermath of the uprisings. Saudi officials took the lead in coordinating the Gulf Cooperation Council (GCC) response to the uprising against the monarchy in Bahrain and claimed that they were doing so to block Iranian aggression. Riyadh concurrently provided material support for the external leadership of the Syrian uprising, although the Saudi authorities proved more reluctant than their Qatari counterparts to supply weapons to the local militias that initiated the armed struggle against the Ba'ath Party–led regime. After Islamist militants seized the initiative on the ground during the winter of 2012–2013, the Saudi government sponsored an assortment of armed formations that competed against the two most prominent radical Islamist formations, the Battalions of the Free of Syria (Kata'ib Ahrar al-Sham) and the Assistance Front for the People of Syria (Jabhat al-Nusrah li Ahl al-Sham).

Egyptian foreign policy became more contentious as well. Officials in Cairo took steps to challenge the upstream states of the Nile River basin, particularly Ethiopia, regarding policies that threatened to diminish Egypt's supply of fresh water. As early as March 2011, Prime Minister 'Isam Sharaf announced that he would travel to Addis Ababa to insist that the Ethiopian authorities guarantee the existing allocation of Nile water. Successive meetings between the two countries' foreign ministers over the winter of 2011–2012 made no progress toward resolving the dispute. On May 28, 2013, Addis Ababa announced that the Blue Nile was going to be diverted so that construction of the Grand

Renaissance Dam could begin in earnest. Liberal and radical Islamist members of the Egyptian Council of Representatives demanded immediate military action if the diversion infringed on Egypt's historical water rights. The rising chorus of bellicose pronouncements from the legislature persuaded President Muhammad Morsi to declare that "Egypt's water security cannot be violated in any way," and that "all options are open" to keep Nile water flowing northward.[5]

Tensions between Cairo and Addis Ababa abated with Morsi's abrupt ouster in July 2013. Egypt's new minister of irrigation and water resources told reporters that the post-Morsi leadership had formulated "a new vision" regarding relations with Ethiopia. Prospects for an amicable resolution of the conflict nevertheless dimmed as the months went by and Ethiopian officials offered no tangible concessions. Ethiopia's minister of water resources remarked in May 2015 that "the dam construction will never stop. We will continue negotiating on [the] hiring of consultants and will continue negotiation on the process of studies, but [all these] processes will not affect the dam construction."[6] By the spring of 2017, senior Egyptian officials expressed mounting frustration over Ethiopia's unwillingness to address their concerns and Sudan's shift toward Ethiopia's position concerning the dam.

Algeria, too, became more assertive following the 2010–2011 uprisings. In the words of the International Crisis Group, Algiers began to "compete with France over shaping [North Africa's] security infrastructure" and emerged as "the lead backer of the Nouakchott Process, launched by the A[frican] U[nion] in March 2013, which [gathered] together eleven Maghreb, Sahel and West African countries to promote regional security cooperation."[7] Algerian officials played a particularly prominent role in convening the Inter-Malian Dialogue, an initiative that brought together the most influential armed factions in northern Mali to discuss possible forms of administrative autonomy. The talks culminated in a provisional agreement that was signed in Algiers in May 2015.

When fighting escalated in Libya during 2011–2012, Algeria warned that outside intervention would produce greater instability throughout North Africa. After the militias active in Libya coalesced into two rival camps in the summer of 2014, the authorities in Algiers cajoled all of the warring parties to take part in a national reconciliation project. Yet Algerian commanders in June 2015 deployed troops along the Libyan frontier and reportedly ordered them to shoot to kill anyone who tried to cross the border. Furthermore, Algiers in

September 2016 dropped its long-standing opposition to the Egypt-led effort to supply arms and equipment to the Cyrenaica-based Libyan National Army (LNA). A senior Algerian commander told reporters: "We have to be realistic. We're not going to wait indefinitely for the political parties to reach an agreement. Libya needs the law to be applied across the land and, above all, a strong army that can guarantee security up to its borders."[8]

Algeria's change of policy regarding external support for the LNA reflected a notable strategic reconciliation with Egypt. In March 2016, the two countries signed a memorandum of understanding that laid the groundwork for more extensive collaboration between their respective internal security forces. Algerian officials balked, however, when the Egyptian foreign ministry went on to suggest that the two states' regular armed forces undertake joint tactical operations in conjunction with contingents of the LNA. Such intervention would have contravened the strict prohibition against interfering in the domestic politics of other countries that is commonly believed to be enshrined in the Algerian constitution.

Meanwhile, Algeria continued to nurture cooperative relations with Iran, which most MENA states considered highly provocative. The authorities in Algiers refused to sever diplomatic ties with Tehran during the Saudi-Iranian crisis of January 2016, and they maintained a working relationship with the Iran-backed regime in Damascus even as other Arab governments voiced support for its adversaries. Rapprochement with the Islamic Republic did raise the prospect that Algeria might act as intermediary in the civil war in Yemen that pitted the Iran-backed Supporters of God movement (Ansar Allah, commonly called the Houthis) against a Saudi-led coalition supporting President 'Abed Rabbo Mansour Hadi. But as the fighting in Yemen intensified, Algiers's campaign to improve ties with Tehran aggravated long-standing tensions with Riyadh. When animosity between Saudi Arabia and Qatar flared during the summer of 2017, the Algerian government adopted a non-committal posture toward the confrontation in the Gulf. Such studied impartiality signaled de facto sympathy for Doha, with whom Algiers had forged strong diplomatic and economic links.

Moreover, Algeria stepped up pressure on Morocco to honor the commitments Rabat had made as part of the 1991 cease-fire that had terminated the fighting over the Western Sahara. President 'Abd al-'Aziz Bouteflika in

November 2013 demanded that the African Union create a mechanism to monitor human rights violations in the disputed territory if the organization opted to readmit Morocco as a full member. The demand prompted the Moroccan government to recall its ambassador from Algiers and to start building a wall along the boundary between the Moroccan-controlled portion of the Western Sahara and the area controlled by the Algerian-backed Polisario movement. Algerian engineers initiated work on a parallel barrier a year later. Animosity flared again in the spring of 2018, when officials in Rabat charged that Hizbullah agents operating out of the Iranian embassy in Algiers had been giving combat training to Polisario cadres.

In short, five primary protagonists in the MENA international arena have pursued markedly combative, if not actually belligerent, foreign policies in the wake of the 2010–2011 uprisings. Each of these states exhibits little, if any, inclination to propose or accept compromise solutions to ongoing regional disputes or to make significant concessions to its adversaries. On the contrary, countries throughout the region display a propensity to engage in truculent behavior and employ inherently coercive tactics in their interactions with their neighbors.[9]

DISPUTE REGULATION THROUGH MILITARY FORCE

MENA states tended to refrain from employing military force as a means of regulating regional disputes in the years following America's 2003 invasion of Iraq. From March 2003 to March 2011, governments there initiated fewer than sixty bilateral militarized interstate incidents, that is, one threat of military force or other bellicose action against surrounding states and nonstate organizations every six or seven weeks. After armed conflict broke out between Hizbullah and Israel in July 2006, for instance, the chief of staff of the Iranian armed forces told reporters that the Islamic Republic would "never militarily" take part in the fighting. Turkey scaled back its armed incursions into northern Iraq and carried out a substantial reduction of military forces stationed along the border with Syria. In much the same way, officials in Riyadh called for multilateral deliberations rather than punitive attacks in the face of clear evidence that Tehran had accelerated its nuclear research program. Only along its exposed southern flank did Saudi Arabia carry out substantial military operations, which took the form of sporadic clashes with Yemen's Supporters of God.

In the aftermath of the 2010–2011 uprisings, by contrast, exercising military force as a means of regulating interstate disputes became common practice for MENA governments. At least 167 bilateral militarized interstate incidents occurred from March 2011 to March 2019—an average of about two every month. The commander of the Islamic Republic's regular army pointedly warned in April 2012, for example, that "in case of any aggression, and if the problem [regarding Abu Musa and the Tunbs] is not resolved through political channels, the military forces are prepared to show Iran's might to the offender state."[10] Iranian warships patrolling the waters of the southern Gulf at the same time stepped up harassment of fishing boats operating out of Saudi Arabia and the UAE.

In August 2014, the Islamic State of Iraq and Syria (ISIS) swept across north-central Iraq and seized the Iraqi town of Jalawlah, not more than 30 kilometers away from the border with Iran. Iranian commanders dispatched units of both the regular armed forces and the IRGC to assist Kurdish fighters (peshmerga) affiliated with the KRG in recapturing the town. Iranian troops then carried out joint operations with KRG-affiliated peshmerga and the Tehran-aligned Badr Organization (Munazzamah Badr) to drive ISIS out of the adjacent towns of Amirli and Sulaiman Bak. Friction subsequently arose between the Iran-sponsored militias that made up the Popular Mobilization and local Kurdish and tribal formations battling ISIS in Diyala, Salah al-Din, and al-Anbar provinces. Nevertheless, IRGC personnel continued to collaborate with Kurdish fighters and Badr Organization cadres to expel ISIS from territory along the KRG's southern boundary, while the Islamic Republic's elite 81st Armored Division fought alongside KRG-affiliated peshmerga units and the militant Kurdistan Workers' Party (PKK) to push ISIS out of the town of Khanaqin on the Iran-KRG border.

Turkish military operations in the MENA escalated even more sharply during the course of the uprisings. Repeated air and ground incursions resumed in northern Iraq. Persistent skirmishes along the border led to a large-scale offensive in northern Syria in August 2016, followed by a more extensive intervention in the fall of 2019. Ankara signed an agreement with Sudan in December 2017, according to whose terms the Turkish navy would modernize the Red Sea port of Suwakin and establish a permanent forward base there. January 2020 saw the deployment of Turkish troops to Libya to protect the leadership in Tripoli from the rapidly advancing LNA.

As Gause recounts in his contribution to this volume, Saudi Arabia took an unprecedented turn toward using the armed forces as a dispute-regulating instrument in the spring of 2011. The Saudi-led effort to prop up the regime in Bahrain entailed direct intervention by Saudi and UAE military units and internal security personnel. In March 2015, Riyadh launched a large-scale air campaign against the Supporters of God in Yemen. Saudi and UAE forces mounted a combined air and ground offensive in southern Yemen four months later. The bombing raids persisted until April 2016, when a truce took effect to allow representatives of the Supporters of God to journey to Kuwait for talks with representatives of President Hadi. The negotiations and attendant cease-fire collapsed after the Supporters of God lobbed ballistic missiles into Saudi territory, prompting Saudi commanders to order air strikes that were even more destructive and indiscriminate than before.

Saudi policy with regard to the Syrian civil war became more bellicose after Russian troops intervened in the conflict at the end of September 2015. Russian air attacks against fighters aligned with the Saudi-sponsored Army of Conquest (Jaysh al-Fath) prompted Foreign Minister 'Adil al-Jubair to threaten that, unless President Bashar al-Assad relinquished power at once, the kingdom would undertake military operations on Syrian territory. At the end of the year, Riyadh put together a thirty-four-nation coalition to combat radical Islamist movements like those active in Syria and Iraq; the coalition's initial operations included joint air and naval maneuvers in the northern Gulf and the deployment of Saudi warplanes to Incirlik in southern Turkey. More extensive exercises took place in February 2016, during the course of which the kingdom reaffirmed its willingness to contribute troops to fight ISIS. When senior commanders of the so-called anti-terrorism coalition finally gathered in Riyadh that March, however, they discussed how to disrupt funding for transnational radical organizations rather than how to conduct military operations against militant Islamists.

By the spring of 2014, Egyptian officials were drawing a connection between the activities of Islamist militants in the Sinai and the civil war raging in Libya. The LNA's General Khalifah Bilqasim Haftar at that point invited Cairo to undertake "all necessary military actions inside Libya" that might help to restore order in the border area between the two countries.[11] Egyptian commanders seized the opportunity to augment ground and naval forces stationed along the frontier. The buildup failed to deter Libyan radicals calling themselves the Supporters of the Islamic Way of Life (Ansar al-Shari'ah) from seizing a cluster of military bases outside Benghazi in early August. Following this offensive, Egyptian warplanes bombed the encampments and supply depots of the Supporters of the Islamic Way of Life and other militias battling the LNA in eastern and central Libya. A second wave of Egyptian air strikes and naval bombardments took place that autumn.

Operations by the Egyptian armed forces inside Libya accompanied an augmentation of Egypt's military presence at the southern end of the Red Sea. Cairo expressed a willingness to contribute troops to the Saudi-led offensive against the Supporters of God, although few, if any, ended up being dispatched. A flotilla of Egyptian warships took up positions in the Gulf of Aden at the end of March 2015. This deployment, in the context of rising animosity between Egypt and Sudan over the Nile River and Cairo's decision to relinquish control over a pair of islets at the mouth of the Gulf of Aqaba to Saudi Arabia, led the Sudanese government to demand that Egypt engage in negotiations to determine the permanent disposition of the disputed border zone known as the Halayib Triangle. Cairo flatly refused, charging that Khartoum was manipulating the dispute over Halayib to compel Egypt to make concessions regarding the future allocation of Nile water. The Sudanese government stood its ground, and in March 2017 it set up a special commission to demarcate the boundary. The day after the commission was created, the head of the National Defense and Security Committee of Egypt's Council of Representatives declared, "Neither the Egyptian people nor the armed forces will let go of a single centimeter of the Egyptian territory."[12] Cairo inaugurated a new ground, air, and naval complex on the Red Sea coast ninety kilometers north of the Halayib Triangle in January 2020 and reached an agreement with Eritrea three months later that allowed Egypt's Southern Fleet to use Nora Island as a forward station.

Algeria's constitutional prohibition against foreign military intervention prevented authorities in Algiers from using the armed forces as a means of regulating regional disputes. Algerian officials consistently criticized the involvement of outside armies in the Libyan civil war, even after radical Islamists based in southwestern Libya raided the massive Algerian natural gas plant at In Aminas in January 2013. Following that attack, it became harder for the Algerian government to maintain strict adherence to the principle of noninterference. Reports began to circulate that units of the Algerian special forces were carrying out clandestine operations inside Libyan territory. More visibly, in May 2014 Algeria "signed a cooperation accord with Tunisia that granted it 'rights of hot pursuit' or the ability to engage in cross-border military actions on Tunisian soil," a move that indicates "Algeria has inched closer to a more flexible attitude as far as intervening militarily on foreign soil" is concerned.[13] Sure enough, May 2020 brought news that the nonintervention clause of Algeria's constitution would be amended so as to permit contingents of the country's armed forces to participate in foreign peacekeeping operations, "within the framework of the United Nations, the African Union and the League of Arab States."[14]

Military force has therefore become a major instrument of dispute management throughout the MENA in the years after the uprisings. Cross-border military operations occur more frequently and on a larger scale than during the eight years following the 2003 Gulf War. More important, states across the region have developed a common predisposition to deploy their armed forces at the first sign of trouble rather than holding back when confronted with a situation that might or might not turn out to be a significant external threat.

EXPANSION OF THE REGIONAL SECURITY COMPLEX

Prior to the 2010–2011 uprisings, the MENA regional security complex consisted of four distinct zones of interstate conflict. The first zone was made up of Iran, Iraq, Saudi Arabia, and the five smaller GCC states (Kuwait, Bahrain, Qatar, the UAE, and Oman); the second included Iran, Iraq, Turkey, and Syria; the third involved Egypt, Israel, Syria, Jordan, Lebanon, Iraq, and Saudi Arabia; and the fourth consisted of Libya, Tunisia, Algeria, and Morocco. In each of these conflict zones, actions undertaken by one state to protect or enhance its own security had a direct impact on the security of the other states. That is to say, security policies implemented by one state generated externalities that imposed a significant cost on the others.

In the aftermath of the uprisings, four additional zones of interstate conflict became incorporated into the MENA regional security complex: the first consists of Turkey, Iran, and the republics of the South Caucasus; the second is made up of Saudi Arabia, the smaller GCC states, Yemen, Sudan, Eritrea, Djibouti, Ethiopia, and Somalia; the third includes Egypt, Sudan, South Sudan,

Ethiopia, Eritrea, Uganda, and Kenya; and the fourth involves Libya, Algeria, Morocco, Mauritania, Mali, Niger, and Chad.

Strategic rivalry between Iran and Saudi Arabia started to spill into the South Caucasus immediately following the dissolution of the Soviet Union, but this trend accelerated after 2010–2011. Tehran forged connections with the countries of the area in response to a series of strategic initiatives by Israel, which cultivated particularly close military and economic ties to Azerbaijan. The Islamic Republic itself looked to Azerbaijan to supply fighters for the Iran-sponsored militias that moved into Syria during 2014–2015. Efforts to strengthen relations with Baku became more pressing for the authorities in Tehran after popular restiveness erupted in predominantly Azerbaijani districts of northern Iran. In April 2015, Iran's minister of defense traveled to the Azerbaijani capital and proposed to set up a bilateral commission to coordinate security policies. The proposal included an offer to supply an assortment of Iranian-made weapons to Azerbaijan's armed forces. Ongoing rapprochement between the two countries set the stage for an October 2017 visit by a pair of Azerbaijani warships to the Iranian naval base at Enzeli on the Caspian Sea and culminated in the initial meeting of the Joint Working Group on Military Cooperation at the end of that month.

Iran's activities in the South Caucasus soon attracted the attention of the GCC states. Saudi officials made a concerted effort to persuade Azerbaijan to join the coalition against radical Islamists that it spearheaded in the spring of 2016, which Tehran strenuously resisted. At the same time, Saudi Arabia and the UAE ordered armaments from Georgia's state-run munitions company. The authorities in Doha welcomed Azerbaijan's President Ilham Aliyev in February 2017, and two months later hosted Armenia's President Serge Sargosyan—who arrived in Qatar from an official visit to the UAE. Riyadh then dispatched the head of Saudi Arabia's new ministry for Gulf affairs to Baku on three separate occasions that spring. The second half of 2017 saw the kingdom undertake to improve relations with both Turkmenistan and Tajikistan. In response, Iran deployed an upgraded missile corvette at Enzeli, increasing to six the number of ships in its Caspian Sea flotilla.

Turkey's military offensive against the predominantly Kurdish enclave of ʿAfrin in northern Syria in early 2018 heightened tensions throughout the South Caucasus. The Kurdish Democratic Federation of Northern Syria circulated appeals for public support in Armenia, while Turkish officials solicited material and moral backing from the population of Azerbaijan. Azerbaijani nationalists reciprocated by distributing inside Turkey photographs of fighters in the disputed territory of Nagorno-Karabakh, who were posing alongside artillery shells that bore the slogan "Karabakh is Turkish, and will remain Turkish." Other pro-Azerbaijan lobbyists claimed that Armenia was providing weapons and supplies to the primary Syrian Kurdish militia, the People's Protection Units (YPG). At least one prominent YPG commander boasted an Armenian family background, although he had been born and raised in Turkey. The spillover from Ankara's 'Afrin offensive prompted a substantial rise in friction along the contested Azerbaijan-Armenia border.

The MENA security complex expanded southward as well. This took place on two battlefronts. In the first, Saudi Arabia, Qatar, and the UAE found themselves drawn to the Horn of Africa by three overlapping developments. The jump in world food prices that occurred during the opening decade of the twenty-first century gave GCC governments a strong incentive to boost investment in agricultural land, and Riyadh, Doha, and Abu Dhabi turned to Sudan, Ethiopia, Uganda, and Kenya as prospective breadbaskets. Qatar pushed matters a step further by proposing to create additional arable land by constructing a massive irrigation scheme in central Sudan that would have siphoned off more than 1 percent of the total annual downstream flow of the Nile River. This project elicited fierce opposition not only from Cairo but also from Riyadh and contributed to the crisis in Saudi-Qatari relations that erupted in March 2014.

At the same time, Saudi Arabia, Qatar, and the UAE moved to confront Iran, which had forged partnerships with Sudan during the late 1980s and with Eritrea and Djibouti after 2007. Beginning in late 2008, Iranian warships routinely called at the Eritrean port of Assab as part of the multinational campaign against Somalia-based pirates. Saudi officials charged that the Iranians took advantage of these stopovers to deliver arms and equipment to be forwarded to the Supporters of God in Yemen. When Riyadh deployed patrol boats along the Yemeni coast to interdict such shipments in November 2009, Iranian commanders announced their intention to station a destroyer at the southern end of the Red Sea. President Mahmud Ahmadi-Nejad traveled to Djibouti that same year and concluded a half dozen bilateral economic agreements.

Qatar riposted to Iranian advances in the Horn of Africa by stepping in to broker an agreement between the government in Khartoum and the secession-ists of Darfur. Doha subsequently mediated a cease-fire between Eritrea and Djibouti regarding the disposition of contested territory, and in June 2010 de-ployed two hundred Qatari troops along the Eritrea-Djibouti border to monitor the truce. Riyadh's counteroffensive against Tehran picked up momentum in early 2014, when Saudi officials abruptly suspended all transactions involving financial institutions based in Sudan. Contingents of the Saudi and UAE armed forces then took up forward positions in Djibouti. Following a violent altercation between UAE representatives and Djiboutian military officers in April 2015, however, the UAE expeditionary force decamped to Assab, shouldering aside the Iranian navy and transforming the sleepy harbor into a combined deepwa-ter port and tactical air base. UAE commanders also set up a training facility for the Somali armed forces and engaged in negotiations with the autonomous administration of Somaliland to obtain access to the port at Berbera.

Furthermore, Saudi Arabia, Qatar, and the UAE became more deeply en-tangled in the Horn of Africa as a result of their joint military intervention in the civil war in Yemen. Warplanes of the Saudi, Qatari, and Emirati air forces took part in the March 2015 bombing campaign, and warships from the three countries began to patrol the waters of the Bab al-Mandab and Gulf of Aden. One thousand Qatari troops backed by two hundred armored vehicles moved into positions along Saudi Arabia's southern border in April and May, and elite units of the UAE armed forces took the lead in pushing the Supporters of God out of Aden that summer.

Trilateral unity started to crumble during the winter of 2015–2016. Qatar and the UAE fell out over the role of the Yemeni Gathering for Reform, with the UAE foreign minister blaming that movement's reluctance to break completely with the Supporters of God for the fact that the latter retained command of the approaches to the central city of Ta'izz. The success of its troops on the battlefield tempted the UAE to consider establishing a long-term presence not only around Aden but also in the extensive oil-producing provinces of Hadramawt and Shabwah. UAE representatives conferred regularly with leaders of the pro-autonomy Southern Movement (al-Hirak al-Junubi) and permitted checkpoints throughout Aden, Dali' and Lahij provinces to display the flag of the old People's Democratic Republic of Yemen. Prospects for the emergence of an autonomous zone in the south brightened after UAE forces gained control of the port city of al-Mukalla in April 2016. Meanwhile, UAE companies invested substantial funds to improve infrastructure on the island of Socotra, which lies off the coast of al-Mukalla.

President Hadi responded to the UAE's drift toward bolstering southern autonomy by dismissing Prime Minister Khalid Bahhah, who enjoyed close ties to the UAE, and refusing to renew the contract for Dubai-based DP World to manage Aden harbor. Emirati commanders retaliated by preventing Hadi's airplane from landing at Aden upon his return from Riyadh, and UAE diplomats treated the president with disdain when he visited Abu Dhabi in April 2017 to try to patch things up. In contrast, Saudi officials joined the Yemeni government in expressing serious misgivings when the UAE helped organize a General Congress of Hadramawt at the end of April. The convention's concluding statement, which called for the establishment of an "independent province" in eastern Yemen, provoked President Hadi to dismiss the governor of Aden and four ministers of state who had aligned themselves with the UAE. As the fissure dividing Saudi Arabia from the UAE widened, Qatar and its allies in the Yemeni Gathering for Reform acquired greater leverage in both domestic and regional affairs. Consequently, the 2017 crisis that pitted Qatar against Saudi Arabia and the UAE reverberated throughout the Horn of Africa conflict zone.

Southward expansion of the MENA security complex also occurred due to intensified rivalry among Egypt, Sudan, and Ethiopia over the allocation of Nile River water and Kenya's more active involvement in Nile Basin affairs. In 2011, the governments of Kenya and South Sudan signed a memorandum of understanding to construct a pipeline that would link the oilfields of the latter to the former's Indian Ocean port of Lamu. After South Sudan signed a bilateral security pact with Egypt in March 2014, and Egypt offered to contribute troops to the new Protection and Deterrence Force (PDF) that had been created by the Inter-Governmental Authority on Development, Kenya riposted by sending contingents of its armed forces to join the PDF. This move flew in the face of Nairobi's long-standing neutrality toward the conflict in South Sudan.

More significant than Kenya's increased involvement in the dispute over the Nile was Uganda's. Kampala sent troops into South Sudan when warfare resumed in late 2013, and its proclivity to back the authorities in Juba over opposition forces led by Riek Machar Teny laid a foundation for sustained security cooperation between Uganda and Egypt. In the late summer of 2014, a delegation of senior Egyptian commanders visited the Ugandan ministry of defense to map out areas of common concern "including the shared resource of the River Nile."[15] At the same time, officials in Kampala cultivated closer ties to Khartoum and hosted Ethiopia's prime minister Hailemariam Desalegn, telling him that Uganda "need[ed] to have equitable use [of the Nile in order to] ensure [greater regional] cooperation."[16]

As a result of these developments, any flare-up in the dispute among Egypt, Sudan, and Ethiopia over the distribution of Nile River water became likely to entangle Kenya and Uganda. Furthermore, the dynamics of the interstate conflict over the Nile became bound up with developments in the South Sudan civil war. Egypt's campaign to establish a strategic partnership with Eritrea further complicated the Nile dispute. Cairo stepped up its military and economic links to Asmara shortly after construction on the Grand Renaissance Dam got underway, and Eritrean officials reciprocated by declaring that they fully backed the existing allocation of Nile water. By the spring of 2015, Egypt and Eritrea were discussing joint military operations as a way to promote regional security in the southern Red Sea.

Finally, expansion took place to the west. Algeria's efforts to restore order in Mali, combined with its resurgent rivalry with Morocco, dragged the Arab states of the southern Mediterranean littoral more deeply than ever into the expansive sub-Saharan region known as the Sahel. Islamist militants based in northern Mali, including the potent Supporters of the Religion (Ansar al-Din) movement, attacked police barracks and oil facilities in Algeria's southern desert during the winter of 2012–2013. Algerian military commanders responded by closing Algeria's lengthy borders with Mali and Niger. The Supporters of the Religion then boosted ties with a number of radical Islamist formations active in Niger and southwestern Libya, one of which claimed responsibility for the January 2013 raid on In Aminas. That same formation went on to attack several uranium-mining operations inside Niger.

Meanwhile, the Supporters of the Religion set up operational links to al-Qaeda in the Arab Maghreb, which enabled the two groups to capture large parts of the Malian cities of Timbuktu, Kidal, and Tessalit. These militants then carried out attacks in central Mali in conjunction with contingents of the Nigeria-based Islamist movement Boko Haram, which also expanded its activities into Niger. Faced with sustained and expanding disorder in the Sahel, the Algerian authorities in October 2017 revivified the regional counterterrorism structure (Comité d'état-major operationnel conjoint, or CEMOC) that they had created seven years earlier. This move also represented a riposte to the French-sponsored Group of Five Sahel Joint Force, which unlike CEMOC included Morocco as a member.

Jockeying between Algeria and Morocco for influence in the Sahel soon became connected to interstate rivalries in other conflict zones of the MENA. The authorities in Algiers have encouraged representatives of Tunisia, Egypt, and Sudan to take an active part in regional planning meetings sponsored by CEMOC. As early as May 2011, the GCC floated a proposal to invite Morocco to become one of its member states. Moreover, Saudi Arabia and the UAE were reported in early 2019 to be funding the activities of the Group of Five Sahel Joint Force.

International relations in the Middle East and North Africa have undergone a profound transformation in the wake of the wave of popular uprisings that took shape during the winter of 2010–2011. States all across the region have become more likely to act truculently in their dealings with one another and more apt to wield military force as a means of regulating interstate disputes. Meanwhile, the MENA regional security complex has enlarged so as to incorporate four adjacent conflict zones.

Consequently, the institutional context of the current MENA international arena differs markedly from the one that governed the pre-uprising regional order. Policy makers have adopted more expansive conceptions of national security, along with a proclivity to press home whatever diplomatic, economic, or military advantage they happen to possess. At the same time, interstate disputes now involve a larger number and wider range of protagonists. This cluster of emergent institutions can be expected to prove significantly less conducive to orderliness than the structural configuration that shaped regional affairs prior to the uprisings.

Chapter 14

PROXY WAR AND THE NEW STRUCTURE OF MIDDLE EAST REGIONAL POLITICS

Marc Lynch

THE ARAB UPRISINGS NOT ONLY DISRUPTED THE DOMESTIC politics of states across the region, the massive wave of popular protest transformed international politics as well. New forms of proxy warfare and competitive intervention defined the post-2011 regional order, affecting the trajectory of almost every conflict and attempted transition. Syria's tragic war was shaped by the aid to rebels from actors such as Turkey, Saudi Arabia, and Qatar and to the regime by Iran and Russia. Support to Libya's revolution from Turkey, Qatar, Egypt, and the United Arab Emirates evolved into ever more direct interventions in support of competing factions, which contributed to the failure of Libya's transition. After Yemen's Gulf Cooperation Council–brokered transition collapsed, a coalition led by Saudi Arabia and the UAE directly intervened and Iran's support to the Houthi rebels increased.

The international effects on regional politics go beyond the proxy wars. The 2017 boycott of Qatar by Saudi Arabia and the UAE had ripple effects across the region and beyond, escalating local conflicts along ideological lines rooted in regional rather than local differences. Saudi Arabia's shocking detention of Lebanon's Prime Minister Saad Hariri in an effort to enforce a tougher line against Hizbullah disrupted Lebanese politics. Iran-backed attacks on Saudi oil facilities and US presence in Iraq repeatedly inflamed the risk of regional warfare. And through it all, Israel has cultivated ever closer and more public ties with leading Arab regimes, even with recurrent violence in Gaza, the paralysis of the peace process, and overt moves toward annexation of the West Bank.

What accounts for these turbulent changes, sudden shifts, and new forms of regional political action? This chapter argues that the Arab uprisings both revealed and generated fundamental changes in the structure of regional international relations in the Middle East. The uprisings, civil wars and troubled transitions created manifold, irresistible opportunities for competitive interventions by regional powers. The resulting shifts in the operation of power and perceptions of threat have created fundamental structural changes which will complicate the reformation of any stable regional order. Efforts to reimpose a regional order based on cooperation between a new Arab core and Israel against Iran are likely to fail because of these profound structural changes.

These changes can be grasped only at the systemic level, not through individual cases. The pattern of failed and weakened states affected the entire regional order in interdependent ways. The unpredictable behavior of key actors, and their seeming inability to correct or move on from terrible mistakes, are rooted in these structural changes. The regional order today is shaped by the profound insecurity felt by all regional elites, regardless of their current power or stability; by the proliferation of failed states and destabilizing forces; by uncertainty about the current or future balance of power; by a persistent crisis of governance; and by consistently counterproductive interventions and proxy wars.

The changes brought about by the Arab uprisings have played out across every level of analysis. The international system is no longer reliably unipolar, and American policy under both the Obama and Trump administrations became far less predictable. The regional balance of power and the lines of political competition have become far less clear and for more complex and contested. There are far fewer normative or practical limits on policies at home or abroad. States across the region may have beaten back popular protest for the time being, but they have been unable to solve any of the underlying economic or political problems, and in most cases have made them worse. As Paul Salem put it, "In an unstable regional order, countries' internal and external conflicts are mutually exacerbating: internal tensions in one country draw in external alignments and contribute to regional proxy conflict, and regional conflict is more likely to impose itself onto domestic contests and push states toward failure and civil war."[1]

THE STRUCTURE OF REGIONAL POLITICAL ORDER

Analysis of international order typically begins from the global level, before moving down toward more regional and local levels of analysis. From this perspective, the Arab uprisings coincided with a significant decline in US hegemony, as the global order shifted from a clearly defined unipolarity into a much murkier condition. The international order after 2011 has not yet become bipolar, despite Russian advances in the Middle East, and has not yet even become multipolar. But the inability of the United States to shape the course of events and the growing evidence of hedging behavior by even the closest American allies clearly suggest that the logic of unipolarity no longer applies.

That logic profoundly shaped regional politics from 1991 until the Arab uprisings. The end of the Cold War decisively shifted the structural logic of regional politics in ways that defined the alliance choices and the foreign policy behavior of every state in the Middle East. This is not to say that the United States achieved ideological hegemony or absolute control over events in the region. Managing the growing US imperium required constant military intervention and deep political management, and invited frequent challenges from allies and adversaries alike.

Nonetheless, the logic of regional order was clearly unipolar. Almost every state in the Middle East came to be aligned with the United States after 1991, while those few that did not (Iran, Syria, and Libya) were defined as rogue states beyond the pale of international order. What is more, both Syria and Libya made an effort to engage with the US-led regional order. Syria participated in American-sponsored peace talks with Israel for almost the entire decade of the 1990s until the death of Syrian President Hafez al-Assad, whereas Libya surrendered its chemical and alleged nuclear programs in 2003 in exchange for international rehabilitation. Iran, which remained defiantly outside the US-led regional order, instead became the patron of "resistance" trends of all varieties—not only Shiʻi or even Islamist, but of all those popular forces arrayed against the status quo.

This logic of unipolarity created expectations of US intervention, even in areas where there were no obvious American interests at stake, driving ever more expensive campaigns along the periphery for which there was little strategic logic or public support. Managing local conflicts and supporting local proxies to sustain the status quo became compelling interests in their own right in this system. Unipolarity meant that allies had considerable range of maneuver: Although they had nowhere else to go, the costs to the United States of cutting them off would be high. Washington might feel somewhat confident in promoting democratic reforms, for instance, because even popular politicians with anti-American views were compelled to remain within the alliance structure. But those allies could indulge in independent foreign policies and could rebuff American pressure, as the United States had little ability to sanction or punish allies. Finally, American unipolarity drove popular anti-Americanism, as well. The US role in sustaining and defending a broadly unpopular regional order made it an appropriate target for popular animosity, a target encouraged by ostensible American allies keen to have the anger of their own people directed elsewhere.

The invasion and occupation of Iraq, intended to demonstrate American unipolar dominance, instead profoundly destabilized the regional order that Washington had spent the previous twelve years holding in place. The occupation of Iraq shifted the local balance of power, removing constraints on Iran and bogging down the United States in an expensive quagmire that largely made other interventions unthinkable. The sectarian civil war spread both radical ideologies and animosities. Structurally, Iraq became a failed state at the center of the Middle Eastern order, inviting competitive intervention by surrounding regional powers. Iran, Saudi Arabia, Syria, and even Jordan were drawn into the Iraqi civil war, supporting local proxies and channeling resources in order to shape internal political outcomes. The Iraq War created the structural precedent for the regional disruptions that came in 2011 and presaged regional dynamics in the period after the uprisings.

The Arab uprisings of 2011 struck at the heart of the unipolar order. Washington found itself trapped between its long-stated democratic aspirations and the hard realities of the autocratic alliance structure it had built and nurtured. The uprisings targeted precisely the autocrats upon whom the United States had relied and in whose stability and security it had invested for decades.

Uprisings against hostile or unloved regimes such as Syria's and Libya's (and to some extent Yemen's) posed more of an opportunity than a problem, but challenges to Egypt's President Hosni Mubarak, Jordan's King Abdullah, and Bahrain's monarchy sharply challenged the core of the American imperium. American efforts to find a middle ground—of rhetorically supporting democratic movements while moving to protect allied monarchs and presidents whenever possible—pleased no one. Arab publics viewed the United States, even under Obama, as obviously and necessarily on the side of the hated status quo, whereas Arab leaders viewed America's rhetorical approval of the uprising as an existential betrayal.

The uprisings led Arab leaders to believe that the United States no longer could, or would, guarantee their survival. Their actions in response drove ever greater distance between them and Washington. Harsh repression against peaceful activists—especially the sectarian crackdown in Bahrain and the brutal massacre of Muslim Brotherhood protesters in Egypt—antagonized those in Washington committed to at least the appearance of democracy. UAE and Saudi support for a military coup in Egypt overturned a democratic transition which the United States had greatly valued. Efforts by regional players to intervene in arenas such as Syria frustrated American diplomats seeking to coordinate policy with America's partners. Gulf and Israeli opposition to the nuclear agreement with Iran angered Obama administration officials who viewed the agreement as their highest strategic priority.

This growing divide between the United States and its partners created opportunities for other international powers, especially Russia, to present themselves as an alternative. The forceful Russian intervention in Syria should have further alienated Moscow from Arab regimes that had spent years supporting the other side in that conflict. Instead, many Arab leaders concluded that Russia might be a more useful military ally given American reluctance to intervene and the growing divergence in preferences and worldview. By 2015, regional leaders—Arab, Iranian, Turkish, and Israeli alike—increasingly engaged with Moscow. These were rarely serious bids to change alliances, given the continuing American preponderance of power and the limited opportunities Russia could offer. But hedging did allow those leaders to play Russia off against the United States, using the flirtation with Russia to compel American behavior, arms sales, or rhetoric.

The United States did not lose any allies, nor did Russia gain any. Nevertheless, the new realities challenged the logic of unipolarity. Regional actors ceased to perceive the United States as the only game in town, and the United States repeatedly proved unable to coordinate policies among its ostensible allies or to dictate their behavior. In case after case, from Bahrain to Yemen to the 2013 Egyptian military coup, Washington found itself bending to the preferences of Saudi Arabia and supporting the kingdom's deeply counterproductive policies. To secure the support of its allies for the Iranian nuclear agreement, Washington had to resort to arms sales, security commitments, and support for otherwise objectionable policies, such as the Saudi-led war in Yemen. In the years following 2011, the United States was a unipolar power at the center of a regional order in which most of its erstwhile partners opposed its policies and resisted its strategies.

Changes in the international level coincided with significant changes in the regional distribution of power. Traditional powers faded from the scene, consumed by domestic problems, while power and influence shifted inexorably to the Gulf. The salience of the Israeli issue for regional politics changed in notable ways as attention shifted to other burning issues, opening up the possibility of open alliance between Arab states and Israel without resolving the Israeli-Palestinian conflict that had previously seemed unthinkable. And Iran's regional position evolved in paradoxical ways, as its power and influence rose even as it faced growing external challenges and domestic turbulence.

The shift of power to the Gulf was driven both by the unprecedented weakness of others and by the effective adaptation of those wealthy states to the new regional structure. The collapse of the traditional powers is as obvious as it is shocking.[2] Core states such as Syria and Iraq, as well as the second-tier power Libya, simply ceased to exist as functional states and instead became arenas within which other powers fought their battles. Another core state, Egypt, did not collapse completely, but, consumed by domestic political upheaval and utterly dependent on financial support from the Gulf, ceased to be an effective independent power.

This power vacuum at the center of the Middle East created opportunities for the powers on the periphery: Israel, Turkey, Iran, and the Gulf states. These states, relatively insulated from the failed states and chaotic wars at the center, were able to project power in various ways while paying limited costs. Their struggles for power and influence were at the heart of the proliferation of proxy wars and competitive interventions that have defined the post-2011 regional order.

Each of these peripheral states could bring different forms of power to bear. Israel enjoyed a qualitative military advantage over its neighbors and used that military power frequently to maintain deterrence against potential adversaries. The Israelis used airpower repeatedly in the post-2011 period against Gaza and, increasingly, against Hizbullah and Iranian targets in Syria. Israel's close relationship with the United States also served as a key source of power. The declining salience of the Palestinian issue in regional politics further enhanced Israeli regional power: Israel became a more palatable alliance partner for Arab states and faced fewer costs for its continued occupation of the West Bank and its violence against Palestinians.

Iran expanded its power during this period but faced new challenges.[3] The negotiation of the nuclear agreement with the P5+1 (the UN Security Council members plus Germany) reduced external pressure and sanctions, providing some limited economic benefits while increasing diplomatic contacts and reducing the immediate threat of war. The Iranian state was far more capable and robust than those of its counterparts in the Arab center. While Iran repeatedly faced rounds of domestic political turbulence, including a remarkable outburst of protest in early 2018, its state and political system proved more than sufficient to sustain regime security. At the same time, Iran developed a distinctive model of proxy warfare that proved very well adapted to the new regional environment. Iran exerted power across the region's failed states through a combination of means: directly deploying IRGC personnel; using relationships with local organizations such as Hizbullah and the Houthis; building local militias in Shi'i communities such as Iraq; deploying Shi'i militias recruited abroad—for example, Iraq and Afghanistan—into war zones, such as Syria. These single-minded, highly organized proxies typically proved more effective and disciplined than those recruited by Iran's Arab and Turkish rivals.

Turkey, for its part, enjoyed significant advantages at the outset of the Arab uprisings. Its robust economy, large military, and NATO membership made it a formidable player by Middle Eastern standards. Its democratically elected moderate Islamist leadership seemed like an attractive model for transitioning

Arab countries, whereas its soap operas and television broadcasts offered a form of soft power. Taking vocal positions critical of Israel while building bridges to Assad's Syria, Erdoğan's Turkey had sought to use its bridging position to become a key broker between Iran and the West. After 2011, it sought to play a pivotal role in Syria and North Africa. Its projection of power into the Syrian war, however, proved catastrophic, although it did emerge as the decisive power for the Syrian uprising by virtue of geography, hosting Syrian political and military organizations along with millions of refugees. Its open-border policy and facilitation of the movement of supplies to Syrian rebels sustained the insurgency but also strengthened radical Islamist groups that ultimately included ISIS. It found itself competing with Saudi Arabia and Qatar for patronage over the Syrian insurgency while paying far more direct costs than its more distant counterparts. Finally, the role of Kurdish groups in the Syrian war intersected dangerously with Turkish domestic politics, ultimately putting Turkey into direct conflict with the United States.

Qatar and the UAE emerged as the prototypical powers of the post-uprisings era. Each enjoyed distinct advantages that were unusually well suited to the new forms of emergent political competition. Each possessed great wealth, a small population, and competent administrators. Their highly effective repressive apparatus enabled them to remain largely insulated from proxy warfare on their own soil; even the concerted efforts of Saudi Arabia and the UAE to destabilize Qatar in 2017 by promoting opposition groups and dissident royal family members amounted to little. Each enjoyed media empires that shaped regional public opinion and gave a platform to preferred proxies and friendly voices. Each had highly professional and well-equipped militaries, which could project direct hard power in ways not typical of historical Arab armies.

The regional structure after 2011, then, became a multipolar one in which surviving states, mostly on the periphery, competed through proxy warfare on the soil of the failed and failing states at the center. The lines of alliance and competition were not completely consistent. The alignment against Iran that grouped Saudi Arabia, Egypt, the UAE, and Israel followed directly on the pre-uprisings regional order. But the anti-Iran coalition was disrupted by the campaign against Qatar, which divided the GCC and prevented the full consolidation of an anti-Iran alliance system. Iranian proxies seemed to advance relentlessly in Syria and Iraq despite the efforts of this Arab coalition, while Hizbullah's position in Lebanon remained unchallenged and the exigencies of war drove Yemen's Houthis closer to Iran for military support.

While Gulf leaders often blamed Iran for all the region's problems, in fact Tehran had little significance in key arenas such as Egypt, Libya or the rest of North Africa. Competition among Gulf states, especially Qatar, Saudi Arabia, and the UAE, mattered as much as or more than the conflict with Iran in driving political rivalries across the region. During the initial Libyan intervention, all the Gulf states were on the same side, supporting the uprising against Qaddafi. However, during the following years Libyan politics divided between factions supported by the UAE and those supported by Qatar. Qatar and Saudi Arabia fought on the same side in Syria but often undermined their own proxies through their relentless competition for leadership and control. Qatar supported the post-Mubarak Egyptian government but was elbowed aside after the 2013 military coup supported by Saudi Arabia and the UAE. Saudi Arabia and the UAE intervened together in Yemen in support of the deposed government, but their interests diverged over time as each focused on its own zones of influence.

A key feature of this regional order that is not fully captured by the description of the rivalries among great powers is the importance of the unification of political space. The Arab uprisings, propelled by diffusion and demonstration effects, spread rapidly from one country to the next. In that environment, anything happening anywhere proved a threat to some and an opportunity to others. Regimes could not afford indifference to protests elsewhere in the region. At the same time, every state knew that others would likely intervene in the transitioning or failing states, meaning that they could ill afford to stand aloof for fear of their rivals taking advantage.

This brings us to the level of domestic politics. The proliferation of failed states and the domestic adaptations made by deeply insecure regimes shaped the post-2011 regional order.[4] Regime security theory has long been a dominant trend in the study of regional international relations. In this tradition, regimes pursue foreign policies primarily to guarantee their own survival rather than in pursuit of a more abstract national interest. Threats to regime survival more often emerge from inside than from outside borders, and foreign policy is typically designed to respond to those domestic threats. Regimes apply themselves to the acquisition of the material resources that will ensure political survival, either to push back against those who would support political opponents materially or ideologically or to deflect foreign political criticism that might resonate with citizens.

Structural changes in the international and regional political order directly affect the perception of those threats and of the possible foreign policy responses. The American response to the Arab uprisings, for instance, convinced many Arab regimes that an alliance with the United States was no longer an effective guarantor of their survival. The hedging behavior and public distancing from Washington may then have been less about specific grievances over Syria or Iran than about America's loss of credibility when it came to protecting its friends. Regionally, increasing interventionism by the peripheral powers made it even clearer that the primary threat to domestic stability may lie abroad. The role of Qatar, Saudi Arabia, and the UAE in Egyptian or Tunisian politics meant that regional competition was deeply interconnected with domestic political outcomes. This made foreign policy even more clearly an instrument for ensuring regime survival than in past eras.

The Arab uprisings also revealed the importance of state strength as a decisive intermediating variable in regional order. Simply put, most Arab regimes faced some sort of popular domestic challenge in 2011, with the diffusion of protests from Tunisia and Egypt clearly adding an international dimension to the threat. Some Arab regimes proved more competent at responding to those challenges than others. While Tunisia and Egypt failed and Libya and Yemen fractured, other regimes had the resources and political acumen to survive. Their responses varied along a continuum from repression to co-optation to political reform, but underlying those responses lay a relatively competent administrative and security apparatus that remained loyal and proved capable of implementing the regime's political strategy. States that lacked such an apparatus ceased to exist as de facto states.[5]

This variation in the state's internal strength is a critical part of international structure in today's Middle East. The hardened, competent, and well-endowed governing apparatus of the GCC are able effectively to control their own territory, blocking efforts at external interference and domestic political challenge alike. Failed or fragmented states, such as Libya, Syria, and Yemen, were unable to control their territory or population and became arenas for competition rather than actors in the new regional political order. And weaker surviving states, such as in Jordan, constantly struggled to maintain order through lucrative external alliances.

THE MEANS OF FOREIGN POLICY: PROXY WARFARE AND INTERVENTION

These structural changes across multiple levels provide the context within which different types of proxy and client networks have emerged. The forms of regional involvement in the Syrian, Libyan, and Yemeni wars have become deeply constitutive of political practice and possibility. Arab regimes now routinely do things that once would have been unthinkable: Egyptian and UAE air strikes in support of one faction in Libya and Turkish intervention in support of the other; relentless Saudi-UAE bombing of Yemen despite massive humanitarian costs and rising international condemnation; acceptance of Israeli air strikes and support for rebels in Syria; open cooperation between Arab states and Israel despite the lack of any progress toward a Palestinian state.

A toxic combination of perceived threat and opportunity generated pressures toward interventionism that were nearly irresistible.[6] The way the Arab uprisings rapidly diffused across very different Arab states in 2011 elicited a perception of the entire region as a unified political space. At the very least, every leader had to consider the possibility that an uprising or civil war in any other Arab country might suddenly and unexpectedly travel to his own. This perception of potential threat led regional powers to seek to block any potential change that might have negative consequences for them anywhere in the region—while also seeking to push changes that were favorable to them. The forceful Saudi response to the Bahraini uprising was, in part, a response to fear that democratic reforms empowering Shi'i movements could empower Iran on the regional stage, and could inspire Saudi Shi'is to demand similar political reforms.[7] The UAE's support for the 2013 military coup in Egypt was, in part, a move to block the consolidation of a pro-Qatar Muslim Brotherhood-led regime, which would have represented a major shift in the regional configuration of alliances.[8] Saudi and UAE intervention in Yemen was, in part, driven by the fear of the consolidation of power by a regime led by an Iran-aligned Houthi movement and a Saudi opponent, former president Ali Abdullah Saleh.

We therefore have to rethink how we measure and evaluate power, interests, and institutions to take into account these new forms of proxy warfare and regional competition. The structural changes described here created almost irresistible pressures toward proxy wars and interventions, trapping states and regimes within a competitive but counterproductive dynamic, even when they understand its failings. As F. Gregory Gause III points out, regional actors "are not confronting each other militarily; rather, their contest for influence plays out in the domestic political systems of the region's weak states. It is a struggle over the direction of the Middle East's domestic politics more than it is a purely military contest. The military and political strength of the parties to civil conflicts, and the contributions that outsiders can make to that strength, is more important than the military balance of power."[9] Such proxy wars tend to be extremely destructive and destabilizing, cutting against the prospects of either democratization or a stabilized regional order.[10]

These new forms of power are not only visible in the war zones. The interests and interventions of external powers quickly polluted democratization during transitions in Egypt, Libya, Tunisia, and Yemen. Coalitions that came to power through elections reflected a potential shift in the balance of proxies. When the Muslim Brotherhood won Egypt's elections in 2012, it not only caused a seismic shift in Egyptian politics but also shifted Egypt from a core position in the Saudi-UAE camp to the crown jewel of the Qatari camp. Qatar and the UAE intervened promiscuously in Tunisian politics, taking advantage of new opportunities to support politicians and friendly media outlets.

In countries where uprisings tipped toward civil war, competing external interventions accelerated state failure and ratcheted up conflict to ever higher levels of destruction.[11] The arming of insurgents and pro-regime militias shifts military power to forces outside the state, eroding any monopoly that had once existed over the means of violence. The proliferation of weapons in the hands of local militias, gangs, or warlords creates pockets within states in which the state is absent, or at least in which governance and authority are contested. The emergence of war economies, which generate illicit rents and black market opportunities, generates a strong interest in perpetuation of conflict.[12]

The negative effects of these interventions are exacerbated because outside powers have interests different from those of the locals, and thus have less incentive to compromise or to tailor policies to local conditions. Whereas

Syrians suffering massive death and displacement might be desperate to stop the fighting, distant powers such as Iran, Saudi Arabia, Qatar, and the United States pay a small price for fueling the Syrian war. Indeed, they often saw value in the continuation of a hurting quagmire. Proxy war is relatively cheap to these distant powers, giving them every incentive to continue. Even local actors who might prefer to compromise might be unable to do so because they depend on support from abroad and need to keep their sponsors satisfied.[13] This is why the political science literature has found that, generally, the more external involvement by competing powers, the longer civil wars continue, the more destructive they are, and the harder they are to resolve. Joint intervention by outside powers can end civil wars quickly and offer, perhaps, a path toward ending such wars. But multiparty external involvement by states with competing interests almost always prolong and intensify conflict.[14]

Countries are not equally good at working with proxies, of course. The very different types of relationships that can be formed should be seen as an important dimension of power in this new regional structure. Iran's ability to draw on experience and successful models of working at different levels of closeness with local Shiʻi militias, political parties, or religious institutions has been a key to its post-2011 projection of power.[15] During the early years of the conflict, Islamist-leaning factions in Syria were better able to draw on a wider range of private supporters across the Gulf to gain access to money and guns than were their more secular or liberal counterparts. Qatar's long-established relationship with the Muslim Brotherhood gave it points of entry into a well-organized and effective partner in almost every political arena.

But ideology and identity manifest in unusual ways. Proxy wars make strange bedfellows, which tends to complicate the grand narratives of regional affairs. Local allies are sometimes ideological allies; in other cases, however, they participate in alliances of convenience. In Libya, for example, the UAE and Qatar have drawn their allies from those who had preexisting business relationships with their sponsors, who then used them as conduits for aid and assistance.[16] Yemeni president Ali Abdullah Saleh, a longtime Saudi ally until he was forced from power, subsequently aligned himself with the Houthis. The fiercely anti-Islamist UAE nonetheless has struck deals with al-Qaeda in the Arabian Peninsula to ensure stability in its southern zones of control, and it welcomes some Islamist militias in its Libyan coalition.

The degree of "proxyness" changes over time and context as well. Before 2007, the Houthis had been almost completely independent from Iran. After years of war and external involvement, however, they became more intimately involved with Tehran.[17] Iran began to provide weapons technology and military advice to the Houthis, which it had never done before, creating new dependencies and new incentives on all sides. Before 2013, the Muslim Brotherhood of Egypt had never been anyone's proxy; following the coup and the Saudi-led listing of the Brotherhood as a terrorist organization, it became more dependent on Qatar and Turkey. Even Iraq's Shi'i Popular Mobilization Forces vary widely in terms of their dependence on Iran and the extent of their local embeddedness.

THE MIDDLE EAST THE UPRISINGS MADE

The Arab uprisings of 2011 have driven the emergence of a fundamentally new structure of regional politics with new methods of implementing policy, which is rapidly evolving. The high level of unpredictability and the incoherence in regional politics are rooted in structural change. There is also a high degree of uncertainty about the real balance of power at every level: international, regional, and domestic. States have discarded long-established norms governing acceptable foreign policy behavior, exacerbating uncertainty. The Arab uprisings left in their wake a profound sense of personal insecurity among Arab leaders, which magnifies the impact of this uncertainty. The unification of the Arab political space makes every development anywhere a measure of regional power and influence, as well as a potential threat to domestic security, raising the stakes of even seemingly marginal conflicts and making it exceptionally difficult for leaders to back down from even obviously disastrous campaigns. And the pattern of failed and transitional states creates an exceptionally large number of potential zones of intervention, generating tremendous complexity.

The responses by leading Arab regimes to these changes have had largely negative effects. Their interference in the post-2011 transitions severely wounded prospects for democracy, reinforcing or restoring autocracy across most transitional states with lasting effects on civil society and the prospects for democratic change. Their interventions into civil wars have contributed to strategic stalemate, radicalization, and humanitarian catastrophe. Their crosscutting battles for influence have undermined all efforts to coordinate effective regional responses to challenges, from the Obama administration's efforts to coordinate Syria policy to the Trump administration's efforts to unify Arab ranks against Iran.

The logic of political competition generated by these new structural conditions make it unlikely that these negative trends will be easily transcended. Current proposals to rebuild regional order and to dampen down the most brutal wars are still primarily road maps for one side's victory rather than serious bids for compromise and rebuilding. Saudi Arabia and the UAE, for instance, have come to accept that the high human costs of their war in Yemen require that the war be ended, but they propose to end it only through their own total victory. Syria's war has slowly ground toward a dispiriting conclusion, with Assad's external backers keeping him in power at tremendous human cost while external backers of the uprising eventually acceded to those imposed realities. The Islamic State has been destroyed as a territorial entity in Iraq and Syria, but its insurgency continues to evolve and adapt. The boycott of Qatar has proved difficult to resolve, and it appears likely to remain a feature of the regional landscape for at least the near term. The Trump administration's unilateral withdrawal from the Iran nuclear agreement and reimposition of sanctions has removed one of the few potential areas of regional cooperation on a matter of shared interest. The regional order made by the crushing of the Arab uprisings will not likely provide for stability or security any time soon.

Chapter 15

INTERNATIONAL LAW, USE OF FORCE, AND THE NEW MIDDLE EAST

Aslı Ü. Bâli

THE MIDDLE EAST AND NORTH AFRICA (MENA) REGION IS OFTEN thought of as exceptional from the perspective of international law. Unlike Europe, the Americas, and Africa, the MENA region has no comparable regional organization to facilitate cooperation and coordination.[1] The states of the MENA region also have relatively low participation in the principal multilateral agreements that make up the fabric of the postwar international legal order such as human rights treaties and multilateral trade agreements.[2] Other normative changes that have marked the international order, such as international environmental and labor protections, have had limited impact. Yet in truth the region has been profoundly marked by international law and is increasingly significant in reshaping core attributes of the international legal order. This is especially true with respect to the rules of the international security order, whether in terms of arms control, counterterrorism, or armed conflict.

A quick survey of the region in 2019 reveals the degree to which it is a crucible for interventions that have produced a New Middle East, while shifting conceptions of sovereignty, humanitarianism, and the prohibition on the use of force in the international order. These changes call into question the viability and legitimacy of the cornerstones of the United Nations–based international security order. In Iraq, the ravages of the 2003 intervention are still evident in the country's debilitated infrastructure and fragile public order some decade and a half after the American invasion and occupation. The fractious sectarian conflict unleashed by regime change in Iraq has metastasized across the region, with spillover effects from Syria to Yemen that have occasioned civil wars and further external interventions under various humanitarian and counterterrorism guises. Moreover, the emergence of the Islamic State of Iraq and Syria (ISIS), itself a consequence of sectarian militarization following the 2003 war, cut a new swath of devastation across Iraq and Syria. Last, humanitarian logics mixed with other motives provided the basis for a UN Security Council–backed intervention in Libya that also resulted in regime change paving the way for a civil war that has called into question the country's territorial integrity. The aerial bombardment campaign that flattened much of the country's infrastructure was justified in the name of a humanitarianism that was nowhere in evidence when the time came to stabilize, let alone rebuild, Libya.

In each of these conflicts, international law has been present in setting the parameters of external intervention and use of armed force as well as placing limits on access to arms and funding for both state and nonstate actors in the region. But the MENA region is not merely a site for the imposition of framings based in international law. The region has also contributed to the production of new interpretations of existing rules and the elaboration of new doctrines in the laws of armed conflict and arms control, as a sort of collateral effect of the so-called war on terror. This jurisgenerative role is evident in the areas of humanitarian intervention, in counterproliferation and counterterrorism doctrines, and in the loosening of the prohibition on the use of force and the ever-expanding exceptions to that prohibition.

The conflicts that have marked the region in the post–Cold War and post-9/11 periods have redistributed power, redefined alliances that shape the region's geopolitics and, in several cases, called into question the territorial integrity of states. To the degree that these conflicts—and attendant external interventions—have been mediated by international frameworks, the New Middle East has both shaped and been shaped by international law.

THE INTERNATIONAL SECURITY ORDER: FROM POSTWAR TO POST–COLD WAR

Public international law has long been the handmaiden of imperial orderings. International law served as the legitimating framework for the colonization of large regions of the world, with a sovereignty regime exclusively reserved for Europeans and their settler colonies.[3] The modern Middle East is itself very much a product of such international law framings, ranging from the nineteenth century colonization of parts of the region by European powers to the creation of the mandates system to the conditions set for decolonization from Palestine to Kuwait.[4] In the aftermath of World War II and the collapse of European empires another international legal order was established by the victorious powers.

The postwar international order, largely authored by the United States, resolved questions concerning borders, sovereignty, and the use of force through the UN Charter, a multilateral treaty creating the defining international organization of the new system. The United Nations provided a framework for decolonization, according sovereignty to all states in the postcolonial order. Sovereignty, in turn, carried the promise of a defense against external intervention and a guarantee that states would control the domestic jurisdiction of their territory. In exchange for these privileges of sovereignty, every member of the United Nations system pledged to abide by the new use-of-force regime whereby military aggression was prohibited. The UN prohibition on the use of force admits only three exceptions: self-defense following an armed attack, consensual uses of force (i.e., intervention at the request of the affected government), and collective self-defense authorized by the UN Security Council. In addition, the UN Charter lists among the objectives of the organization the protection and promotion of human rights, provisions that over time set constraints on states' domestic jurisdiction by universalizing minimum standards of conduct.

The institutional design of the UN collective security system rests on the twin pillars of the prohibition on the use of force and the executive primacy of the Security Council over judgments about maintenance of international peace. Moreover, the security architecture of the system deliberately accords its most powerful members the ability to prevent—that is, veto—any collective action that might compromise their interests. By adopting asymmetric voting rights for the permanent members—presumptively the most powerful states in the international system, each a recognized nuclear power—the UN Charter prioritizes peace (or at least the avoidance of cataclysmic conflict among its permanent members) above all other values. During the second half of the twentieth century the rivalry between the United States and the Soviet Union gave rise to indirect conflict and proxy wars, not nuclear exchanges.

When a great power engaged directly in peripheral conflicts, it was generally justified as intervention by invitation at the request of a local ally.

The covert interventions and proxy wars of the Cold War caused extreme violence from Africa to the Middle East to Southeast Asia to South and Central America, despite remaining formally consistent with the UN parameters. In the Middle East, the competition between the United States and the Soviet Union for influence and control over resources resulted in interventions like the overthrow of the democratically elected Iranian prime minister through a covert operation backed by the United States and United Kingdom in 1953. In addition, great powers competed to supply arms to various client states, with arms sales to Iraq in the 1980s prolonging and intensifying the Iran-Iraq War.

With the end of the Cold War, a region that (with the notable exceptions of postrevolutionary Iran, Syria, North Yemen, Libya, and, to a lesser extent, Iraq) was already largely in the pro-Western camp might have expected a significant peace dividend. The beginning of the 1990s was marked by optimism that the collective security model of the United Nations, paralyzed during the Cold War by the dueling vetoes of rival powers, might operate to enforce the prohibition on the use of force and realize the humanitarian potential of the UN Charter's design.

At first, a more progressive international order seemed at hand with reinvigorated transnational civil society movements advocating for human rights and environmental protections and new multilateral initiatives to better integrate a globalizing world in areas from trade to travel. For the Middle East, however, the newly unbridled collective security order proved destabilizing.

The invasion of Kuwait by Iraq in 1990 resulted from a series of grievances related to the Iran-Iraq War, which had ended two years earlier. Partly funded by loans from the Gulf Arab states, Iraq claimed that the Iran-Iraq War had defended those Gulf states from the threat of postrevolutionary Iran. At the end of that war, Baghdad balked at demands for repayment of the loans and began to complain of economic warfare. Iraq accused Kuwait of seizing oil assets from a disputed oil field on the border between the two countries and of pumping in excess of its OPEC quota, driving down oil prices. Attempts at a mediated resolution failed and Iraq invaded Kuwait in clear violation of its sovereignty and the UN prohibition on the use of force. Within less than six months of the invasion, the UN Security Council authorized coercive action by a multinational coalition led by the United States to liberate Kuwait.

The Iraq-Kuwait dispute was a jurisgenerative moment. Legal innovation from within the UN Charter framework enabled a devastating sanctions regime to be put in place that commanded worldwide adherence.[5] The United States built the case for war through incremental Security Council resolutions. When, in November 1990, the Security Council agreed to a resolution threatening enforcement action should Iraq fail to comply by a set deadline,[6] control of the collective security apparatus passed from the United Nations to the United States. With that resolution in place, the United States was able to adopt a unilateral definition of compliance and block others on the Security Council from slowing progress toward war.[7] The UN secretary-general, seeking a negotiated solution, lamented that the Security Council resolutions left him in a straitjacket.[8] In a few short years, the United Nations went from peacemaker in the Iran-Iraq War to an instrument of renewed military action in the Gulf.

The imprimatur of United Nations–based collective security enabled the United States to assemble, between November and January, a broad coalition that would participate in the military operation and crucially underwrite its costs. Beneath the rosy view of the 1991 Gulf War as a successful instance of Security Council–backed action lies a more complicated account of the relationship between international law and hegemony. The details of that account are contained in missed opportunities to resolve the conflict short of war and the punitive embargo that immiserated Iraq for more than twelve years. One lesson was that a reinvigorated Security Council would not necessarily be a stabilizing force if authority for coercive action became an irreversible delegation of power to the United States.

Between the August 1990 invasion of Kuwait and the UN-backed war in January 1991, there was immense pressure on the Baghdad regime, which resulted in several attempts by Iraq to negotiate over its withdrawal from Kuwait.[9] American opposition to a negotiated withdrawal that would have allowed Iraq to preserve its military capacities was a major stumbling block.[10] The invasion of Kuwait furnished the United States with an opportunity to accomplish several goals through military action against Iraq, which a negotiated withdrawal would thwart. Chief among these was asserting the indispensable role of the

United States in securing the flow of oil from the Gulf to allies in Europe and Asia and establishing the terms of a new Pax Americana.[11]

The US-led military operation centered on one of the most extensive aerial bombardment campaigns in history, with forty-two days of bombardment, followed by a ground campaign that is estimated to have resulted in as many as one hundred thousand Iraqi combatant deaths and the killing of thousands of civilians.[12] The war also resulted in the destruction of most of Iraq's infrastructure, both military and civilian, provoking a public health catastrophe across the country. At the end of the war, the embargo imposed on the country was not lifted but extended as a means of compelling Iraqi disarmament, making the rebuilding of the country nearly impossible and leaving the civilian population entirely dependent on the regime for subsistence rations. The sanctions remained in place for almost thirteen years, producing high rates of infant mortality and malnutrition and the spread of preventable diseases, the result of the collapse of the country's water, sewage, sanitation, and electricity systems.[13]

The war marked the beginning of what President George H. W. Bush termed the "new world order."[14] For the duration of the 1990s—notwithstanding the devastation of Iraq—there was a palpable sense of global optimism that the unipolar post–Cold War period would provide relative stability and prosperity worldwide. The Security Council became the premier forum for addressing conflicts and humanitarian crises from Somalia to Rwanda to Yugoslavia. Whatever the failings of the Security Council to prevent atrocities, new mechanisms, like the creation of international criminal tribunals, held the promise of accountability and multilateral cooperation that generated faith in the United Nations as a viable framework for international peace and security.

The Kosovo War brought the 1990s interlude of multilateralism to an end. From the collapse of the Soviet Union in 1991 through much of the decade, Russia was consumed with domestic turmoil. While Russia maintained its traditional alliance with Serbia during the Yugoslav Wars, it joined Western powers in supporting the Dayton Agreement and the deployment of a UN mission in Bosnia. But when a rebellion began in the Serbian province of Kosovo, Russia opposed multilateral military action through the United Nations. The Security Council passed a resolution calling on all parties to cease hostilities, but the threat of a Russian veto meant that use of force would not be authorized. Ultimately, NATO undertook a ten-week military campaign against

Yugoslavia without UN authorization. The NATO intervention in Kosovo was deemed "illegal but legitimate" by its defenders:[15] illegal because it was a direct violation of the United Nations' use-of-force regime but legitimate for having prevented atrocities against the Kosovar population.

After Kosovo, the return of competing vetoes signaled the end of multilateral cooperation in support of US hegemony. In its stead, the United States and its allies sought to forge a more permissive use of force regime. The attacks by al-Qaeda on the United States on September 11, 2001, dashed hopes that post–Cold War unipolarity had eliminated threats of a global scale. Initially, state fears of large-scale terrorist attacks produced a period of renewed cooperation. The Security Council rapidly passed a series of far-reaching resolutions mandating worldwide counterterrorism coordination.[16] Exactly eleven years to the day after President George H. W. Bush's "new world order" speech to Congress, the September 11 attacks ushered in a period in which his son, President George W. Bush, would preside over the emergence of a new international security order centered on counterterrorism, counterproliferation, and preventive self-defense—an order that would destabilize and transform the Middle East.

THE MENA AS A ZONE OF LEGAL INNOVATION: PREVENTIVE SELF-DEFENSE AND COLLECTIVE SECURITY

The war in Afghanistan that began a month after the September 11 attacks was fought on traditional self-defense grounds: The United States held al-Qaeda, headquartered in Afghanistan, responsible for the attacks. The US informed the Security Council that it was invoking article 51 of the UN Charter to attack al-Qaeda and associated forces in Afghanistan.[17] Some questioned the legitimacy of targeting the Taliban, but the initial self-defense argument for the war had a firm legal basis in the UN Charter.[18] By contrast, when the Bush administration soon began planning a second war, this time against Iraq, it did so on the basis of an unprecedented new doctrine combining the threats of terrorism and weapons of mass destruction into a potent new argument to authorize force.

The 2003 Iraq War was transformative; it set in motion events that would contribute to the redistribution of power among the states in the region, the spread of sectarian conflict, and arguably the unraveling of a number of states over the following decade. The invasion and occupation of Iraq was also illegal.

In this basic sense, one might argue that, in contrast to the 1991 Gulf War, international law took a back seat in the war that most shaped the New Middle East. Yet in fact the architects of the war went to great lengths to offer legal arguments in its defense. These arguments were not deemed broadly persuasive when first proffered, but they have had durable effects. The precedent set in Iraq has weakened the prohibition on the use of force; produced a model for unilateral counterproliferation enforcement; and demonstrated that international law is an instrument that, when wielded by a global hegemon, can be deployed to ratify the outcome of a war of aggression.

Three arguments were offered in defense of the legality of the war. The principal American argument centered on a broad doctrine of anticipatory (sometimes also described as preventive) self-defense. The UN Charter recognizes self-defense in response to an armed attack as a lawful basis for the use of force. The permissibility of preemptive self-defense is more controversial, but the minimum basis for invoking self-defense preemptively is the threat of an imminent attack. The argument for a far broader scope of allegedly defensive action was introduced by President Bush *fils* in June 2002 and further articulated in the National Security Strategy published three months later.[19] The "Bush doctrine" argued that the concept of imminence be adapted to the changing character of armed conflict: "Rogue states and terrorists . . . rely on acts of terror and, potentially, the use of weapons of mass destruction—weapons that can be easily concealed, delivered covertly and used without warning. . . . The greater the threat, the greater is the risk of inaction—and the more compelling the case for taking anticipatory action to defend ourselves, even if uncertainty remains as to the time and place of the enemy's attack."[20] The broadest version of the US case for attacking Iraq rested on the view that the combination of an alleged arsenal of weapons of mass destruction (WMD) and purported ties to terrorist organizations gave rise to a legitimate right of "preemptive" action to counter a projected Iraqi threat to American national security.[21]

The United Kingdom did not embrace the American position, determining that Iraq did not pose a sufficiently imminent threat to use force in self-defense. Instead, the British advanced a second argument, one that depended no less on creative lawyering. The United Kingdom acknowledged the requirement of Security Council authorization for the war to be legal and offered an interpretation of existing Security Council resolutions as providing the requisite authority. In the fall of 2002, British and American efforts to build the case against Iraq had resulted in Security Council Resolution 1441, which found Iraq in material breach of its disarmament obligations and required renewed arms control inspections.[22] At the time that the resolution passed, the US ambassador to the United Nations stated that the resolution entailed "no automaticity" with respect to use of force should Iraq fail to comply; the UK ambassador agreed that "if there is a further Iraqi breach of its disarmament obligations, the matter will return to the Council for discussion."[23] Thus, there was consensus among the permanent members that if Iraq did not fully comply with Resolution 1441, a second resolution would be required to authorize the use of force.

Nonetheless, when weapons inspections results were deemed inconclusive, the United Kingdom advanced the view, with American support, that a combination of the "serious consequences" threatened in Resolution 1441 and a finding of material breach of the underlying obligation to disarm was sufficient to "revive" the council's original authorization to use force against Iraq in 1991. On this argument, despite the public opposition by France, Russia, and China to use force against Iraq in 2003, their support for the war in 1991 created an irrevocable authorization that was then "revived."[24] Then British attorney general Peter Goldsmith had rejected this position as late as January 2003, but he changed his position in March 2003, apparently persuaded by American representations concerning the gravity of the threat of Iraqi WMD.[25]

A third line of argument in defense of the legality of the Iraq War was raised retroactively, when it became apparent that intelligence concerning Iraqi WMD had been exaggerated and that the regime of Saddam Hussein did not have ties to al-Qaeda. With the grounds for action based on self-defense or material breach of disarmament obligations no longer plausible, the war was instead justified as a regime change intervention for humanitarian purposes. The absence of evidence of a humanitarian motivation in the run-up to the war was largely sufficient to dismiss this argument. There were other criticisms of the cynical invocation of humanitarianism as well: the role of the United States in supporting the Baghdad regime throughout the 1980s despite its record of human rights atrocities and chemical weapons use; the failure to pursue "humanitarian" regime change in 1991 while military action was legally authorized; and the US role in producing a humanitarian crisis in

Iraq through harsh sanctions. In short, whatever the legality of humanitarian intervention more generally, few accepted the relevance of the doctrine to the war against Iraq in 2003.

The principal American and British legal arguments in defense of the war—anticipatory self-defense and "revived" Security Council authorization—were also dismissed as implausible by most international lawyers and scholars, including those in the United States and the United Kingdom. The logic advanced by the Bush doctrine that any regime with access to WMD and suspected of collaborating with nonstate actors may be liable to attack on "preventive self-defense" grounds was especially troubling. Allowing "abstract risks of an uncertain nature" to be treated as an armed attack effectively removes the prohibition on unilateral uses of force.[26]

The Iraq War undermined the UN use-of-force regime in two ways; first, the willingness of the United States and United Kingdom to do an end run around the Security Council—despite their own asymmetric advantage as permanent members—cast into question the authority of the collective security mechanism.[27] Second, the discovery that Iraq did not possess WMD demonstrated the degree to which the United Nations could be instrumentalized to advocate war on the basis of distorted intelligence. The Iraq War also sowed the seeds for the unsettling claim that interventions for regime change may be justified on humanitarian grounds if the regime is sufficiently odious.

Despite the consensus that the war had been illegal, its aftermath witnessed a sort of legitimation when the Security Council authorized the creation of a multinational force to secure postwar Iraq under US leadership, effectively providing legal authority for the occupation, if not the invasion, of the country.[28] The United Nations also called on other countries to contribute to this multinational force, thereby providing a mechanism for the United States to distribute the costs of the occupation and counterinsurgency. The UN-backed multinational force was authorized in October 2003 and extended until 2008, when the United States signed a bilateral agreement with Iraq to keep American forces in the country at Baghdad's invitation.[29] In some sense, then, despite the nearly unanimous international view that the Iraq War was illegal, the United States nonetheless succeeded in deploying the United Nations to lend legitimacy to subsequent efforts to stabilize Iraq while mitigating its own costs.

THE MENA AS LABORATORY: HUMANITARIAN INTERVENTION

The Iraq War was enormously consequential for the distribution of power in the Middle East. The fall of Saddam Hussein and efforts to rebuild Iraq on more democratic terms empowered the plurality Shi'i community in Iraq and enhanced Iran's influence in the country. As the Bush administration touted the demonstration effect of Iraqi democratization, the combination of Iraq's new political order and the expansion of Iranian influence unnerved the Gulf Arab monarchies. As sectarian conflict raged in Iraq, support for Sunni insurgents began to have spillover effects elsewhere in the region. Meanwhile, the Bush administration during its second term placed American democracy promotion on the back burner,[30] while popular grievances about authoritarianism, corruption, and economic mismanagement were expressed with increasing regularity by restive publics across the region.

These developments came to a head with the eruption of the Arab uprisings of 2010–2011. Gulf Arab states' fears that demands for democratization would destabilize their regimes led to brutal counterrevolution in Bahrain, "managed transition" in Yemen, and covert support for a military overthrow of the first democratically elected president in Egypt.[31] But the uprising in Libya represented a different kind of turning point. Once again, the Middle East provided a zone for legal innovation where a confluence of regional and international factors, and the position taken by powerful states, produced new precedent in international law: a United Nations–authorized intervention to promote regime change on humanitarian grounds.

There are several critical elements worth noting to understand how Libya became the first case of a Security Council–backed use of force for humanitarian ends. Doctrinal developments in international law following the Kosovo intervention, the flat-footed international response to uprisings in Tunisia and Egypt, and the specificities of Libya's position regionally and internationally combined to create a highly unusual window of opportunity.

In terms of doctrinal developments, during the twelve years between the Kosovo intervention and the Libyan uprising, the United Nations convened two commissions, one to investigate Kosovo and another to examine the policy question of humanitarian intervention. The Kosovo Commission found the intervention against the Serbs to have been "illegal but legitimate," in its memorable formulation, and the second commission concluded that the tension between humanitarian intervention and sovereignty was best resolved through a redefinition of sovereignty.[32] The result was a new doctrine known as the "responsibility to protect" (widely referred to by the acronym R2P), which holds that sovereignty entails the responsibility to protect the humanitarian welfare of the civilian population of the sovereign's territory. If the sovereign fails in that responsibility, a secondary responsibility arises in the international community to use diplomatic, humanitarian, or other means to provide civilian protection.

The R2P doctrine was imagined as embracing nonmilitary means to address humanitarian crises and reinforcing sovereignty by making explicit the international obligation to help states meet their existing responsibilities. Should military means be required, acting on the basis of R2P would require an authorizing Security Council resolution. The R2P concept was embraced first by a UN General Assembly resolution in 2005, then by the Security Council in 2006 in a resolution concerning peacekeeping (rather than coercive use of force) in Darfur.[33]

The Libyan uprising began on February 17, 2011, following the Tunisian uprising against the authoritarian regime of Zine el-Abidine Ben Ali and the fall of Egypt's dictator, Hosni Mubarak.[34] The fast pace of events that removed Ben Ali and Mubarak from office occurred within weeks of the first spontaneous protests. External supporters of the regimes—France, in the case of Tunisia, and the United States and the Gulf monarchies, in the case of Egypt—were largely sidelined by events that saw the long-standing dictators overthrown.

When protests erupted in Libya against Muammar Qaddafi's regime, there was a clear sense that history was on the side of the uprising and that the Arab world was being swept up by a leaderless revolution. Former members of the Bush administration claimed that the so-called Arab Spring was in part a consequence of their "freedom agenda" of democracy promotion following the Iraq War.[35] In many ways, Libya was the low-hanging fruit of the Arab uprisings—a regime whose fall would have few adverse consequences for members of the Security Council or their remaining allies in the Middle East. This presented a rare opportunity for European countries and the United States to act on the "right side of history," in support of popular demands for democratization rather than the authoritarian stability they had long backed.

The result of the conjuncture of the Libyan uprising with the mainstreaming of R2P was uncharacteristically swift and coordinated action by the Security Council. Within less than ten days of the beginning of the uprising, the Security Council passed a resolution authorizing coercive action in Libya, including the imposition of an arms embargo, a travel ban, an asset freeze on members of the Qaddafi regime, and referral to the International Criminal Court for investigation.[36] When this resolution was passed on February 26, 2011, the Qaddafi regime had made clear its intention to repress the uprising but no atrocities had occurred. Within nineteen days, the Security Council acted again on Libya, this time with the ostensible goal of stopping the Qaddafi regime from committing threatened atrocities in Benghazi. It imposed a no-fly zone over the country, modified the arms embargo to enable weapons supplies to rebels, and authorized all necessary means to protect civilians short of a "foreign occupation force."[37]

The resolution used the language of R2P (civilian protection) as the basis of the authorization to use force rather than the Security Council's traditional authority to respond to threats to international peace and security. China and Russia abstained in the vote but allowed the resolution, backed by the United States, Britain, and France, to pass. A military intervention by those three countries began on March 19, with command of the operation later transferred to NATO. The precipitous action by the Security Council resembled a highly accelerated version of the 1991 Gulf War authorization, complete with sanctions, a no-fly zone, and coercive intervention. All this took place within a month and in the absence of an act of aggression against any other state by the Libyan government.

The legality of the Libyan intervention is clear insofar as it was authorized by the Security Council. Moreover, the scope of the authorization to use force was so broad as to permit any military action that could be alleged to further the goal of protecting civilians. Even the provision excluding a "foreign occupation force" did not preclude the introduction of ground forces so long as they could be described as protecting civilians rather than undertaking an occupation. Shortly after the beginning of the intervention, public statements by American, British, and French officials made clear that regime change was being pursued and this, too, did not exceed the mandate (so long as the regime could be presented as a threat to civilians).[38] An important lesson of the Libya intervention echoed the 1991 Iraq War: once force is authorized, the Security Council effectively delegates all decisions about the scope and nature of the intervention to the multilateral coalition acting to enforce it. If such a coalition includes permanent members of the Security Council, a second resolution to narrow the scope of authority or otherwise reign in the interveners is all but precluded.

As the Libya intervention shifted focus from civilian protection to regime change, many states questioned its legitimacy.[39] Some argued that the R2P doctrine's conditions were not satisfied in the case of Libya. Use of force was authorized in anticipation of rather than in response to a high-casualty humanitarian crisis; it was not a last resort as diplomatic efforts had not been exhausted, and there was little evidence that resort to force had a reasonable prospect of improving humanitarian conditions for the civilian population.[40] The reliance on aerial bombardment resulted in the destruction of much of the infrastructure necessary to secure the welfare of civilians. Further, the arming of opposition groups left the country awash in weapons distributed among a fractured landscape of militias.[41] But perhaps the greatest source of illegitimacy in the eyes of many in the international community was the objective of regime change.

The Libya intervention demonstrated that concerted action to avert a humanitarian catastrophe—at least in cases where no great power interest would be adversely affected—remained possible. The R2P precedent in Libya is another step in the direction of a more permissive use of force regime, with increased scope for nondefensive action and the expansion of Security Council authority to act in the absence of a threat to international peace and security. At the same time, responses to the intervention made clear international reluctance to authorize force for the purpose of regime change.

Once Qaddafi was killed and the NATO mission ended, those who participated in the intervention failed to follow through on civilian protection by committing sufficient aid to rebuild the country's damaged infrastructure and secure the weapons that had been provided to rebels.[42] In fact, not even the regime assets frozen by the Security Council at the beginning of the uprising were made available to assist with reconstruction.[43] While R2P had been introduced as a doctrine to enhance sovereignty through international assistance, in Libya the R2P-based intervention was widely held responsible for turning the country into a failed state.[44] An inversion of the Kosovo formulation of "illegal but legitimate" may best capture the ultimate verdict on the Libya intervention: "legal but illegitimate."

Criticism of the Libya intervention has cast a pall over R2P more generally, leading one commentator to conclude "R2P, RIP."[45] But the supporters of the doctrine prefer the characterization of R2P as "down but not out,"[46] insisting that its framework still provides the best model for collective action in cases of extreme humanitarian crisis. One prominent legal scholar has even argued that Libya represents a "multilateral constitutional moment" that will consolidate rather than undermine transformations in the international law system's approach to sovereignty and civilian protection.[47] The likelihood that states may yet make recourse to the "Libya precedent" for future interventions cannot be gainsaid. The history of external intervention in the Middle East has a long record of purportedly humanitarian motivations, and the availability of the R2P doctrine has provided a lawful new bottle for old wine.

THE MENA AS CAULDRON: THE UNWILLING OR UNABLE DOCTRINE

In Libya, an uprising against a regime with few allies produced an almost-instant military mobilization to prevent potential abuses. At the same time, elsewhere in the region uprisings were met with atrocities that occasioned no UN-backed intervention because they were committed by authoritarians with powerful allies on the Security Council. Perhaps the premier example of humanitarian double standards is Syria. The beginning of the Syrian uprising coincided with the Libya intervention, but the increasingly violent repression of the protests by Syrian dictator Bashar al-Assad's regime did not trigger an R2P-based response by the United Nations.

States that opposed intervention in Syria—notably Russia and China—openly cited NATO's actions in Libya as having broken trust that R2P could serve as the basis of a constrained and strictly humanitarian effort to protect civilians.[48] The states that led the intervention in Libya were also slow to suggest coercive measures in Syria. An aerial bombardment campaign in Syria comparable to the one in Libya might have produced state collapse on Israel's doorstep while further aggravating an already-severe refugee crisis with significant costs to Jordan, Lebanon, and Turkey. Pointing the finger at Russia for shielding its Damascus ally from Security Council action obscures the fact that none of its permanent members ever proposed humanitarian intervention in Syria.[49]

That does not mean, however, that there has been a dearth of intervention—and legal arguments in defense of such actions—in Syria. Russia and Iran have intervened directly and extensively at the request of the Syrian government. But Western powers opposed to the Assad regime have also found legal grounds to support their own interventions. Beyond the covert supply of funds and arms to rebels in Syria, US and European forces have engaged in military action on a number of fronts.[50] Limited air strikes targeting Syrian military infrastructure in response to chemical weapons attacks—undertaken both unilaterally by the United States in 2017 and multilaterally by the United States, United Kingdom, and France in 2018—have garnered the most attention. The air strikes against Syria have been cited by some as an international precedent for a "right of humanitarian intervention to protect against repeat chemical weapons use."[51] This argument draws together and builds on earlier interventionist innovations in the region, including the counterproliferation-based preventive intervention in Iraq and the humanitarian precedent set in Libya. That said, few international law scholars agree that such a right of WMD-based humanitarian intervention now exists.[52] For its part, the United States has not offered an explicit *international* legal rationale for the strikes, although it did reference a vital interest in preventing chemical weapons use.[53] Still, the cumulative jurisgenerative effect of international law–based interventions in the Middle East is evident in the muted international response to the air strikes—a nondefensive use of force on sovereign territory—despite their manifest illegality.[54]

Beyond the strikes on chemical weapons facilities, however, the United States and its allies have engaged in a protracted air and ground campaign in Syria since 2014. This Syria intervention does not target the Assad regime but disregards Syrian sovereignty claims altogether while undertaking major military action on Syrian territory. The basis for the intervention is the counterterrorism campaign against ISIS. In framing the authority to conduct this campaign, the United States and others cited the Iraqi government's request for assistance to justify use of force against ISIS in Iraq.[55] Syria, meanwhile, was depicted as a cauldron of humanitarian catastrophe and state failure. Extending the multilateral campaign against ISIS to Syrian soil, by this logic, is an outgrowth of collective self-defense justified by Syria being "unable or unwilling" to meet the threat.[56]

As we have seen throughout this chapter, the traditional United Nations use-of-force regime provides three lawful bases for coercive action on the territory of a state: self-defense in response to an armed attack, consent to the use of force by the state whose territory is implicated, or Security Council authorization. One issue that arises under this regime is when and how self-defense may be invoked against a nonstate actor (NSA) operating from the territory of a state. If that NSA has the support of the state on whose territory it is located, the actions of the NSA may be imputed to its state sponsor. But if the NSA is operating on the territory of a state without that state's support, as is the case of ISIS in Syria, then the applicability of a self-defense justification for action against the territorial state becomes more complicated. There is some debate about the conditions that must be met for counter-NSA action on the territory of another state, but there is agreement, at a minimum, that consent of the territorial state must be sought.[57] In the case of Syria, not only did the United States not request permission from Syria's government; the Assad regime's attempts to offer consent on condition of consultation and coordination were ignored.[58]

The "unable or unwilling" doctrine is an outgrowth of the American framing of the war on terror with its presumption of a global battlefield in which the need to take defensive action admits no territorial boundaries. In such a conflict, the argument goes, states that are themselves nonthreatening may nonetheless become "hosts" to an NSA, against which a legitimate right of self-defense may be invoked. To address this possibility, the doctrine holds that defensive action is lawful if it can be shown that the host state does not have the capacity to address the threat or is unwilling to do so. Although this argument remains controversial, the posture in Syria goes well beyond the bounds of even this permissive doctrine. The novel legal issue presented in Syria is a circumstance in which "the host state . . . is willing and able to deal with the nonstate group (ISIS) through military cooperation with the threatened state (US) but the latter (the United States) doesn't want to associate itself with the host state for potentially unrelated reasons."[59]

To solve this challenge, some legal scholars initially argued that Syria was, in effect, offering "passive consent" to the anti-ISIS military campaign on its territory.[60] Whatever its merits, such a theory became unsustainable when the Syrian government sent letters to the United Nations making explicit its position that the failure to seek its consent for military action on its soil is a violation of Syrian sovereignty.[61] The decision nonetheless to ignore or rebuff the Syrian offer of conditional consent represents another unprecedented and hence innovative approach to intervention in the post-9/11 era.[62]

Two arguments were tentatively made in defense of military action on Syrian territory without seeking consent. The first was that the Assad regime had lost effective control over the territory and hence was no longer in a position to provide valid consent. The second was that the atrocities committed by the Assad regime were of a sufficient severity to deny the government the right to serve as the legitimate representative of the state.[63] Both arguments foundered, however, on the reality that Assad government officials remained seated as the internationally recognized representatives of the Syrian state at the United Nations and other key international institutions. Moreover, none of the states in the anti-ISIS coalition recognized a different legitimate representative of Syria, nor did they argue that any other party to the Syrian civil war exercised a greater degree of control over Syrian territory. By international law standards, this means that the Assad regime remains the relevant government of Syria for purposes of consent.

At least one scholar has argued that the true basis for the failure to seek Syrian consent involves a novel amalgamation of the logics underlying the two arguments. On the one hand, Syria is treated as a sort of quasi-failed state, thus "unable" to meet the ISIS threat. On the other hand, the logic of humanitarianism dictates treating Syria as a pariah state whose willingness to cooperate should be set aside on the basis of the odiousness of the regime.[64] The challenge of this posture should be clear: If disapproval of a state's government can become the basis for disregarding its sovereignty, there will be few constraints left against engaging in coercive military force on the territory of an adversary. Absent the requirement of seeking consent, the already-permissive doctrine of defensive strikes against NSAs will simply be a license for discretionary unilateral intervention.

THE MENA AS JURISGENERATIVE CRUCIBLE

The Middle East has been the site of external interventions almost too numerous to chronicle in the post–Cold War and post-9/11 periods.[65] The region has been profoundly transformed by interventions that have collapsed states that once defined the balance of power in the Middle East. Moreover, the chaos that has engulfed postintervention Iraq and Libya, to name just two examples, has produced new sources of transnational destabilization—weapons transfers, refugee flows, and competing nonstate groups with transnational reach—as well as new forms of regional competition that continue to unfold in unpredictable ways. The Middle East and the conflicts engendered in it by external interventions have also transfigured the basic rules of the postwar collective security order. The jurisgenerative character of these interventions has introduced new justificatory logics and doctrinal innovations that have fundamentally and profoundly challenged—and quite possibly irretrievably undermined—international law governing the use of force.

The prohibition on the use of force was the cornerstone of the international order designed to prevent the recurrence of world war in a nuclear age. But with each new intervention, the primacy of the Security Council as the forum for resolving competition between great power interests has eroded. The logics of humanitarianism and counterterrorism are available for any powerful state to invoke in defense of its prerogative to intervene globally at its own discretion. The Middle East has come to serve not only as a laboratory for what it means to intervene but also as a crucible for the international law doctrines that provide the justificatory infrastructure for interveners. And in the process the New Middle East offers perhaps the best evidence that according powerful states the discretion to unilaterally assess when force is necessary to achieve preventive, humanitarian, or counterterrorist ends results in abuse and escalation that produces humanitarian suffering and geopolitical destabilization on an unprecedented scale.

Afterword

THE FOURTH DREAM

Moncef Marzouki

I FIND MYSELF ASKING, AT TIMES, WHETHER I AM WITNESSING the failure of what I call the fourth dream of the Tunisian people, the democratic project. To understand why I call democracy our fourth dream and to provide context about my concern for its future, let me put this project in its historical context. I begin by outlining the three preceding projects, the failure of which paved the way for the appearance of the democratic project in the Arab world.

Over the past half century, from when I was a young student who was involved in politics from an early age to when I became a head of state, I have witnessed in Tunisia and in most Arab countries the high and low tide of three ideological waves: nationalism, pan-Arabism, and political Islam. An ideological wave consists of the hope, illusion, and belief that the solution for all problems is within reach. All of these psychological elements find some representation in the intellectual leaders of the day and the political parties seeking power to fulfill dreams and promises. Our fathers would be extremely surprised and probably shocked if they knew how the nation-state projects for which they fought their whole lives had turned into the corrupt, oppressive, and incompetent bureaucracy the people rose up to overturn. The dream of our parents' generation turned gradually into a nightmare.

In 1991, I wrote a book that was banned in Tunisia but published in Beirut, the title of which was *The Second Independence.* My thesis at that time was that the nation-state, born in 1956 in Tunisia, and over the course of the second half of the twentieth century in other Arab countries, freed us from foreign occupation but not from oppression. It was just the first step. Democracy would be our second independence, because it would free the people from a new internal occupation, represented by a state that hijacked the dreams of our fathers and the sacrifice of our martyrs.

It would be too simplistic to explain the obvious failure of the nationalist state only by the fact that it was run by greedy elites hoarding their own privileges by imposing a harsh and brutal dictatorship on the people, dependent on a fragile and corrupt economy. An artificial state—created by foreigners and governed by local elites that adopted the mentality of their conquerors and struggled only to maintain their own status and privileges—could never succeed in meeting the aspirations of its people. This explains the birth and rapid expansion of the wave of pan-Arab nationalism, represented by the Egyptian leader Gamal Abdel Nasser. This wave began in the 1950s and reached its peak in the 1960s and early 1970s. The end of the United Arab Republic, uniting Syria and Egypt in 1961, as well as the humiliating military defeat of 1967 and the struggle between factions of the same Ba'ath Party in Iraq and Syria quickly buried the dream of uniting a strong Arab nation capable of liberating the remaining Arab people without a state, the Palestinians.

In fact, the failure of the dream was preordained because dictatorships do not unite. Each dictator seeks to claim the sole mantle of the savior. Let us remember that the European Union was built on the ruins of dictatorships in Germany, Italy, Spain, and, later, the communist dictatorships of the Eastern European countries. The projects of political Islam and democracy have flourished in the ruins of failed nationalist and pan-Arab ideologies. These subsequent projects reached their peak in the 1980s and found themselves in competition.

Three decades later, the failure of political Islam can no longer be denied. Its armed wing has resorted to terrorism and its record is catastrophic. Armed Islamists have been responsible for the murder of countless thousands of innocent people, mostly Muslims, the return of foreign forces to Arab soil, and the reinforcement of dictatorship. Equally damaging has been the harm done to the millions of Muslims living in the West and the tarnishing of Islam's image worldwide. As for the peaceful branch of political Islam, it has renounced violence and armed resistance everywhere and established instead the goal of changing the terms of the existing Arab political system. The strategic choice—whether in Tunisia, Algeria, Morocco, or Jordan—is to allow this reformist movement in political Islam to join the political fray through political participation. The unfortunate exception to this broader trend has been Egypt, where the established system refused to accept the incorporation of political Islam.

Now, what about the democratic wave that reached its peak during the Arab uprisings between 2011 and 2013? Is it starting to decline, and is it experiencing the same fate as nationalism, pan-Arabism, and militant political Islam? This is the question, the most important question.

Here, there is no need to recite well-known facts about the trajectory of democratic transition in the region. The transition to democracy has stalled, if not failed, because of the massive intervention of regional powers, as well as some of the social characteristics of the states in which uprisings occurred. Others in this book have addressed proxy wars, which are a good example of the kind of external intervention that doomed transitions in countries that now are mired in conflict. The premier example may be the trajectory of Libya, where external intervention has led the country to chaos and civil war. In January 2018, the main leader of the counterrevolution in Libya, General Khalifa Haftar, said in an interview to the magazine *Jeune Afrique*, "Libya is not sufficiently mature for democracy which may be a project for future generations."

Nor do I need to remind my readers of the fate of democracy in Egypt after July 2013. Following the externally sponsored counterrevolution that brought Abdel Fattah al-Sisi to power, it was interesting to see how Western nations reacted to presidential elections in Egypt. What is clear is that the political system that took hold in Egypt in the aftermath of a counterrevolutionary coup is not merely a classic dictatorship but more akin to a fascist state.

This brings me to Tunisia.

How do we account for Tunisia, which is now widely considered the only success story among the Arab Spring countries? I understand that friends of my country might not like the idea that even Tunisia is failing to achieve a democratic transition. However, my own assessment is that there is a real possibility that Tunisia might not be able to consolidate its democracy.

So far, Tunisians have been fortunate for reasons quite distinct from the naïve narratives about the country often aired by analysts in the West. If we have not suffered the fate of Libya, Egypt, Syria, or Yemen, it is not because we are different, smarter, or more moderate. Rather, it is because fortunately the very structure of Tunisian society did not lend itself to the developments witnessed in those countries. Unlike Syria, we are a mostly homogeneous society without ethnic or religious minorities. Unlike Libya or Yemen, Tunisia is a society with limited tribal influence and a history of strong civil society. Tunisia is also a country dominated by a very large, modern, and Westernized middle class. Contrary to Egypt, we have an army that is not involved directly or indirectly in politics or business. The peaceful transition in Tunisia was also the product of an agreement struck between the secular parties, including mine, and the Islamist party, Ennahda, itself based on the political experience of leaders who spent long periods in exile and in conversation with one another. Tunisia fortuitously had all the cards in its favor to achieve a peaceful democratic transition. Unfortunately, things have not gone as the democrats had hoped.

From the beginning of my term as the first democratically elected president of Tunisia in December 2011 until the end of my term in December 2014, I watched in astonishment and anger how anti-democratic factions seized the mechanism of democracy to pervert it and to subvert its channels of power to enable a comeback for the corrupt system that was defeated by the revolution. Freedom of expression has been widely used by the erstwhile journalists and media of the dictatorship to attack the revolution, spreading all kinds of rumors and false accusations. Even worse, the revolution was undermined and the people mobilized against the government even as it sought to grapple with the social and economic legacy left by the dictatorship, and with the new threat of terrorism. The very freedoms of our society were deployed against us. Suddenly, suspicious businesspeople established political parties using money from unknown sources—money that in fact flowed into Tunisia from the Gulf and particularly the United Arab Emirates. The concerted effect of media propaganda and voting corruption produced a shocking result in the 2014 parliamentary elections: a mere three years after the revolution, the remnants of the dictatorship won more seats than the parties that fought for years against repression.

In the aftermath of the election, many people would ask, "Why did you not take the necessary steps to protect the fledgling democracy?" In fact, the measures to combat a corrupt media spreading disinformation are difficult to distinguish from attacks on press freedom. The prohibition of corrupt, foreign-funded political parties would appear to be a form of political repression. Moreover, there was not yet in place any legal basis for the banning of such parties. One must not forget that we had against us not only the worsening economic situation and corrupt media but also the deep state left by the dictatorship and a business community that never accepted the revolution. To make the situation more complicated, there was a deep divergence of views within the government itself. I was a proponent of a policy of firmness vis-à-vis the forces of counterrevolution. Ennahda, the Islamist party, was, by contrast, afraid of provoking a new confrontation with the still-active political system mainly represented by the deep state.

Here I come to the main reason that anti-democratic forces were able to use the very mechanism of democracy to come back to power democratically and then dismantle from within the democratic project they have always despised. The main reason is a shocking and surprising alliance between the counter-revolution's political parties and the Islamist party that owed its own access to power to the revolution. To understand this alliance, which is today the pillar of the government in place, we must return to the coup in Egypt in July 2013.

The Islamist party came to the conclusion that the Arab Spring had been crushed by civil war in Libya, Syria, and Yemen and by the coup d'état in Egypt, and was motivated by the fear that they would probably experience the same fate one way or another in Tunisia. Therefore, they decided that it would be safer for them to reach a consensus with the representatives of the counterrevolution. Thus, an electoral agreement between the remnants of the dictatorship and the party with the greatest share of seats in Parliament brought back to power the architects of the repression the uprising sought to end.

It is true that the election of the Constituent Assembly, which in turn elected the president of the republic, was free and fair for the first time in Tunisian history. However, the complaints that I sought to litigate in court in 2014 about numerous instances of fraud during the presidential election have never been investigated largely because of political pressure on the judiciary. In fact, Tunisia is the victim of an incredible paradox. The revolution brought democracy and democracy brought back the counterrevolution. Now the counterrevolution is taking control of democracy and may destroy it from within.

This is the paradox. I do not offer this assessment as a political opposition figure who is embittered over the loss of the last presidential election. This assessment is grounded in much more complex and structural features than anything attendant to a single election.

On January 17, 2018, the French newspaper *Libération* ran the headline, "Essebsi in the Footsteps of Ben Ali." The title of the article may seem shocking and exaggerated, but it succinctly conveys the concerns of the population and foreign observers concerning the regime's drift toward autocracy. On January 11, 2018, the International Crisis Group published a report echoing concerns about the slowdown or even reversal of the democratic process. They describe a government tempted by the return to authoritarianism. In response, the International Crisis Group advised the president to speed up the implementation of the constitution and the establishment of the constitutional court. That court is provided for by the constitution but has still not been brought into existence.

The president's response to international criticism makes clear that he will not act on the International Crisis Group's recommendation. Indeed, his attacks on foreign media are reminiscent of Ben Ali's strategy of casting aspersions on international critics for allegedly failing to understand Tunisia. Freedoms, including freedom of expression and the press, have declined precipitously in Tunisia. Many bloggers, journalists, and protesters are in prison. Tunisian journalists declared February 3, 2018, a Day of Anger to protest the growing harassment of the press in the country.

The government is trying to display a bright image of itself and Tunisia. In fact, the country's image has been tarnished by the inclusion of Tunisia on a European Union list published in December 2017 of seventy countries considered illicit tax havens. The government gave the European Union assurances that it would address the issues that led to the listing, and Tunisia was moved from a blacklist to a gray list. I learned later that Tunisia had been added to a *new* blacklist of countries that were laundering money and funding terrorists.

Despite fierce opposition from Tunisia's youth and a large part of the political class, in 2017 the parliament voted in favor of an amnesty law forgiving corruption offenses in the civil service. The establishment of the Truth and Dignity Commission, an independent structure for transitional justice, was a great achievement of the revolution, but the current government has done everything to sabotage the commission's work, including the application of immense pressure to pass the amnesty law. For the public, the arrests from time to time of corrupt businesspeople are mere struggles between groups within a deeply corrupt political class, best represented by the president's ruling party.

With regard to the economic and social situation in the country, demonstrations have taken place throughout the country, including in the suburbs near Tunis, since 2018. These nightly demonstrations have been quite violent, sometimes reminiscent of the early days of the revolution in 2010. This is perhaps unsurprising when we consider that the main problem that led to the revolution—widespread poverty in the peripheral regions and massive unemployment among young educated people—persists. During the 2019 presidential campaign, the president-elect promised to put an end to the economic problems that had not been solved by the troika government that ruled the country from 2011 to 2013. Nevertheless, since then the government's record on socioeconomic accomplishments has been very thin and worrying for the future. Economic growth has not been stimulated, unemployment has worsened, and the standard of living of the middle class is declining year after year as the country's debt explodes. For most Tunisians, the question is very simple: Have we gone from corrupt dictatorship to corrupt democracy that paves the way to the return of dictatorship as occurred in Egypt? This is the main question and the main concern to Tunisians.

When we contemplate this general picture, two attitudes emerge: Those who feel sympathy for the Arabs are invariably saddened by such a distressing record. Racists rejoice, confirmed in their prejudice that democracy is a Western value and that Arabs are not able to create and maintain democratic regimes for cultural or even genetic reasons. We owe some gratitude to those who have sympathy with our plight. As for the rest, there is no need to argue with them; one just has to ignore them. To place the circumstance I have described in historical perspective, we would do well to remember the hardship endured by the Chinese people between 1840 and 1940 or those experienced

by Europeans between 1914 and 1945 to understand that all nations are subjected to the iron fist of history before reaching a certain equilibrium. There
is little reason to expect the Arab world to attain such an equilibrium without
obstacles.

At times, I imagine the Arab world as a collective entity engaged in a giant
experiment, repeating to itself: "Well, let us try nationalism. It doesn't work.
Throw it away. Let us try pan-Arabism. It doesn't work either. Throw it away,
too. Why not try political Islam? It's not more functional. Throw it away. How
about democracy? Does it work? No problem. We will have to find something
else." In fact, we are dealing not with a succession of failures, but with the slow
and chaotic evolution toward more complex and mature economic, political,
and social structures.

In this march toward the solution of eternal problems, there will always be
both small victories and significant setbacks—always. For instance, of course
the nationalist state failed to secure freedom and prosperity for its citizens.
However, at least this era accomplished independence. That independence
now required of Arab people the wherewithal to confront their own corrupt
elites and demand to take power back from them and wield it instead in ways
that serve the majority of the people.

Of course, the pan-Arab ideology has failed to create united Arab states,
but it has created a strong sense across the Arabic-speaking world of shared
belonging. It is not by luck that the Tunisian revolution had such significant
follow-on effects with a huge impact on Egypt, Libya, Yemen, and Syria, rather
than inspiring events in Peru or Zimbabwe.

Of course, political Islam has nowhere been able to create the perfect
Islamic state of its dreams. However, it has created social solidarities that
compensate for the inadequacy of the state, maintaining the hope of a better
world, and restoring to those who are disoriented by globalization a sense of
identity and dignity.

And finally, of course democracy is not fulfilling all its promises, but even
in Egypt, I think, there will be something gained in the long run from the
experience of what has happened in the past four or five years.

Behind the political scenes in Tunisia are extraordinary phenomena, such
as the empowerment of women, the rise of the middle classes, the bastion of
what I call the e-generation for freedom of expression, and the growing role

of civil society. This is why I do believe that behind the obvious failures, the democratic process, even when it is diverted for a time, is still powerful enough to resume its course.

However, one must not be naïve; democracy is not an inescapable fate. What I have learned in opposition and as a head of state is that democracy has to meet three conditions to survive in Tunisia or in any Arab country. First, democracy must be linked to social justice for the poor and middle classes. Social and economic crises take precedence over freedom of speech and freedom of association. A broad swath of the public would accept a Chinese-style regime if it brings them prosperity more than they would accept a British-style regime if it brings them only poverty and instability, as in Iraq. We must not forget that in the 1950s countries like Egypt, Iraq, and Syria experienced parliamentary regimes swept away by coups d'état that few regretted because the parliamentary regimes had brought only more privileges to the minority and more poverty to the majority.

Second, democracy must have a local and regional support system, so that it is under the protection of as many political and social actors as possible. Dictatorship is based on a centralized state where all power is in the hands of a minority. Democracy can be based only on a decentralized state in which political power is shared among the largest number of citizens. The national parliament is not enough. Regional structures are needed. This is why I have enshrined in the Tunisian constitution the principle of decentralization and the distribution of political power between the state and the elected representatives of the regions. And this is the reason the current government is against this constitution and would like especially to remove this part of the constitution addressing decentralization.

Third, democracy must protect itself against corruption through tough rules and an independent judiciary under the watch of a very demanding civil society.

These are the general conditions, and they are valid for all Arab countries, but there are conditions specific to each country apart. For instance, I do not see viable democracy in Egypt with an army that is involved in politics and business.

The question, then, is who will achieve these conditions? It is obvious that risky, complex, and long-term policies need to be put together and carried out by democratic forces that are constantly struggling against those powerful forces that are determined to sabotage democracy or to pervert and use it for the benefit of the same corrupt elite associated with the overthrown dictatorships. When we examine the social and economic policies and the political forces necessary for the establishment of a true and lasting democracy, we may always make the same observation: the forces that can win democracy are the same ones that can destroy it.

For instance, many democratic parties today in Tunisia are riddled with corruption, simply because they cannot exist without the support of suspicious businesspersons or even foreign dictatorships. The same situation also pertains to many nongovernmental organizations. One cannot imagine democracy without free media, but the level of its corruption in Tunisia or Egypt, especially in Egypt, also threatens democracy. It is very curious that in our country media could be a major threat to democracy. Because this is very new, we have to elaborate a new theory about the role of media, the role of nongovernmental organizations, and the role of political parties in promoting democracy. I am afraid that each of these essential forces necessary to enable democracy can also serve to destroy it. Similarly, the business community, which has the most to gain from the rule of law and alone can provide the political stability it needs, often prioritizes short-term interests that damage the rule of law. Finally, the youth whom I call the e-generation are largely filled with democratic values and committed to the quest for democracy. Unfortunately, these youth have also come to despise politics and politicians. By refusing to vote, a large part of the youth is steering us awry: their passivity leaves room for the older generation, which systematically votes for the most backward and anti-democratic social forces.

I am not saying that democracy is a hopeless case in Tunisia or in any Arab country. I am simply saying that within the political parties, nongovernmental organizations, media, economic community, youth, there are forces pushing toward the acceleration of democratization and others within these same structures pushing against it. We can be certain that a gigantic experiment is in progress, but nobody is able to predict the result or even the direction. The very serious economic and environmental crises that set developments in motion are evolving in their own way while the political processes are increasingly on a divergent trajectory.

In the end, the portrait I have depicted is my own rendition of the political problem that I personally face in my capacity as a political player in contemporary Tunisia. These are also the political problems of most of the class of politically involved actors of my generation. The conundrum we all face is how to make the next move. What do you do when you do not know, and when at every crossroad you have no choice but to decide what to do?

As far as I am concerned, I have some very simple principles. First, stick to moral values. Ideas change constantly. What was true or believed to be true yesterday can be proved wrong tomorrow. But values are stable. Values that were true centuries ago will remain true in the centuries to come. One can always rely on values because they summarize the whole human experience across generations.

Second, keep going with one's dream. Democracy is currently my dream, the dream of my generation, so we have to stick to this dream because it is our last hope. Democracy should be given every chance despite and because it is the worst political system except all the others, as Winston Churchill put it.

Third, accept that negative forces of destruction are part of the natural process of our world. The destruction of ideology, states, and whatever—however terrible the price—is sometimes necessary for the purpose of building something better and more sustainable. This is exactly what I hope for in the Arab world when I observe the destructive forces attacking countries, dismantling states, and obliterating populations. To accept these destructive forces is a terrible thing, but it may also be inevitable.

Fourth, be confident in the positive forces of construction that are always at work, even in the darkest phases of history.

Fifth, be open to all the surprises that are ahead. The only thing that must not surprise us is surprise itself. That is probably the most important feature of our current social, technological, and political environment.

Sixth, be convinced that we fail not because we cannot reach our objectives but simply because we abandon them. To combat discouragement, one has to accept that trying to change the world might be naïve but to stop trying is criminal.

Notes

INTRODUCTION

1. "Transcript: Secretary Rice Holds a News Conference," *Washington Post*, July 21, 2006, http://www.washingtonpost.com/wp-dyn/content/article/2006/07/21/AR200 6072100889.html.

2. "Full Text: George Bush's Iraq Speech," *The Guardian*, June 28, 2005, https:// www.theguardian.com/world/2005/jun/29/iraq.usa.

3. The figures are for the years 2003–2011. Amy Hagopian, Abraham D. Flaxman, Tim K. Takaro, Sahar A. Esa Al Shatari, Julie Rajaratnam, Stan Becker, Alison Levin-Rector et al., "Mortality in Iraq Associated with the 2003–2011 War and Occupation: Findings from a National Cluster Sample Survey by the University Collaborative Iraq Mortality Study," *PLOS Medicine* (October 15, 2013), http://journals.plos.org/plosmed-icine/article?id=10.1371/journal.pmed.1001533#abstract1.

4. According to the Economist Intelligence Unit, by 2019 Iraq had slipped from a "hybrid" (simulated) democracy to full-blown authoritarianism. "Democracy Index 2019: A Year of Democratic Setbacks and Popular Protest" (London: Economist Intel-ligence Unit, 2019), http://www.eiu.com/Handlers/WhitepaperHandler.ashx?fi=De-mocracy-Index-2019.pdf&mode=wp&campaignid=democracyindex2019.

5. For a more detailed account of the Arab uprisings, see James L. Gelvin, *The Arab Uprisings: What Everyone Needs to Know*, 2nd ed. (New York: Oxford University Press, 2015).

6. UN High Commissioner for Refugees, *Regional Summaries: Middle East and North Africa* (Geneva: UNHCR, 2019), http://reporting.unhcr.org/sites/default/files/ga2019/pdf/Chapter_MENA.pdf.

7. Zeina Karam, "Millions of People Are Being Starved to Death as Food Is Used as a Weapon across the Middle East," *Business Insider*, February 1, 2016, http://www.business insider.com/millions-are-being-starved-to-death-across-the-middle-east-2016-2.

8. Antonio Gramsci, *Selections from the Prison Notebooks of Antonio Gramsci*, ed. and trans. Quentin Hoare and Geoffrey Nowell Smith (London: Lawrence and Wishart, 1971), 481–95.

9. See information from the World Bank's DataBank from 2018 for the Middle East, at https://data.worldbank.org/region/middle-east-and-north-africa?view=chart, and for Turkey, at https://data.worldbank.org/country/Turkey.

10. *Arab Human Development Report 2016: Youth and the Prospects for Human Development in a Changing Reality* (New York: UN Development Programme, 2016), http://www.arab-hdr.org/reports/2016/english/ExecutiveENG.pdf.

11. Jane Harrigan and Chengang Wang, "The Economic and Political Determinants of IMF and World Bank Lending in the Middle East and North Africa," *World Development* 34, no. 2 (2006): 255, 261.

12. See, e.g., Michael Schwartz, "The Egyptian Uprising: The Mass Strike in the Time of Neoliberal Globalization," *New Labor Forum* 20, no. 3 (Fall 2011): 33–43.

13. *Arab Human Development Report 2009: Challenges for Human Security in the Arab Region* (New York: UN Development Programme, 2009), http://www.undp.org/content/undp/en/home/librarypage/hdr/arab_human_developmentreport2009.html.

14. "A Dangerous Deterioration: Egypt under al-Sisi, A Conversation with Dr. Ashraf El Sherif," *Project on Middle East Democracy* (June 2017), https://pomed.org/wp-content/uploads/2017/06/Ashraf_QA_FINAL.pdf; Nathan J. Brown and Mai el-Sadany, *How a State of Emergency Became Egypt's New Normal* (Washington, DC: Carnegie Endowment for International Peace, October 30, 2017), https://carnegieendowment.org/2017/10/30/how-state-of-emergency-became-egypt-s-new-normal-pub-73587.

15. Frederic Wehrey, *The Forgotten Uprising in Eastern Saudi Arabia* (Washington, DC: Carnegie Endowment for International Peace, June 14, 2013), https://carnegieendowment.org/2013/06/14/forgotten-uprising-in-eastern-saudi-arabia-pub-52093; *World Report 2019* (New York: Human Rights Watch, 2019), https://www.hrw.org/sites/default/files/world_report_download/hrw_world_report_2019.pdf.

16. Alex Ward, "Thousands of Algerians Are Protesting to Force Their Ailing Dictator

to Step Aside," *Vox*, March 5 2019, https://www.vox.com/world/2019/3/5/18251527/algeria-protest-term-pouvoir-bouteflika.

17. See UN Information Centre in Cairo, *Syria: UN-Arab League Envoy Warns of Limited Options, Dangers of Fragmentation* (December 30, 2012), http://www.unic-eg.org/eng/?p=5140.

18. Rasmus Alenius Boserup and Virginie Collombier, *Militarization and Militiaization: Dynamics of Armed Group Proliferation in Egypt and Libya* (Barcelona: Barcelona Centre for International Affairs, October 2018), https://www.cidob.org/en/publications/publication_series/menara_papers/working_papers/militarization_and_militia_ization_dynamics_of_armed_group_proliferation_in_egypt_and_libya.

19. Imad K. Harb, *Is Partition Becoming a Reality in Yemen?* (Washington, DC: Arab Center Washington DC, May 22, 2019), http://arabcenterdc.org/policy_analyses/is-partition-becoming-a-reality-in-yemen/.

20. *All According to Plan: The Rab'a Massacre and Mass Killings of Protesters in Egypt* (New York: Human Rights Watch, August 12, 2014), https://www.hrw.org/report/2014/08/12/all-according-plan/raba-massacre-and-mass-killings-protesters-egypt. For Bahrain, see Mahmoud Cherif Bassiouni, Nigel Rodley, Badria Al-Awadhi, Philippe Kirsch, and Mahnoush H. Arsanjani, *Report of the Bahrain Independent Commission of Inquiry* (Manama: Bahrain Independent Commission of Inquiry, December 10, 2011), http://www.bici.org.bh/BICIreportEN.pdf.

21. See, e.g., Shadi Hamid, William McCants, and Rashid Dar, *Islamism after the Arab Spring: Between the Islamic State and the Nation-State* (Washington, DC: Brookings Institution, January 2017), https://www.brookings.edu/wp-content/uploads/2017/01/islamism-after-the-arab-spring_english_web_final.pdf.

22. See Sami Zubaida, "Class and Community in Urban Politics," in *Islam, the People and the State: Political Ideas and Movements in the Middle East* (London: I. B. Tauris, 2009), 83–98.

23. *Endless Torment: The 1991 Uprising in Iraq and Its Aftermath* (New York: Human Rights Watch, June 1992), https://www.hrw.org/reports/1992/Iraq926.htm.

24. Musa al-Gharbi, "The Myth and Reality of Sectarianism in Iraq," *al-Jazeera America*, August 18, 2014, http://america.aljazeera.com/opinions/2014/8/iraq-sectarianismshiassunniskurdsnourialmalaki.html.

25. *Arab Human Development Report 2004: Towards Freedom in the Arab World* (New York: UN Human Development Programme, 2005), http://hdr.undp.org/en/content/arab-human-development-report-2004.

26. See Heiko Wimmen, *Syria's Path from Civic Uprising to Civil War* (Washington, DC: Carnegie Endowment for International Peace, November 22, 2016), https://carnegieendowment.org/2016/11/22/syria-s-path-from-civic-uprising-to-civil-war-pub-66171.

27. R. Green, "Dispute over Takfīr Rocks Islamic State," *MEMRI*, August 4, 2017, https://www.memri.org/reports/dispute-over-takfīr-rocks-islamic-state. Although more commonly rendered "al-Qaeda in Iraq," the term "al-Qaeda in Mesopotamia" is a more accurate rendering of the Arab name and alludes to the disdain al-Qaeda leaders have for the contemporary nation-state system in the Islamic world.

28. Emile Hokayem, "Lebanon's Little Syria," *Foreign Policy*, May 15, 2012, https://foreignpolicy.com/2012/05/15/lebanons-little-syria/; Mona Alami, *The Impact of the Syria Conflict on Salafis and Jihadis in Lebanon* (Washington, DC: Middle East Institute, April 18, 2014), https://www.mei.edu/publications/impact-syria-conflict-salafis-and-jihadis-lebanon; *Turkey's Syrian Refugees: Defusing Metropolitan Tensions* (Brussels: International Crisis Group, January 29, 2018), https://www.crisisgroup.org/europe-central-asia/western-europemediterranean/turkey/248-turkeys-syrian-refugees-defusing-metropolitan-tensions.

29. See "Report of the Bahrain Independent Commission"; Bruce Riedel, *Who Are the Houthis, and Why Are We at War with Them?* (Washington, DC: Brookings Institution, December 18, 2017), https://www.brookings.edu/blog/markaz/2017/12/18/who-are-the-houthis-and-why-are-we-at-war-with-them/; Frederic Wehrey, *The Forgotten Uprising in Eastern Saudi Arabia* (Washington, DC: Carnegie Endowment for International Peace, June 14, 2013), https://carnegieendowment.org/2013/06/14/forgotten-uprising-in-eastern-saudi-arabia-pub-52093.

30. Abdulaziz H. al-Fahad, "From Exclusivism to Accommodation: Doctrinal and Legal Evolution of Wahhabism," *New York University Law Review* 79, no. 2 (May 2004): 487, 517.

31. See Jeffrey Goldberg, "The Obama Doctrine," *The Atlantic*, April 2016, http://www.theatlantic.com/magazine/archive/2016/04/the-obama-doctrine/471525/.

32. "Offshore balancing" refers to a policy whereby the United States depended on its proxies to maintain the status quo in the region while the United States acted as the ultimate guarantor of their security.

33. See Prince Turki al-Faisal, "Mr. Obama, We Are Not 'Free Riders,'" *Arab News*, March 14, 2016, http://www.arabnews.com/columns/news/894826.

34. Aaron David Miller and Richard Sokolsky, "Trump Isn't Just Reversing Obama's Foreign Policies. He's Making It Impossible for His Successor to Go Back to Them,"

Politico, April 23, 2019, https://www.politico.com/magazine/story/2019/04/23/trump-obama-foreign-policy-226708.

35. David Barbuscia, "Saudi Arabia Would Need Oil at $80–$85 a Barrel to Balance Budget: IMF Official," *Reuters*, February 11, 2019, https://www.reuters.com/article/us-saudi-economy-imf/saudi-arabia-would-need-oil-at-80-85-a-barrel-to-balance-budget-imf-official-idUSKCN1Q01N0.

36. "Saudi Activist Says Money Given to Egyptian General to Oust Morsi," *UPI*, July 30, 2013, https://www.upi.com/Top_News/World-News/2013/07/30/Saudi-activist-says-money-given-to-Egyptian-general-to-oust-Morsi/53881375183115/; Marina Ottaway and David Ottaway, "Egypt's Durable Arab Spring," *Foreign Affairs*, January 24, 2016, https://www.foreignaffairs.com/articles/egypt/2016-01-24/egypts-durable-arab-spring.

37. UN Security Council Resolution No. 1973 (2011), https://www.securitycouncil-report.org/atf/cf/%7B65BFCF9B-6D27-4E9C-8CD3-CF6E4FF96FF9%7D/Libya%20S%20RES%201973.pdf.

38. "Memorandum of Conversation, Washington, April 4, 1977," *Foreign Relations of the United States, 1977–1980*, vol. 8, *Arab-Israeli Dispute, January 1977–August 1978*, https://history.state.gov/historicaldocuments/frus1977-80v08/d25.

39. See, e.g., James L. Gelvin, "No, Trump Is Not Like Obama on Middle East Policy," *Salon*, January 9, 2019, https://www.salon.com/2019/01/09/no-trump-is-not-like-obama-on-middle-east-policy_partner/.

40. *Russian Strategy in the Middle East* (Santa Monica, CA: RAND Corporation, 2017), https://www.rand.org/pubs/perspectives/PE236.html; Scott Wilson, "Obama Dismisses Russia as 'Regional Power' Acting out of Weakness," *Washington Post*, March 25, 2014, https://www.washingtonpost.com/world/national-security/obama-dismisses-russia-as-regional-power-acting-out-of-weakness/2014/03/25/1e5a678e-b439-11e3-b899-20667de76985_story.html?utm_term=.a77e90287fe2.

41. *Shared Vision, Common Action: A Stronger Europe, European Union Global Strategy* (n.p.: European Union, June 2016), https://eeas.europa.eu/sites/eeas/files/eugs_review_web_0.pdf; Anthony Dworkin, *League and Nations: Europe's Unity Struggle at the Sharm El-Sheikh Summit* (London: European Council on Foreign Relations, February 15, 2019), https://www.ecfr.eu/article/commentary_league_and_nations_europes_unity_struggle_at_the_sharm_el_sheikh.

42. Jeffrey Goldberg, "Saudi Crown Prince: Iran's Supreme Leader 'Makes Hitler Look Good,'" *The Atlantic*, April 2, 2018, https://www.theatlantic.com/international/archive/2018/04/mohammed-bin-salman-iran-israel/557036/.

43. Patrick Wintour, "US Backtracks on Iran-Focused Conference in Poland after Objections," *The Guardian*, January 23, 2019, https://www.theguardian.com/world/2019/jan/23/us-backtracks-on-iran-focused-conference-in-poland-after-objections.

44. See James L. Gelvin, *The New Middle East: What Everyone Needs to Know* (New York: Oxford University Press, 2018), 137–67.

CHAPTER 1

1. "Thousands of Tunisians Celebrate Anniversary of Revolution," *France 24*, January 14, 2020, https://www.france24.com/en/20200114-thousands-of-tunisians-celebrate-anniversary-of-revolution.

2. *OECD Economic Surveys, Tunisia* (Paris: OECD, March 2018), http://www.oecd.org/economy/surveys/Tunisia-2018-OECD-economic-survey-overview.pdf.

3. Gilbert Achcar, *The People Want: A Radical Exploration of the Arab Uprising* (Berkeley: University of California Press, 2013), 74.

4. The Arab New Left has been revisited in several recent conferences and publications: "The Arab Left: Mapping the Field," Orient-Institut Beirut, September 30–October 1, 2011; "The Arab Left in Egypt and Lebanon," special issue, *Arab Studies Journal* 24, no. 1 (2016): 90–227; Jamil Hilal and Katja Hermann, eds., *Mapping of the Arab Left: Contemporary Leftist Politics in the Arab East* (Palestine: Rosa Luxemburg Stiftung Regional Office, 2014); and Sune Haugbolle, "The New Arab Left and 1967," *British Journal of Middle Eastern Studies* 44, no. 4 (2017): 497–512.

5. Vincent Geisser, "Interview inédite de Rached Ghanouchi, leader historique du mouvement tunisien 'Renaissance,'" *Oumma*, January 30, 2011, https://oumma.com/interview-inedite-de-rached-ghanouchi-leader-historique-du-mouvement-tunisien-renaissance/.

6. Hisham Mubarak, *Al-Irhabiyun qadimun: Dirasa muqarina bayna mawqif al-ikhwan al-muslimin wa-jama'at al-jihad min qadiyat al-'unf, 1928–1994* (Cairo: Markaz al-Mahrusa li'l-Nashr wa'l-Khadamat al-Sahafiyya, 1995), 123–40; Geneive Abdo, *No God but God: Egypt and the Triumph of Islam* (Oxford: Oxford University Press, 2000), 117–18, 121–22.

7. John Walton and David Seddon, *Free Markets and Food Riots: The Politics of Global Adjustment* (Oxford, UK: Blackwell, 1994), 39–40.

8. See the website of the Arab Organization for Industrialization, at https://fas.org/nuke/guide/egypt/agency/aoi.htm.

9. Samia Saʿid Imam, *Man yamluk misr? Dirasa tahliliyya li-usul nukhbat al-infitah al-ijtimaʿiyya, 1974–1980* (Cairo: Dar al-Mustaqbal al-ʿArabi, 1987), 205, 211, 280–309.

10. Melani Cammett, Ishac Diwan, Alan Richards, and John Waterbury, *A Political Economy of the Middle East*, 4th ed. (Boulder, CO: Westview Press, 2015), 340–41.

11. Cammett et al., 504.

12. Clement Henry Moore, "Islamic Banks and Competitive Politics in the Arab World and Turkey," *Middle East Journal* 44, no. 2 (1990): 238.

13. ʿAbd al-Qadir Shuhayb, *Al-Ikhtiraq: Qissat sharikat tawzif al-amwal fi misr* (Cairo: Sinaʾ liʾl-Nashr, 1989), 29, 60, 80, 84, 98; Robert Springborg, *Mubarak's Egypt: Fragmentation of the Political Order* (Boulder, CO: Westview Press, 1989), 47, 59.

14. Moore, "Islamic Banks and Competitive Politics," 236.

15. Shaimaa Al-Aees, "Islamic Banking Takes Upward Trend in Egypt," *Daily News Egypt*, January 10, 2015, https://dailynewsegypt.com/2015/01/10/islamic-banking-takes-upward-trend-egypt/.

16. Adam Hanieh, *Capitalism and Class in the Gulf Arab States* (New York: Palgrave Macmillan, 2011), 151–57.

17. Karen Pfeifer, "How Tunisia, Morocco, Jordan and Even Egypt Became IMF 'Success Stories' in the 1990s," *Middle East Report*, no. 210 (1999): 23–27.

18. Jeremy N. Sharpe, "Egypt: Background and U.S. Relations" (Washington, DC: Congressional Research Service, June 7, 2018), 23–24, https://fas.org/sgp/crs/mideast/RL33003.pdf.

19. Quoted in Yezid Sayigh, "Above the State: The Officers' Republic in Egypt" (Washington, DC: Carnegie Endowment for International Peace, 2012), 9.

20. An important exception was the AFL-CIO's Solidarity Center, which commissioned me to write *The Struggle for Worker Rights in Egypt* (Washington, DC: Solidarity Center, 2010).

21. *Most Improved in Doing Business 2008* (Washington, DC: World Bank, 2008), http://www.doingbusiness.org/Reforms/Top-reformers-2008; *Most Improved in Doing Business 2009* (Washington, DC: World Bank, 2009), http://www.doingbusiness.org/Reforms/Top-reformers-2009; *Most Improved in Doing Business 2010* (Washington, DC: World Bank, 2010), http://www.doingbusiness.org/Reforms/Top-reformers-2010.

22. Quoted in Emma Murphy, *Economic and Political Change in Tunisia: From Bourguiba to Ben Ali* (London: Macmillan, 1999), 130.

23. Joel Beinin, *Workers and Thieves: Labor Movements and Popular Uprisings in Tunisia and Egypt* (Stanford, CA: Stanford University Press, 2016), 72.

24. Chômage Gafsa 2004, https://upload.wikimedia.org/wikipedia/commons/b/b4/ Ch%C3%B4mage_Gafsa_2004-edit.svg; Habib Ayeb and Ray Bush, "Small Farmer Uprisings and Rural Neglect in Egypt and Tunisia," *Middle East Report* 44, no. 272 (2014): 6.

25. Achcar, *The People Want*, 11, 14.

26. *Arab Human Development Report 2003: Building a Knowledge Society* (New York: UN Development Programme, 2003), 139.

27. *Arab Human Development Report 2009: Challenges to Human Security in the Arab Countries* (New York: UN Development Programme, 2009), 113–14.

28. Achcar, *The People Want*, 24.

29. Achcar, 26–27.

30. Yara Bayoumy, "Obama Administration Arms Sales Offers to Saudi Top $115 Billion: Report," September 7, 2016, https://www.reuters.com/article/us-usa-saudi -security/obama-administration-arms-sales-offers-to-saudi-top-115-billion-report -idUSKCN11D2JQ.

31. Bruce Reidel, "The $110 Billion Arms Deal to Saudi Arabia Is Fake News," *Markaz* (blog of the Brookings Institution), June 5, 2017, https://www.brookings.edu/blog/ markaz/2017/06/05/the-110-billion-arms-deal-to-saudi-arabia-is-fake-news/; Aria Bendix, "U.S. Approves $1.4 Billion Military Sale to Saudi Arabia," *The Atlantic*, June 6, 2017, https://www.theatlantic.com/news/archive/2017/06/us-approves-14-billion -sale-to-saudi-arabia/529257/.

32. Sam Kimball, "Tunisia's Getting More Guns Than Democracy," *Foreign Policy*, April 21, 2016, https://foreignpolicy.com/2016/04/21/tunisias-getting-more -guns-than-democracy/.

33. Christine Lagarde, "The Arab Spring, One Year On," *IMFBlog*, December 6, 2012, https://blogs.imf.org/2011/12/06/the-arab-spring-one-year-on/.

34. Central Bank of Egypt, *Monthly Statistical Bulletin* (January 2014, 2015, 2017): 93–94.

35. Sebastian Sons and Inken Wiese, "The Engagement of Arab Gulf States in Egypt and Tunisia since 2011: Rationale and Impact," *DGAPanalyse* 9 (October 2015): 29.

36. Central Bank of Egypt, *Monthly Statistical Bulletin*, 93–94.

37. Sons and Wiese, "Engagement of Arab Gulf States," 25–26.

38. Sons and Wiese, 41; Toby Matthiesen, "Renting the Casbah: Gulf States' Foreign Policy towards North Africa since the Arab Uprisings," in *The Changing Security Dynamics of the Persian Gulf*, ed. Kristian Coates Ulrichsen (London: Hurst & Co., 2017), 45.

39. Sons and Wiese, "Engagement of Arab Gulf States," 41.

40. Sons and Wiese, 34; Matthiesen, "Renting the Casbah," 45.

41. "UAE Ranked World's Top Aid Donor for Third Consecutive Year," *Gulf News*, April 11, 2017, https://gulfnews.com/news/uae/aid/uae-ranked-world-s-top-aid-donor-for-third-consecutive-year-1.2009870.

42. "UAE to Build Egypt's New Capital City," *Gulf Business*, March 15, 2015, http://gulfbusiness.com/uae-to-build-egypts-new-capital-city/.

43. Egypt, General Authority for Investment and Free Zones, "Saudi Arabia Accounts for 27 percent of Arab Investments in Egypt," March 3, 2015, http://www.gafi.gov.eg/English/MediaCenter/News/Pages/Saudi-Arabia-accounts-for-27-Percent-of-Arab-Investments-in-Egypt.aspx.

44. "Qatar's $1B Investments in Egypt at Risk Amid Diplomatic Rift," *Albawaba*, June 8, 2017, https://www.albawaba.com/business/qatars-1-billion-investments-egypt-risk-amid-diplomatic-rift-984112.

45. "Saudi Investments in Egypt Stable: GAFI," *Egypt Today*, November 5, 2017, https://www.egypttoday.com/Article/3/31087/Saudi-investments-in-Egypt-stable-GAFI.

46. "Crown Prince Signs $10 Billion Deal on Mega-City during Cairo Visit," Reuters, March 4, 2018, https://www.reuters.com/article/us-saudi-egypt/crown-prince-signs-10-billion-deal-on-mega-city-during-cairo-visit-idUSKBN1GG0QD.

47. "IMF Executive Board Approves US$12 billion Extended Arrangement under the Extended Fund Facility for Egypt," *IMFBlog*, November 11, 2016, https://www.imf.org/en/News/Articles/2016/11/11/PR16501-Egypt-Executive-Board-Approves-12-billion-Extended-Arrangement.

48. Sons and Wiese, "Engagement of Arab Gulf States," 51, 54, 58; World Bank, *Global Economic Prospects Middle East and North Africa*, June 2015, 5, http://www.worldbank.org/content/dam/Worldbank/GEP/GEP2015b/Global-Economic-Prospects-June-2015-Middle-East-and-North-Africa-analysis.pdf.

49. "Qatar's QNB Buys Further 49.96 Pct in Tunisian Qatari Bank," *Reuters*, January 23, 2013, https://www.reuters.com/article/us-qatar-qnb-tunisia/qatars-qnb-buys-further-49-96-pct-in-tunisian-qatari-bank-idUSBRE90M0OR20130123; Matthiesen, "Renting the Casbah," 55–56.

50. Kristian Coates Ulrichsen, *Qatar and the Arab Spring: Policy Drivers and Regional Implications* (Washington, DC: Carnegie Endowment for International Peace, September 24, 2014, https://carnegieendowment.org/2014/09/24/qatar-and-arab-spring-policy-drivers-and-regional-implications-pub-56723.

51. Tunisie, Agence de Promotion de l'Investissement Extérieur, *Bilan 2016 des investissements étrangers en Tunisie*, 47.

52. Matthiesen, "Renting the Casbah," 56.

53. Arab Export and Investment Credit Guarantee Corporation, "Tunisia: Inward and Outward FDI," February 2016, http://dhaman.net/wp-content/uploads/2016/02/Tunisia.pdf; Tunisie, Agence de Promotion de l'Investissement Extérieur, *Bilan 2016*, 47.

54. "IMF Survey: Tunisia Gets $2.9 Billion IMF Loan to Strengthen Job Creation and Economic Growth," *IMF News*, June 2, 2016, https://www.imf.org/en/News/Articles/2015/09/28/04/53/sonew060216a.

55. "Tunisia to Accelerate Reforms as IMF Freezes Loan: Minister," *Reuters*, February 26, 2017, https://www.reuters.com/article/us-tunisia-economy/tunisia-to-accelerate-reforms-as-imf-freezes-loan-minister-idUSKBN16508T.

56. Fadil Alireza, "'Two Classes Left—Rich And Poor': Sinking Tunisia's Currency," *Middle East Eye*, May 5, 2018 https://www.middleeasteye.net/news/two-classes-left-rich-and-poor-sinking-tunisias-currency.

57. "Regional Partners Pledge Billions in Help for Tunisia," *Reuters*, November 28, 2016, https://www.reuters.com/article/us-tunisia-economy-investment/regional-partners-pledge-billions-in-help-for-tunisia-idUSKBN13N1KC.

58. R. J. Reinhart and Iman Berrached, "Tunisia's New Government Faces Daunting Challenges," November 25, 2019, https://news.gallup.com/poll/268502/tunisia-new-government-faces-daunting-challenges.aspx.

CHAPTER 2

1. Kiren Aziz Chaudhry, *The Price of Wealth: Economies and Institutions in the Middle East* (Ithaca, NY: Cornell University Press, 1997).

2. See, e.g., Steven Heydemann, ed., *Networks of Privilege in the Middle East: The Politics of Economic Reform Revisited* (New York: Palgrave, 2004); Ishac Diwan, Adeel Malik, and Izak Atiyas, eds., *Crony Capitalism in the Middle East: Business and Politics from Liberalization to the Arab Spring* (Oxford: Oxford University Press, 2019).

3. Mushtaq H. Khan, "Political Settlements and the Governance of Growth-Enhancing Institutions" (unpublished paper, July 2010), https://eprints.soas.ac.uk/9968/1/Political_Settlements_internet.pdf.

4. Douglass C. North et al., "Violence and the Rise of Open-Access Orders," *Journal of Democracy* 20, no. 1 (2009): 55–68.

5. Most countries in the MENA region grew at between 2 percent and 4 percent

per capita during the 2000s. Melani Cammett, Ishac Diwan, Alan Richards, and John Waterbury, *A Political Economy of the Middle East*, 4th ed. (Boulder, CO: Westview Press, 2015). This is in contrast to lower growth rates during the long adjustment phase of the 1980s and 1990s. However, this performance did not keep up with the average of developing countries during this period (5 percent) and was far below the rates of 6 percent and above observed in the fast-growing economies of East Asia.

6. Most recent studies have shown that the size of the middle class—defined as the three middle quintiles of the income distribution—has been remarkably stable in most MENA countries over the past two decades, but that the nature of this group has changed over time, with a smaller share of public servants and a higher share of individuals working in the private sector. See Ishac Diwan, "Understanding Revolution in the Middle East: The Central Role of the Middle Class," *Middle East Development Journal* 5, no. 1 (2013): 4–8.

7. Eva Bellin, "The Robustness of Authoritarianism in the Middle East: Exceptionalism in Comparative Perspective," *Comparative Politics* (2004): 139–57.

8. In particular, consumption subsidies rose to extraordinary levels in the late 2000s on the back of the oil boom.

9. Steffen Hertog, "The Role of Cronyism in Arab Capitalism," in *Crony Capitalism in the Middle East*, 57–59.

10. Bellin, "Robustness," 148.

11. Gary W. Cox, Douglass C. North, and Barry R. Weingast, "The Violence Trap: A Political-Economic Approach to the Problems of Development," *Journal of Public Finance and Public Choice* 34, no. 1 (2019): 3–19.

12. Ragui Assaad, Caroline Krafft, and Djavad Salehi-Isfahani, "Does the Type of Higher Education Affect Labor Market Outcomes? Evidence from Egypt and Jordan." *Higher Education* 75, no. 6 (2018): 945–95.

13. See Cammett et al., *A Political Economy*, 319–51.

14. Clement Moore Henry and Robert Springborg. *Globalization and the Politics of Development in the Middle East*, 2nd ed. (New York: Cambridge University Press, 2010), 67–73.

15. Steve L. Monroe, "Ethnic Politics and Business Politics in Jordan," in *Crony Capitalism in the Middle East*, 263.

16. Ishac Diwan and Jamal Ibrahim Haidar, "Clientelism, Cronyism, and Job Creation," in *Crony Capitalism in the Middle East*, 119.

17. Seda Demiralp, "The Rise of Islamic Capital and the Decline of Islamic Radicalism in Turkey," *Comparative Politics* 41, no. 3 (2009): 315–35.

18. Lant Pritchett, Kunal Sen, and Eric Werker, *Deals and Development: The Political Dynamics of Growth Episodes* (New York: Oxford University Press, 2018).

19. Ishac Diwan, "A Landing Strategy for Saudi Arabia," *POMEPS Studies 33: The Politics of Rentier States in the Gulf,* ed. Marc Lynch (Washington, DC: Project on Middle East Political Science, 2019), https://pomeps.org/wp-content/uploads/2019/02/POMEPS_Studies_33.pdf.

CHAPTER 3

1. *Arab Human Development Report, 2016: Youth and the Prospects for Human Development in a Changing Society* (New York: UN Development Programme, 2016), http://www.arab-hdr.org/Reports/2016/2016.aspx.

2. *Arab Human Development Report, 2003: Building a Knowledge Society* (New York: UN Development Programme, 2003), http://hdr.undp.org/sites/default/files/rbas_ahdr2003_en.pdf.

3. Shahrbanou Tadjbakhsh, "In Defense of a Broad View of Human Security," in *Routledge Handbook of Human Security*, ed. Mary Martin and Taylor Owen (New York: Routledge, 2014), 44.

4. *Arab Human Development Report, 2009: Challenges to Human Security in the Arab Countries* (New York: UN Development Programme, 2009), 137.

5. Ministry of National Education, *Basic Education in Turkey: Background Report* (Ankara: Republic of Turkey, Ministry of National Education, 2005), 17–18.

6. Ministry of National Education, 37.

7. See, e.g., letters of the Middle East Studies Association's Committee on Academic Freedom (CAF) of April 29, 2009; October 3, 2011; November 21, 2011; August 7, 2012; September 4, 2012; December 12, 2012; and January 24, 2013, at http://mesana.org/committees/academic-freedom/intervention/letters-turkey.html.

8. The high-profile trials that resulted from these investigations targeted 275 people, many of whom were military officers, journalists, and opposition members of parliament charged with belonging to an alleged secularist clandestine organization called Ergenekon, which was purportedly plotting against the government. Owing to an absence of evidence to substantiate even the existence of Ergenekon, the convictions were overturned in April 2016.

See CAF letter of October 4, 2013, on three mass trials of academics, at http://mesana.org/committees/academic-freedom/intervention/letters-turkey.html.

9. See CAF letters of February 28, 2013; May 8, 2013; May 6, 2014; and January 7, 2016, on state interference in faculty governance and higher education administration, at http://mesana.org/committees/academic-freedom/intervention/letters-turkey.html.

10. See CAF letter October 4, 2013, on reports of reprisals against university students and professors, at http://mesana.org/committees/academic-freedom /intervention/letters-turkey.html.

11. For the English version of the petition, see http://bianet.org/english/human-rights /170978-academics-we-will-not-be-a-party-to-this-crime.

12. See especially the detailed list of abuses in the CAF letter of February 22, 2016, at http://mesana.org/committees/academic-freedom/intervention/letters-turkey.html.

13. For more on the coup, see Henri J. Barkey's chapter "Erdogan, Turkish Foreign Policy, and the Middle East" in this volume.

14. For full details of the Emergency Decree of September 1, 2016, see the CAF letter of September 6, 2016, at http://mesana.org/committees/academic-freedom /intervention/letters-turkey.html.

15. For more details on the elimination of university self-governance, see the CAF letter of November 7, 2016, at http://mesana.org/committees/academic-freedom/in-tervention/letters-turkey.html.

16. For more details on the faculty dismissals, see the CAF letters of January 12, 2017; January 17, 2017; and February 8, 2017, at http://mesana.org/committees/academ-ic-freedom/intervention/letters-turkey.html

17. Umar Farooq, "Post-Coup Purge Will Affect Turkey's Education Sector for Decades," *Los Angeles Times*, http://www.latimes.com/world/europe/la-fg-turkey-education -purge-2016-story.html.

18. Judith Tucker, "July 8th Emergency Decree 701 Removing 206 Academics and 52 Administrators," *MESA CAF*, https://mesana.org/advocacy/committee-on-academic -freedom/2018/07/17/july-8th-emergency-decree-701-removing-206-academics -and-52-administrators.

19. On the origins of "Berber," see Ramzi Rouighi, *Inventing the Berbers: History and Ideology in the Maghreb* (Philadelphia: University of Pennsylvania Press, 2019).

20. On French colonial narratives, see, e.g., Abdel-Majid Hannoum, *Colonial Histories, Post-Colonial Memories: The Legend of the Kahina, a North African Heroine* (New York: Heinemann, 2001).

21. See Laurie A Brand, *Official Stories: Politics and National Narratives in Egypt and Algeria* (Stanford, CA: Stanford University Press, 2014), 117–52.

22. Brand, 176.

23. Nacer Djabi, "The Algerian Constitution: Lip-Service to Safeguards" (Paris: Arab Reform Initiative, October 2016), https://www.arab-reform.net/publication/the-algerian-constitution-lip-service-to-safeguards/.

24. Fatima Arab, "Des changements qui promettent dans les manuels scolaires," *DjaZairess*, September 18, 2017, https://www.djazairess.com/fr/elwatan/552887.

25. Omar Arbane, "Depuis deux and, Tamazight est enseignée dans 37 wilayas," *El Watan*, December 10, 2017, http://www.elwatan.com/actualite/depuis-deux-ans-tamazight-est-enseignee-dans-37-wilayas-10-12-2017-358310_109.php. The number of provinces was increased to fifty-eight in December 2018.

26. M. Ouyougoute, "Colère des étudiants contre la baisse du budget du haut commissariat à l'amazighité," *Liberté*, December 5, 2017, https://www.liberte-algerie.com/actualite/colere-des-etudiants-contre-la-baisse-du-budget-du-haut-commissariat-a-lamazighite-282578.

27. "Al-Jazaʿir tusdur awwal bayyan rasmi biʾllughah al-amazighiyyah wa jadal hawla kitabatiha bi-il harf al-latini," *al-Quds al-Arabi*, http://www.alquds.co.uk/?p=858656.

28. See Palestinian Ministry of Education, "The Myth of Incitement in Palestinian Textbooks," *Electronic Intifada*, June 13, 2005,

https://electronicintifada.net/content/myth-incitement-palestinian-textbooks/5626; Nathan J. Brown, "Democracy, History and the Contest over the Palestinian Curriculum," Adam Institute, November 2001, https://home.gwu.edu/~nbrown/Adam_Institute_Palestinian_textbooks.htm.

29. "Infographic: Palestinian Population Worldwide by Place of Residence at the Beginning of 2017," *Al-Zaytouna Center for Studies and Consultations*, https://eng.alzaytouna.net/2017/04/05/infographic-palestinian-population-worldwide-by-place-of-residence-at-the-beginning-of-2017/.

30. Ibtisam Abu-Duhou, "Schools in Palestine under the Occupation and the Palestinian National Authority," *Palestine-Israel Journal of Politics, Economics and Culture* 3, no. 1 (1996): http://www.pij.org/details.php?id=566.

31. Nubar Hovsepian, "Palestinian Education in a Virtual State," in *Trajectories of Education in the Arab World: Legacies and Challenges*, ed. Osama Abi Mershed (New York: Routledge, 2010), 128–35.

32. Right to Education Campaign, *The Right to Education Campaign's Submission to the United Nations Human Rights Council's Universal Periodic Review of Israel December 2008*, https://www.google.com/url?sa=t&rct=j&q=&esrc

=s&source=web&cd=&cad=rja&uact=8&ved=2ahUKEwjNocD5usTsAhWVuJ4KHUC
3AVgQFjAAegQIBxAC&url=https%3A%2F%2Flib.ohchr.org%2FHRBodies%-
2FUPR%2FDocuments%2FSession3%2FIL%2FR2EC_ISR_UPR_S3_2008_TheRight
toEducationCampaign_uprsubmission.pdf&usg=AOvVaw2ref5LZeZJlm-pZP_bcePO.

33. See CAF letter of February 25, 2015, regarding destruction of Palestinian educational institutions at, https://mesana.org/advocacy/committee-on-academic-freedom/2015/02/25/israels-destruction-of-palestinian-educational-institutions-in-july-and-august-2014.

34. For a report dealing solely with the material, human, and educational damage visited upon Gaza during the Israeli assaults of July 7–August 26, 2014, see UNESCO, "Rapid Assessment of Higher Education Institutions in Gaza: Data Analysis Report," 2015, https://unispal.un.org/pdfs/UNESCO_HIGHERED.pdf.

35. See, inter alia, CAF letter of February 9, 2016 regarding repeated incursions into Palestinian universities by the Israeli army at https://mesana.org/advocacy/committee-on-academic-freedom/2016/02/09/outrageat-the-repeated-israeli-army-incursions-at-palestinian-universities.

36. See CAF letter of August 6, 2018, on the arbitrary conditions placed on foreign nationals working in Palestinian universities at https://mesana.org/advocacy/committee-on-academic-freedom/2018/08/06/arbitrary-demands-on-foreign-national-academics-working-in-palestinian-universities.

37. UN Office of the High Commissioner for Human Rights, "Summary Prepared by the Office of the High Commissioner for Human Rights, in Accordance with Paragraph 15(C) of the Annex to Human Rights Council Resolution 5/1," 2008, https://www.un.org/unispal/document/auto-insert-184027/. See also Leo Wiggen-Bush, "The Detention of Palestinian Children and Its Impact on Their Education and Development," *Jadaliyya*, January 3, 2018, https://www.jadaliyya.com/Details/34933/The-Detention-of-Palestinian-Children-and-Its-Impact-on-Their-Education-and-Development?mc_cid=3a1529956d&mc_eid=aaa3ac55ea.

38. Right to Education Campaign, *The Right to Education Campaign's Submission*.

39. UNESCO, "Rapid Assessment of Higher Education."

40. UNESCO, "Iraq: Education in Transition: Needs and Challenges" (Paris: UNESCO, 2004), https://unesdoc.unesco.org/ark:/48223/pf0000138665.

41. UNESCO, "Iraq."

42. UNESCO, "Iraq."

43. UNESCO, "Iraq."

44. Christina Asquith, "A New History of Iraq," *The Guardian*, November 24, 2003, https://www.theguardian.com/education/2003/nov/25/schools.schoolsworldwide.

45. Global Education Monitoring Report Team, *The Hidden Crisis: Armed Conflict and Education* (Paris: UNESCO, 2011), https://unesdoc.unesco.org/ark:/48223/pf0000190743.

46. For a detailed discussion of the impact on universities and archives, see Keith Watenpaugh, Edouard Méténier, Jens Hanssen, and Hala Fattah, "Opening the Doors: Intellectual Life and Academic Conditions in Post-War Baghdad," *Iraqi Observatory*, July 15, 2003, https://www.h-net.org/about/press/opening_doors/opening_doors.pdf.

47. Asquith, "New History of Iraq."

48. Asquith.

49. Adnan Abu Zeed, "Iraqi State Education Increasingly Religious," *Al-Monitor*, January 27, 2015, https://www.al-monitor.com/pulse/en/originals/2015/01/iraq-state-education-religious-curricula.html.

50. Abu Zeed.

51. *Arab Human Development Report, 2016: Youth and the Prospects for Human Development in a Changing Reality* (New York: UN Development Programme, 2016), table 1, p. 231. and table 4, 234.

52. *Syria Crisis Education Strategic Paper: London 2016 Conference* (New York: UNICEF, 2016), http://www.oosci-mena.org/london-education-conference-2016.

53. "Urgent Measures Needed to Stop Iraq's Displaced Children Being Left Behind," Norwegian Refugee Council, December 3, 2019, https://www.nrc.no/resources/briefing-notes/urgent-measures-needed-to-stop-iraqs-displaced-children-being-left-behind/.

CHAPTER 4

My thanks to Zep Kalb and Daniel Tavana for assistance on data analysis in this chapter.

1. E.g., Sadegh Zibakalam, "Tabaghe-ye motavaset kojast?" *Shargh*, January 15, 2013; Alireza Raisi, "The Puzzle of Populism in Iran's Electoral Politics," *Democratization* 26, no. 6 (2019): 916–34.

2. Göran Therborn, "Class in the 21st Century," *New Left Review* 2, no. 78 (2012): 5–29, at 20.

3. Hagen Koo, "Middle Classes, Democratization, and Class Formation: The Case of South Korea," *Theory and Society* 20, no. 4 (1991): 485–509; Dietrich Rueschemeyer,

Evelyne Huber Stephens, and John D. Stephens, *Capitalist Development and Democracy* (Chicago: University of Chicago Press, 1992); Vivek Chibber, *Postcolonial Theory and the Specter of Capital* (London: Verso, 2013).

4. Arjun Jayadev, Rahul Lahoti, and Sanjay Reddy, "The Middle Muddle: Conceptualizing and Measuring the Global Middle Class," in *Toward a Just Society: Joseph Stiglitz and Twenty-First Century Economics*, ed. Martin Guzman (New York: Columbia University Press), 67.

5. Gay Seidman, "Guest Editor Introduction: The Politics of the Middle Class in Developing Countries," *Political Power and Social Theory* 21 (2010): 95–98, at 97. Also see Diane Davis, "The Sociospatial Reconfiguration of Middle Classes and Their Impact on Politics and Development in the Global South: Preliminary Ideas for Future Research," *Political Power and Social Theory* 21 (2010): 241–67.

6. Raka Ray, "'The Middle Class': Sociological Category or Proper Noun?" *Political Power and Social Theory* 21 (2010): 313–22, at 316.

7. Rogers Brubaker, *Ethnicity without Groups* (Cambridge, MA: Harvard University Press, 2004), 8.

8. See the collection of essays in *Civil Society and Democracy in Iran*, ed. Ramin Jahanbegloo (Lanham, MD: Lexington Books, 2011).

9. Fatemeh Sadeghi, "Ostoreh-ye tabaghe-ye motavaset," *Shargh*, March 5, 2013.

10. Given the paucity of surveys in Iran, we should ask whether data from the ISS is reliable. The ISS was designed and implemented to produce benchmarks for demographic, social, and political indicators in contemporary Iran based on robust survey methods carried out in middle-income countries in MENA and other regions. For the methodology of the ISS, see Kevan Harris and Daniel Tavana, "Voter Behavior and Political Mobilization in Iran: Findings from the Iran Social Survey" (Lund, Sweden: European Middle East Research Group, 2018), https://doi.org/10.26369/re.2018.001.

11. Frank Newport, "Americans' Identification as Middle Class Edges Back Up," *Gallup*, December 15, 2016, https://news.gallup.com/poll/199727/americans-identification-middle-class-edges-back.aspx.

12. Ronelle Burger, Cindy Lee Steenekamp, Servaas van der Berg, and Asmus Zoch. "The Emergent Middle Class in Contemporary South Africa: Examining and Comparing Rival Approaches," *Development Southern Africa* 32, no. 1 (2015): 25–40; Rodolfo Elbert and Pablo Pérez. "The Identity of Class in Latin America: Objective Class Position and Subjective Class Identification in Argentina and Chile (2009)," *Current Sociology* 66, no. 5 (2018): 724–47.

13. Hossein Adibi, *Tabaghe-ye Motavaset-e Jadid dar Iran* (Tehran: Ja'meh Publishing, 1979); Mohammad Hossein Bahrani, *Tabaghe-ye Motavaset va Tahavolat-e Siasi dar Iran-e Mo'aser (1320–1380)* (Tehran: Agah Publishing, 2010).

14. See Nils Gilman, "Modernization Theory Never Dies," *History of Political Economy* 50, no. S1 (2018): 133–51.

15. For example, see Aghil Daghagheleh, "Ambivalent Voting Behavior: Ideology, Efficacy, and the Socioeconomic Dynamic of Voter Turnout in Iran, 1997–2005," *Sociological Forum* 33, no. 4 (2018): 1023–44. This article puts forth a plausible claim that voter turnout among Iran's middle class—as defined by income and education higher than the median—varies across presidential elections from 1997 to 2005. The evidence used is a state-administered 2005 survey that asks selected individuals to recall whether they voted or not as far back as 1997, but not for whom they voted. Unfortunately, the survey instrument does not allow for testing any claim that middle-class voters cast ballots disproportionately for reformist or moderate candidates. This undermines the key argument of the paper about the coherence of middle-class voting behavior, which remains an untested a priori assumption. Furthermore, as survey methodologists and social psychologists have repeatedly argued, asking individuals in the present about voting behavior during long-past events, especially among low-information citizens, suffers from high levels of "recall inaccuracy." See Erika van Elsas, Emily M. Miltenburg, and Tom W. G. van der Meer, "If I Recall Correctly: An Event History Analysis of Forgetting and Recollecting Past Voting Behavior," *Journal of Elections, Public Opinion and Parties* 26, no. 3 (2016): 253–72. Given the lack of stable partisan identification, the absence of long preelection campaigns, and the low incumbency rates in Iranian politics, bias in survey response due to recall inaccuracy could be far higher than in wealthier democracies. For survey evidence on the low levels of partisan identification among many Iranians, a finding common in many Middle Eastern cases, see Harris and Tavana, "Voter Behavior and Political Mobilization."

16. M. Bahrani, "Why Did the Middle Class Choose Rouhani in the June 14 Election?" (in Persian), *Islamic Republic News Agency*, June 11, 2014, https://www.irna.ir/news/81196515/.

17. Is self-reported electoral behavior from the ISS reliable? According to Iran's Ministry of Interior, 72.9 percent of the 50.4 million Iranians eligible to participate in the 2013 presidential election voted. In the 2016 ISS, 76.3 percent of age-eligible respondents reported that they voted in the 2013 presidential election. Survey research shows that measurement of electoral behavior often overestimates voting for

the incumbent and underestimates voting for unsuccessful candidates as a result of pro-incumbent bias. This is no different for the Iranian case in the raw data of the ISS. In addition, 13 percent of respondents who reported voting in the 2013 election also reported that they did not recall whom they voted for. A relevant inquiry is whether these two discrepancies—pro-incumbent bias and refusal or nonrecollection—affect the relative frequencies of vote share for the categories of interest. If more educated or higher-income voters reported "I don't know" more frequently than other types of respondents when asked who they voted for in 2013, then the estimates on relative vote share for these groups for any candidates might be further skewed in the survey data. Yet this is not the case in the ISS data. The "I don't know" category correlates mostly with ISS respondents who are older, poorer, and less educated than the average respondent—sometimes called "low-information voters" among pollsters. Conversely, younger, more educated, and higher-income respondents were more likely to report who they voted for, which arguably advantages the data in the ISS for this analysis.

18. Iranians are eligible to vote in elections once they reach eighteen years of age. It is relatively easy to vote on election day as well, since voters can cast their vote in any polling station in the country rather than at a specific registered site. Since the mid-1990s, between 60 percent and 80 percent of the electorate has turned out to vote in national-level elections in Iran. The 2013 election was similar in this regard, with a high reported turnout according to official sources. The ISS was the only nationally representative postelection survey to independently verify the government's reported turnout.

19. As also seen in Figure 4, the main discrepancy between the official results and the ISS is a slight increase in the relative share of votes for the election winner, Hassan Rouhani. Survey research in democratic contexts has shown a pro-incumbent respondent bias in retrospective recollection of vote choice. See Oliver Heath and Robert Johns, "Measuring Political Behaviour and Attitudes," in *Social Measurement through Social Surveys: An Applied Approach*, ed. Martin Bulmer, Julie Gibbs, and Laura Hyman (Surrey, UK: Ashgate Publishing, 2010), 47–68.

20. Although three cohorts are shown, using different age cohorts within younger respondents does not shift the main trends shown in Figure 5.

21. E.g., Mohammad Reza Farzanegan, Pouya Alaedini, and Khayam Azizmehr, "Middle Class in Iran: Oil Rents, Modernization, and Political Development" (MAGKS Papers on Economics No. 201756, Faculty of Business Administration and Economics, Philipps-Universität Marburg, 2017).

22. See, for example, the analysis by Mohammad Ali Kadivar and Vahid Abedini, "Electoral Activism in Iran: A Mechanism for Political Change," *Comparative Politics* 52, no. 3 (2020): 493–514.

CHAPTER 5

1. Aomar Boum, "Youth, Political Activism and the Festivalization of Hip-Hop Music in Morocco," in *Contemporary Morocco: State, Politics and Society under Mohammed VI*, ed. Bruce Maddy-Weitzman and Daniel Zisenwine (New York: Routledge, 2013), 161–77.

2. David Seddon, "Winter of Discontent: Economic Crisis in Tunisia and Morocco," *MERIP*, 14, no. 127 (September–October 1984): 7–16; "Riot in Rebellion in North Africa: Political Responses to Economic Crisis in Tunisia, Morocco and Sudan," in *Power and Stability in the Middle East*, ed. Berch Berberoglu (London: Zed Books, 1989), 114–35.

3. François Burgat, "Les harraga algériens," *Migrations Société* 24, no. 143 (2012): 105–20.

4. Meriem Verges, "'I Am Living in a Foreign Country Here': A Conversation with an Algerian 'Hittiste,'" *Middle East Report* 192 (January–February 1995), 14.

5. Luis Martinez, "Youth, the Street and Violence in Algeria," in *Alienation and Integration of Arab Youth: Between Family, State and Street*, ed. Roel Meijer (Richmond, UK: Curzon, 2000), 83–106. Also see Mounia Bennani-Chraïbi, "Youth in Morocco: An Indicator of a Changing Society," in *Alienation and Integration of Arab Youth: Between Family, State and Street*, ed. Roel Meijer (Richmond, UK: Curzon, 2000), 143–60.

6. For an excellent discussion of Rai music and its political use from the colonial period to the recent present, see Malika Mehdid, "For a Song-Censure in Algerian Rai Music," in *Popular Music Censorship in Africa*, ed. Michael Drewett and Martin Cloonan (London: Routledge, 2006), 199–214. Also see Bouziane Daoudi and Hadji Miliani, *L'aventure du raï: Musique et société* (Paris: Découverte, 1997).

7. Christa Jones, "Raï and Politics Do Not Mix: Musical Resistance during the Algerian Civil War," *French Review* 86, no. 3 (2013): 474–84.

8. Bezza Mazouzi, *La musique algérienne et la question raï* (Paris: La revue musicale, 1992), 78.

9. For a detailed discussion of this song, see Ted Swedenburg, "Beur/Maghribi Musical Interventions in France: Rai and Rap," *Journal of North African Studies* 20, no. 1 (2015): 109–26; Heidrun Friese, "'Ya l'babour, ya mon amour': Raï, Rap and the Desire to Escape," *Music, Longing and Belonging: Articulations of the Self and the Other*

in the Musical Realm, ed. Magdalena Waligórska (Newcastle, UK: Cambridge Scholars Publishing, 2013), 176–201.

10. Mark A. Tessler, "Alienation of Urban Youth," in *Polity and Society in Contemporary North Africa*, ed. I. William Zartman and William Mark Habeeb (Boulder, CO: Westview Press, 1993), 71–101.

11. Abderrahim Bourkia, *Des ultras dans la ville: Étude sociologique sur un aspect de la violence urbaine* (Casablanca: Éditions la Croisée des chemins, 2018); David Seddon, "The Politics of 'Adjustment' in Morocco," in *Structural Adjustment in Africa*, ed. Bonnie K. Campbell and John Loxley (New York: St. Martin's Press, 1989), 234–65.

12. Leola Johnson, "Silencing Gangsta Rap: Class and Race Agendas in the Campaign against Hardcore Rap Lyrics," *Temple Political and Civil Rights Review* 3 (1993–1994): 25–44.

13. "El Général Rais El Bled," YouTube video, 3:58, posted by djstey, January 30, 2011, https://www.youtube.com/watch?v=EIKygYHGzJ8. English translation is adopted from Sean O'Keefe, "El Général—Rais lebled," Revolutionary Arab Rap: The Index (*blog*), August 30, 2011, http://revolutionaryarabraptheindex.blogspot.com/2011/08/el-general-rais-lebled.html.

14. Nouri Gana, "Rap and Revolt in the Arab World," *Social Text* 30:4, no. 113 (2012): 25–53.

15. Aomar Boum, "The Culture of Despair: Youth, Unemployment and Educational Failures in North Africa," in *Educators of the Mediterranean: Up Close and Personal Critical Voices from South Europe and the MENA*, ed. Ronald G. Sultana (Rotterdam: Sense Publishers, 2011), 242; Norma Mendoza-Denton and Aomar Boum, "Breached Initiations: Sociopolitical Resources and Conflicts in Emergent Adulthood," *Annual Review of Anthropology* 44 (2015): 295–310.

16. Eric Drott, "Resistance and Social Movement," in *The Routledge Reader on the Sociology of Music*, ed. Kyle Devine and John Shepherd (New York: Routledge, 2015), 171–79.

17. Boum, "Youth, Political Activism."

18. Taieb Belghazi and Abdelhay Moudden, "*Ihbat*: Disillusionment and the Arab Spring in Morocco," *Journal of North African Studies* 21, no. 1 (2016): 37–49.

19. Khalil Hindi, "Profile: Ahmed Fouad Negm," *Index on Censorship* 8, no. 2 (1979): 50–51. Also see Elliott Cola, "Egyptian Movement Poetry," *Journal of Arabic Literature* 51 (2020): 53–82.

20. Jennifer Hill Boutz, *Hassan Ibn Thabit, a True Mukhadram: A Study of the Ghassanid Odes of Hassan ibn Thabit* (PhD diss., Georgetown University, 2009).

21. "Lotfi Double Kanon Kamikaz," YouTube video, posted by Kamikazlo, 4:19, July 1, 2007, https://www.youtube.com/watch?v=Ulgi2z3mvkQ.

22. Moulay Driss El Maarouf and Taieb Belghazi, "The Urban and Virtual Rhetoric of *tcharmil*: Display Violence and Resistance," *Journal of North African Studies* 23, nos. 1–2 (2018): 292–310.

23. Aomar Boum and Mohamed Daadaoui, *Historical Dictionary of the Arab Uprisings* (Lanham, MD: Rowman and Littlefield, 2020).

24. Zakia Salime, "I Vote I Sing: The Rise of Aesthetic Citizenship in Morocco," *International Journal of Middle East Studies* 47, no. 1 (2015): 136–39.

25. Cristina Moreno Almeida, "Unravelling Distinct Voices in Moroccan Rap: Evading Control, Weaving Solidarities, and Building New Spaces for Self-Expression," *Journal of African Cultural Studies* 25, no. 3 (2013): 319–32; Almeida, *Rap beyond Resistance: Staging Power in Contemporary Morocco* (London: Palgrave Macmillan, 2017).

26. Marilyn Booth, "Sheikh Imam the Singer: An Interview." *Index on Censorship* 14, no. 3 (1985): 19.

27. Norma Mendoza-Denton and Aomar Boum, "Breached Initiations: Sociopolitical Resources and Conflicts in Emergent Adulthood," *Annual Review of Anthropology* 44 (2015): 295–310.

28. "Lotfi DK nouvelle generation," YouTube video, posted by zaki mort, 3:38, May 21, 2016, https://www.youtube.com/watch?v=jQRINnSGG_s.

29. Souad Halila, "Rap and Islamism in Post-Revolutionary Tunisia: Local Idiosyncrasies and Global Reverberations," in *Islamism and Cultural Expression in the Arab World*, ed. Abir Hamdar and Lindsey Moore (London: Routledge, 2015), 230–31.

30. "Guiton'n- ya-mchad," YouTube video, posted by Elhiwar Ettounsi, 5:08, February 19, 2014, https://www.youtube.com/watch?v=UP5etJQ9KcY&list=RDUP5etJQ9KcY&start_radio=1&t=0.

31. On Palestine, see Aomar Boum, "'Soundtracks of Jerusalem': YouTube, North African Rappers, and the Fantasies of Resistance," in *Modernity, Minority and the Public Sphere: Jews and Christians in the Middle East*, ed. S. R. Goldstein-Sabbah and H. L. Murre-van den Berg (Leiden: Brill, 2016), 284–310.

CHAPTER 6

1. For the classic account of political opportunity structures, see Charles Tilly, *From Mobilization to Revolution* (Reading, MA: Addison-Wesley, 1978).

2. Monica Marks, "Why do Tunisia's Islamists Support an Unpopular Law Forgiving Corruption?" *Washington Post*, May 5, 2017, https://www.washingtonpost.com/

news/monkey-cage/wp/2017/05/05/why-do-tunisias-islamists-support-an-unpopu-lar-law-forgiving-corruption/?utm_term=.05f6b7860b4f.

3. Stacey Philbrick Yadav, "How War Is Changing Yemen's Largest Islamist Co-alition," *Washington Post*, March 27, 2017, https://www.washingtonpost.com/news/monkey-cage/wp/2017/03/22/how-war-is-changing-yemens-largest-islamist-coali-tion/?utm_term=.5de6a653b8dd.

4. The term "ikhwanist" denotes political movements organizationally indepen-dent from, but broadly inspired by, the ideological roots of the Ikhwan al-Muslimin, or Muslim Brotherhood.

5. Pew Forum on Religion and Public Life, "Beliefs about Sharia," in *The World's Muslims: Religion, Politics, and Society* (Washington, DC: Pew Research Center, April 30, 2013), chap. 1, http://www.pewforum.org/2013/04/30/the-worlds-muslims-reli-gion-politics-society-beliefs-about-sharia/.

6. See the Arab Barometer Wave IV (2016–2017), http://www.arabbarometer.org.

7. For a broad overview of the *wasatiyya* movement, see Raymond William Baker, *Islam without Fear: Egypt and the New Islamists* (Cambridge, MA: Harvard University Press, 2006).

8. Vali Nasr, "The Rise of Muslim Democracy," *Journal of Democracy* 16, no. 2 (April 2005): 13–27.

9. See Rachid Ghannouchi, "Participation in Non-Islamic Government," in *Liberal Is-lam: A Sourcebook*, ed. Charles Kurzman (New York: Oxford University Press, 1998), 89–95.

10. Arguably even Algeria is still dealing with the legacy of the 1990s conflict in ways that structure and constrain political outcomes, including the political fortunes of Islamist parties.

11. Shadi Hamid, *Temptations of Power: Islamists and Illiberal Democracy in a New Middle East* (New York: Oxford University Press, 2014); Nathan Brown, *When Victory Is Not an Option: Islamist Movements in Arab Politics* (Ithaca, NY: Cornell University Press, 2012).

12. See Shadi Hamid and William McCants, "Islamists on Islamism today: An Interview with Mustafa Elnemr, Muslim Brotherhood Youth Activist," *Markaz* (blog of the Brookings Institution), April 4, 2017, https://www.brookings.edu/blog/markaz/2017/04/04/islamists-on-islamism-today-an-interview-with-mustafa-elnemr-muslim-brotherhood-youth-activist/.

13. On post-Islamism, see Olivier Roy, *The Failure of Political Islam* (Cambridge, MA: Harvard University Press, 1994); Roy, *Globalized Islam: The Search for a New Ummah* (New York: Columbia University Press, 2004).

14. Carrie Wickham, *The Muslim Brotherhood: Evolution of an Islamist Movement* (Princeton, NJ: Princeton University Press, 2013); Khalil Al-Anani, *Inside the Muslim Brotherhood: Religion, Identity, and Politics* (Oxford: Oxford University Press, 2016).

15. Avi Spiegel, *Young Islam* (Princeton, NJ: Princeton University Press, 2015).

16. Peter Mandaville, *Political Pluralism in the Middle East and North Africa* (Washington, DC: Hollings Center for International Dialogue, March 2018), https:// hollingscenter.org/wp-content/uploads/2018/03/PPMENA-Report-Final.pdf.

17. Shadi Hamid, "Syria's Most Important Rebels Are Islamists, and We Have to Work with Them Anyway," Brookings Institution, October 8, 2013, https://www.brookings .edu/opinions/syrias-most-important-rebels-are-islamists-and-we-have-to-work-with -them-anyway/.

18. "Muslim Brotherhood Popularity Declines," Pew Research Center Global Attitudes and Trends, May 21, 2014, http://www.pewglobal.org/2014/05/22/one-year -after-morsis-ouster-divides-persist-on-el-sisi-muslim-brotherhood/egypt-report-13/.

CHAPTER 7

1. For a brief analysis of the use of the term *dawla* by the Islamic State—and its resonance not only with the modern state but also with the Abbasid caliphate—see Will McCants, *The Isis Apocalypse* (New York: Picador, 2015), 15.

2. Ghaith Abdul-Ahad, "The Bureaucracy of Evil: How Islamic State Ran a City," *The Guardian*, January 29, 2018, https://www.theguardian.com/cities/2018/jan/29/ bureaucracy-evil-isis-run-city-mosul.

3. I first described this challenge in "Shari'a and State in the Modern Muslim Middle East," *International Journal of Middle East Studies* 29, no. 3 (1997): 359–76.

4. See, e.g., Wael B. Hallaq, *The Impossible State: Islam, Politics, and Modernity's Moral Predicament* (New York: Columbia University Press, 2014). For some critiques of Hallaq's argument, see Nathan J. Brown, "A Discussion of Wael Hallaq's Islam, Politics, and Modernity's Moral Predicament," *Perspective on Politics* 12, no. 2 (2014): 461–67.

5. Clark B. Lombardi, *State Law as Islamic Law in Modern Egypt* (Leiden: Brill, 2006).

6. See, e.g., Hussein Agrama, *Questioning Secularism: Islam, Sovereignty, and the Rule of Law in Modern Egypt* (Chicago: University of Chicago Press, 2012); Jocelyn Cesari, *The Awakening of Muslim Democracy: Religion, Modernity, and the State* (Cambridge: Cambridge University Press, 2014); Iza Hussin, *The Politics of Islamic Law: Local*

Elites, Colonial Authority, and the Making of the Muslim State (Chicago: University of Chicago Press, 2016).

7. See Frank E. Vogel, *Islamic Law and Legal System: Studies of Saudi Arabia* (Leiden: Brill, 2000); Nathan J. Brown, "Why Won't Saudi Arabia Write Down Its Own Laws," *Foreign Policy*, January 23, 2012, http://foreignpolicy.com/2012/01/23/why-wont-saudi -arabia-write-down-its-laws.

8. See the full list of regulations on the official website of the religious police at http://www.pv.gov.sa. On the religious police specifically, as well as for a very thorough history of Saudi religious institutions, see Nabil Mouline, *The Clerics of Islam: Religious Authority and Political Power in Saudi Arabia* (New Haven, CT: Yale University Press, 2014).

9. For Qutb, the term *jahiliyya* refers to the modern world in which mankind submits to other humans rather than to God.

10. Ellis Goldberg, "Smashing Idols and the State: The Protestant Ethic and Egyptian Sunni Radicalism," *Comparative Studies in Society and History* 33, no. 1 (January 1991): 3–35.

CHAPTER 8

1. Martin Sökefeld, "Mobilizing in Transnational Space: A Social Movement Approach to the Formation of Diaspora," *Global Networks* 6, no. 3 (2006): 271.

2. Jolle Demmers, "New Wars and Diasporas: Suggestions for Research and Policy," *Journal of Peace, Conflict & Development* 11 (November 2007): 9; Garrett Wallace Brown, "Diaspora, Transnationalism, and Issues in Contemporary Politics," in *A Companion to Diaspora and Transnationalism*, ed. Ato Quayson and Girish Daswani (Malden, MA: Wiley Blackwell, 2013), 77.

3. Barbara Whitmer, *The Violence Mythos* (Albany, NY: SUNY Press, 1997), 48.

4. Albert O. Hirschman, *Exit, Voice and Loyalty: Responses to Decline in Firms, Organizations and States* (Cambridge, MA: Harvard University Press, 1970), 77–78.

5. Stephen Lubkemann, "Where to Be an Ancestor? Reconstituting Socio-Spiritual Worlds among Displaced Mozambicans," *Journal of Refugee Studies* 15, no. 2 (2002): 204–6.

6. Hirschman, *Exit, Voice and Loyalty*, 77–78, 96.

7. Amnesty International, *The Long Reach of the Mukhabaraat: Violence and Harassment against Syrians Abroad and Their Relatives Back Home* (London: Amnesty International, October 2011), 5.

8. Robin Cohen, *Global Diasporas: An Introduction* (Seattle: University of Washington Press, 1997), 155–75; Demmers, "New Wars," 7; Terrence Lyons, "Diasporas and Homeland Conflict," in *Territoriality and Conflict in an Era of Globalization*, ed. Miles Kahler and Barbara F. Walter (Cambridge: Cambridge University Press, 2006), 111.

9. Demmers, "New Wars" 3; Hazel Smith, "Diasporas in International Conflict," in *Diasporas in Conflict: Peace-Makers or Peace-Wreckers?*, ed. Hazel Smith and Paul Stares (New York: United Nations University Press, 2007), 3–5.

10. Lisa Wedeen, "Acting 'As If': Symbolic Politics and Social Control in Syria," *Comparative Studies in Society and History* 40, no. 3 (July 1998): 503–23.

11. Cecilia Baeza and Paulo Pinto, "Building Support for the Asad Regime: The Syrian Diaspora in Argentina and Brazil and the Syrian Uprising," *Journal of Immigrant and Refugee Studies* 14, no. 3 (2016), 334–52; Cecilia Baeza and Paulo Pinto, "The Syrian Uprising and Mobilization of the Syrian Diaspora in South America," *Middle East Report* 284–85 (Fall–Winter 2017): 27.

12. Eva Østergaard-Nielsen, *Diasporas and Conflict Resolution—Part of the Problem or Part of the Solution?* (Copenhagen: Danish Institute for International Studies, March 2006), 1; Smith, "Diasporas," 13.

13. Gabriel Sheffer, *Diaspora Politics: At Home Abroad* (Cambridge: Cambridge University Press, 2003), 69; Smith, "Diasporas," 7.

14. UN Office for the Coordination of Humanitarian Affairs, *Response Plan for the Syrian Humanitarian Operations from Turkey* (New York: UN Office for the Coordination of Humanitarian Affairs, July 2014–June 2015), 1; Eva Svoboda and Sara Pantuliano, *International and Local/Diaspora Actors in the Syria Response: A Diverging Set of Systems?* (London: Overseas Development Institute, March 2015), 10.

15. Mehrunisa Qayyum, *Syrian Diaspora: Cultivating a New Public Space Consciousness* (Washington, DC: Middle East Institute, August 2011); Dana M. Moss, "The Ties That Bind: Internet Communication Technologies, Networked Authoritarianism, and 'Voice' in the Syrian Diaspora," *Globalizations* 15, no. 2 (2018): 265–82; Kathleen Newland, *Voice after Exit: Diaspora Advocacy* (Washington, DC: Migration Policy Institute, November 2010); Demmers, "New Wars"; Østergaard-Nielsen, "Diasporas"; Roschanack Shaery-Eisenlohr, "From Subjects to Citizens? Civil Society and the Internet in Syria," *Middle East Critique* 20, no. 2 (Summer 2011): 127–38.

16. Nora Ragab, "The Engagement of the Syrian Diaspora in Germany in Peacebuilding," *IS Academy Policy Brief* 13 (Maastricht, Netherlands: Maastricht Graduate School of Governance, United Nations University, 2013); see also Newland, *Voice*, 10.

17. Kari Andén-Papadopolous and Mervi Pantti, "The Media Work of Syrian

Diaspora Activists: Brokering between the Protest and Mainstream Media," *International Journal of Communication* 7 (2013): 2185–2206.

18. Moss, "Ties," 274; Newland, *Voice*, 19.

19. Andén-Papadopolous and Mervi Pantti, "The Media Work of Syrian Diaspora Activists," *International Journal of Communication* 7 (2013): 2185–2206.

20. Svoboda and Pantuliano, "International," 9–13.

21. Moss, "Ties," 266.

22. Karel Layla Asha, "'Mothers at Home and Activists on the Street?' The Role of Women in the Syrian Revolution of 2011–2012," *McGill International Review* 2, no. 3 (Spring 2013): 50–65.

23. Newland, *Voice*, 8, 15; Demmers, "New Wars," 10; Sheffer, *Diaspora Politics*, 3; Giulia Sinatti, Rojan Ezzati, Matteo Guglielmo, Cindy Horst, Petra Mezzetti, Päivi Pirkkalainen, Valeria Saggiomo et al., *Diasporas as Partners in Conflict Resolution and Peacebuilding* (The Hague: African Diaspora Policy Centre, 2010), 26–30.

24. Moss, "Ties," 277.

25. "Q&A: Syria's New Property Law," Human Rights Watch, May 29, 2018, https://www.hrw.org/news/2018/05/29/qa-syrias-new-property-law.

26. Benedict Anderson, *Imagined Communities: Reflections on the Origin and Spread of Nationalism* (New York: Verso, 2006).

27. Georges Fahmi, "Most Syrian Christians Aren't Backing Assad (or the Rebels)," Chatham House (London), December 20, 2016, https://www.chathamhouse.org/expert/comment/most-syrian-christians-aren-t-backing-assad-or-rebels.

28. "Abuse of the Opposition Forces, 'Ethnic Cleansing' of Christians in Homs, Where Jesuits Remain," *Agenzia Fides*, March 21, 2012, http://www.fides.org/en/news/31228-ASIA_SYRIA_Abuse_of_the_opposition_forces_ethnic_cleansing_of_Christians_in_Homs_where_Jesuits_remains; Martin Chulov, "Iran Repopulates Syria with Shia Muslims to Help Tighten Regime's Control," *The Guardian*, January 13, 2017, https://www.theguardian.com/world/2017/jan/13/irans-syria-project-pushing-population-shifts-to-increase-influence; Molly Jackson, "Turkey Says Russia Is 'Ethnically Cleansing' Turkmen: Who Are They?" *Christian Science Monitor*, December 9, 2015, https://www.csmonitor.com/World/Global-News/2015/1209/Turkey-says-Russia-is-ethnically-cleansing-Turkmen.-Who-are-they.

29. On Syrian internet use, see Shaery-Eisenlohr, "From Subjects," 127–38.

30. Primo Levi, *The Drowned and the Saved* (New York: Vintage International, 1989), 42.

31. Østergaard-Nielsen, "Diasporas," 1; Smith, "Diasporas in International Conflict,"

9. See also Ragab, "The Engagement"; also Stephen Castles, Hein de Haas, Mark J. Miller, *The Age of Migration: International Population Movements in the Modern World* (New York: Guilford Press, 2014); Bassma Kodmani, *The Syrian Diaspora, Old and New* (Paris: Arab Reform Initiative, December 5, 2018), https://www.arab-reform.net/wp-content /uploads/pdf/Arab_Reform_Initiative_en_the-syrian-diaspora-old-and-new_2068 .pdf?ver=c925c67d906b8911a8751c1f3558a576 ; Sinatti et al., "Diasporas as Partners."

32. On integrating, see Sheffer, *Diaspora Politics*, 1.

33. Kodmani, *The Syrian Diaspora*, 7.

34. Lyons, "Diasporas and Homeland Conflict," 113.

CHAPTER 9

1. For examples of profiles of Muhammad bin Salman in the Western press, by and large positive, see Dexter Filkins, "A Saudi Prince's Quest to Remake the Middle East," *The New Yorker*, April 9, 2018, https://www.newyorker.com/magazine/2018/04/09/a-sau-di-princes-quest-to-remake-the-middle-east; and "Saudi Arabia's Heir to the Throne Talks to 60 Minutes," CBS News *60 Minutes*, https://www.cbsnews.com/news/saudi-crown-prince-talks-to-60-minutes/.

2. For an early assessment of the Salman era, see Madawi Al-Rasheed, ed., *Salman's Legacy: The Dilemmas of a New Era in Saudi Arabia* (London: Hurst and Company, 2018).

3. I discuss the regional crisis in "Beyond Sectarianism: The New Middle East Cold War" (Brookings Doha Center Analysis Paper No. 11, Doha, July 2014), https:// www.brookings.edu/research/beyond-sectarianism-the-new-middle-east-cold-war/.

4. Sean Yom and F. Gregory Gause, III, "Resilient Royals: How Arab Monarchies Hold On," *Journal of Democracy* 23, no. 4 (October 2012): 74–88.

5. Christopher Phillips, "Eyes Bigger Than Stomachs: Turkey, Saudi Arabia and Qatar in Syria," *Middle East Policy* 24, no. 1 (Spring 2017): 36–47.

6. On the 2011 transition in Yemen, see "Yemen: Enduring Conflicts, Threatened Transition" (International Crisis Group Report No. 125, Brussels, July 3, 2012), https:// www.crisisgroup.org/middle-east-north-africa/gulf-and-arabian-peninsula/yemen/ yemen-enduring-conflicts-threatened-transition.

7. Peter Salisbury, "Yemen and the Saudi-Iranian 'Cold War'" (research paper, Chatham House, London, February 2015), https://www.chathamhouse.org/sites/default/ files/field/field_document/20150218YemenIranSaudi.pdf.

8. "Crude Oil Prices down Sharply in Fourth Quarter of 2014," *Today in Energy*, US

Department of Energy, Energy Information Administration, January 6, 2015, https://www.eia.gov/todayinenergy/detail.php?id=19451.

9. *Statistical Review of World Energy 2020* (London: BP, 2020), 26, https://www.bp.com/content/dam/bp/business-sites/en/global/corporate/pdfs/energy-economics/statistical-review/bp-stats-review-2020-full-report.pdf.

10. *The Saudi Economy in 2018* (Riyadh: Jadwa Investment, February 2018), 28, http://www.jadwa.com/en/researchsection/research/economic-research/macroeconomic-reports.

11. On this period in Saudi history, see Sarah Yizraeli, *The Remaking of Saudi Arabia: The Struggle between King Sa'ud and Crown Prince Faysal, 1953–1962* (Tel Aviv: Moshe Dayan Center, 1997); Robert Vitalis, *America's Kingdom: Mythmaking on the Saudi Oil Frontier* (Stanford, CA: Stanford University Press, 2007); Robert Lacey, *The Kingdom: Arabia and the House of Saud* (New York: Avon, 1981).

12. "Saudi Arabia Names New Interior Minister," *Arab News*, June 21, 2017, http://www.arabnews.com/node/1118321/saudi-arabia.

13. Simon Henderson, "Meet the Next Generation of Saudi Rulers," *Foreign Policy*, November 10, 2017, https://foreignpolicy.com/2017/11/10/meet-the-next-generation-of-saudi-rulers/.

14. Hugh Miles, "Saudi Arabia: Eight of King Salman's 11 Surviving Brothers Want to Oust Him," *The Independent*, October 23, 2015, http://www.independent.co.uk/news/world/middle-east/saudi-arabia-power-struggle-between-king-salman-and-mohammed-bin-salman-could-bring-down-the-a6706801.html; Rori Donaghy, "Senior Saudi Royal Urges Leadership Change for Fear of Monarchy Collapse," *Middle East Eye*, September 22, 2015, http://www.middleeasteye.net/news/saudi-arabia-senior-royal-urges-change-amid-fears-monarchy-collapse-1612130905; "Dissident Prince: Sacking Bin Salman by Ruling Family a Matter of Time," MideastWire.com, June 29, 2018, https://mideastwire.com/page/articleFree.php?id=67059.

15. "Saudi Crown Prince Promises 'Return to Moderate Islam'," *Al Jazeera*, October 25, 2017, https://www.aljazeera.com/news/2017/10/saudi-crown-prince-promises-return-moderate-islam-171024182102549.html.

16. Margherita Stancati, "Mohammed bin Salman's Next Saudi Challenge: Curtailing Ultraconservative Islam," *Wall Street Journal*, January 10, 2018, https://www.wsj.com/articles/mohammed-bin-salmans-next-saudi-challenge-curtailing-ultraconservative-islam-1515525944.

17. Stephane Lacroix, "Between Islamists and Liberals: Saudi Arabia's New 'Islamo-Liberal' Reformists," *Middle East Journal* 58, no. 3 (Summer 2004): 345–65.

18. On the issue of gender in Saudi state building, see Madawi Al-Rasheed, *A Most Masculine State: Gender, Politics, and Religion in Saudi Arabia* (Cambridge: Cambridge University Press, 2013).

19. Filkins, "A Saudi Prince's Quest."

20. Kristin Smith Diwan, "Let Me Entertain You: Saudi Arabia's New Enthusiasm for Fun," Arab Gulf States Institute in Washington, March 9, 2018, http://www.agsiw.org/let-me-entertain-you-saudi-arabias-new-enthusiasm-for-fun/.

21. Jane Kinninmont, "Vision 2030 and Saudi Arabia's Social Contract: Austerity and Transformation" (research paper, Chatham House, London, July 2017), https://www.chathamhouse.org/sites/files/chathamhouse/publications/research/2017-07-20-vision-2030-saudi-kinninmont.pdf.

22. "Saudi Arabia Makes 2 Billion Riyal Payment in Citizens Account Program," *Reuters*, December 21, 2017, https://www.reuters.com/article/us-saudi-allowances/saudi-arabia-makes-2-billion-riyal-payment-in-citizens-account-program-idUSKBN1EF0S2?il=0.

23. "Threefold Increase in Electricity Bills from Today," *Saudi Gazette*, January 1, 2018, http://saudigazette.com.sa/article/525167/SAUDI-ARABIA/Threefold-increase-in-electricity-bills-from-today; "Saudi Arabia's Water Minister Sacked after Complaints over Tariffs," *The National*, April 24, 2016, https://www.thenational.ae/world/saudi-arabia-s-water-minister-sacked-after-complaints-over-tariffs-1.138178; Simeon Kerr and Ahmed Al Omran, "Saudi Arabia and UAE Introduce 5% VAT in Bid to Narrow Deficits," *Financial Times*, January 2, 2018, https://www.ft.com/content/b1742920-efd0-11e7-b220-857e26d1aca4.

24. Kate Kelly and Stanley Reed, "How Aramco's Huge IPO Fell Short of Saudi Prince's Wish," *New York Times*, December 6, 2019, https://www.nytimes.com/2019/12/06/business/energy-environment/saudi-aramco-ipo.html.

25. Zahraa Alkhalisi, "Saudi Arabia Eases Austerity after 'Very Negative' Response," *CNN*, January 9, 2018, http://money.cnn.com/2018/01/09/news/economy/saudi-arabia-austerity-backlash/index.html; Ben Hubbard, "Saudi Arabia Restores Public Sector Perks amid Grumbling," *New York Times*, April 23, 2017, https://www.nytimes.com/2017/04/23/world/middleeast/saudi-arabia-king-salman.html.

26. "Saudi Arabia's 2018 Fiscal Budget" (Riyadh: Jadwa Investment, December 19, 2017).

27. Jay Solomon and Summer Said, "Why Saudis Decided Not to Prop Up Oil," *Wall Street Journal*, December 21, 2014, http://www.wsj.com/articles/why-saudis-decided-not-to-prop-up-oil-1419219182.

28. Ben Hubbard, "Saudi Arabia Says Detainees Handed Over More Than $100 Billion," *New York Times*, January 30, 2018, https://www.nytimes.com/2018/01/30/world/middleeast/saudi-arabia-corruption.html.

29. "Saudi Corruption Cash Settlements Will Help Finance Royal Handouts: Finance Minister," *Reuters*, January 24, 2018, https://www.reuters.com/article/us-saudi-finance/saudi-corruption-cash-settlements-will-help-finance-royal-handouts-finance-minister-idUSKBN1FD17B.

30. Nicolas Parasie, "Saudi Arabia Takes Reins of Construction Giant Binladin Group," *Wall Street Journal*, January 13, 2018, https://www.wsj.com/articles/saudi-arabia-takes-reins-of-construction-giant-binladin-group-1515773084; Ben Hubbard, "Saudi Arabia Frees Media Mogul, But His Company's Fate Remains a Mystery," *New York Times*, January 26, 2018, https://www.nytimes.com/2018/01/26/world/middleeast/saudi-mbc-corruption-crackdown.html.

31. Nicolas Pelham, "The Crown Prince and the New Saudi Economy," *New York Times*, January 24, 2018, https://www.nytimes.com/2018/01/24/opinion/crown-prince-saudi-economy.html.

32. Jeffrey Goldberg, "The Obama Doctrine," *The Atlantic*, April 2016, https://www.theatlantic.com/magazine/archive/2016/04/the-obama-doctrine/471525/.

33. Michael Knights and Alexandre Mello, "The Saudi-UAE War Effort in Yemen (Part 1): Operation Golden Arrow in Aden" (Policy Watch 2464, Washington Institute for Near East Policy, August 10, 2015, https://www.washingtoninstitute.org/policy-analysis/view/the-saudi-uae-war-effort-in-yemen-part-1-operation-golden-arrow-in-aden.

34. Ben Hubbard, "Shiite Cleric Gained in Status as a Rivalry Deepened," *New York Times*, January 4, 2016, https://www.nytimes.com/2016/01/05/world/middleeast/shiite-cleric-gained-in-status-as-a-rivalry-deepened.html.

35. David D. Kirkpatrick, "As U.S. and Iran Seek Nuclear Deal, Saudi Arabia Makes Its Own Moves," *New York Times*, March 30, 2015, https://www.nytimes.com/2015/03/31/world/middleeast/saudis-make-own-moves-as-us-and-iran-talk.html.

36. Ellen Knickmeyer and Maria Abi-Habib, "Saudis Pledge $3 Billion to Support Lebanon's Army," *Wall Street Journal*, December 29, 2013, https://www.wsj.com/articles/no-headline-available-1388340244?mod=searchresults&page=1&pos=1&tesla=y.

37. Daniel Nikbakht and Sheena McKenzie, "The Yemen War Is the World's Worst Humanitarian Crisis, UN Says," *CNN*, April 3, 2018, https://www.cnn.com/2018/04/03/middleeast/yemen-worlds-worst-humanitarian-crisis-un-intl/index.html.

38. "Saudi Arabia Halts $3 Billion Package to Lebanese Army, Security Aid," *Reuters*, February 19, 2016, https://www.reuters.com/article/us-saudi-lebanon/saudi-arabia-halts-3-billion-package-to-lebanese-army-security-aid-idUSKCN0VS1KK.

39. "Iraq's Muqtada al-Sadr Makes a Rare Saudi Visit," *al-Jazeera*, July 31, 2017, https://www.aljazeera.com/news/2017/07/iraq-muqtada-al-sadr-rare-saudi-visit-170731073908238.html.

40. "Saudi Arabia: Back to Baghdad" (Report No. 186, International Crisis Group, Brussels, May 22, 2018), https://www.crisisgroup.org/middle-east-north-africa/gulf-and-arabian-peninsula/iraq/186-saudi-arabia-back-baghdad.

41. Kristian Coates Ulrichsen, "How Qatar Weathered the Gulf Crisis," *Foreign Affairs*, June 11, 2018, https://www.foreignaffairs.com/articles/middle-east/2018-06-11/how-qatar-weathered-gulf-crisis.

42. Ben Hubbard and Hwaida Saad, "Saad Hariri Steps Back from Resignation in Lebanon," *New York Times*, November 22, 2017, https://www.nytimes.com/2017/11/22/world/middleeast/lebanon-saad-hariri-resignation.html.

43. Mark Mazzetti, Ronen Bergman, and David D. Kirkpatrick, "Trump Jr. and Other Aides Met With Gulf Emissary Offering Help to Win Election," *New York Times*, May 19, 2018, https://www.nytimes.com/2018/05/19/us/politics/trump-jr-saudi-uae-nader-prince-zamel.html.

44. Mark Lander and Mark Mazzetti, "Trump's Preferred Candidate Wins Again, This Time in Saudi Arabia," *New York Times*, June 21, 2017, https://www.nytimes.com/2017/06/21/world/middleeast/trump-saudi-arabia-mohammed-bin-salman.html

45. F. Gregory Gause, III, *After the Killing of Jamal Khashoggi: Muhammad bin Salman and the Future of U.S.-Saudi Relations*, CSIS Briefs, Center for Strategic and International Studies, December 12, 2018, https://www.csis.org/analysis/after-killing-jamal-khashoggi-muhammad-bin-salman-and-future-us-relations.

46. Margherita Stancati and Summer Said, "Saudi Arabian Arrest Wave Shows Crown Prince's Bid to Control Change," *Wall Street Journal*, June 5, 2018, https://www.wsj.com/articles/saudi-arabian-arrest-wave-shows-crown-princes-bid-to control-change-1528191000.

47. "Saudi Arabia: Unrelenting Crackdown on Activists," Human Rights Watch,

June 20, 2018, https://www.hrw.org/news/2018/06/20/saudi-arabia-unrelenting-crack down-activists.

48. Jamal Khashoggi, "Saudi Arabia's Reformers Now Face a Terrible Choice," *Washington Post*, May 21, 2018, https://www.washingtonpost.com/news/global-opinions/wp/2018/05/21/saudi-arabias-reformers-now-face-a-terrible-choice/?utm_term=.577535a2d229.

49. Natasha Turak, "Gulf Monarchies Pledge $2.5 Billion in Aid to Jordan in an Attempt to Quell Large-Scale Protests," *CNBC*, June 11, 2018, https://www.cnbc.com/2018/06/11/gulf-monarchies-pledge-2-point-5-billion-in-aid-to-jordan-amid-protests.html.

50. Steffen Hertog, "Mohammed bin Salman Isn't Wonky Enough," *Foreign Policy*, March 14, 2018, http://foreignpolicy.com/2018/03/14/mohammad-bin-salman-isnt-wonky-enough/.

CHAPTER 10

1. "Erdogan Says Turkey Came under 'Economic Attack,'" *al-Jazeera*, September 14, 2018, https://www.aljazeera.com/news/2018/09/erdogan-turkey-economic-attack-180914074205694.html; Berat Albayrak, "America Can't Be Trusted to Run the Global Economy," *Foreign Policy*, September 7, 2018, https://foreignpolicy.com/2018/09/07/america-cant-be-trusted-to-run-the-global-economy/.

2. Kim Lane Scheppele, "Constitutional Legalism," *University of Chicago Law Review* 85, no. 2 (March 2018): 545–83.

3. Marianne Kneuer, "Legitimation beyond Ideology: Authoritarian Regimes and the Construction of Missions," *Zeitschrift für Vergleichende Politikwissenschaft* 11, no. 2 (June 2017): https://www.researchgate.net/publication/314773897.

4. Peter Klimek, Raúl Jiménez, Manuel Hidalgo, Abraham Hinteregger, and Stefan Thurner, "Forensic Analysis of Turkish Elections in 2017–2018," *PLOS One*, October 5, 2018, https://doi.org/10.1371/journal.pone.0204975.

5. Zulfikar Dogan, "Erdogan Achieves His Dream to Run Turkey as a Corporation," *Ahval*, September 13, 2018, https://ahval.me/turkish-wealth-fund/erdogan-achieves-his-dream-run-turkey-corporation?amp&__twitter_impression=true.

6. Mehul Srivastava, "Erdogan Sews Up Turkey's 'Second Revolution,'" *Financial Times*, February 27, 2017, https://www.ft.com/content/6337eb16-f85a-11e6-bd4e-68d53499ed71.

7. Pinar Tremblay, "The (De-)Evolution of Turkey's Foreign Ministry," *Al-Monitor*, January 28, 2019, https://www.al-monitor.com/pulse/originals/2019/01/turkey-diplomats-suffocating-under-erdoganism.html.

8. "Turkey's Erdogan Calls Dutch Authorities 'Nazi Remnants,'" *BBC News*, March 11, 2017. https://www.bbc.com/news/world-europe-39242707.

9. Gencer Özcan, *2000'li yillarda Turkiye dis politikasi (2002–2016)* (Istanbul: Bogazici Universitesi TUSIAD Dis Politika Forumu Arastirma Raporu, 2017), 26–27.

10. See, e.g., Ibrahim Karagül, "ABD Türkiye için düşman ülkedir: Bir gün, binlerce insan İncirlik'i de kuşatır," *Yeni Şafak*, January 26, 2018, https://www.yenisafak.com/yazarlar/ibrahimkaragul/abd-turkiye-icin-dusman-ulkedir-bir-gun-binlerce-insan-incirliki-de-kusatir-2043139.

11. For a clear articulation of foreign policy during the first half decade of AKP rule, see Ahmet Davutoğlu, "Turkey's Foreign Policy Vision: An Assessment of 2007," *Insight Turkey* 10, no. 1 (2008): 77–96.

12. "Turkey Exports by Country and Region, 2018," WITS: World Integrated Trade Solution, World Bank, n.d., https://wits.worldbank.org/CountryProfile/en/Country/TUR/Year/LTST/TradeFlow/Export/Partner/all/; *World Trade Statistical Review 2019* (Geneva: World Trade Organization, 2019), https://www.wto.org/english/res_e/statis_e/wts2019_e/wts19_toc_e.htm.

13. "Turkey's Trade with Middle East Surpasses $40 Billion," *Hürriyet Daily News*, April 15, 2019, https://www.hurriyetdailynews.com/turkeys-trade-with-middle-east-surpasses-40-billion-142666.

14. "Syria War: Afrin Looted by Turkish-Backed Rebels," *BBC News*, March 19, 2018, https://www.bbc.com/news/world-middle-east-43457214.

15. Ben Hubbard, Charlie Savage, Eric Schmitt, and Patrick Kingsley, "Abandoned by U.S. in Syria, Kurds Find New Ally in American Foe," *New York Times*, October 13, 2019, https://www.nytimes.com/2019/10/13/world/middleeast/syria-turkey-invasion-isis.html.

16. Kneuer, "Legitimation," 4.

17. Lisel Hintz, "'Take It Outside!' National Identity Contestation in the Foreign Policy Arena," *European Journal of International Relations* 22, no. 2 (2016): 1–27, at 12.

18. "Erdogan: Issue Not about Myself, But Turkey, Islam, *Anatolian Agency*, August 26, 2018, https://www.aa.com.tr/en/todays-headlines/erdogan-issue-not-about-myself-but-turkey-islam/1239555.

19. "Dünya 5'ten Büyüktür; BM Küresel ve Bölgesel Sorunlara Ağırlığını Koymalıdır," Türkiye Cumhuriyeti Cumhurbaşkanlığı (Ankara), September 24, 2014,

https://www.tccb.gov.tr/haberler/410/1373/dunya-5ten-buyuktur-bm-kuresel-ve-bolge-sel-sorunlara-agirligini-koymalidir.

20. "BM Güvenlik Konseyi'nin Demokratik, Şeffaf, Adil ve Etkin Bir Yapıya Ka-vuşmasını İstiyoruz," Türkiye Cumhuriyeti Cumhurbaşkanlığı (Ankara), Septem-ber 19, 2017, https://www.tccb.gov.tr/haberler/410/83544/bm-guvenlik-konseyinin -demokratik-seffaf-adil-ve-etkin-bir-yapiya-kavusmasini-istiyoruz. Erdogan repeated these calls during the 2018 General Assembly meetings.

21. Emily B. Landau and Shimon Stein, "Turkey's Nuclear Motivation: Between NATO and Regional Aspirations" (in Hebrew; INSS Insight No. 1225, November 7, 2019), INSS, http://www.inss.org.il/he/publication/turkeys-nuclear-motivation-between-na-to-and-regional-aspirations.

22. Kneuer, "Legitimation," 29.

23. Albayrak, "America."

24. "Turkey Eager to Use Local Currencies in Trade: FM," *Anatolian Agency*, Sep-tember 22, 2018, https://www.aa.com.tr/en/americas/turkey-eager-to-use-local-cur-rencies-in-trade-fm/1261513.

25. For the time being, members of this middle class are voting with their feet and the brain drain out of Turkey is accelerating. See Kadri Gürsel, "'Gezi Generation' Fleeing Turkey," *al-Monitor*, September 21, 2018, https://www.al-monitor.com/pulse/ originals/2018/09/turkey-brain-drain-young-generation-fleeing.html.

26. Borzou Daragahi, "Turkey Arrests Spark Fears of Widening Crackdown on Erdogan's Political Foes," *The Independent*, November 23, 2018, https://www.indepen-dent.co.uk/news/world/europe/turkey-arrests-academics-activists-erdogan-crack-down-protest-gezi-park-human-rights-a8647836.html.

CHAPTER 11

1. See Jonathan Wittall, "Starving, Bombing Civilians in the Name of 'Fighting Terrorism,'" *al-Jazeera*, May 18, 2018, https://www.aljazeera.com/indepth/opinion/ starving-bombing-civilians-fighting-terrorism-180517081243029.html.

2. Amr Abu Hamed, "Syria's Local Coordination Committees: The Dynamo of a Hijacked Revolution," *Knowledge Programme Civil Society in West Asia Special Bulletin* 5 (May 2014), https://mena.hivos.org/news/syrias-local-coordination-committees -the-dynamo-of-a-hijacked-revolution/.

3. Glenn Kessler, "Are Syrian Opposition Fighters 'Former Farmers or Teachers or Pharmacists'?" *Washington Post*, June 26, 2014, https://www.washingtonpost.com

/news/fact-checker/wp/2014/06/26/are-syrian-opposition-fighters-former-farmers
-or-teachers-or-pharmacists/?utm_term=.f634622c6abc.

4. James T. Quinlivan, "Coup-Proofing: Its Practice and Consequences in the Middle East," *International Security* 24 (Autumn 1999): 131–65.

5. *Arab Human Development Report 2004: Towards Freedom in the Arab World* (New York: UN Development Programme, 2005), http://www.arab-hdr.org/contents/index.aspx?rid=3.

6. Heiko Wimmen, *Syria's Path from Civic Uprising to Civil War* (Washington, DC: Carnegie Endowment for International Peace, May 2016), https://carnegieendowment.org/files/CEIP_CP290_Wimmen_Final.pdf.

7. See, e.g., Hakim Khatib, "Assad and the Rise of ISIS," *Orient Net*, March 10, 2017, https://www.orient-news.net/en/news_show/133225/0/Assad-and-the-rise-of-ISIS.

8. Aron Lund, *Who Are the Pro-Assad Militias?* (Washington, DC: Carnegie Middle East Center, March 2, 2015), https://carnegie-mec.org/diwan/59215.

9. "'We Live as in War': Crackdown on Protesters in the Governorate of Homs, Syria," Human Rights Watch, November 11, 2011, https://www.hrw.org/report/2011/11/11/we-live-war/crackdown-protesters-governorate-homs-syria#; "Syrie: Les forces du régime accusées de massacre," *Le Monde*, September 13, 2013, https://www.lemonde.fr/proche-orient/article/2013/09/13/syrien-les-forces-du-regime-accusees-de-massacre_3476955_3218.html; Liam Stack and Hania Mourtadadec, "Members of Assad's Sect Blamed in Syria Killings," *New York Times*, December 12, 2012, https://www.nytimes.com/2012/12/13/world/middleeast/alawite-massacre-in-syria.html.

10. Paul Bucala, *Iran's New Way of War in Syria*, AEI/Institute for the Study of War, February 2017, https://www.criticalthreats.org/wp-content/uploads/2017/02/Iran-New-Way-of-War-in-Syria_Final.pdf.

11. Borzou Daragahi, "Iranian-Backed Militias Set Sights on U.S. Forces," *Foreign Policy*, April 16, 2018, https://foreignpolicy.com/2018/04/16/iranian-backed-militias-set-sights-on-u-s-forces/; Ali Alfoneh, *Fractured Iraqi Shii Militias in Syria* (Washington, DC: Arab Gulf States Institute in Washington, August 22, 2018), https://agsiw.org/fractured-iraqi-shia-militias-in-syria/.

12. Aron Lund, *How Assad's Enemies Gave Up on the Syrian Opposition* (New York: Century Foundation, October 17, 2017), https://tcf.org/content/report/assads-enemies-gave-syrian-opposition/?agreed=1.

13. Anne Bernard, "As Syria's Revolution Sputters, a Chaotic Stalemate," *New York Times*, December 27, 2014, http://www.nytimes.com/2014/12/28/world/as-syrias-revolution-sputters-a-chaotic-stalemate.html.

14. Ali Nehmé Hamdan, "On Failing to 'Get It Together,'" *Middle East Research and Information Project* 277 (Winter 2015): https://merip.org/2016/03/on-failing-to-get-it-together/.

15. Bill Chappell, "Russia Begins Airstrikes In Syria After Assad's Request," *NPR*, September 30, 2015, https://www.npr.org/sections/thetwo-way/2015/09/30/444679327/russia-begins-conducting-airstrikes-in-syria-at-assads-request.

16. Cindy Saine, "US: 85 to 90 Percent of Russian Airstrikes Hitting Syrian Rebels," *VOA News*, November 4, 2015, https://www.voanews.com/a/putin-erdogan-discuss-syrian-crisis/3036177.html.

17. I. William Zartman, "The Timing of Peace Initiatives: Hurting Stalemates and Ripe Moments," *Global Review of Ethnopolitics* 1, no. 1 (September 2001): https://peacemaker.un.org/sites/peacemaker.un.org/files/TimingofPeaceInitiatives_Zartman2001.pdf.

18. Bennett Ramberg, "Fight to the End," *New York Times*, February 27, 2009, https://www.nytimes.com/2009/02/27/opinion/27iht-edramberg.1.20481678.html.

19. "Syria: UN-Arab League Envoy Warns of Limited Options, Dangers of Fragmentation," UN Information Centre in Cairo, December 30, 2012, http://www.unic-eg.org/eng/?p=5140.

20. Jennifer Cafarella and Genevieve Casagrande, *Syrian Opposition Guide*, Institute for the Study of War, October 7, 2015, http://www.understandingwar.org/sites/default/files/Syrian%20Opposition%20Guide_0.pdf.

21. Khaled Turkawi, "The War Economy in Syria: Funding and Inter-Trade Relations between the Conflicting Forces in Syria," *Jusoor for Studies*, November 2018, http://jusoor.co/details/War%20Economy%20in%20Syria/457/en; Armenak Tokmajyan, *The War Economy in Northern Syria* (Budapest: Aleppo Project, December 2016), https://www.thealeppoproject.com/wp-content/uploads/2016/12/War-Economy-2.pdf.

22. Malik al-Abdeh, "Rebels, Inc.," *Foreign Policy*, November 21, 2013, http://foreignpolicy.com/2013/11/21/rebels-inc/.

23. Alan George, "Patronage and Clientelism in Bashar's Social Market Economy," in *The Alawis of Syria: War, Faith and Politics in the Levant*, ed. Michael Kerr and Craig Larkin (Oxford: Oxford University Press, 2015), 159–81; Lahcen Achy, *Syria: Economic Hardship Feeds Social Unrest* (Washington, DC: Carnegie Middle East Center, March 31, 2011), http://carnegie-mec.org/2011/03/31/syria-economic-hardship-feeds-social-unrest-pub-43355.

24. *Economic Challenges and Reform Options for Syria: A Growth Diagnostics Report* (Washington, DC: World Bank/National Team, Syria, February 21, 2011), http://siteresources.worldbank.org/INTDEBTDEPT/Resources/468980-1218567884549/5289593-1224797529767/5506237-1270144995464/DFSG03SyriaFR.pdf.

25. Tobias Schneider, *Debt-Ridden and Broke: The Syrian Regime's Colossal Reconstruction Challenge* (Washington, DC: Middle East Institute, July 18, 2017), https://www.mei.edu/publications/debt-ridden-and-broke-syrian-regimes-colossal-reconstruction-challenge.

26. *The Cost of Conflict for Children: Five Years of the Syria Crisis* (Uxbridge, UK: Frontier Economics/World Vision International, March 2016), https://www.wvi.org/sites/default/files/The%20Cost%20of%20Conflict%20for%20Children%20report%20-%20online%20version.pdf; Greg Robb, "It May Cost $180 Billion to Rebuild Syria, World Bank's Kim Says," *Market Watch*, April 14, 2016, https://www.marketwatch.com/story/it-may-cost-180-billion-to-rebuild-syria-world-banks-kim-says-2016-04-14. Another source assesses the damage to Aleppo alone at $100 billion to $200 billion: "Investing in Syria's Future," Stratfor (Austin, TX), February 6, 2017, https://worldview.stratfor.com/article/investing-syrias-future.

27. Gardiner Harris and Ben Hubbard, "U.S. Will Not Spend $230 Million Allocated to Repair Devastated Syrian Cities," *New York Times*, August 17, 2018, https://www.nytimes.com/2018/08/17/us/politics/syria-stabilization-foreign-aid.html.

28. "Investing in Syria's Future."

29. Schneider, "Debt-Ridden and Broke."

30. Guy Burton, "China and the Reconstruction of Syria," *The Diplomat*, July 28, 2018, https://thediplomat.com/2018/07/china-and-the-reconstruction-of-syria/.

31. *The Toll of War: The Economic and Social Consequences of the Conflict in Syria*, (Washington, DC: World Bank Group, July 10, 2017), https://www.worldbank.org/en/country/syria/publication/the-toll-of-war-the-economic-and-social-consequences-of-the-conflict-in-syria.

32. For more recent economic projections, see "BTI 2018 Country Report—Syria" (Gütersloh, Germany: Bertelsmann Stiftung, 2020), https://www.bti-project.org/content/en/downloads/reports/country_report_2020_SYR.pdf.

33. "Statement by Panos Moumtzis, Regional Humanitarian Coordinator for the Syria Crisis, on Growing Displacement" (United Nations, New York, April 10, 2018), https://reliefweb.int/sites/reliefweb.int/files/resources/RHC%20Statement%20on%20Syria%20Displacement%2010%20April%202018.pdf.

34. Omer Karasapan, *Syria's Mental Health Crisis*, Brookings Institution, April 25, 2016, https://www.brookings.edu/blog/future-development/2016/04/25/syrias-mental-health-crisis/.

35. This figure was compiled by the United Nations. Karin Laub, "Aleppo Confronts

Vast Destruction Left by 4 Years of War," *Washington Post*, December 23, 2016, https://web.archive.org/web/20161224165001/https://www.washingtonpost.com/world/middle_east/aleppo-confronts-vast-destruction-left-by-4-years-of-war/2016/12/23/e20e8670-c8da-11e6-acda-59924caa2450_story.html?utm_term=.12794fffda25.

36. *Syria Regional Refugee Response* (Geneva: UNHCR, January 1, 2019), https://data2.unhcr.org/en/situations/syria. These numbers comprise those refugees registered with the UNHCR and do not necessarily reflect the total number of refugees hosted by a given state. The Lebanese government, for example, estimates that as of 2019, there were five hundred thousand unregistered Syrian refugees in Lebanon. See Barnaby Papadopulos, "Time Is Running Out for Syrians in Lebanon," *Foreign Policy*, August 14, 2019, https://foreignpolicy.com/2019/08/14/time-is-running-out-for-syrians-in-lebanon/.

37. Sevil Erkuş, "Migrants Day: Turkey Hosts Largest Number of Refugees in the World," *Hürriyet*, December 18, 2018, http://www.hurriyetdailynews.com/migrants-day-turkey-hosts-largest-number-of-refugees-in-the-world-139803.

38. Eric Le Borgne and Thomas J. Jacobs, *Lebanon: Promoting Poverty Reduction and Shared Prosperity* (Washington, DC: International Bank for Reconstruction and Development/World Bank, 2016), http://documents.worldbank.org/curated/en/951911467995104328/pdf/103201-REPLACEMNT-PUBLIC-Lebanon-SCD-Le-Borgne-and-Jacobs-2016.pdf. While Lebanese politicians like to blame refugees for Lebanon's financial woes, it should be noted that 65 percent of the government's budget goes to pay for public-sector employees, and refugees actually contribute to government revenue by paying a consumption tax.

39. By Svein Erik Stave and Solveig Hillesund, *Impact of Syrian Refugees on the Jordanian Labour Market: Findings from the Governorates of Amman, Irbid and Mafraq* (Geneva: International Labour Organization, 2015), https://www.ilo.org/wcmsp5/groups/public/---arabstates/---ro-beirut/documents/publication/wcms_364162.pdf; *Assessment of the Jordanian Marketplace* (Geneva: UNHCR/Norwegian Refugee Council, 2018), https://data2.unhcr.org/es/documents/download/61728.

40. Kareem Chehayeb and Sarah Hunaidi, "Turkey's Deportation Policy Is Killing Syrian Refugees," *Foreign Policy*, August 8, 2019, https://foreignpolicy.com/2019/08/08/turkeys-deportation-policy-is-killing-syrian-refugees-assad-erdogan-akp-chp/; *Syria Conflict at Seven Years: "A Colossal Human Tragedy"* UNHCR/US, March 9, 2018, https://www.unhcr.org/en-us/news/press/2018/3/5aa1ad2e4/syria-conflict-7-years-colossal-human-tragedy.html.

41. Conor Finnegan, "Confusion, Questions Linger over Possible US-Russia Deal on Syrian Refugees," *ABC News*, July 26, 2018, https://abcnews.go.com/Politics/confusion -questions-linger-us-russia-deal-syrian-refugees/story?id=56811531.

42. *Syria Regional Refugee Response: Durable Solutions* (Geneva: UNHCR, n.d.), https://data2.unhcr.org/en/situations/syria_durable_solutions.

43. Omar al-Muqdad, "Russian-US Repatriation Plan Not Supported by Syrian Refugees," Center for Migration Studies, New York, August 29, 2018, https://doi.org/10.14240/ cmsesy082918; Anchal Vohra, "A Deadly Welcome Awaits Syria's Returning Refugees," *Foreign Policy*, February 6, 2019, https://foreignpolicy.com/2019/02/06/a-deadly -welcome-awaits-syrias-returning-refugees/; Anchal Vohra, "Russia's Payback Will Be Syria's Reconstruction Money," *Foreign Policy*, May 5, 2019, https://foreignpolicy. com/2019/05/05/russias-payback-will-be-syrias-reconstruction-money/.

44. See, e.g., Turkey's Syrian Refugees: Defusing Metropolitan Tensions (Brussels: International Crisis Group Europe Report, January 29, 2018), https://d2071andvipowj. cloudfront.net/248-turkey-s-syrian-refugees.pdf; Raphaël Lefèvre, *The Roots of Crisis in Northern Lebanon* (Washington, DC: Carnegie Endowment for International Peace, 2014), https://carnegieendowment.org/files/crisis_northern_lebanon.pdf; Ben Taub, "Iraq's Post-ISIS Campaign of Revenge," *The New Yorker*, December 24–31, 2018, https:// www.newyorker.com/magazine/2018/12/24/iraqs-post-isis-campaign-of-revenge; Louisa Loveluck and Zakaria Zakaria, "Syrian Rebels Are Using the Turkish Offensive to Take Revenge against Kurds," *Washington Post*, March 7, 2018, https://www .washingtonpost.com/world/syrian-rebels-are-using-the-turkish-offensive-to-take -revenge-against-kurds/2018/03/06/85c36eea-1e2d-11e8-8a2c-1a6665f59e95_story .html?utm_term=.a1408d19484e.

45. Jeffrey Goldberg, "The Obama Doctrine," *The Atlantic*, April 2016, https://www .theatlantic.com/magazine/archive/2016/04/the-obama-doctrine/471525/.

46. "Transcripts," *CNN*, January 2, 2019, http://www.cnn.com/TRANSCRIPTS /1901/02/cnr.05.html.

47. Yaniv Kubovich, "Israel's Extensive Strike against Iran in Syria: What We Know," *Haaretz*, January 21, 2019, https://www.haaretz.com/israel-news/israel-s-extensive- strike-against-iran-in-syria-what-we-know-1.6855660.

48. Recep Tayyip Erdogan, Twitter post, October 9, 2019, https://twitter.com/rter- dogan?lang=en. For more details on the Turkish/PKK struggle, see the chapter by Henri J. Barkey in this volume.

49. "Charter of the Social Contract in Rojava (Syria)," Kurdish Institute of Brussels, n.d., https://www.kurdishinstitute.be/en/charter-of-the-social-contract/.

CHAPTER 12

1. "Al-Baghdadi: Suria Layset lilsurien wal Iraq lasa lil Iraqiyeen," *BBC Arabic*, July 1, 2014, http://www.bbc.com/arabic/middleeast/2014/07/140701_isis_leader_call.

2. Hanna Batatu, "Of the Diversity of Iraqis, the Incohesiveness of their Society, and Their Progress in the Monarchic Period Toward a Consolidated Political Structure," in *The Modern Middle East: A Reader*, ed. Albert Hourani, Philip S. Khouri and Wilson Mary C. (Berkeley: University of California Press, 1993), 503–25, 513.

3. An insightful account of the influence of modernization on Iraqi society and relations between old and new classes can be found in Hanna Batatu, *The Old Social Classes and the Revolutionary Movements in Iraq* (London: Saqi Books, 1978).

4. Examples of this discourse can be found in Mājid Shubbar, *Khuṭab al-zaʿīm ʿAbd al-Karīm Qāsim, [1958–1959]* (London: Dar Al-Waraq, 2007).

5. Isam al-Khafaji, "War as a Vehicle for the Rise and Demise of a State-Controlled Society: The Case of Baʿthist Iraq," in *War, Institutions and Social Change in the Middle East*, ed. Steven Heydemann (Berkeley: University of California Press, 2000), 258–91.

6. Rolf Schwarz, "From Rentier State to Failed State: War and the De-formation of the State in Iraq," *A Contrario* 5, no. 1 (2008): 102–13.

7. al-Khafaji, "War as a Vehicle," 3.

8. For more on the impact of economic sanctions, see Abbas al-Nasrawi, "Iraq: Economic Sanctions and Consequences, 1990–2000," *Third World Quarterly* 22, no. 2 (April 2001): 205–18.

9. See, e.g., Hasan al-Alawi, *As-Shiʿa wal dawla al-Qawmiyya fil Iraq* (unknown publisher, 1991).

10. Eric Davis, *Memories of State: Politics, History and Collective Memory in Modern Iraq* (Berkeley: University of California Press, 2005).

11. See, e.g., "The Concluding Statement of Iraqi Opposition Conference," *Aljazeera. net*, December 12, 2012, http://www.aljazeera.net/news/arabic/2002/12. The British and American governments facilitated the conference.

12. Arend Lijphart, "Consociational Democracy," *World Politics Journal* 21, no. 2 (January 1969): https://www.jstor.org/stable/2009820; "Constitutional Design for Divided Societies," *Journal of Democracy* 15, no. 2 (2004): 96–109.

13. Rahman Dag, "The Failure of the State (Re-)Building Process in Iraq," in *Neoliberal Governmentality and the Future of the State in the Middle East and North Africa*, ed. Emel Akcal (London: Palgrave, 2016), 32–43.

14. Lijphart, "Constitutional Design."

15. For other interpretations for this phenomenon, see Frédéric Volpi, ed., *Political Islam: A Critical Reader* (London: Routledge, 2011).

16. See Harith Hasan, "Sectarian Identities, Narratives and Political Conflict in Baghdad," *Levantine Review* 4, no. 2 (Winter 2015): 177–200.

17. For further details, see Fanar Haddad, *A Sectarian Awakening: Reinventing Sunni Identity in Iraq after 2003* (Washington, DC: Hudson Institute, August 4, 2014), https:// www.hudson.org/research/10544-a-sectarian-awakening-reinventing-sunni-identity -in-iraq-after-2003.

18. Interview with the author, Baghdad, November 2016.

19. John McGarry and Brendan O'Leary, "Iraq's Constitution of 2005: Liberal Consociation as Political Prescription," *International Journal of Constitutional Law* 5, no. 4 (October 2007): 670–98.

20. Shi'is are about 60–65 percent of the Iraqi population. However, this understanding of majoritarianism is reductive as it equates ethnoreligious majority with political majority. As the 2019–2020 protests have demonstrated, this understanding does not correspond with the way many Shi'is tend to identify themselves politically.

21. Paul Iddon, "Can Majoritarian Governance Work in Iraq?" *Rudaw*, March 24, 2018, http://www.rudaw.net/english/analysis/23032018.

22. Fanar Haddad, "Shia-Centric State Building and Sunni Rejection in Post-2003 Iraq," Carnegie Endowment for International Peace, January 7, 2016, https://carne gieendowment.org/2016/01/07/shia-centric-state-building-and-sunni-rejection-in -post-2003-iraq-pub-62408.

23. See Harith Hasan, "The Formal Marja': Shi'i Clerical Authority and the State in Post-2003 Iraq," *British Journal of Middle Eastern Studies* 46, no. 3 (February 2, 2018): 481–97.

24. Jack Watling, "The Shia Militias of Iraq," *The Atlantic*, December 22, 2016, https:// www.theatlantic.com/international/archive/2016/12/shia-militias-iraq-isis/510938/.

25. "Thousands of Iraqis Protest against Corruption and Power Cuts," *The Guardian*, August 7, 2015, https://www.theguardian.com/world/2015/aug/07/iraq-protest -corruption-power-cuts.

26. "Hundreds Arrested in Iraqi Kurdistan since Anti-Corruption Protests," *Financial Tribune*, December 28, 2017, https://financialtribune.com/articles/interna- tional/78814/hundreds-arrested-in-iraqi-kurdistan-since-anti-corruption-protests.

27. Gero Erdmann and Ulf Engel, "Neopatrimonialism Revisited—Beyond a Catch-All Concept" (GIGA Working Paper No. 16, German Institute of Global and Area Studies, Hamburg, February 1, 2006), https://papers.ssrn.com/sol3/papers.cfm?ab- stract_id=909183.

28. Maaz Farhan, "Reality versus the Rules: Kurdish Parties Bend Iraq's Electoral Rules on Politics with Guns," *Niqash*, http://www.niqash.org/en/articles/politics/5830/Kurdish-Parties-Bend-Iraq's-Electoral-Rules-On-Politics-With-Guns.htm.

29. For further details, see Harith Hasan, "Sistani, Iran and the Future of Shi'i Clerical Authority in Iraq" (Policy Brief No. 105, Crown Center for Middle East Studies, Waltham, MA, January, 2017), https://www.brandeis.edu/crown/publications/meb/MEB105.pdf.

30. Mudhir Muhammed Salih, workshop on Iraq's political economy: Challenges and Solutions, Baghdad, March 7, 2018.

31. Ali Mirza, "The Rentier Trap in Iraq: Comments and Recommendations," *Iraqi Economists Network*, http://iraqieconomists.net/ar/wpcontent/uploads/sites/2/2018/05/Merza_Rentier_Trap_In_Iraq_Journal_of_Strategic_Issues_number_6_2018.pdf.

32. *The State of Job Market in Iraq* (Baghdad: Central Body for Statistics, Ministry of Planning, December 2011). The problem is worse in Kurdistan. See "Kurdistan's Public Sector Is Double What It Should be," *Rudaw*, September 30, 2016, http://www.rudaw.net/english/business/30092016.

33. Further information about this issue is included in the White Paper published by the Iraqi government in October 2020. An English summary of the White Paper is published here: https://gds.gov.iq/iraqs-white-paper-for-economic-reforms-vision-and-key-objectives/

34. Salam Jabbar, workshop on Iraq's Political Economy: Challenges and Solutions, Baghdad, March 7, 2018.

35. Ali Abdul Amir, "The Demographic Indicators and Socioeconomic Development in Iraq" (paper presented at panel on Iraq's Political Economy, Baghdad, March 7, 2018).

36. Amir.

37. *Iraq Country Poverty Brief* (Washington, DC: World Bank Group, October 2017), http://databank.worldbank.org/data/download/poverty/B2A3A7F5-706A-4522-AF99-5B1800FA3357/9FE8B43A-5EAE-4F36-8838-E9F58200CF49/60C691C8-EAD0-47BE-9C8A-B56D672A29F7/Global_POV_SP_CPB_IRQ.pdf.

CHAPTER 13

1. Steven R. Ward, "The Continuing Evolution of Iran's Military Doctrine," *Middle East Journal* 59 (Autumn 2005): 559–76, at 574.

2. Ali E. Hillal Dessouki, "Regional Leadership: Balancing Off Costs and Dividends in the Foreign Policy of Egypt," in *The Foreign Policies of Arab States*, ed. Bahgat Korany and Ali E. Hillal Dessouki (Cairo: American University in Cairo Press, 2008), 181.

3. F. Gregory Gause III, "Saudi Arabia's Regional Security Strategy," in *International Politics of the Persian Gulf,* ed. Mehran Kamrava (Syracuse, NY: Syracuse University Press, 2011), 180.

4. "Iran Has Rockets 'To Attack Saudi Arabia'," *Middle East Monitor,* October 3, 2015, https://www.middleeastmonitor.com/20151003-iran-has-rockets-to-attack-saudi -arabia/.

5. Fred H. Lawson, "Egypt, Ethiopia and the Nile River: The Continuing Dispute," *Mediterranean Quarterly* 27 (March 2016): 114. 97-121

6. Lawson, 119.

7. *Algeria and Its Neighbours: Middle East and North Africa Report No. 164* (Brussels: International Crisis Group, October 12, 2015), 11.

8. *Algeria and Its Neighbours,* 12.

9. See also Yael Teff-Seker, Aviad Rubin, and Ehud Eiran, "Israel's 'Turn to the Sea' and Its Effect on Israeli Regional Policy," *Israel Affairs* 25 (2019): 234–55; Nael Shama, *The Geopolitics of a Latent International Conflict in Eastern Mediterranean* (Doha: Al Jazeera Centre for Studies, December 23, 2019), https://studies.aljazeera.net/sites/default/files/articles/documents/2020-01/8a79585b90e9471c9d883a2ab5ba4f57_100.pdf.

10. Najmeh Bozorgmehr, Camilla Hall, and Michael Peel, "Iran Commander Escalates Gulf Islands Dispute," *Financial Times,* April 19, 2012, https://www.ft.com/content/ee83997e-8a21-11e1-a0c8-00144feab49a.

11. Mohamed Elmenshawy, *Egypt's Emerging Libya Policy,* Middle East Institute Policy Analysis, Washington, DC, August 27, 2014, https://www.mei.edu/publications/egypts-emerging-libya-policy.

12. Khalid Hassan, "Land Dispute Continues to Threaten Egypt-Sudan Ties," *al-Monitor,* April 10, 2017, https://www.al-monitor.com/pulse/originals/2017/04/sudan-expel -egyptians-halayeb-shalateen-triangle.html.

13. Jalel Harchaoui, *Too Close for Comfort: How Algeria Faces the Libyan Conflict,* Security Assessment in North Africa Briefing Paper, Small Arms Survey, Geneva, July 2008.

14. Dalia Ghanem, "Why Is Algeria Breaking with Half a Century of Non-Interference?" *Middle East Eye,* May 19, 2020, https://carnegie-mec.org/2020/05/19/why-is-algeria-breaking-with-half-century-of-non-interference-pub-81832.

15. Dalton Kaweesa, "UPDF Considers Training, Feeding Partnership with Egyptian Army," *URN,* August 25, 2014, https://ugandaradionetwork.net/story/updf-considers -training-feeding-partnership-with-egyptian-army.

16. Frederic Musisi, "Museveni Wants End to R. Nile Deal Deadlock," *Daily Monitor* (Kampala), March 3, 2017, https://www.monitor.co.ug/News/National/Museveni-wants-end-to-R-Nile-deal-deadlock/688334-3834794-8ttojn/index.html.

CHAPTER 14

1. Paul Salem, "Working toward a Stable Regional Order," *Annals of the American Academy of Political and Social Sciences* 668 (2016): 36–52.

2. Marc Lynch, "Failed States and Ungoverned Spaces," *Annals of the American Academy of Political and Social Sciences* 668 (2016): 24–35.

3. Shahram Akbarzadah, "Iran's Uncertain Standing in the Middle East," *Washington Quarterly* 40, no. 3 (2017): 109–27.

4. Yezid Sayigh, *Crumbling States: Security Sector Reform in Libya and Yemen* (Washington, DC: Carnegie Middle East Center, 2015).

5. Ariel Ahram and Ellen Lust, "The Decline and Fall of the Arab State," *Survival* 58, no. 2 (2016): 7–34.

6. Idean Saleyhan, Kristian S. Gleditsch, and David E. Cunningham, "Explaining External Support for Insurgent Groups," *International Organization* 65, no. 4 (Fall 2011): 709–44.

7. Toby Matthiesen, *Sectarian Gulf: Bahrain, Saudi Arabia and the Arab Spring That Wasn't* (Palo Alto, CA: Stanford University Press, 2013).

8. David D. Kirkpatrick, *Into the Hands of the Soldiers: Freedom and Chaos in Egypt and the Middle East* (New York: Viking, 2018).

9. F. Gregory Gause III, *Beyond Sectarianism: The New Middle East Cold War* (Washington, DC: Brookings Doha Center, 2014), 1.

10. Katherine Sawyer, Kathleen Gallagher Cunningham and William Reed, "The Role of External Support in War Termination," *Journal of Conflict Resolution* 61, no. 6 (2017): 1174–1202.

11. Kristian Gleditsch, "Transnational Dimensions of Civil War," *Journal of Peace Research* 44, no. 3 (2007): 293–309.

12. Samer Abboud, "Social Change, Networks, and Syria's War Economies," *Middle East Policy* 24, no. 1 (2017): 92–107.

13. David Cunningham, "Veto Players and Civil War Duration," *American Journal of Political Science* 60, no. 4 (2006): 875–92.

14. See Kenneth Pollack and Barbara Walter, "Escaping the Civil War Trap in the Middle East," *Washington Quarterly* 38, no. 2 (2015): 29–46; Aysegul Aydin and Patrick

M. Regan, "Networks of Third-Party Interveners and Civil War Duration," *European Journal of International Relations* 18, no. 3 (2012): 573–97.

15. Laurent Louer, *Transnational Shi'i Politics: Religious and Political Networks in the Gulf* (New York: Oxford University Press, 2012).

16. Frederic Wehrey, *The Burning Shores: Inside the Battle for the New Libya* (New York: Macmillan, 2017).

17. Thomas Juneau, "Iran's Policy towards the Houthis in Yemen: Limited Return on a Modest Investment," *International Affairs* 92, no. 3 (2016), 647–63.

CHAPTER 15

1. The European Union, the Organization of American States, and the African Union are all intergovernmental regional institutions that encompass all states in the relevant region. In Asia, the Association of Southeast Asian Nations (ASEAN) is developing into a broader regional organization.

2. The World Trade Organization has 164 members as of 2019, but a surprisingly large proportion of countries in the MENA region remain outside of it (Algeria, Iran, Iraq, Lebanon, Libya, South Sudan, Sudan, Syria, and Yemen). Similarly, a large proportion of the forty-three countries that are nonsignatories to the 1951 Refugee Convention are located in the MENA region. These include Bahrain, Iraq, Jordan, Kuwait, Lebanon, Libya, Oman, Qatar, Saudi Arabia, Syria, and the United Arab Emirates.

3. See, e.g., Antony Anghie, *Imperialism, Sovereignty and the Making of International Law* (Cambridge: Cambridge University Press, 2005).

4. Michelle Burgis, "Mandated Sovereignty? The Role of International Law in the Construction of Arab Statehood during and after Empire," in *Sovereignty after Empire*, ed. Sally N. Cummings and Raymond Hinnebusch (Edinburgh: Edinburgh University Press, 2011), 104–26.

5. The sanctions were imposed by Security Council Resolution No. 661 on August 6, 1991, four days after the invasion of Kuwait, and remained in effect until May 22, 2003. For an assessment of the unprecedented character of the sanctions, see Hans-Christof von Sponeck, "Iraq: Burden of UN Sanctions," *Economic and Political Weekly* 40, no. 47 (November 19–25, 2005): 4902–5.

6. UN Security Council Resolution No. 678, UN Doc. S/RES/678 (November 29, 1990).

7. The bare-knuckled approach taken by the United States included both vote buying and threats against countries who might vote against the US push. Then secretary

of state James Baker famously told colleagues that Yemen's vote against the authorization to use force was "the most expensive no vote you ever cast." Thomas L. Friedman, "How U.S. Won Support to Use Mideast Forces," *New York Times*, December 2, 1990, A1. Shortly thereafter, the US cut foreign aid to the country. Axel Dreher, Valentin Lang, B. Peter Rosendorff and James Raymond Vreeland, "Dirty Work: Buying Votes at the UN Security Council," *Vox EU*, November 24, 2018, https://voxeu.org/article/buying-votes-un-security-council.

8. Vidal Silva, "Perez de Cuellar Campaigns for Peace in Gulf War," *United Press International*, February 1, 1991, https://www.upi.com/Archives/1991/02/01/Perez-de-Cuellar-campaigns-for-peace-in-gulf-war/9464665384400/.

9. See, e.g., Knut Royce, "Iraq Willing to Leave Kuwait in Exchange for Certain Conditions, Officials Say—Offer Includes Link to Palestinian Issue," *Baltimore Sun*, January 3, 1991, https://www.baltimoresun.com/news/bs-xpm-1991-01-03-1991003085-story.html.

10. The United States rejected any conditional offer that was linked to Israel-Palestine or would allow Baghdad to preserve its military capacity. Raymond Hinnebusch, *The International Politics of the Middle East*, 2nd ed. (Manchester: Manchester University Press, 2015), 241–43.

11. John Sigler, "Pax Americana in the Gulf: Old Reflexes and Assumptions Revisited," *International Journal* 49, no. 2 (Spring 1994): 277–300.

12. Patrick E. Tyler, "US Officials Believe Iraq Will Take Years to Rebuild," *New York Times*, June 3, 1991, A1.

13. Denis Halliday, "The Deadly and Illegal Consequences of Economic Sanctions on the People of Iraq," *Brown Journal of World Affairs* 7, no. 1 (Winter–Spring 2000), 229–33.

14. President George H. W. Bush, "Speech before a Joint Session of Congress," September 11, 1990, https://millercenter.org/the-presidency/presidential-speeches/september-11-1990-address-joint-session-congress.

15. See, e.g., Independent International Commission on Kosovo, *The Kosovo Report: Conflict, International Response, Lessons Learned* (Oxford: Oxford University Press, 2000), 4.

16. The most significant of these was Resolution No. 1373, recognizing "the need to combat by all means, in accordance with the Charter of the United Nations, threats to international peace and security caused by terrorist acts" and calling on all states to cooperate "to prevent and suppress terrorist attacks and take actions against

perpetrators of such acts." UN Security Council Resolution 1373, UNSC Res. 1373, preamble, UN Doc. S/RES/1373 (2001).

17. Letter from the Permanent Representative of the United States of America to the United Nations President of the Security Council (October 7, 2001), UN Doc. S/2001/946 (2001).

18. For a discussion of the controversy over targeting the Taliban, see Jordan J. Paust, "Use of Armed Force against Terrorists in Afghanistan, Iraq and Beyond," *Cornell International Law Journal* 35, no. 3 (Winter 2002): 533–57.

19. George W. Bush, speech given at the United States Military Academy West Point, New York, June 1, 2002, https://www.nytimes.com/2002/06/01/international/text-of-bushs-speech-at-west-point.html; and *National Security Strategy of the United States* (September 2002), https://2009-2017.state.gov/documents/organization/63562.pdf.

20. *National Security Strategy*, 15.

21. Jay Bybee, "Authority of the President under Domestic and International Law to Use Military Force against Iraq," US Department of Justice (October 23, 2002), https://fas.org/irp/agency/doj/olc/force.pdf.

22. UN Security Council Resolution No. 1441 (November 8, 2002).

23. UN Security Council Verbatim Report 4644 S/PV.4644 (November 8, 2002), 3 (US ambassador John Negroponte) and 4 (UK ambassador Jeremy Greenstock).

24. The fact that the United States and United Kingdom had continued to "enforce" no-fly zones over Iraq from 1991 to 2003 and had engaged in limited air strikes against the country twice in the 1990s, invoking the authority of the original 1991 use-of-force resolution, was cited as precedent favoring this interpretation by both the United States and the United Kingdom.

25. Oona Hathaway, "What the Chilcot Report Teaches us about National Security Lawyering," *Just Security*, July 11, 2016, https://www.justsecurity.org/31946/chilcot-report-teaches-national-security-lawyering/.

26. Andreas Paulus, "The War against Iraq and the Future of International Law: Hegemony or Pluralism?" *Michigan International Law Journal* 25, no. 3 (2004): 691–733.

27. Subsequent unilateral interventions without Security Council authorization by other permanent members attest to this concern. The Russian intervention in Georgia over South Ossetia (2008) and French actions in Mali (2012) were both premised on variations of self-defense and humanitarian arguments that echoed US and UK positions.

28. UN Security Council Resolution No. 1511, S/RES/1511 (2003).

29. Feisal Istrabadi, "The Limits of Legality: Assessing Recent International Interventions in Civil Conflicts in the Middle East," *Maryland Journal of International Law* 29, no. 1 (2014): 119-160, at 149.

30. Aslı Bâli and Aziz Rana, "American Overreach: Strategic Interests and Millennial Ambitions in the Middle East," *Geopolitics* 15, no. 2 (2010): 210–38.

31. For an early account of counterrevolutionary responses to the uprisings, see Hussein Agha and Robert Malley, "The Arab Counterrevolution," *New York Review of Books*, September 29, 2011, https://www.nybooks.com/articles/2011/09/29/arab-counterrevolution.

32. International Commission on Intervention and State Sovereignty, *The Responsibility to Protect* (December 2001), https://idl-bnc-idrc.dspacedirect.org/bitstream/handle/10625/18432/IDL-18432.pdf?sequence=6&isAllowed=y.

33. UN General Assembly Resolution on the 2005 World Summit Outcome Document, UN Doc. A/RES/60/1 (2005 24 October); UN Security Council Resolution 1706, UN Doc. S/RES/1706 (2006 31 August).

34. See Najla Abdurrahman, "What If Libya Staged a Revolution and Nobody Came?" *Foreign Policy*, February 17, 2011, https://foreignpolicy.com/2011/02/17/what-if-libya-staged-a-revolution-and-nobody-came-2/.

35. See Judy Keen, "Condoleezza Rice Reflects on Bush Tenure, Gadhafi in New Memoir," *USA Today*, October 30, 2011, http://usatoday30.usatoday.com/news/washington/story/2011-10-31/condoleezza-rice-memoir-bush/51006960/1.

36. UN Security Council Resolution 1970, UN Doc. S/RES/1970 (2011 26 February). The referral to the ICC included a specific carveout (para. 6) that the court should not have jurisdiction over alleged acts or omissions by nationals of a country other than Libya, whose state is not a party to the Rome Statute. This exemption would apply to Americans but not Europeans who are parties to the Rome Statute and hence subject to the ICC's jurisdiction. The inclusion of this impunity paragraph strongly suggests that the United States was contemplating the presence of its personnel—most likely as part of a military action—in Libya when the first resolution was being negotiated.

37. UN Security Council Resolution 1973, UN Doc. S/RES/1973 (2011). Ten countries voted in favor and five abstained. The latter group included China, Russia, India, Brazil, and Germany. Abstaining countries reportedly favored a diplomatic solution but feared that blocking the resolution might result in a massacre in Benghazi.

38. Allegra Stratton, "Obama, Cameron and Sarkozy: No Let-up in Libya

until Gaddafi Departs," *The Guardian*, April 14, 2011, https://www.theguardian.com/world/2011/apr/15/obama-sarkozy-cameron-libya.

39. See, e.g., Thorsten Benner, "NATO's Libya Mission Could Cause a Political Backlash," *Deutsche Welle*, September 8, 2011, https://www.dw.com/en/natos-libya-mission-could-cause-a-political-backlash/a-15371687; Philippe Bolopion, "After Libya, the Question: To Protect or Depose?," *Los Angeles Times*, August 25, 2011, https://www.latimes.com/opinion/la-xpm-2011-aug-25-la-oe-bolopion-libya-responsibility-t20110825-story.html.

40. See, e.g., Mary Ellen O'Connell, "The Libyan Intervention: A Victory for War?" *Peace Policy*, October 5, 2011, https://peacepolicy.nd.edu/2011/10/05/the-libyan-intervention-a-victory-for-war/; Anne Orford, "What Kind of Law Is This?" *London Review of Books*, March 29, 2011, https://www.lrb.co.uk/blog/2011/march/what-kind-of-law-is-this.

41. The coalition mandate in Libya was civilian protection, but civilians targeted by armed opposition groups for their alleged support for Qaddafi were not protected. A prominent example is the ongoing plight of Tawerghan civilians who faced arrests, torture, killings, and forced displacement at the hands of Misratan militias. UN Human Rights Council, Report of the International Commission of Inquiry on Libya, UN Doc. A/HRC/19/68 (2012 8 March), at 12–14.

42. Ethan Chorin, "NATO's Libya Intervention and the Continued Case for a 'Responsibility to Rebuild,'" *Boston University International Law Journal* 31, no. 2 (2013): 365–86.

43. On the continuing freeze of state assets and their impact on Libya's trajectory, see Jacob Mundy, "The Globalized Unmaking of the Libyan State," *Middle East Report* 49, no. 1 (Spring 2019): 3–7.

44. See, e.g., Alan J. Kuperman, "Obama's Libya Debacle," *Foreign Affairs* (March–April 2015), https://www.foreignaffairs.com/articles/libya/2019-02-18/obamas-libya-debacle.

45. David Rieff, "R2P, R.I.P.," *New York Times*, November 7, 2011, https://www.nytimes.com/2011/11/08/opinion/r2p-rip.html.

46. Gareth Evans, "R2P Down but Not Out after Libya and Syria," *Open Democracy*, September 9, 2013, https://www.opendemocracy.net/en/openglobalrights-openpage/r2p-down-but-not-out-after-libya-and-syria/.

47. Catherine Powell, "Libya: A Multilateral Constitutional Moment?" *American Journal of International Law* 106, no. 2 (2012): 298–316.

48. "China Defends Veto on Syria Resolution," *France 24*, February 6, 2012, https:// www.france24.com/en/20120206-china-defends-syria-resolution-veto-un-security -council-assad-russia-libya.

49. Russia cast twelve vetoes to prevent Security Council action on Syria between 2011 and 2018, but the subject of those draft resolutions never included coercive enforcement, let alone intervention. Rather, the following actions were contemplated: chemical weapons investigations, calls for cease-fires, condemnations of human rights abuses, referral to the International Criminal Court, and proposals for sanctions. The closest any Security Council member came to proposing enforcement action was when France and Spain introduced a resolution to halt the bombing of Aleppo by barring military flights over the city. The draft stopped short of imposing a no-fly zone. United Nations, "Security Council Fails to Adopt Two Draft Resolutions on Syria" (press release), October 8, 2016, https://www.un.org/press/en/2016/sc12545.doc.htm.

50. Mark Mazzetti, Adam Goldman, and Michael S. Schmidt, "Behind the Sudden Death of a $1 Billion Secret CIA War in Syria," *New York Times*, August 2, 2017, A1.

51. Michael P. Scharf, "Striking a Grotian Moment: How the Syrian Airstrikes Changed International Law," *Chicago Journal of International Law* 19, no. 2 (2019): 586–614.

52. See, e.g., Dapo Akande, "The Legality of the UK's Air Strikes on the Assad Government in Syria," opinion provided to Deputy Leader of the Labour Party, Member of Parliament Tom Watson, April 16, 2018, https://www.ejiltalk.org/humanitarian-intervention-responsibility-to-protect-and-the-legality-of-military-action-in-syria/.

53. "April 2018 Airstrikes against Syrian Chemical Weapons Facilities," Department of Justice Office of Legal Counsel Opinion, May 31, 2018, https://www.justice.gov/olc/opinion/april-2018-airstrikes-against-syrian-chemical-weapons-facilities.

54. For a tally of state responses to the airstrikes, see Alonso Gurmendi Dunkelberg, Rebecca Ingber, Priya Pillai, and Elvina Pothelet, "Mapping States' Reactions to the Syria Strikes of April 2018," *Just Security*, April 22, 2018, https://www.justsecurity.org/55157/mapping-states-reactions-syria-strikes-april-2018/.

55. "Iraq Formally Asks US to Launch Air Strikes against Rebels," *BBC*, June 18, 2014, https://www.bbc.com/news/world-middle-east-27905849.

56. Then US ambassador to the United Nations Samantha Power explicitly made this claim in submitting an Article 51 letter laying out the self-defense logic to the anti-ISIS military campaign. Marty Lederman, "The War Powers Resolution and Article 51 Letters Concerning Use of Force in Syria against ISIL," *Just Security*, September 23,

2014, https://www.justsecurity.org/15436/war-powers-resolution-article-51-letters-force-syria-isil-khorasan-group/.

57. See, e.g., Daniel Bethlehem, "Self-Defense against an Imminent or Actual Armed Attack by Nonstate Actors," *American Journal of International Law* 106, no. 4 (2012): 770–77.

58. The statement by the Syrian representative to the Security Council is cited in Amy Baker Benjamin, "Syria: The Unbearable Lightness of Intervention," *Wisconsin International Law Journal* 35, no. 3 (2018): 515–48.

59. Ryan Goodman, "International Law on Airstrikes against ISIS in Syria," *Just Security*, August 28, 2014, https://www.justsecurity.org/14414/international-law-airstrikes-isis-syria/.

60. See, e.g., Monika Hakimi, "Assessing (Again) the Defensive Operations in Syria," *Just Security*, January 22, 2015, https://www.justsecurity.org/19313/assessing-again-defensive-operations-syria/.

61. Raphaël Van Steenberghe, "From Passive Consent to Self-Defence after the Syrian Protest against the US-led Coalition," *European Journal of International Law Blog*, October 23, 2015, https://www.ejiltalk.org/13758-2/.

62. On the Syrian offer to "cooperate and coordinate" with the multilateral anti-ISIS military campaign, see Justin Sink, "White House Won't Commit to Asking Congress for Syria Strike," *The Hill*, August 25, 2014, https://thehill.com/policy/defense/215905-white-house-wont-commit-to-asking-congress-for-syria-strike.

63. For a discussion of both arguments, see Karine Bannelier-Christakis, "Military Interventions against ISIL in Iraq, Syria and Libya, and the Legal Basis of Consent," *Leiden Journal of International Law* 29, no. 3 (2016): 743–75.

64. This amalgamated argument is critically examined in Baker Benjamin, "Syria."

65. In addition to interventions that challenge the use of force regime, there have also been targeted killings, the proliferation of unmanned aerial vehicles (or drones) routinizing violations of sovereign airspace, and counterterrorism finance rules that sever transnational remittance arrangements.

CPSIA information can be obtained
at www.ICGtesting.com
Printed in the USA
LVHW100842241122
733903LV00001B/131